The British Defeat of
the French in Pennsylvania, 1758

D1567595

ALSO BY DOUGLAS R. CUBBISON

The American Northern Theater Army in 1776:
The Ruin and Reconstruction of the Continental Force
(McFarland, 2009)

The British Defeat
of the French
in Pennsylvania, 1758

A Military History of the Forbes
Campaign Against Fort Duquesne

DOUGLAS R. CUBBISON

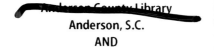

McFarland & Company, Inc., Publishers
Jefferson, North Carolina, and London

LIBRARY OF CONGRESS CATALOGUING-IN-PUBLICATION DATA

Cubbison, Douglas.
The British defeat of the French in Pennyslvania, 1758 : a military
history of the Forbes campaign against Fort Duquesne /
Douglas R. Cubbison.
p.   cm.
Includes bibliographical references and index.

ISBN 978-0-7864-4739-8
softcover : 50# alkaline paper ∞

1. Forbes Expedition against Fort Duquesne, 1758.
2. Forbes, John, 1710–1759.   3. United States—History—French
and Indian War, 1755–1763—Campaigns.   I. Title.
E199.C957   2010   973.2'6—dc22   2010000618

British Library cataloguing data are available

On the cover: *Forbes Arrives at Fort DuQuesne,*
by Nat Youngblood (courtesy Fort Pitt Museum)

Manufactured in the United States of America

*McFarland & Company, Inc., Publishers
Box 611, Jefferson, North Carolina 28640
www.mcfarlandpub.com*

To the memory of my grandfather R.M. "Cubby" Cubbison,
and my mother and father,
Shirley Evans Cubbison (1930–2002)
and William Charles Cubbison (1928–1983).
All three were lifelong residents
of western Pennsylvania, historians, and educators.
Their assistance and enthusiasm provided me
with every opportunity that I could ever have desired.

Acknowledgments

First, this book could not have been completed without the great assistance of my very close friend for forty years, Dr. Walter L. Powell of Gettysburg, Pennsylvania. Walt accompanied me on numerous visits to the historic sites of this campaign over a period of more than three decades, assisted me with navigation across the back roads of western Pennsylvania, helped me to obtain obscure sources, and was a sounding board for my interpretation. Walt's wife, Sue Kinsey Powell, also assisted me with research when necessary, and has fed me innumerable meals and provided considerable hospitality while I passed through Gettysburg in my frantic wanderings throughout western Pennsylvania.

The formidable accomplishments of previous historians who have trod the Forbes Road before me must be acknowledged. Dr. Alfred Proctor James, architect Charles Morse Stotz, Dr. Francis Jennings, Alfred Butler Hulbert, Edward G. Williams, Niles Anderson, and the various editors of *The Papers of Henry Bouquet* and *The Papers of George Washington* have all made great contributions to the comprehension of this campaign, and my debts to them are inestimable.

I also wish to acknowledge the assistance of Ms. Deborah DeSilvo, Ms. Heather Bischoff, Ms. Sharon Gillespie, and the other members of the Inter-Library Loan Department of the U.S. Military Academy Library, West Point, New York; and Ms. Wendy Newell and other members of the Fort Drum Library, Fort Drum, New York, who located numerous references and sources for me that would have otherwise been unobtainable. This book could not have been prepared without their generous and always uncomplaining assistance. Ms. Katherine Ludwig, Librarian, Mr. Greg Johnson, and the other members of the David Library of the American Revolution, Washington's Crossing, Pennsylvania, provided me with assistance on numerous occasions, to include the care and feeding of their overworked microfilm reader/printer machines, and I appreciate their friendly aid. My brother, the Rev. Robert Kaylor, an elder in the United Methodist Church, generously assisted with interpretation of the sermons of the Reverend Barton during this campaign. Others who have assisted me include Mr. Alan Aimone, Reference Librarian, U.S. Military Academy Library; and my lifelong friend Mr. Bruce Egli, who reviewed an early version of this manuscript. Ms. Nancy Watt assisted me with research on historic fabrics used as Indian trade goods.

My wife, Rebecca Jordan, has been of considerable assistance in ensuring that I remained fed while in the obsessive throes of preparing this manuscript, and cheerfully accepted my self-imposed exile in my office, remaining supportive even as I consumed prodigious numbers of cigars and innumerable cups of whiskey and coffee while attempting to unravel the threads of a complicated and convoluted story through the fog of two and a half centuries. This book could not have been completed without her support and understanding.

Per Tot Discrimina, Ohio Brittanica Consilio Manuque.

("Through So Many Hazards, Ohio, British by Thought and Deed."
Forbes's own testimony to his campaign.)

Table of Contents

Introduction

The campaign directed by Brigadier General John Forbes in 1758 to drive the French out of the Forks of the Ohio is among the most important in American history. As an integral component to his campaign, Forbes directed the construction of a wagon road leading from Philadelphia to the Ohio Valley — a road that traversed all intervening ridges of the Allegheny Mountains, established either fords or bridges over all waterways, and connected a series of small posts that provided respite and security at regular intervals along the route west. This road would subsequently serve as the conduit for trade, commerce, and expansion of the Middle Colonies of the Crown, and then the Mid-American States of the fledgling United States of America. Forbes's Road would become a national road over the mountains, and its location and presence directly influenced the growth and development of the nation.

The year 2008 marked the 250th anniversary of this campaign. Surprisingly and sadly, the year passed without seeing the publication of even a single comprehensive history of Forbes's campaign. Numerous well-researched and carefully prepared periodical articles exist, along with the exemplary and lengthy transcriptions of a number of important primary sources. The campaign has received coverage in numerous histories, but is still waiting for a dedicated treatment in its own right.

The author grew up and attended schools in western Pennsylvania. My father, a historian, a Korean War veteran with the famous 28th "Keystone" Division of the Pennsylvania National Guard and a lifelong educator, took my family on a visit to the reconstructed Fort Ligonier very early in my life. I well remember the thrill and excitement in my heart as I walked up to the towering pointed pickets of the fort, the distinctive smell of freshly cut and preserved wood in my nose, while my father regaled me with the tale of a brave Scotsman who built a road and led an army through the wilderness. To a young boy, it seemed like an amazing accomplishment.

Throughout my years of high school, the highlight of every fall was the annual parade and battle reenactment of Fort Ligonier Days. It was always a weekend to be anticipated, and it never failed to satisfy all of my expectations. I shared it with many of my friends, and still return to a significantly expanded fort with those same comrades every fall. There has always been something special about Fort Ligonier and the Forbes Road.

Forty years later, with ten years of service as a U.S. Army Officer, and a lifetime spent exhaustively studying military art and science, sometimes upon the very fields of conflict while hostilities were in progress, I still find the accomplishments of Forbes and his army both exciting and thrilling. As a professional soldier, I'm still amazed and impressed by the campaign.

This treatise presents the first focused study of this campaign. It is a military history of the campaign, and is presented exclusively from the English and provincial standpoint. Forbes's army set the tempo and held the initiative throughout 1758. Until the very end, the French were almost bystanders, deeply interested, but never able to really influence the campaign. This study is focused upon the British military and leadership aspects of the campaign. Additionally, because of the absence of adequate primary sources, it is an operational history of the campaign, and makes no attempt to present a detailed tactical description of individual activities, actions and engagements. What it is intended to do is to describe how Brigadier General John Forbes planned and executed one of the most challenging, and most important, military campaigns in the history of North America.

This missive is not intended to be a social or political history, or a history of Native American participation or diplomacy. Other historians have more than adequately addressed these topics, and the reader is referred to the superlative works of Francis Jennings, Michael McConnell, Matthew Ward, Holly Mayer, and others for these aspects of the Forbes Campaign.

And although these other branches of Pennsylvania and Virginia history are intriguing, and reveal important pieces of the momentous events of 1758, it must not be forgotten that the Forbes Campaign was first, foremost, and always a military operation. It was directed by a seasoned, professional military officer; and was executed by subordinate leaders and soldiers with the assistance of adept Native American warriors. The campaign was a purely military movement focused upon guiding a train of artillery, stockpiles of supplies, and several thousand well-armed, disciplined and highly trained men across a series of formidable obstacles to arrive as a cohesive, powerful fighting force before a piece of key terrain of international significance, defended by a determined, deadly foe.

Throughout this study I have permitted the actual participants to tell the story in their own words, to the maximum extent feasible. As a result, this narrative contains many quotations, only utilizing my own narrative to place their accounts into perspective, and to provide necessary interpretation and explanation.

This study serves as my personal testimony of my sincere admiration and respect for a superb soldier who has never received adequate recognition for his accomplishments, skills and courage: Brigadier General John Forbes of the Royal Scots Grays, the 17th Foot, Scotland, Great Britain and points west.

ONE

"A lion heart of courage"

The Appointment of Brigadier General John Forbes to Command the Expedition

The Allegheny Mountains' lush green escarpments rise west of the Atlantic Ocean, towering over the rolling plains of the Atlantic Piedmont, spectacularly illuminated with glistening golden rays at sunrise, and throwing long dark shadows at sunset. Their weather-worn rock remains strong, steep and impressive, and forms palisades of stone rising in the face of any westbound traveler. These mountains constitute a great obstacle to travel and commerce, running up the eastern seaboard of North America from the Gulf of Mexico to the Atlantic Ocean far to the north. To the east, water runs from the mountains' lush, green ridges that never end into the ocean itself. To the west, a series of progressively greater waterways carry the runoff into the Mississippi River. The Allegheny Mountains are ancient mountains, weathered by millenia, but their lofty elevations are still impressive, and combine to create a rolling wave of endless ridges, steep slopes, powerful rushing streams of water, massive slabs of rock, and precipitous descents. When the European arrived they were covered with a thick old-growth forest of towering maples, chestnuts and pines. They had never been crossed, except by Native Americans on narrow foot trails, or English traders leading small strings of pack horses heavily laden with valuable goods to exchange with these natives for furs that could be readily converted into great wealth in Europe.

By 1750, thirteen large and prosperous English colonies existed to the east of the Alleghenies. The ridges of the Alleghenies formed a nearly impenetrable obstacle that rose between the English colonies and the undiscovered lands that promised growth and expansion to the west, and this impassive solid wall of rock and trees precluded both communications and commerce. It would have to be overcome before the colonies could further expand.

But another obstacle, this one man-made instead of natural, had also manifested itself. The French colony of New France occupied the St. Lawrence and Richelieu river valleys to the north. To form a connection to the French colonies on the Gulf of Mexico and in the Illinois country, and to prevent an English expansion from sundering these colonies, the French had determined to occupy the Ohio Valley, and they had done so in convincing fashion. Beginning in 1753, the French had dispatched a military force down the St. Lawrence River, Lake Ontario, Niagara River, Lake Erie, French Creek and eventually the Allegheny River to become the first European power to seize control of the Ohio Country.

The English colonies viewed this development with alarm and consternation, particularly as many prominent Englishmen and Virginian colonists owned stock in a land development venture organized as the "Ohio Company." This venture promised its investors land, and thus wealth, that encompassed the Ohio Valley. Alarmingly to their financial prospects, this was land that the French now seemed bent upon possessing for themselves. Diplomatic overtures had been tried and failed, and had in turn been displaced by a military expedition mounted by the Virginia militia, in which the French had dispatched overwhelming force and readily gained the upper hand. In these early actions a vigorous, redheaded young Virginia gentleman of good breeding and even greater ambition, who just incidentally happened to be a member of the Ohio Company, had gained some small measure of renown, if not success. His name, of course, was George Washington.

Eventually, to turn their claims of sovereignty into solid possession by virtue of force of arms, the French established a fortification at the point where the Allegheny and Monongahela Rivers joined to create the Ohio River. Known as Fort Duquesne, this fortification was small and inconsequential as a piece of military engineering, a flimsy stockade of a few logs and some few shovelfuls of dirt, defended by an under-strength and under-armed garrison, commanded by rising ground and regularly battered by spring freshets. Yet its strength lay in dominance of presence, rather than military might. So long as the French occupied this fort on this piece of ground, the Ohio Company was stymied, and the English colonies were trapped behind the Allegheny Mountains. Another military expedition, again by the Virginia militia, was mounted and several small but vicious firefights erupted across the forests and glades of the Alleghenies, in which young Washington again played his part. Again, the French committed overwhelming force and persevered. Finally, Great Britain dispatched an expansive military expedition consisting of a powerful, well-equipped, and well-financed army under the command of British Major General Edward Braddock. Braddock was a skilled soldier of long service with the Royal Guards, and his capabilities were highly regarded by the English Crown. Young Washington eagerly accepted his invitation to tutor under a professional English officer. Braddock's army penetrated the Allegeheny Mountains in rapid order in the early summer of 1755, and he seemed poised to expel the French from the Forks of the Ohio.

On the hot afternoon of July 9, 1755, the plans and dreams of Braddock, Washington, the Ohio Company, Great Britain and its colonies collapsed in a maelstrom of gunfire, choking clouds of black powder smoke, Indian war cries, and blood. Braddock's army was slaughtered in an afternoon's violence, and the survivors fled in panic and consternation back across the very mountains that they had crossed with so much toil and struggle.

Now the frontiers of the colonies of Maryland, Pennsylvania and Virginia lay exposed to Indian war parties that poured across the mountains, many of them utilizing the very road that Braddock had constructed for British conquest of the forks. Numbers of these Indians were motivated by their traditional warrior ethos to perform deeds of martial valor, and to gain prisoners, plunder and wealth. But many more of them were seething to gain revenge upon the British colonies that had consistently exploited and cheated them, and driven them out of their homes and lands. In short order, the frontiers of these colonies were engulfed in an orgy of death, destruction, fire, and viciously executed but highly focused acts of violence.[1]

For the British, the years of 1755, 1756 and 1757 would be a continuous string of misadventures, fiascos, failures, and blunders intermingled with the occasional outright disaster. Braddock's defeat on the Monongahela had been the most momentous and stunning of these disasters, but there had been other reverses. In 1755 Governor William Shirley's expedition against Fort Niagara had only reached the mouth of the Oswego River on Lake

Ontario, where he had constructed a set of rickety fortifications as his sole accomplishment. Militia Colonel William Johnson of the New York colony's Mohawk Valley led another expedition against the French Fort St. Frederick on Lake Champlain. Johnson's ragged assemblage of provincials had only reached the southern terminus of Lake George by mid–September. There, he repulsed a poorly executed and clumsy French attack, sustaining heavy casualties and being wounded in the process, and his expedition ground to a cessation at this precise location. His army remained languidly in camp while the French, uninhibited by Johnson's army, constructed a considerably larger and more substantial fortification named Fort Carillon at Ticonderoga south of St. Frederick on Lake Champlain. Johnson in turn constructed his own rude log fortification, Fort William Henry, atop his battlefield and returned home, leaving both the old French threat at Fort St. Frederick, and the new French threat of Fort Carillon, in place. So desperate was the British Crown for any success whatsoever that even this meager and valueless victory gained Johnson a Baronetcy.

The year 1756 started off just as poorly for the English, and it never really improved. An audacious French expedition launched from Fort de La Presentation on the St. Lawrence River had traversed the frozen wastelands of the western Adirondacks in March and destroyed the British line of communications to Oswego. This debacle set the stage for British fortunes that year. In August the new French commander, the Marquis de Montcalm, turned to Lake Ontario with a stout French army and in short order destroyed the English toehold on the lake at Oswego. A British relief column on the Mohawk River precipitously fled at the news, causing nearly as much damage in their own panic as Montcalm had inflicted in his offensive. In attempt to reverse their fortunes, the British dispatched considerable reinforcements to North America, but they accomplished nothing except squandering the year's campaign season indecisively floundering about the Hudson River Valley.

This abysmal record, now well established, continued in 1757. Montcalm returned with his small but skilled French battalions, this time moving south from Forts St. Frederick and Carillon to lay siege to and destroy Johnson's Fort William Henry. A British expedition against Louisburg bobbed aimlessly about the North Atlantic, and failed to achieve a single thing except to absorb English strength and focus. And meanwhile, throughout 1755, 1756 and 1757, the Indian raiding parties swept out of Fort Duquesne and the native villages of the Ohio country, rolling back the Pennsylvania, Maryland and Virginia frontier scores of miles. Literally hundreds of settlements were disrupted, family members killed or captured, structures burned, farm fields abandoned. The Ohio Valley seemed secure in French hands, and they were clearly winning the war in a fashion marked by pillars of smoke on the frontier that marched steadily and without interruption towards the great English settlements of the coast, taunting their shattered dreams of expansion and growth.

All of this changed late in 1757 when a temperamental, eccentric and abrasive British politician named William Pitt grasped Great Britain's reins of power. For Pitt was easily all of these things, but he was also a brilliant, articulate, perceptive, organizationally gifted visionary who was committed with his heart and soul to achieving not just British victory in the war, but building a British empire, and establishing British global preeminence. Pitt was particularly adept as a Parliamentary orator, and he was extremely popular with the common Englishman. He had briefly formed a government in the winter of 1756–1757, but had shortly been dismissed. But Pitt's leadership was preeminent, and shortly thereafter Pitt had formed a government in which he served as secretary of state for the Southern

Department, while the Duke of Newcastle served as treasurer. But for all practical purposes Pitt was the head of the government. Mere obstacles such as French armies and navies, and incompetent British commanders, held little fear for Pitt. He aggressively ordered a series of coordinated campaigns throughout the world, and consulted with General John Ligonier, the newly appointed British commander in chief, to identify determined, energetic military leaders who would carry campaigns through to victory, regardless of the odds against them and the challenges that they faced.

On December 30, 1757, Pitt dispatched letters to North America regarding the direction that military affairs were to take in that theater of operations. This simple set of instructions may well be among the most important letters in world history, for they initiated a series of events that would alter the global military, political, social and economic landscape. These instructions were received at British Headquarters in New York City on March 4, 1758, when the adjutant general of British Forces in North America, Colonel John Forbes of the 17th Foot, wrote to his friend General John Campbell, Lord Loudon, then commanding general of British Forces in North America:

> The Squirrel Man of War came into this port about 12 this forenoon, and in a very short time I had the News brought to me of your being recaled and Gen Abercrombie [James Abercromby] appointed Commander in Chieff, in your place.[2]

Pitt ordained three principal avenues of attack in the instructions that Forbes opened on that chilly, brisk March day in New York Harbor. Colonel Jeffery Amherst, a vigorous officer who had served under Ligonier in the previous war, was catapulted over the head of senior but dilatory officers and promoted to command an expedition against the French maritime fortress of Louisbourg, Cape Breton Island, Novia Scotia. Louisbourg controlled the important and lucrative French fisheries of the North Atlantic, whose loss would prove a considerable blow to French finances. Louisburg was also well positioned to serve as a base of future operations against the heart of New France along the St. Lawrence River basin. A long-serving, rotund, unimaginative and fabulously incompetent British general, James Abercromby, was given overall British command, and was particularly entrusted with leadership of the British army operating in the Hudson Valley. However, Pitt ensured that Abercromby was fortified with the presence of a young firebrand who was a member of the British peerage and an accomplished officer of incalculable promise, Brigadier General Lord George Augustus Howe. The combination of Abercromby and Howe would move against the French strongholds of Carillon and St. Frederick on Lake Champlain.

Finally, to address the grimly decaying situation on the frontiers of the Middle Atlantic colonies, another officer well known to Ligonier was selected to follow in the footsteps of the ill-fated Braddock against Fort Duquesne. Colonel John Forbes, commanding officer of the 17th Regiment of Foot, an accomplished British officer of considerable experience currently serving in North America, and of greatest import a grimly determined Scottish warrior, was promoted to brigadier general. Forbes was assigned the mission to once again lead a British army across the Allegheny Mountains and seize Fort Duquesne and the Ohio Valley. Pitt's intent was that these three expeditions, simultaneously aimed at the strategic center and both flanks of New France, would first fragment and then overwhelm the French defenses.

Of the three expeditions, that assigned to Forbes was unquestionably the most arduous. Lord Loudon, as British commander in the North American colonies during 1756 and 1757, had already assembled the fleet and army that Amherst would employ against Louisbourg. In fact, he had led this very fleet against Louisburg in 1757, but bad luck and a range of other circumstances had frustrated him. Loudon provided Amherst with an already formed and organized army and navy in New York Harbor, simply waiting for Amherst to assume the reins of command. And once embarked, Amherst could utilize his naval power to land him literally within cannon shot of Louisbourg. Loudon had also assembled a large army based on the inland harbor and mercantile center of Albany, north of New York City on the Hudson River, and had constructed a formidable advanced depot at Fort Edward at the northern extremity of the river, specifically to facilitate an advance upon Lake Champlain. As with the army destined for Louisburg in New York City, this command was also organized and established, and was simply waiting for Abercromby and Howe to issue the order to advance. A large flotilla of bateaux and wagons had been constructed to maintain the line of communications between Albany and Fort Edward. A difficult but relatively short portage did exist between Fort Edward and Lake George. But this portage featured a well-established and well-worn road that had been in nearly daily use for three years before the destruction of Fort William Henry in August 1757, so it constituted a minor obstacle at worst. With the exception of this portage, Abercromby and Howe could use bateaux and small ships to move their army towards the North Star.

No such preparations had been made for Forbes. In fact, he didn't even have an army, and only a single subordinate officer was initially assigned to him. Even when the army was eventually formed, it would still be by far the smallest of the three major British columns that year. And unlike the other two expeditions, he would be unable to depend upon the highly efficient water transportation provided by the Royal Navy, or bateaux, to move. Rather, Forbes would have to construct his own road across the looming Allegheny Mountains. No advanced logistical base had been established, and the endless ridges of the mountains constituted a formidable adversary in their own right, even without the daunting presence of the French and their skilled Indian allies. Braddock had been given the same assignment three campaign seasons ago, and he had been killed and his army butchered in a debacle that resonated throughout the British Empire. It was a daunting challenge. Anybody but a fighting Scotsman would have quailed before it.

Pitt and Ligonier had appointed just such a man to command this

Brigadier General John Forbes. This portrait depicts Forbes as a younger officer with the Scots Grays. At the time of the 1758 Campaign, he would have been older and showing the debilitating effects of his terminal illness (courtesy Fort Ligonier Museum).

Pittencrieff House, Fife, Scotland. Forbes's Boyhood Home — where John Forbes, the "merry little cout," grew to manhood (courtesy Fife Council Libraries and Museums).

most difficult expedition. Forbes had been one of Ligonier's staff officers and an intimate of his in Europe during the War of the Austrian Succession. As a Lieutenant Colonel Forbes had played an important role, and had ridden with Ligonier at the head of the renowned charges of the British Cavalry at the Battle of Laffeldt on July 2, 1747.[3] At that engagement Ligonier had led two glorious cavalry charges, the first consisting of an assault of sixty squadrons of British cavalry against over twice the number of French cavalry squadrons, absolutely routing them. Later in the day, these same cavalry squadrons, still under Ligonier's command, successfully covered the withdrawal of the British army at great sacrifice. Ligonier felt comfortable appointing a fellow officer who had demonstrated such great courage on that battlefield under his own eye, and with whom he had served closely with under such adverse conditions.[4] On March 14, 1758, General Abercromby formally informed Forbes of his appointment, promoted him to the rank of brigadier general while on service in North America, and ordered him to repair to Philadelphia to take immediate charge of the preparations for the campaign.[5]

The newly promoted Brigadier General John Forbes was born on September 5, 1707, in the Parish of Edinburgh, Edinburgh County, Scotland.[6] As such, he was properly considered to be a Lowland Scots, and not a Highlander, although it must be observed that the Forbes family roots did, in fact, extend deeply into the rugged hills of Scotland. His parents were Lieutenant Colonel John Forbes of Pittencrieff and Elizabeth Graham Forbes. He grew up in Pittencrieff, Dunfermline, Shire of Fife, Scotland. He was a younger son, and two of his brothers lived to adulthood. Arthur Forbes was the older sibling and remained at home in Pittencrieff, for his name shows up on deeds from the Shire of Fife in 1732, 1758, and 1763.[7] Hugh Forbes became a prominent attorney in Edinburgh. The Forbes clan is one of the oldest and most powerful of the Scottish Lowlands, and is well known for its military service, although historically this service had not always been to the standing Crown of England.

Almost nothing is known of Forbes's childhood and education. The only remaining clue to his life as a young man is a simple sentence engraved in a pane of window glass in his boyhood home of Pittencrieff, "Jo. Forbes Merry little cout."[8] Cout, pronounced "coot," is an old Scots word derived from "colt" which suggests that he must have been a "lively"or "naughty" youth.[9] According to his 1759 Philadelphia obituary, "in his younger days he was bred to the profession of physic." Forbes certainly received medical training, for he began his military career at the age of 22 when he was commissioned as surgeon with the Royal Regiment of North British Dragoons (Scots Greys) on September 25, 1729.[10] It appears that the man that the "Merry little cout" had become found the military life better suited to his temperament, for on July 5, 1735, Forbes was commissioned a "Gentleman Cornet" in the same regiment. Forbes would stay with this regiment for over twenty years. He was commissioned a lieutenant on April 23, 1742. The regiment was sent to the Continent to participate in the War of Austrian Succession, and was heavily engaged on the British left flank at the Battle of Dettingen, Germany, on June 16, 1743. This engagement was notable because it was the last field of battle in English history in which the army was personally led by a monarch, King George II. Shortly thereafter, Forbes was promoted to captain on September 25, 1744. On May 11, 1745, Forbes would have been present with his regiment at the Battle of Fontenoy, although they were not heavily engaged there. Forbes must have caught the eye of senior officers, for he would record in a letter written late in 1757 or early in 1758:

> That during the whole last war (where he was present at every action) he had the happiness to be always distinguished for his diligence and capacity by his General having served Aide de Camp to Sir John Campbell to his death, and afterwards was sent for by the Earl of Stair, to who he was Aide de Camp, until your Majesty was pleased to appoint him Deputy Quarter Master General in Flanders, where he served to the peace. And for his diligence in executing the dutys of that important employment he refers himself to H.R.H. The Duke [The Duke of Cumberland, George II's son and Captain General of the British Army] Sir John Ligonier and all the other General Officers.[11]

Forbes was appointed "Deputy Quarter Master General" with the rank of Lieutenant Colonel on December 4, 1745. Because this was an office that only existed while the army was campaigning in Europe, he was also permanently commissioned a major in the Scots Greys on February 3, 1746. Among the officers that Forbes served with on Ligonier's staff was a young subaltern named Jeffery Amherst. It was as deputy quartermaster general for the British Cavalry under Ligonier that Forbes had played his prominent part at Laffeldt. As deputy quartermaster general throughout several years' campaigns in Europe, Forbes had gained considerable logistical and transportation experience that was later integral to his command responsibilities in Pennsylvania.[12]

Regrettably, almost nothing is known of his personal life. He never married and had no children. Little of his personality is exposed by his professional letters, although several lines that he wrote on November 29, 1754, to Lord Charles Hayes shows that he clearly had a sense of humor, and was willing to enjoy a few vicarious pleasures:

> So much for business. And now to inquire how your old honour does in this cold weather.... I am afraid I shall hear of you, as I found my bottle this morning: Froze to the Centre. — So you may

guess that in this most miserable cold place, I scarce have more spirits than enough — however, warm punch & a warm Lass helps out the long nights, That you were able to enjoy both or either shall be always [my] sincere wish....[13]

With the end of the war in 1748, Forbes returned to Scotland and was again promoted to lieutenant colonel of the Scots Greys on November 29, 1750. Because the colonel of a British Regiment was predominantly an administrative and financial position by the mid–18th century, Forbes had now risen to be the tactical and military commander of the regiment in only fifteen years, having held every rank in the regiment from ensign to lieutenant colonel. Certainly Forbes had demonstrated considerable military and leadership skills, but to rise in the ranks so rapidly he also needed some measure of political connections, which can only be guessed at today. His close relationship with Ligonier was extremely important to him. He was also a lifelong friend with his neighbor and contemporary Colonel Sir Peter Halkett, of Pitfirrane, Scotland, the commanding officer of the 44th Foot; and John Montague, 4th Earl of Sandwich, Lord of the Admiralty and quite well positioned at the court of King George II.[14] He had unquestionably caught the eye of the Duke of Cumberland, King George's son and at the time the captain general of the British Army.

Forbes continued his meteoric rise, being promoted Colonel of the 17th Regiment of Foot on February 25, 1757, a prestigious and lucrative post that could only be obtained through royal favor. Forbes joined John Campbell, 4th Earl of Loudon, in North America early in 1757. He served as Loudon's adjutant general, primarily in New York City, throughout the remainder of that general's term of service in North America. In this position, Forbes became familiar with the majority of the senior British and provincial officers in North America, and would have been aware of nearly every military activity, logistical requirement, or tactical action on the continent. Forbes departed New York on April 15, 1758, and arrived in Philadelphia on the evening of Tuesday, April 18, 1758, to initiate the campaign.[15]

Upon his appointment to command of the expedition against Fort Duquesne in March 1758, Forbes was 51 years old, possessing 29 years of military service encompassing his entire adult life. He had served in every officer rank of the British Army from ensign to colonel. He had participated in every campaign of the British Army in the War of Austrian Succession on the European Continent between 1744 and 1748, which had been the longest and most sustained combat that the British Army had seen since the campaigns of Marlborough. He had gained considerable logistical experience as deputy quartermaster general with Ligonier's Cavalry, had personally served with the Duke of Cumberland, Lord Ligonier and other notable English army officers, and had been given a full year to obtain familiarity with North America. Forbes was a seasoned, experienced professional officer, clearly well regarded in the British Army, and he would prove an excellent selection to lead what was certain to be a difficult and arduous campaign.

Forbes had consistently complained of ill health throughout the 1757 and 1758 campaigns, referring to a range of ailments, sometimes with his legs, but most often with his digestive system. As early as April 27, 1757, he wrote to his brother Hugh Forbes, asking him to "figure to yourself my misery, Lame & Sick neither able to eat, drink, write or think." Forbes complained of being "very much out of order" on December 10 and December 21 of 1757 and February 3, 1758.[16] Clearly, by the beginning of the campaign in the spring of 1758, Forbes was extremely ill with a debilitating digestive ailment (probably stomach cancer, although insufficient information is available for a legitimate diagnosis) that was well into the long, painful process of killing him. He solicited medical assistance, principally from Lieutenant James Grant of the 77th Foot, throughout the campaign.

Forbes employed a "Four Wheel Chariot" during the early parts of the campaign that he had purchased from Lord Loudon upon his departure from the colonies in April 1758.[17] Once beyond a point where this carriage was practicable, Forbes had a litter devised that could carry him slung between two horses across the Allegheny Mountains. Although Forbes was dying during the campaign, his courage remained undaunted. His Native American allies expressed their distrust of the leadership of a warrior that had to be carried. But Forbes's officers explained "that he was of so fierce and explosive a disposition that they thought it safe only to let him out on the battlefield."[18]

Two descriptions of Forbes document the strength of will, mental fortitude in the face of adversity, determination to persevere, and force of personality that he possessed. His comrade in arms, and by the termination of the campaign his good friend, Henry Bouquet would write:

> The glory of our success must after God be allowed to our General, who from the beginning took those wise measures which deprived the French of their chief strength, and by the treaty of Easton kept such a number of Indians idle during the whole campaign, and procured a peace with those inveterate enemies, more necessary and beneficial to the Provinces than the driving the French from the Ohio. His prudence in all measures, in the numberless difficulties he had to surmount, deserves the highest praises.[19]

One of the most ringing descriptions of Forbes is provided by a man who never knew him, Episcopal Bishop Cortlandt Whitehead of Pittsburgh:

> A lion heart of courage unparalleled must have been his who in physical weakness and distress, and in the face of this great undertaking through the wilderness, and moreover with the enervating memory of former disasters in the same region, proceeded to carry out his plans.[20]

Two

"A gathering from the scum of the worst of people, in every Country"

The Organization and Leadership of the Forbes Campaign

As Lord Loudon's adjutant general, Forbes had previously communicated with an experienced Swiss officer, Lieutenant Colonel Henry Bouquet, commander of the First Battalion of the Royal American Regiment (60th Foot), then serving as the English military commander in Charleston, in the colony of South Carolina. The earliest documented correspondence between Forbes and Bouquet was a set of General Orders that Forbes issued to Bouquet on December 2, 1757.[1] Bouquet had been appointed to serve as Forbes's second in command for the expedition, although they had never met in person prior to the commencement of the campaign. They two men had much in common, having both been well tempered in the military cauldron of the European Continent, and it was probably natural that they shortly established a strong working relationship.

Henry Bouquet had been born at Rolle, a small town on the northern shore of Lake Geneva in Switzerland, in 1719.[2] His grandfather had been the proprietor of a prominent local hotel, the "Hotel de la Tete Noire [Negro Head Hotel]" in Rolle, and had been both a longstanding member and president of the Town Council. On April 24, 1736, at the age of 17, Bouquet entered the company of Captain Crousaz in the Swiss Regiment of Constant as a cadet. The captain-lieutenant of this company was Louys Bouquet, Henry Bouquet's uncle, who would rise to the rank of general. Presumably, this uncle had a great influence on Bouquet's early adulthood. He was discharged from the company, apparently having completed his rudimentary military training "on the job" as it was then performed, on April 4, 1739.

Bouquet joined the Company Rodel of Herr Roguin, lieutenant colonel in the Swiss regiment of Colonel von Diesbach in the service of his Royal Majesty of Sardinia, as a second lieutenant on September 1, 1739. Bouquet would subsequently transfer to the Swiss regiment of Colonel Roy, also in service to the King of Sardinia, as a lieutenant in 1743. He served five years in this position, throughout most of the War of Austrian Succession, in which Sardinia served as an ally to Maria Theresa of Austria. Much of the Sardinian Theater of this war occurred in the mountains of northern Italy, and provided Bouquet with valuable experience in warfare in rugged terrain roughly similar to the Allegheny Mountains of Pennsylvania.[3] Bouqet is noted to have distinguished himself at the Siege and Battle of Cony, Italy, in late September and October 1744. Beginning on March 8, 1745, Bouquet served as a regimental adjutant, a position of great responsibility that entailed managing the correspondence and administration of a regiment nearly single-handedly. Hostilities concluded with the Second Treaty of Aix-la-Chapelle, whose negotiations started on April 24, 1748; and Bouquet left the service of Sardinia shortly thereafter on May 1, 1748.

Following the termination of his military responsibilities, Bouquet went on the obligatory "grand tour of Europe" of which every European gentleman was supposed to partake. It has been suggested that Bouquet spent sufficient time with eighteen-year-old George Broderick, Viscount Midleton of the Irish peerage, on this tour both to develop a friendship with Lord Midleton, and to acquire a familiarity with the English language. Subsequently he would enlist in the service of the Prince of Orange of Holland, in that prince's regiment of Swiss Guards. Bouquet was a company commander in that regiment with the rank of lieutenant colonel when he transferred to English service with the Royal American Regiment.

Unfortunately, very little is actually known regarding Bouquet's European military experience. His early papers were apparently destroyed in a fire in November 1758. As a result, attempting to ascertain the types of engagements and campaigns that he participated in, his leadership roles, his military education and mentors, how much experience he had with constructing roads over difficult terrain, whether he fought against or directed partisans, is all speculative.[4] Based upon Bouquet's performance during the Forbes Campaign, and in subsequent campaigns in North America, it is apparent that he possessed considerable military acumen by the start of the Seven Years' War in 1755.

In that year James Prevost, a Swiss soldier and adventurer — and of greatest import a friend of the Duke of Cumberland, son of King George II and at that time the captain general of the British Army — proposed raising four battalions of infantry under a unique concept. To reduce the dependence on British manpower, Prevost's concept was that Germans could be enlisted for service in North America, and then augmented by recruiting additional soldiers from the large number of German immigrants in America, particularly in the colony of Pennsylvania. Prevost's scheme was, not surprisingly given King George's affinity for matters German, accepted. "The Royal American Regiment" or 62nd Foot (later renumbered the 60th Foot), was organized beginning in 1755. An accomplished Swiss officer possessing years of experience in European conflicts, Frederick Haldimand, was given command of one of the battalions of this regiment. Haldimand had been born in the canton of Neuchatel, Switzerland, in October 1718, and he had served with Frederick the Great of Prussia in the renowned Prussian Army in the 1740s. Accordingly, he was a natural selection to command a battalion of predominantly German troops. Haldimand recommended his good friend, Lieutenant Colonel Henry Bouquet of the Dutch Swiss Guards, as Lieutenant Colonel of the First Battalion. It is likely that Bouquet's friendship with Lord Midleton, who in turn was an intimate with the Duke of Cumberland, facilitated the acceptance of Haldimand's recommendation. Eager for active service, and doubtless seeking more rapid promotion in the challenging military environment of North America, Bouquet accepted the position, raised his battalion, and soon found himself in Charleston.

Bouquet first congratulated Forbes on his having "the honor of serving under your command" from New York City on April 23, 1758.[5] Bouquet also informed Forbes that he was leaving for Philadelphia on Friday, May 5. Shortly thereafter they met for the first time. At this meeting Forbes established their respective command functions that would drive the campaign. Forbes of course maintained overall leadership of the expedition, but also assumed the onerous but integral logistics and transportation functions. These would have to be managed from the support base of Philadelphia, which meant that Forbes would have to initially direct the campaign from the rear, rather than the more traditional front. Clearly, Forbes saw that the critical point of the campaign would not be at the head of the column, at least not until the final movement on Fort Duquesne, but rather would be the trail of the army from where all of his supplies must be drawn. Braddock had failed to pay proper attention to this aspect of his campaign in his haste to reach the Forks of the Ohio, and it was not an error that Forbes intended to repeat. In the meantime, Bouquet would serve as Forbes's operational or tactical commander, responsible for driving the front of the column forward across the endless ridges of the Allegheny Mountains, while Forbes pushed the logistics to the fore. This would rapidly become a highly successful, and extremely effective, command relationship. Forbes carefully ensured that Bouquet understood his commander's intent for every aspect of the campaign, and then entrusted Bouquet with the authority to supervise the daily activities of the advance. As the campaign progressed, it becomes apparent that Forbes and Bouquet forged a close personal bond, and worked together extremely well. These two professional soldiers comprised a leadership team that consistently and continuously overcame the many obstacles, challenges, and difficulties that were presented by "an immense Forest of 240 miles of Extent, intersected by several ranges of Mountains, impenetrable almost to any thing human save the Indians who have foot paths ... through those deserts."[6]

Forbes effectively functioned as a brigade commander throughout this campaign. To assist him, only two principal staff officers were available. This was not uncommon, for in the 18th century the concept of modern military staff officers and sections was unknown. Forbes's brigade major was Captain Francis Halkett of the 44th Foot. Brigade major was one of the few established staff positions in an 18th-century army. The officer assigned as brigade major was detailed from his usual position with the line, and was to receive greater pay and allowances for the significantly increased workload and responsibilities that the position entailed. The brigade major's functions were similar to those of the adjutant general of the modern army. Essentially, he was responsible for all of the administrative duties and functions of the brigade headquarters, including but not limited to the preparation and dissemination of orders, compilation of reports, maintenance of official brigade papers, and organizing and preparing the correspondence of the commanding officer of the brigade. The brigade major was also directed to assist a brigade commander, however it was deemed to be appropriate and necessary.

Halkett was the middle of three sons of Colonel Sir Peter Halkett, of Pitfirrane, Scotland, the commanding officer of the 44th Foot. Forbes and Halkett's father were the same age, from the same hometown, and remained close personal friends throughout their lifetimes. Colonel Sir Halkett had been killed at Braddock's defeat on the Monongahela, along with his third son James, a lieutenant in the 44th Foot. Upon the colonel's death the peerage was passed to the eldest son, also Peter Halkett, who had remained in Scotland. Captain Francis Halkett had served as Braddock's brigade major on that campaign, so he was experienced with the responsibilities and duties of the position, the provincial troops that Forbes would have to deal with, and the Allegheny Mountains that Forbes would have to traverse. Quite possibly, Halkett was also motivated by the desire to gain revenge upon the French at Fort Duquesne. Halkett had served as a secretary to Forbes in New York beginning not later than October 1757, and he regularly appears in Forbes's official and personal correspondence throughout the winter of 1757–1758.[7] Forbes's relationship with Halkett was probably akin to that of an uncle and nephew, and Halkett remained unwaveringly loyal to the general throughout the entire campaign.

Although Brigade Major Francis Halkett played a pivotal role in the campaign, almost nothing is known of the man. Most information on Halkett is derived from a memorial that he prepared in 1758, in an attempt to gain a promotion into Forbes's 17th Foot, with Forbes's patronage. Since this is the only available biographical sketch of Halkett, it is reproduced in its entirety:

- That he bought his Lieutenancy & Company.
- That he is the eldest Captain in the Regiment but one, has been five campaigns upon service and by the 2 day of May next will be of 7 years standing, that he has constantly attended his duty, and has discharged it to the satisfaction of all his Commanders.
- That he has acted as Major of Brigade since the troops first came over to this Country, and always had the honour, to attend the person of the Commander in Chief.
- That his Father was Colonel of the 44th Regiment, and killed in the battle of the Monongahela.
- That from the courtesies your Lordship has been pleased to show him, and the inclination to serve him that your Lordship was pleased to express, he flatters himself, your Lordship would have taken the first proper opportunity of providing for him.
- That he has reason to believe he likewise possessed the good graces of General Shirley whilst under his Command, from his raising of his own account, offer'd him one of the Majority, when he had orders from the Government to raise 2,000 men, but upon the Royal Americans being established, it put a stop to the leavying of this Corps.
- As your Lordship may not think his pretentions are sufficient to be provided for in the 35th, 40th or 47th Regiments, when the Lieutenant Colonelcys are now vacant, he would think it very sufficient, and one of the greatest Honour, and obligation, your Lordship joining with Brigadier Forbes to intercede with General Abercromby, to allow me to purchase the Majority of the 17th Regiment, upon Lieutenant Colonel Morris retiring.[8]

Given his qualifications, his already close personal relationship with Forbes, and his determination to conquer the French, Halkett was an excellent selection for the post of brigade major. He provided Forbes with superlative service throughout the campaign. Since Forbes was ill for much of the year, he frequently had to verbally issue his orders and instructions to Halkett, who then transcribed them into written format. This constituted an absolutely critical service that required Halkett to clearly convey not only Forbes's direct instructions, but also Forbes's intent and purpose behind the directions.

Forbes's second principal staff officer was his quartermaster general, Lieutenant Colonel John St. Clair. Like Bouquet, St. Clair held his commission in the Royal American Regiment, although he had continuously served as a deputy quartermaster general at different times and places in North America since his arrival with Braddock's Expedition in the spring of 1755. Little is known of St. Clair's life before the Braddock Expedition, except that he possibly was not of the Scottish peerage as was generally assumed by both his contemporaries and historians, who consistently referred to him as Sir John St. Clair.[9] Like Forbes, St. Clair had been with the British Army throughout the War of Austrian Succession, and by 1758 was an experienced officer with extensive military service on both the Continent and North America.[10]

In the English Army of 1758, the quartermaster general was a position of immense importance. The quartermaster was responsible for providing and managing all food for the soldiers; locating and providing all forage for the animals; contracting for and coordinating wagons and carts, with drovers to drive them, and horses and/or oxen to pull them; contracting for and controlling other transportation such as pontoons to cross water obstructions, and bateaux and canoes to utilize waterways; selecting camping sites for an army; laying out and organizing these campgrounds; and acquiring and issuing clothing and military equipment (except for arms, ammunition and accouterments, which were handled by artillery officers for the Board of Ordnance). In short, the quartermaster had a myriad of duties that were primarily logistical, supply and transportation in nature. If the quartermaster was remiss in his duties, an army could not possibly be fed, clothed or even moved.

At the beginning of the campaign, Forbes issued the following instructions to St. Clair, which was to guide his actions and activities to facilitate Forbes's advance. These orders provide a record of St. Clair's responsibilities, as Forbes would have them understood:

> As the Season of the Year advances very fast you are hereby desired to repair to the Provinces of Pennsylvania, Maryland & Virginia, where you will give such orders and directions as shall seem necessary to you, for the accelerating the Military Operations that are to be carried on during the ensuing Campaign.
>
> Giving particular attention to the state of the roads, and ordering provendor of all kinds for horses, at proper places upon those roads and taking care that the bridges be repaired and floats made where necessary. You will inform yourself how we can be supplyed with carriages of all kinds, and in all bargains or contracts made, that there must be large pecuniary fines in case of failure. You will cause the provinces to establish posts for horses for the special communication of all intelligence. And you will constitute a small number of Guides of the most intelligent people who know the Country that can be found.
>
> And as it will be necessary to have a certain number of waggons attending the army, you will inform yourself whether the gaining of them by contract or purchasing them will be most expedient, and you will take notice that they are to be covered with oil cloathes & numbered and that the horses & drivers are to be able and sufficient. You will hasten the working tools, bespoke by Mr. Howell at Philadelphia, as likewise to provide scythes and sickles with some grinding stones. You will remember to determine if there can be water carriage from Conegocheegee [Conococheague Creek] to Will's Creek, and to get the roads betwixt them repaired, and forage laid in at different stages. And to get as much as possible laid in at Fort Cumberland [at the intersection of Wills Creek and the Potomac River, in the colony of Virginia].
>
> You will hasten as much as possible the new Levies, and inforce with all your arguments the forming of ranging companies, and the Governours must be required to send orders to all troops & others under their command to obey your directions, and when you learn where their troops are, you will make a disposition of the Pensilvania and Maryland forces all along those roads leading to Conigockey where a deposite for the provisions should be made, and the Virginia forces may be posted upon the road from thence up to Fort Cumberland. If there be any Cherokee Indians arrived at Winchester or [letter torn and word missing] you will give them all sorts of incouragement in going out upon scouting parties, joining some of the provincials with them, by which our convoys may be kept free of the enemys scouting parties, and our march and designs be kept secret from them. The provincial forces of Pensilvania and Maryland as soon as leveyed are to be ready to march to Conagocheegee, in order to be reviewed, and in the meantime to assist in escorting the provisions stores &c and the men unfit for that service are immediately to be taken notice of and the provinces acquainted that better men may be sent in their place.
>
> The Virginia people are to be employed from Conegocheegee to Fort Cumberland where they must be assembled & reviewed likewise, and as the Kings provisions can not easily be furnished to either upon those routes they will be allowed four pence sterling & Rum. N.B.: Virginia has six months provisions for 1200 men at Winchester. A proper person ought to be appointed to reside with [letter torn word missing] of the provinces in order to solicit what may be wanted and to give intelligence how they proceed.
>
> Enquiry ought to be made immediately about proper people used to deal with the Indians, in order to send two, three or more of them (unknown to one another) up to Fort Duquesne, and the Ohio, to get intelligence and to bring us a state of the enemys strength & situation.
>
> As the magazines for provisions and for forage must be your first and principle [letter torn word missing] there must be no time lost in getting them ready with all the diligence possible.[11]

When Forbes heard in October 1754 that St. Clair had been appointed to be quartermaster for Braddock, he would write a confidant that he knew St. Clair to be "a mad sort of Fool."[12] During the Braddock Campaign, St. Clair had rendered good service, and nearly worked himself to exhaustion for Braddock, but he had also revealed a short temper charitably described as irascible, that significantly inhibited his effectiveness. Still, St. Clair was the most experienced quartermaster general in the North American colonies. His previous experience with the Pennsylvania, Virginia and Maryland Provincial soldiers, Colonial leaders, and their governments, and his extensive services west of the Allegheny Mountains during the Braddock Campaign should have made him a valuable asset to Forbes.

However, Forbes was extremely nonplussed with St. Clair's performance as quartermaster throughout the campaign. Forbes wrote Abercromby as early as June 15, "For I see my friend Sir Jno. St. Clair does not value what expence he runs into, which I must moderate as much as possible."[13] And he complained again to Abercromby regarding St. Clair's temper on June 27, "My friend Sir John having almost disoblidged the whole Virginians with their new Governour [Francis Fauquier] in to the bargain." Regarding St. Clair's inefficiency, Forbes wrote from Carlisle on July 9: "...gott here July the 4th. Where (God grant I may keep my temper) I found everything a heap of Confusion, and Sir John St. Clair at Variance with every mortall."[14] Forbes and other officers, both British regulars and particularly provincials, would complain regularly during the campaign of St. Clair's incompetence, poor management skills, recurring interference with other officers, irregular assumption of command, acrimonious disposition, and inability to cooperate with either civilians or soldiers. His profanity and temper were legendary in both Braddock's and Forbes's armies. The renowned historical architect Charles Morse Stotz, who made his life's work the study of eighteenth-century military affairs in western Pennsylvania, referred to St. Clair as a "vacillating incompetent."[15] St. Clair would cause Forbes great problems during the campaign; he routinely imposed substantial delays, and incurred additional labors for Forbes's already overworked soldiers. At one point St. Clair single-handedly disrupted the entire unity and cohesion of Forbes's forward momentum when he arrested a senior Virginia officer. Finally, in what must only have been utter and complete exasperation, Forbes would write to Bouquet on September 4, "He is a very odd Man, and I am sorry it has been my fate to have any Concerns with him."[16]

The Fort Ligonier Museum possesses a portrait from life of St. Clair by the renowned royal artist Allan Ramsey, which reveals an angry pair of stone-cold blue eyes, and a visage that almost reeks of confrontation. Even 250 years after it was painted, his gaze is so fierce, hostile and penetrating that the janitorial staff at the museum prefers not to work in the same room alone with it. It almost certainly is a stunningly accurate portrait, for it forcibly projects the personality of a man who provided such very poor service indeed to John Forbes.

When Forbes was given direction of the Duquesne expedition in March, he had an impressive command assigned to him consisting of no less than two regular battalions, a detachment of Royal Artillery, and provincial forces from Pennsylvania, the Lower Counties of Pennsylvania (today's Delaware), Maryland, Virginia, and North Carolina. Although this force must have looked imposing on paper, Forbes lamented to his friend Lord Loudon on April 23, 1758, from Philadelphia: "I am here these six days by my self alone, having no mortall but Halkett. In short necessity will turn me into a Cherokee, and don't be surprised if I take F: duQesne at the head of them; and them only, For to this day I have no orders to command any troops nor has any troops orders to receive my Commands."[17] Forbes's first and most pressing requirement was to actually assemble something vaguely resembling an army.

The initial component available to him was a strong detachment from the 1st Battalion of the 60th Foot, otherwise known as the Regiment of Royal Americans. This would prove to be the core of his army, for it was commanded and trained by Bouquet. The battalion contained a great proportion of experienced and capable officers and noncommissioned officers (NCOs). A typical officer was Lieutenant Lewis Ourry, born on February 21, 1717, to a French Huguenot refugee family (another well-known French Huguenot in service to England was Lord Ligonier). His father had served under George I and George II, and Ourry's three brothers all served in the Royal Navy. Ourry was commissioned a 2nd lieutenant in Churchill's Marines in 1747, and in 1750 he had become fort adjutant in Jersey. He served as adjutant until 1756, when he joined the Royal Americans as a lieutenant. Ourry had over a decade of military service when the Forbes campaign commenced, to include considerable time in the responsible position of adjutant. His numerous letters, both before and after the 1758 campaign, reveal Ourry to be an educated, well-lettered professional officer with a sense of humor and considerable capability in such diverse fields as logistics, coordination with provincial citizens and militia, military leadership, and even bridge building.[18]

Once raised in 1755, Bouquet's First Battalion of the Royal Americans had been initially dispatched to South Carolina, where they had performed primarily garrison duties in 1756 and 1757. Although the battalion had not seen any active campaigning, yet their sojourn in the Carolinas had provided Bouquet with an opportunity to train and discipline them to his own high personal standards. Certainly this was needed, for Bouquet was none too impressed with the quality of soldiers under his command, despairing at one point: "We have gotten a Number of such drunken dirty fellows that we shall never make anything of them."[19] The Royal Americans had not found the Carolina climate to be to their liking, and Forbes would comment on May 3, "...these companies are very sickly, coming from Carolina, and very much want some Days of rest and Refreshment."[20]

Bouquet was originally to have had available the five companies of the Royal Americans that he had commanded in Charleston, but only four companies were finally marched to Philadelphia. The company of Major John Tulleken remained in New York Colony throughout the 1758 campaign.[21] The strength of the four companies of Royal Americans was recorded at Carlisle on July 17, 1758, to be one Colonel (Bouquet), sixteen other officers, sixteen sergeants, 8 drummers, and 381 rank and file for a total of 422 soldiers.[22]

Forbes's second regular battalion was a sturdy and large regiment of Highlanders. This regiment had been formed under a plan originally proposed by the Duke of Cumberland late in 1756, and subsequently approved by the King, to raise two thousand loyal Scottish Highlanders for service in North America. The First Highland Battalion, as it was formally designated, was to be under the active command of Archibald Montgomery, the son of Alexander Montgomery, the 9th Earl of Eglinton.[23] Born into a Scottish family with a commendable record of military service on May 18, 1726, Montgomery had been educated at Eton College and Winchester School, had entered military service in 1743, and had seen considerable service as a captain and major with the 36th Foot. Montgomery had no difficulties raising his regiment, originally ten companies, and his recruiting was so successful that he was able to increase his regiment by an additional three companies in 1757. By the start of the Forbes Campaign, Montgomery would command a thirteen-company battalion of over one thousand tough Highlanders from a number of different clans including many of his own Montgomerys, augmented by loyal clansmen from the Stuarts, Frasers, MacDonalds, Camerons, MacLeans, and MacPhersons. Montgomery received his commission as lieutenant colonel on January 4, 1757.[24]

The leadership of Montgomery's regiment was extremely mature.[25] His two majors were Sir James Grant, the 4th Earl of Ballindalloch; and Alexander Campbell. Grant, born in 1720, had entered military service as an ensign with the 1st Foot (the Royals) in 1741. Grant had been on continuous service with the grenadiers of the Royals, and had fought in Flanders during the War of Austrian Succession. In particular, he had been a participant in the bloody and tumultuous Battle of Fontenoy in May 1745. Grant would note of his own service in a memorial that he had prepared while attempting to obtain the majority with Montgomery's new regiment:

> has had a Company six years, which he purchased, as well as every other Commission, that he has been abroad upon Service every Campaign of the War, and was Aide de Camp to General St. Clair both with the Army in Flanders & at Turin, that there are very few Captains who served abroad & who are of so long outstanding, unprovided for & not one Officer imployed for so long a time in the station of Aide de camp, who has not been promoted.[26]

Campbell started his military career as an Ensign with the loyal Argyllshire Militia in 1745. He had served as the captain of an independent company in the East Indies in 1747, and then with the 1st Foot. The known military records for eight captains present with Forbes in July 1758 reveals that seven of them had previous service, most of them possessing nearly fifteen years of leadership experience, the majority of this service being acquired with the Dutch-Scots Brigade:

- John Sinclair: Considerable service in the Dutch-Scots Brigade, as an ensign, lieutenant and captain;
- Hugh Mackenzie: 15-year veteran of the Dutch-Scots Brigade, as an ensign, lieutenant and captain;
- John Gordon: Entered service as a 2nd lieutenant with the 1st Foot in 1746, promoted to captain upon raising Company in 77th Foot;
- Alexander Mackenzie: Ten years service with the Dutch-Scots Brigade, joined British Army in 1756 when 4th Foot was expanded;
- William MacDonald: No previous experience;
- George Munro: Fifteen years previous service with the Dutch-Scots Brigade;
- Roderick Mackenzie: Veteran of the Dutch-Scots Brigade; and
- Allen MacLean: Experienced officer with the Dutch-Scots Brigade, had been wounded at the Siege of Bergen-op-Zoom.

The exemplary quality of leadership in the Highland Regiment would have made it a particularly robust corps.

The regiment was subsequently renumbered the 77th Regiment of Foot. Ten companies of the regiment were originally dispatched from Cork, Ireland, on June 30, 1757, to Charleston, South Carolina, to reinforce Bouquet's garrison there. Montgomery had been so successful in recruiting that he had too many men, and upon their arrival on September 3, 1757, some two hundred soldiers were "draughted," or forcibly transferred, out of his regiment into the Royal Americans.[27] Lord Loudon noted that a number of "Low Country Men" (or Scottish men from the lower counties of Scotland and not the Highlands) had enlisted in Montgomery's Regiment, and he recommended that these men be particularly drafted for the Royal Americans. Upon Montgomery's arrival in Charlestown, Bouquet reported, "They were very healthy when they arrived.... That Battalion is in extreme good order." [28] Colonel William Byrd III of Virginia, then in South Carolina assisting Southern Indian Superintendent Edmond Atkin with enlisting Native warriors to support the British cause, wrote to Forbes on March 21: "I think 'tis pitty so fine a battalion should lay the summer in garrison here, for it is really the finest I ever saw, but the hot weather disagrees very much with them."[29]

Three additional companies were raised in Scotland in 1757. These companies were sent directly to Philadelphia, where they arrived on April 22, 1758. Their voyage from

England had apparently been long and difficult, for Forbes recorded that upon their arrival these companies "have one third sick."[30] They were formed as a temporary battalion under the command of Captain Allen McLean, the most senior captain, until they were joined with the remainder of Montgomery's regiment. These companies moved up from Philadelphia to Carlisle in early May, McLean informing Forbes from Lancaster on May 2: "I have the pleasure of acquainting you that I arrived here Saturday last [April 29, 1758] with the three additional Companies of Colonel Montgomerys. I left none upon the road, tho the situation they were in at Philadelphia seem'd to promise otherwise. They complain now of being beatten in the feet on account of the hardness of the Roads; but that is a malignity so easily got over; that their rest here will render them fit enough for duty."[31]

Montgomery's full battalion was subsequently ordered to join Forbes's expedition, and the main body of the regiment landed at Philadelphia on June 8, 1758.[32] Upon their arrival Montgomery's regiment mustered one colonel (Montgomery), two majors (Grant and Campbell), seven captains (John Sinclair, Hugh Mackenzie, John Gordon, Alexander Mackenzie, William McDonald, George Munro, Roderick Mackenzie), thirty-one other officers, forty sergeants, twenty drummers, and 999 rank and file.[33]

Although both regular battalions, the Royal Americans and Montgomery's Highlanders, had every appearance of being more than satisfactory, neither had seen any active service previous to this campaign. Their effectiveness on the march, and in the field, remained to be proven.

The majority of Forbes's army would be provincial troops, predominantly provided by the colonies of Pennsylvania and Virginia. Pennsylvania, in large part because of its Quaker roots, did not have a military tradition or even a militia prior to the onset of the Seven Years' War. However, Braddock's defeat and the resulting swarm of raids and assaults by Native American warriors on the Pennsylvania frontier had led to the establishment of a provincial military force in the colony. Although outside the scope of this study, the establishment of such a force had not been accomplished without strident and fervent debate and argument that graphically demonstrated the rift between the predominantly Scotch-Irish settlers on the frontier, and the Quakers who constituted the majority of the Pennsylvania Assembly. Further confounding the issue was a longstanding and bitter feud between the Penn family as proprietors, and the Colonial Assembly.[34]

Not without experiencing even more friction, Pennsylvania would recruit a three-battalion-strong Pennsylvania regiment to support Forbes in the spring of 1758, although it never functioned as a single regiment but rather operated as three distinct and separate battalions. The First Battalion would be commanded by Colonel John Armstrong, a veteran officer best known for leading a daring and successful attack upon the Indian village of Kittanning in September 1756, which had been the only bright spot in the annals of English arms that year. Born in Ireland on October 13, 1717, Armstrong was a responsible, mature founding citizen of Carlisle, Pennsylvania, and he provided exemplary leadership to the Pennsylvanians entrusted to his care. Colonel James Burd commanded the Second Battalion. Born in Edinburgh, Scotland, in 1726, Burd and his family moved to Philadelphia in 1748, where he became a merchant with strong connections to a number of prominent Pennsylvania families including the Shippens, the Willings, and the Allens. Burd had served as an engineer and work party commander constructing a road from Pennsylvania to Fort Cumberland during the Braddock Campaign, had entered provincial service as a captain in January 17, 1756, and had become a colonel and the commander of the Pennsylvania forces on the Fort Augusta frontier in the summer of 1757. Along with Armstrong, he possessed as much military command time as any provincial officer available in Pennsylvania, and his political and social connections were invaluable. The Third Battalion's commanding officer was Colonel Hugh Mercer. Born on January 17, 1726, near Rosehearty, at the manse of Pitsligo Kirk, Aberdeenshire, Scotland, to a Presbyterian minister, Mercer had attended the University of Aberdeen and graduated as a physician. Mercer served as a surgeon with the Jacobite Army in the 1745 Rebellion, and had been forced to flee to America after the Stuart defeat at Culloden. He moved to Mercersburg, Pennsylvania, as a founding citizen of that community, participated as a volunteer in Braddock's expedition, accepted a captain's commission in the Pennsylvania Provincials early in 1756, and had accompanied Armstrong on the raid to Kittanning, where he had distinguished himself. Mercer was a mature civic and community leader with considerable military experience. Taken together, the Pennsylvania Provincials had superb battalion-level leadership.

To augment these three battalions, Pennsylvania also contributed a small detachment of artillerymen, and a troop of fifty light horsemen. Pennsylvania did not benefit from a previous military record, and the colony did not even possess a militia until November 1755. Only a single battalion had served in mostly small detachments guarding frontier posts since April 1756. For a colony that only three years before had never even had a county militia, the military establishment provided Forbes by Pennsylvania was actually quite impressive. Pennsylvania recruited a significant number of soldiers, over two thousand officers and enlisted ranks, and would comprise the largest single contingent with Forbes. Although raising and managing this force was not performed without many challenges, Forbes had no reason to complain of Pennsylvania's commitment to his campaign.

Recruiting for this mass of Pennsylvania soldiers had progressed satisfactorily, primarily because the war had adversely affected the Pennsylvania economy. In particular, large numbers of indentured servants, or individuals who had recently completed their terms of servitude and needed cash to start life on their own, were available for enlistment.[35]

The Pennsylvania battalions were initially hampered by shortages of equipment, arms in particular. Burd noted during a visit to one of the Pennsylvania frontier forts in February 1758: "Here I found a target erected, I ordered the Company to shoot at the same. ... some of them shot tolerably bad, most of their arms are very bad."[36]

The absence of an established militia, or participation in previous campaigns, meant that the pool of experienced officers, NCOs and soldiers was extremely limited. In a famous quotation, Forbes would lament of the Pennsylvania provincial forces:

> [A] few of the principle Officers excepted, all the rest are an extream bad Collection of broken Innkeepers, Horse Jockeys & Indian traders, and that the men under them, are a direct copy of their Officers, nor can it well be otherwise, as they are a gathering from the scum of the worst of people, in every Country.[37]

Still, these Pennsylvanians provided Forbes with dependable service throughout the campaign. The total strength of these three battalions was recorded on July 17, 1758, as three colonels, 135 other officers, 88 sergeants, 44 drummers, and 2,006 rank and file for a total of 2,276 soldiers.[38]

The most experienced provincials in Forbes's army would be provided by the colony of Virginia. Its colonel, young George Washington, also possessed more knowledge of the Ohio country than any other officer with Forbes's army, having traversed the area as early as 1753 while carrying a message from the Virginia governor to the French military commandant of the area. Washington had repeatedly been over the same country on numerous occasions between 1754 and 1755. The First Virginia Regiment had been in service since

1754. Some of its soldiers had served with Washington at the early skirmishes at Jumonville and Fort Necessity that year, many had participated in Braddock's expedition, and since that time they had fought an epic struggle to safeguard the frontier against the hordes of Indian raiders issuing forth from the French posts in the Ohio country. Washington had served as one of Braddock's aides-de-camp during the 1755 expedition, and had gained considerably from the opportunity to closely observe a seasoned professional British senior officer managing a complex campaign traversing difficult terrain. Washington's services at the Battle of Monongahela and subsequent retreat were nothing short of heroic. He had gained considerable command experience, and he and a select few of his Virginia subalterns were the only officers in the British Army who had literally been engaged in the Seven Years' War from the very first shot.

Since Braddock's defeat, Washington had commanded the solitary regiment attempting to defend the frontiers of his colony. In this role, Washington had to manage a myriad of desperately challenging command problems such as surly, unpaid soldiers; difficult logistical challenges including road building; and the design, construction and maintenance of defensive positions. At the same time Washington had to address tactical issues including establishing an effective patrol system against a skilled, deadly, and tenacious opponent. Washington was well respected by most British officers. Governor James Glen of South Carolina would write to his cousin, John Forbes, "Washington is a cool sensible modest young man."[39] But he would reveal during this campaign that he was still a Virginian in his allegiances, first and foremost; and he was also a most reckless and ambitious young man.

As a result of four campaigns under arms, the First Virginia Regiment provided a base of experienced officers, NCOs, and soldiers. It was already well formed and fully organized in the spring of 1758, although Washington noted that his regiment would require one hundred fifty men to complete it to full strength.[40] Washington's lieutenant colonel was Adam Stephen, who had been born in 1718 in Scotland, had graduated from King's College, University of Aberdeen as a physician, and had served as a surgeon with the Royal Navy during the War of Austrian Succession. He had immigrated to the colony of Virginia, where he practiced medicine in Fredericksburg before serving as a company commander under Washington during the 1754 campaign.[41] Stephen commanded a company of rangers in the Braddock expedition, and was every bit as experienced and capable as Washington.

To support Forbes's expedition, the Virginia Assembly passed an act on March 1, 1758, to not only maintain Washington's regiment, but to raise a second regiment of 1,000 men, in addition to other measures.[42] Virginia's Second Regiment was to be commanded by fifty-year-old Colonel William Byrd III, a socially well-placed and prominent Virginian, the eldest son of one of the wealthiest and most preeminent families in the colony. Byrd possessed considerable experience on the frontier, particularly regarding negotiations with Native Americans. Before his appointment as Colonel of this regiment, Byrd was serving as the assistant to Edmond Atkin, the British Indian Superintendent to the Southern Indians, so he was familiar to and experienced in dealing with the Cherokee and Catawba Indians who would join the Forbes expedition.[43] His lieutenant colonel was George Mercer, a native-born twenty-five-year-old Virginian. Mercer had attended William and Mary College in Williamsburg, Virginia, was a trained surveyor, and as with the other senior Virginian officers he was a member of one of Virginia's leading families. He had been wounded while serving under Washington at Fort Necessity in 1754, had commanded a company of carpenters on the Braddock Campaign, and had served as Washington's aide-de-camp in the 1st Virginia Regiment in 1756. Mercer had commanded a Virginia company serving in South Carolina with Bouquet in 1757, and had already started to build a positive working relationship with that officer.[44]

Unlike the Pennsylvania regiment that was predominantly recruited from servants who were interested in escaping or improving their economic and social position, the Virginia regiments consisted of men from the lower stratum of society. Typically, Virginia's recruits were those too poor to afford a substitute, vagrants, unemployed workers, landless farmers, and other undesirables or unfortunates who had been either pressed or pressured into service.[45] As a result, desertion was particularly rampant in the Virginian regiments. Still, Forbes would obtain excellent service from these two regiments.

St. Clair inspected Washington's and Byrd's regiments in mid–May, and reported their state of readiness at that time to Forbes in two letters:

> I have seen the 4 Companys of Colonel Washington's Regiment who are in garrison at Fort Loudon, if the other Companys are in as good order as those are you may expect a great deal of service from them. That Regiment does Honour to its Colonel. They are in want only of tents which cannot be provided any where else but at Philadelphia; so that if the Colony should be prevailed upon to pay for them, they ought to be made at Philadelphia.
>
> As to the 2nd Regiment I hear they are compleat, I have reviewed the Captain's Complement of three Companys of 70 men each, who are good men and shall review about 300 more tomorrow, who are on their march: So that it is certain that in 4 or 5 days we shall have 200 of them here, but where to put them I cannot tell. I have sent to the Countys to see if I can collect arms for them, but I despair of getting one third part. I have wrote a very strong Letter to Mr. Blair *by your Order* [underlined in original] or in his absence to the Council of Virginia, requiring them to send up the arms for the Regiment from Williamsburg. I have quoted your Right in having all arms and artillery at your disposal, and that you had made a tryal of it at Philadelphia, even in ordering arms out of their stores; tho' purchased by the Province, and those were taken from them for other uses than arming their Provincial Troops. This Regt. are in want of every thing, which can be got no where but at Philadelphia. I think I shall be able to get them arms and blankets in Virginia.[46]
>
> My situation at present is, that I am at this place with Colonel Washington's four Companys, who are in want of Tents. That I have reviewed 633 men of the 2nd Virginia Regiment and there is near 200 more about town who I am to see this day. Those are in want of everything as I told you in my Letter of the 19th. I do not know where I can put them having no room in this place, nor can I march them out of it, lest they should become a sacrifice to our enemys who are daily scouting about us, at this moment there are a party of 100 Indians and 60 of the Virginia forces after them.
>
> I am not able to form the 2nd Regiment having neither seen nor heard from Mr. Blair since I left you, nor is there a list of the Officers been sent up here to Colonel Mercer.[47]

Colonel Byrd would report on the status of his regiment on several occasions to Forbes. On May 29 he reported, "The colony of Virginia has done me the honor to appoint me to command a regiment of a thousand new raised men (fine young fellows) which I have accepted of. They are quite raw at present & you are no stranger to my inexperience, but under your direction I hope they may prove of service to the cause...."[48] On June 3 he wrote in a similar vein: "The regiment the country has sent to my care is a body of fine stout fellows; officers & men intirely raw & undisciplined & I myself unexperienced. I can not by any means procure serjeants who know their duty to instruct them, but will do our best."[49] Still, by late in the summer Byrd had clearly proven his leadership skills, for on August 22, 1758, he wrote to Forbes:

> I have all my men in great obedience, they fire well at marks, & are very active fellows. They are awkward at the manual exercise & I believe Sir you can not expect them to be otherwise, when I tell you I have neither Sergts or Drills who were ever in the Service before.[50]

Virginia would also contribute a company of artificers, trained craftsmen such as wheel-wrights, carpenters, blacksmiths, tinsmiths, carriage makers, collar makers, etc. who were instrumental to keeping Forbes's army functioning. This company, commanded by Captain John Possey of the 2nd Virginia Regiment, would provide essential services to the army as it advanced into the wilderness.[51] They were at work on the roads not later than August 8, 1758. To provide scouts for Forbes's army, Virginia additionally raised a troop of fifty light horsemen under the command of Captain Robert Stewart. These men were recruited from Washington's First Regiment, and the men then replaced from the Second Regiment, and the cavalrymen carried against the rolls of Byrd's regiment. Stewart's Light Horse joined Forbes's army in early July.[52]

By July 17, Virginia counted the following soldiers with Forbes: two colonels (Washington and Byrd), eighty-nine other officers, eighty-five sergeants, thirty-five drummers, and 1,793 rank and file for a total of 2,004 soldiers.[53]

Maryland provided a relatively small force, approximately 350 soldiers, but rarely were soldiers provided by a province under such great difficulties, and in such a convoluted manner. By the Seven Years' War, the two houses of the Maryland Assembly were engaged in an acrimonious debate that almost reached the level of internecine warfare, and which effectively hobbled the ability of the colony to pass any legislation or raise any funds. In 1757, Maryland maintained two small forces to defend its hard-pressed frontiers, approximately 220 men at Fort Cumberland, and 114 men at Fort Frederick. The Assembly of Maryland had ceased to pay or feed these men after October 8.[54] Accordingly, Lord Loudon had accepted them into English service. The Proprietary Governor Horatio Sharpe held hopes that the spring 1758 session of the Assembly would resolve this logjam. In the event, Sharpe was to be bitterly disappointed:

> I doubt not but that the [Lower House of the] Assembly will as usual profess the utmost Readiness on their Part to comply with the General's Requisition & to do every thing that can be reasonably decided of them but I am thorowly convinced that they will never grant any Money for that or any other purpose unless upon Terms which they know the Upper House will never agree to & which if they would I am peremptorily forbidden by my Instructions [as Proprietary Governor] to accept.[55]

Forbes continued the arrangements that Loudon had made, telling Brigadier General Stanwix, "The Maryland Assembly broke up without giving one man or one sixpence. ... their 300 men who will now disband which is a pity to allow off at this critical time. So think they ought to be kept as they are: At the Expence of the Government for the rest of this campaign."[56] Accordingly, although these soldiers are routinely identified as "Maryland" troops during this campaign, they were more properly Royal soldiers raised in Maryland, paid for, equipped and armed by the Crown, but serving under Maryland provincial officers rather than Royal officers. Although never formally referred to as such during the campaign, it was essentially the "Royal" Maryland Battalion.

Maryland Governor Horatio Sharpe ordered Maryland militia to march to the two forts to relieve the more experienced Maryland veterans, who then joined Forbes. Sharpe set the example himself, personally leading these militiamen to the forts and serving with them at both Fort Frederick and Fort Cumberland at different times. By June 14 Sharpe was writing letters from Fort Frederick.[57] Sharpe was active throughout the campaign, and proved to be a consistent supporter of Forbes.

These Maryland soldiers were generally well regarded. Forbes would record that as these soldiers "have been used to the Woods and the Indian manner of fighting, I thought it would be a great loss to allow them to disband." Forbes would also note, upon promoting the senior company commander, Captain John Dagworthy, to lieutenant colonel to command this battalion, "he commands some of the briskest people I have seen...."[58] The "Royal" Soldiers from Maryland, as they in fact were, gave excellent service to Forbes. On July 17 their numbers were sixteen officers, eight sergeants, four drummers, and 248 rank and file for a total of 276 soldiers.[59]

Two other colonies provided small numbers of soldiers. North Carolina dispatched a battalion of three companies, a total of three hundred soldiers. Forbes noted on June 16, 1758:

> Governor Dobbs without orders has sent 200 of the North Carolina people by sea to Alexandria, and marches 100 more by land to Winchester, so you will give orders for their being taken care of and victualled, and order them directly up to join us.[60]

By early July the two companies that had come by way of Alexandria had joined Forbes. Quartermaster John St. Clair reported: "I have sent orders for the N. Carolina Provincials to march from Alexandria to Fort Frederick, and have sent them a Commissary, those who arrive at Winchester march to Fort Cumberland the 8th of July with a convoy from Mr. Walker."[61] The battalion of three companies was commanded by Major Hugh Waddell, who had previously served as a captain with the North Carolina Company in the 1754 Fort Necessity campaign with Washington.[62] On July 17, 1758, the strength of this detachment was recorded as nine officers, twelve sergeants and two hundred rank and file, for a total of 221 soldiers.[63]

Forbes was surprised to see these soldiers show up, as they had arrived "without a scrape of a pen" from North Carolina Governor Arthur Dobbs.[64] At the time, the colony of North Carolina had "neither Bullion nor Coin ... by which the Troops can be paid when they go out of the province." [65] As a result, the North Carolina soldiers were so poorly equipped, clothed and armed that Forbes had to march them to Fort Loudon to be properly outfitted at the Crown's expense. Forbes would complain that they were "in such absolute want of everything" that "I must either give them a kind of Cloathing or get no Service from them."[66] Forbes also had to assume full responsibility for paying them, and in fact he had to fulfill all of their financial needs, which would eventually require the expenditure of no less than five hundred pounds sterling, a relatively large sum for so few soldiers.[67] This ragged band of southern provincials arrived at Fort Loudon on July 20 to be outfitted.[68] Upon their arrival Waddell provided a complete return to Forbes to facilitate his battalion's being armed, clothed and equipped, which indicated that already thirty-three men had deserted, three had died, and eleven were too sick to perform their duties.[69] This large number of desertions and sick, so shortly after their enlistment and before the campaign had even begun, suggests that these soldiers were not of the best quality, although their shortages of clothing and camp equipage doubtless contributed to both absence and illness. Another officer described the Carolina companies "in a pitiable condition, and lack health, uniforms and everything. I have never seen such misery. I believe they are good only for eating our provisions or guarding a fort."[70] Forbes would write to Bouquet on July 14 with "no news only the beggary and desertion of the North Carolina Forces."[71]

The three "Lower Counties" of Pennsylvania, New Castle, Kent and Sussex (now the state of Delaware), raised three companies of volunteers to assist Forbes. These companies joined Forbes comparatively early, which is not surprising since they were so close to Philadelphia. They departed for Lancaster on May 30, 1758.[72] Captain Richard Wells commanded the battalion, in addition to one of the companies. Wells's commission was dated

April 17, 1758, and he would be promoted to major in June. A Pennsylvania official would note of Wells, "His Age, figure and circumstances, make him abundantly better qualified for it [the Majority commanding]. He has also the honour of being a Justice of the Peace for Kent [County]." The other two companies were commanded by Captain John McClughan, commissioned April 16, 1758, and Captain Benjamin Nixon, commissioned April 15, 1758. Nixon would resign and be replaced by Jacob Gooding Jr. on June 13, 1758. These companies were ready for service by May 23: "We have requested Mr. Chew to procure the Drums & Colours, etc. necessary for our three Companies; they are already provided with Cloathing & most of the other necessaries for their March, when your Honour pleases to Command." The three companies consistently mustered about 235 officers and other ranks. Unlike the other provincial soldiers, of whom Forbes and other officers would regularly grumble, no disparaging comments regarding the Delaware soldiers have been located, suggesting that they were a solid body of reliable infantry. One observer noted, "I have view'd his [Captain Wells's] men, and think them the finest set of fellows I ever saw, most of them from their size being fit for Grenadiers."[73]

One of the most important components of Forbes's army was a strong detachment of the Royal Artillery. Should Forbes manage to reach Fort Duquesne, the artillery would be essential to defeat that fortification. Additionally, the artillery with his column would enable Forbes to prepare strong defensive positions, which would be impervious to small French raiding parties principally composed of Indian warriors. The Royal Artillery detachment with Forbes arrived the second of week of June in Philadelphia harbor, and was rapidly unloaded and organized to join the expedition. It was a comparatively small party; when it mustered upon its arrival at Philadelphia on June 13 it consisted of:

Captain Lieutenant	1
Lieutenant Fireworkers	2
Sergeant of Miners	1
Miners	6
Bombadiers	2
Gunners	12
Matrosses	12
Drummer	1
Total	37

[Note: these are military]

Clerk of Stores	1
Conductors	3
Carpenters	2
Wheelers	2
Smiths	2
Collar Maker	1
Cooper	1
Total	12

[Note: these are civilian employees of the Board of Ordnance][74]

However, it should be noted that the artillerymen were only responsible for actually maintaining, loading, aiming and firing the cannon. Normally infantrymen would be assigned to the cannon, along with teams of contracted horses and civilian drovers, who would be tasked with actually maneuvering the cannon and handling the ammunition. Captain-Lieutenant George Anderson commanded the artillery on the expedition. The names of his lieutenants and other Royal Artillerymen are not known, except for that of Lieutenant-Fireworker George Wright.[75]

To augment the Royal Artillery, a detachment of Pennsylvania Provincials "trained for this service" also manned artillery pieces constituted as "the Royal Artillery Train of Pennsylvania." A small number of bronze artillery pieces, four 6-pounder cannon and two Royal (5½") howitzers previously purchased by the colony of Pennsylvania and located at Lancaster, were manned by these soldiers, and participated throughout the command as the "Provincial Train." Commanded by Captain Lieutenant David Hay, this detachment consisted of Ensign Martin Heydler, Sergeant John Mayer, and fifty-five men.[76]

The complete artillery train consisted of the following, based upon an undated list which appears to have been a compilation of the ordnance equipment unloaded from a Royal store ship upon its arrival in Philadelphia:

Ordnance, Heavy Brass Mounted, 24-Pounders	18
Ordnance, Heavy Brass Mounted, 12-Pounders	12
Ordnance, Light Brass Mounted, 12-Pounders	4
Ordnance, Light Brass Mounted, 6-Pounders	14
Ordnance, Light Brass Mounted, 3-Pounders	4
Brass Howitzers Mounted, 8-Inch	4
Howitzers, Royal, Mounted, 5 ½-Inch	4
Powder, Corn, Copper Hooped Barrels	2,996
New York Powder, Copper Hooped Barrels	270
New York Powder, Hazel Hooped Barrels	328
Shot For the Highlanders, Barrels	165
Flints, Musquet	124,000
Flints, Carbine	2,000
Flints, Pistol	1,250
Flints for the Highlanders Carbine	41,600
Flints for the Highlanders Pistol	43,600
Paper, Fine, Rhims [Reams]	279
Paper, Fine, for the Highlanders, Rhims [Reams]	108
Musquets with Bayonets & Slings	1,000
Carbines w/Rifled Barrels & Bayonets & Molds	100
Mortars Brass with Beds, 13-Inch	2
Mortars Brass with Beds, 10-Inch	2
Mortars Brass with Beds, 8-Inch	4
Mortars Brass with Beds, 4⅖-Inch	30[77]

This was an extremely large train of artillery, which would have been quite ponderous, and in fact would have overwhelmed the ability of Forbes's army to transfer it across the Allegheny Mountains. Accordingly, the heavier artillery was left behind to defend the Delaware River, and Forbes carried the following ordnance forward with him on the campaign, including both Royal Artillery cannons offloaded from the store ship and the small Pennsylvania Provincial Train of Artillery:

Light Bronze 12-pounder cannons	6
Light Bronze 6-pounder cannons	8
Bronze 8" Howitzers	2
Bronze 5½" (Royal) Howitzers	2
Bronze 8" Mortar	1
Bronze 5½" (Royal) Mortars	2
Bronze 4⅖" (Coehorn) Mortars	12[78]

The flints, powder, ball and stacks of arms also accompanied Forbes across the mountains. Although a relatively minor participant in the campaign, for they would only be engaged on one occasion at Loyalhanna Creek in October, their contributions on this date would be integral to the defense of the post. Their stellar performance defending the Loyalhanna Encampment suggests that the artillery was well organized and commanded throughout the campaign. The artillery stores were heavy and considerable, and moving the artillery successfully across the Pennsylvania mountain ranges was a challenging task that would occupy much of the campaign's efforts and energies.

Perhaps the most important soldiers with Forbes were the military engineers assigned to the expedition, although they consisted of a bare handful of officers. Ensign Charles Rhor, actually a subaltern from Bouquet's Royal Americans, served as Forbes's chief engineer. In this capacity Rhor would be responsible for selecting the route of the road from Philadelphia to Fort Duquesne, supervising the creation of all portions of this road including bridges and fords, choosing the location and designing the various defensive posts upon which Forbes based his entire campaign, and supervising their construction. It was an extremely important task, and both Forbes and Bouquet were quite impressed with Rhor's efforts.[79] Writing to Forbes on August 26, Bouquet would note of Rhor: "...although a young man — has a great deal of judgement, and I know from experience that he sees things clearly, without prejudice, and I can depend on his report."[80] Rhor was not only popular with his commanding officers, but he fostered an excellent relationship with the provincials on the working parties who would have to execute his plans and actually perform the grueling manual labor of clearing and construction. Lieutenant Colonel Adam Stephen told Bouquet, "I am Charmd with Rhor & will give him Officers & men that he can depend on."[81] Rhor made a number of significant contributions to the campaign, and in large part the advance of Forbes's army from Philadelphia to Loyalhanna was directly a result of Rhor's skills and efforts. Unfortunately, Rhor would be killed in September.

Recognizing that it would be impossible for Rhor to perform all the engineering functions for an entire campaign by himself, Forbes intended that he should be assisted by a number of other officers from the Royal Americans who possessed some knowledge of military engineering and construction. Lieutenant Emanuel Hess was one of these men, but Forbes noted that Hess was "dying of a deep consumption [tuberculosis]" at Philadelphia in June 1758. Hess would write Bouquet from Lancaster on September 20, 1758, "I must give up all hope of making this campaign."[82] Because of his illness, Engineer Hess was never on active service with Forbes's army. Another engineering officer was Lieutenant Thomas Basset, but he was also in poor health during the campaign, Forbes reporting to Abercromby on October 8 that he was dying, although he in fact apparently recovered.[83] The third officer was Captain Harry Gordon, with whom Forbes was not particularly impressed, but who succeeded to serve as Forbes's chief engineer upon Rhor's demise.[84] A fourth officer was Captain Richard Dudgeon, "a new Engineer from England" that Forbes sent to assist Bouquet on June 16.[85] With Rhor's loss, Forbes and Bouquet would struggle with his few remaining engineering officers, but Gordon, Basset and Dudgeon still managed to guide the operations of the army successfully to the Forks of the Ohio.

The final component of Forbes's army was the most difficult to control, and the least dependable, but was still one that Forbes expended considerable efforts and funds upon. Specifically, this portion of his army was composed of primarily Cherokee and Catawba Native American warriors, with some few members from other Indian nations, who had marched from the southern colonies of North Carolina and South Carolina to join Forbes. These Indians had predominantly been recruited by William Byrd III, then serving as an assistant to Southern Indian Superintendent Edmond Atkin, at the instigation of Lord Loudon.[86]

Unfortunately, these Natives had decided to join Forbes on their own schedule, early in the spring, which was their traditional time for war parties to depart. They arrived in Virginia and Pennsylvania in late April and early May to find that Forbes's army was still assembling, and that no accommodations had been made to receive them. Surprised to find no British army, and disturbed to find no provisions, arms, ammunition or other presents awaiting them, they almost immediately began to lose interest in participating in the campaign. Forbes went to great length to retain the Indians, for he well recognized their skills in reconnaissance and patrolling, and that they could provide his advancing columns with a screen of protection. Forbes immediately ordered thousands of pounds' sterling worth of gifts. In fact, once the need was identified, Forbes provided a veritable cornucopia of weapons, clothing, ammunition, equipment, food and drink, and other objects of great value to the Natives. A compilation of the mass of goods that were provided to the Cherokee and Catawba warriors is documented in Appendix A. At the same time as he was working so strenuously to obtain and distribute these presents, Forbes appointed Captain Abraham Bosomworth of the Royal Americans to serve as Indian agent to them, and also solicited the assistance of other officers who had had previous dealings with the Natives to support Bosomworth. Forbes would record, "I think the Cherokees of such Consequence that I have done everything in my power to provide them in their necessarys."[87] At one time Forbes had nearly three hundred Natives available to him, although their numbers began to dwindle at the same time as Forbes began his advance in earnest. Colonel Washington would advise Forbes on April 23 regarding these Natives: "There are two things I can find tho, that will contribute greatly to their ease, and contentment of mind; namely, an early Campaigne, and plenty of Goods."[88] Forbes was extremely disappointed in his dealings with the Cherokees and Catawbas to ascertain just how accurate Washington's advice was, for Forbes found them very difficult to satisfy and manage. The records of this campaign are replete with letters and discussions regarding efforts to retain the Natives, and attempts to employ them successfully.

Forbes reported that he had about two hundred Indians still with him in mid–July, and when he began his final advance in late October "that I have not now left with me above fifty."[89] The fact that Forbes still managed to retain so many warriors through the campaign season attests to his great efforts, and to his commitment to maintaining good relationships with the Indians. In fact, Forbes had more Native warriors, and employed them to better purpose, with his army than any other British establishment in North America during the Seven Years' War, except for those in which the redoubtable Sir William Johnson was directly involved. The Native Americans' numbers were always variable, their term of service indefinite, their reliability questionable, but Forbes counted them an important element of his force.

Forbes adapted this army, as appropriate, to the exigencies of wilderness warfare. One example of Forbes's adaptations was the use of rifles with his army. Although the traditional impression of a British Regular Army is that they were only armed with the relatively inaccurate smoothbore muskets, Forbes's army positively did carry and utilize rifles, for sixteen "rifled carbines" with rifle molds were issued to the Royal Americans under Colonel Bouquet on May 6, 1758.[90] These were probably drawn from the three hundred rifled carbines that Colonel Prevost had manufactured for the Royal American Regiment in Germany, and that had been brought to North America by Prevost in January 1757.[91] An additional one hundred "Carbines with Rifled Barrels & Bayonets & Molds" also arrived aboard the store ship from the Board of Ordnance that arrived at Philadelphia in early June.[92] These were rifles purchased by the Board of Ordnance, and shipped from the stores at the Tower of London. Aside from the sixteen rifles issued to the Royal Americans, how these rifles were used, or to which specific units they were assigned, is unknown. Bouquet was aware that these rifles with the army required higher quality powder than the smoothbore muskets, for he wrote Forbes on June 3: "There are 37½ barrels of very good powder at Harris's Ferry, intended for Fort Augusta. Half of it is fine powder for rifles, and Indians, and it is no longer possible to buy it. If you should consider it wise to take possession of it, you would be able to replace it with ordinary powder."[93]

One rifle documented to this campaign survives today. This is a musket-bore rifle made by London gunsmith Benjamin Griffin for Lieutenant Colonel Montgomery of the 77th Highlanders. The barrel of this musket is quite short, just beneath 24," and it is an impressively massive .70 caliber. The gun has a wooden patch box typical of early rifles, but is equipped with a distinctive front sling swivel and rear sling attachment more representative of military arms than a hunting rifle. This gun is quite similar to German rifles of the 18th century, and may have been a private hunting arm that Montgomery had manufactured, possibly for deer hunting in Scotland. However, given its distinctive swivels, it is much more likely that this rifle was designed specifically for military use in North America.[94] It is probably a finer rifle than would have been carried by a common provincial soldier, or would have been issued out from Board of Ordnance stores, but it is still representative of the European manufactured rifles in use by Forbes's army.

The Pennsylvania provincials serving with Forbes also carried rifles. Unlike the shorter European rifles, the rifles that these men carried were the more familiar Pennsylvania long rifles. Most of these rifles were probably manufactured by Pennsylvania craftsmen. Bouquet wrote on June 3 to George Stevenson, who was the Recruiting Officer for the Pennsylvania Regiment:

> With respect to the Defficiencies justly complained of in the new Levies, I hope they will soon be Supplyed particularly in point of view of Money: And we expect, dayly to receive some arms.... But in the interim, I think it advisable to persuade every Man that has a good Gun, or a Rifle to bring it with him, and it shall be Appraised, that in case it shou'd be lost, or destroyed on real Service, the owner may be paid the just Value of his Arms.[95]

When Bouquet gave orders to Captain George Ashton of the 3rd Battalion of the Pennsylvania Provincials on May 25, 1758, he specifically noted:

> And as a sufficient Number of Arms cannot yet be provided for your men, you are hereby desired to engage them to take their own Fuzees or Rifles (with Ammunition) which Fuzees or Rifles shall be appraised in Case they shall happen to be lost or destroyed on real Service, they shall be paid by the Crown.[96]

Bouquet wrote Forbes on June 7: "A large part of the provincials are armed with grooved rifles and have their molds. Lead in bars will suit them better than bullets—likewise the Indians—but they also need fine powder FF."[97]

Further evidence that rifles were carried on this campaign by the Pennsylvania Provincials is an invoice approved by Bouquet on October 15, 1758, for an expenditure of 4 pounds, 15 shillings to replace a "rifel gun" from the 2nd Pennsylvania Battalion that had been "snatched away by an Indian" while delivering a flag of truce to Fort Duquesne after Grant's defeat.[98] Suggesting that the Virginia, North Carolina, Maryland or Lower County provincials also carried at least some rifles with them, brigade orders were issued by Colonel George Washington during the final advance on Fort Duquesne on November 24: "A return to be given in of the best Marksmen in each Corps also of the Number of Rifles in each Corps."[99] Rifles were an integral component of Forbes's army, and well over one hundred were probably carried by his soldiers on the campaign. Even the positively known numbers of rifles, which certainly do not account for the majority of the rifles with the army, document that an absolute minimum of one out of every forty arms (2.5 percent) with Forbes's army were rifles.

Still, even with these adjustments to reflect the realities of wilderness warfare, Forbes's army was, in fact, no such thing. The force had not even existed in April, and was not completely recruited, armed, and equipped until early in July. The entire command would never be united until it collectively reached Loyalhanna Creek in early November. The two regular regiments were newly raised, of excellent material, but had never proven themselves in combat. The provincials, also of excellent material, were from five different provinces: Pennsylvania, Maryland, Virginia, the Lower Counties (Delaware), and North Carolina. Two of these colonies, Virginia and Pennsylvania, were actively competing against the other for the route to the Ohio country to be established through their territory. The Maryland soldiers suffered from political controversy in their colony that denied them adequate funding, and in fact had to enter into Royal service to be paid and supported. The North Carolina companies were desperately underfunded from their inception, as their state was relatively poor and possessed little available currency. Many of the provincial officers were experienced, but few of them had previously held commands at the levels that they now found themselves. Only a handful of officers had proven themselves with similar responsibilities in active operations, among this number being Forbes, Bouquet, Washington, Halkett and St. Clair. It was a daunting prospect, and Forbes and Bouquet would find themselves repeatedly challenged by the exigencies of managing and maneuvering this fractious army. But it was the only force available to Forbes, and this was the army that Forbes had to push and Bouquet had to pull across the tangled wilderness of the Allegheny Mountains.

Among the many challenges faced by Forbes and Bouquet on this campaign would be to forge this diverse and relatively inexperienced force into a unified, responsive instrument of their collective will. For as Forbes doubtless informed Bouquet in early May, he had a definite plan of campaign that Forbes considered almost certain of success. But its implementation would demand much of the soldiers and leadership of this newly recruited and established army.

• THREE •

"By which I shall have a constant Supply"

Forbes Plans a Campaign

Forbes based his campaign plan upon a set of precepts espoused by Count Turpin of France, as Forbes articulated to Southern Secretary William Pitt in a letter on October 20, 1758:

> [A]s the Enemy's Numbers had all along been represented to me, not only equall, but even to exceed what I could carry against them, so it was absolutely necessary that I should take precautions by having posts along my route, which I have done from a project that I took from *Turpin's Essay Sur La Guerre*. Last Chaptre 4th Book. Intitled *Principle Sur Lequel on peut etabler un project du Campagne*, if you will take the trouble of looking into his Book, you will see the Generall principles upon which I have proceeded.[1]

The military treatise that Forbes referred to was written by the French Count Lancelot Turpin de Crissé, *An Essay on the Art of War*. Turpin, a widely experienced French general, had written this essay in French in 1754, and it was one of the more widely read studies of warfare in the middle of the 18th century. British Brigadier General James Wolfe maintained a copy of Turpin in his library, as did a certain young Virginia gentleman with military aspirations.[2] In 1758 this book had not yet been translated into English, although Captain Joseph Otway would publish such an edition in 1761.[3] The chapter that Forbes referenced, "A Principle On which the Plan of a Campaign may be established," employed the expedient of comparing a campaign to a siege. Relevant sections of Turpin's study, as subsequently translated by Otway, are provided. These passages provided Forbes with "the general principles" upon which he proceeded. In fact, they are integral to comprehending Forbes's intent throughout the campaign. Although lengthy, the applicable portions of this treatise that Forbes applied on this campaign are provided in their entirety. Count Turipin began:

> War could not be termed a science, were it not founded upon invariable principles; nevertheless, it would be rashness to affirm them to be absolutely fixed, or to pretend to conduct their operations to such a certain point, as to assure their success, without indulging notions too chimerical [imaginary or unreal]. Why could there not be some general method established, which, being accommodated to the circumstances of time and place, would render the event of the operations more certain, and their success less dubious? Art is now brought to that perfection, that there is almost a certainty of carrying a place when the siege of it is properly formed; why therefore, with regard to the conducting of a campaign, cannot there be certain methods resolved on beforehand, for making the operations conducive to the end proposed, and from whence new ones may also be derived, if necessary? A general who proposes succeeding by such a method, will find prudence more necessary than bravery, and genius with an extensive foresight, more requisite than intrepidity.

By one unexpected movement of the enemy, the deepest-laid plans, and best concerted measures, may be destroyed. If, in order to make conquests, advancing was the only thing necessary, the general who was most daring would gain the greatest reputation, and every officer commanding an army would act after that manner; but it is not sufficient only to advance, the reason for doing it should be well considered, and the proper measures taken for retreating in safety.

Thus, Turpin indirectly criticizes Braddock's plan of campaign, in which he had advanced with no measures implemented to secure his logistical rear. Forbes certainly took notice of Braddock's shortcomings.

Count Turpin continued:

The wars of Italy under Charles VIII, under Louis XII, and Francis I sufficiently prove the danger of incursions and sudden invasions in distant countries, which may not only occasion the ruin of the army, but of the state also. The necessity of establishing general and probable principles for the prevention of such mistakes for the future, and from whence also combinations for every particular operation of a campaign may be produced, becomes evident. In order to establish a principle of this nature, it is necessary to suppose that the officer who is to carry it into execution, is thoroughly experienced in every thing relative to the science of war. The first thing a general should do, is to examine the map of the country through which his army is to march; he should use the same precautions generally practiced to gain the knowledge of the ground round a place that is to be attacked, and over which the trenches are to be directed.[4]

One method that Forbes employed almost immediately to gain knowledge of the "country through which his army is to march" was to obtain the letter book of St. Clair from his services directing the quartermaster operations for Braddock's Campaign. Forbes could reasonably expect that St. Clair's letters would be extremely revealing regarding the logistical, topographical, transportation, and financial aspects of Braddock's Campaign. By obtaining St. Clair's letter book, Forbes was able to garner an unbiased documentation of the challenges that Braddock had faced only three years earlier in penetrating the Allegheny Mountains to Fort Duquesne.[5] On March 23, Colonel James Montrose, a senior British engineer in New York, met with Forbes and "shewed him the Proportion of Stores sent with General Braddock."[6] Clearly, Forbes left no stone unturned in gathering his information on the Braddock Campaign and Pennsylvania.

One of the intriguing aspects of Count Turpin's guidance was that he compared the conduct of a successful campaign with that of a formal siege. By the middle of the 18th century, siegecraft had become a science of established techniques that if adhered to were almost certain to result in the capture of any fortress, no matter how well designed, constructed or defended. John Muller, Chief Master of the Royal Military Academy in Woolwich, stated in 1757:

The Art of Attacking is rendered so superior to that of Defending, that those Places which were formerly esteemed impregnable, can scarce stop a victorious Army a Month: And nothing but great Garrisons, and large Places well fortified, and provided with a sufficient Quantity of Artillery, and every Necessary for a good Defence, can have any chance of making a tolerable Resistance.[7]

Thus, if a campaign could be conducted to the same standards, its success would be equally as certain as any well-conducted siege. As Turpin expounded:

The operations for carrying on war offensively may be compared with those of a siege.... It is an established rule, that a general should never think of forming a second or a third parallel, to advance nearer the body of the place, till the first is entirely perfected and established, and the magazines of the trenches placed within reach.... These magazines are intended for supplying the troops more speedily with whatever is necessary for carrying on the attack of the works. If they have not a free communication with the tail of the trenches, they will be very soon exhausted and unable to supply the heads of the advanced parallels; and if these parallels are not properly provided, the siege will be retarded, and the intended attacks come to nothing. If the batteries which are erected to destroy the defenses of the place, do not take in the whole front of the works; if there is not a strict communication kept up between them and the tails of the trenches; if they are not supported and protected by the parallels, or not well served; they will never be able to silence the fire of the enemy, and will also be in danger of being taken, occasioned by the difficulty the troops will find in coming to their assistance.

The reason for advancing these different principles, which, in reality, are the rudiments for conducting the operations of a siege, is to mark their analogy with those of a campaign. The province, or country to be conquered, hath always some principal point, which it must be the general's endeavour to arrive at [in Forbes's case, Fort Duquesne at the Forks of the Ohio]: therefore, when a general is advancing into a country, why may not he form a first parallel and a general magazine for subsistence, in the same manner as that at the tail of the trenches? The communications with the general magazine of subsistence should be kept open, and supported on the right and the left of the first parallel that is established in the enemy's country. In order to form this parallel, the general should have the right or left of it towards some advantageous post, which he should take possession of; and before he thinks of advancing further, this parallel should be strongly supported by taking possession of the rivers and towns in the direction of it. It should also be observed as a rule never to begin the second parallel till the first is completely established, and the communications between the general magazines and the rivers and towns perfectly secured. The same rule should be observed in advancing from a first to a second, and from a second to a third parallel.

As magazines of the trenches within reach of the zigzags, are necessary for carrying on the operations of a siege, in the same manner, also, intermediate magazines of provision and ammunition should be formed in the first parallel established in the enemy's country; by which means everything necessary will be conveyed with ease from the general magazine to every part of the parallel.

The success of a campaign whose plan is formed upon this maxim, seems to be almost certain; and if by any unforeseen events, the general's expectations should not be fully answered, he need not be apprehensive of any bad consequences, as he will always remain in possession of that part of the country, where the first parallel is established. Even if the whole season has been employed in establishing the first parallel, it should not be looked upon as time thrown away, as it will be the means of securing the winter-quarters, and facilitating the execution of the measures concerted for the ensuing campaign....

...in carrying on an offensive war, some unexpected successes may prevent favorable opportunities of establishing two or even three parallels in the course of the same campaign; nevertheless, a prudent general will never suffer himself to be so much elated by a fortunate beginning, as to lose sight of his principal object; and his principal care will always be to have the parallels he has established in the enemy's country, secured after such a manner, as to render the communication between them and his winter-quarters perfectly free and open, as well as that the communication between them and the general magazine shall remain entirely free and uninterrupted. This general magazine will serve to establish the several intermediate ones necessary for pushing on another parallel the following campaign....

The batteries in a siege should find their effect, by keeping up a fire superior to that of the place. The view of a detachment should be to keep back the enemy and harass him, to protect the forage, and extend contributions over a province. When a battery is well served, the soldier is always animated; and when detachments return successful, it raises the general's credit with the army. The batteries of the trenches have yet another object, which is to cover the attack of a work, and to assist in pushing on the branches, which are to establish the third parallel upon the covered way. In the same manner, large detachments are designed to advance, and take possession of the right or left of a country, to cover the body of the army by which it is followed, In order to establish the intended parallel. As a battery whose platform is placed too far before the parallel, may easily be taken; in the same manner a detachment too far advanced before the army, instead of answering the end intended, is exposed to the danger of receiving a check, by which the whole operations of a campaign are often retarded.... every general commanding an army, should lay it down as a rule, never to hazard large bodies in front, unless he is certain they will not be forced to return. It is more pardonable in a general to neglect seizing a post, than to take possession of ground that he is forced to abandon....

In all the different events with which both ancient and modern history furnishes us, it may be remarked, that the defeat of an army, and the loss of an extent of country, after an unfortunate defeat, are generally owing to the neglect of generals in securing to themselves the places from whence they set out, or causing the posts necessary for retreating through to be secured. There are but few examples where the losses of battles have not been in some measure owing to one or another of the above mentioned neglects. It hath been sufficiently proved, that if much advantage is not gained, there can at least no ill consequences attend the pursuing of this method, which is here proposed for the advantage of those who may hereafter have an opportunity of carrying it into execution.[8]

In addition to Count Turpin's cautiously considered approach to military campaigns, Forbes was clearly influenced by the direction, or rather the misdirection, that the Braddock Campaign had taken.

Shortly after his arrival in the colony of Virginia, Braddock had chaired a critical meeting with numerous Colonial Governors and Colonel William Johnson, Superintendent to the Iroquois Confederation of the Six Nations, at the John Carlyle residence in Alexandria, Virginia, on April 14–15, 1755. This was an event that Carlisle regarded as "the Grandest Congress held at my home ever known on this Continent." At this meeting Braddock had committed with the King's colonial governors and Johnson to arrive at the Forks of the Ohio "upon the end of June, nearly in July." [9] To maintain this all but impossible timetable, a schedule that he had artificially imposed upon himself, Braddock had been forced to drive his command rapidly over the Allegheny Mountains, and had not taken time to construct any magazines, depots, or fortifications along his route. His supply and transportation situation had deteriorated so badly that he had eventually been forced to segment his force, proceeding with a large advanced party while leaving Colonel Thomas Dunbar of the 48th Foot with a greatly reduced main body in a camp near Jumonville Glen.

Although Braddock had made rapid progress, and had adhered to the schedule that he had agreed upon with the Royal governors, he had done so at the expense of establishing an effective supply system, functional transportation assets, or safeguarding his line of communications. Lt. Colonel Adam Stephen, who had commanded a company of Virginia rangers with Braddock, would write Bouquet regarding this on May 26, 1758:

> I have often reflected on the dismal Situation of the Grand Detachment, under Command of the Brave General Braddock, for want of Provisions, about three days before the Engagement. They depended entirely upon a Convoy which I carryd up to them, escorted by one hundred men; and I think it was a hundred to One, that even the Enemy permitted us to join the General; We came up with his Excillency in the Evening of the Sixth of July & next morning were attackd in the Rear, by upwards of three hundred French & Indians, who had been detachd from Fort duQuesne, then about twenty miles distant, on purpose to intercept the Convoy. At the Same time, Flour was So Scarce at Col. Dunbar's Camp that he could not have Spar'd another Supply to the General Before he had recei'd it from Fort Cumberland; So that Even Successful, we Should have been distressed before a fresh Supply Could have Arriv'd.[10]

Forbes's cousin, Governor James Glen of South Carolina, wrote in August, "A Virginia Gentleman who was in Braddocks Expedition, when he heard you had fixed your rout, came to me, honestly expressing his satisfaction, assuring me that if that general had succeeded at DuQuesne he had been undone, as his Army must have perished for want of provisions."[11] Bouquet would report on June 11, although he did not note his source of intelligence, "I am told that Braddock's army went 3 days without finding grass for the horses, which made them unfit to carry provisions; and he would have been likely to die of hunger, if he had beaten the enemy."[12] Forbes also read in St. Clair's August 15, 1755, letter to Sir Francis Napier in England, "I am still of Opinion that an Expedition might be carried on to the Ohio even from this Country and with a moral certainty of success, but we must follow different methods from what we observed in our last, particularly building small Forts in well Chosen places and at proper distances, this I proposed frequently before, but was as often laughed at on account of the time and Expence they must take up, but we went then upon an unhappy supposition of Certain success, and that it depended upon our presence only, without the formality of observing Military precautions and the Dictates of Common Sense."[13] Forbes had absolutely no intentions of repeating Braddock's mistakes. He was not going to simply advance to the Forks of the Ohio; he was going to advance to stay.

First, Forbes determined to establish Philadelphia as his main supply base. Philadelphia's deep-water harbor on the Delaware River provided better piers, unloading capability, storage capacity, and logistical facilities than had been available to Braddock along the Potomac River in the colony of Virginia. By 1758, Philadelphia was the single most prosperous and busiest port in North America. Historian James Flaxner Walzer has noted:

> The Philadelphia trading area was the largest and most populous and dominated primarily by the merchants of a single maritime entrepot. Inland trade was more highly centralized here than in any other part of the thirteen colonies, and it was because of this that Philadelphia had by-passed the older colonial cities of New York and Boston to become the largest and busiest commercial seaport in British North America.[14]

A 1774 foreign visitor to Philadelphia described the scene as he arrived: "The voice of industry perpetually resounds along the shore, and every wharf within my view is surrounded with groves of masts, and heaped with commodities of every kind, from almost every quarter of the globe."[15] The city also had a well-developed mercantile community, which meant that nearly every article of war that Forbes's army required could be manufactured by artisans, or procured from active merchants, in the city. As is documented in Appendix B, Forbes drew nearly every item of Indian trade goods directly from the vendors of Philadelphia. Having this port with its well-developed merchant, commercial and transportation system immediately available would provide Forbes with a well-founded support base that could easily feed, sustain, arm, and equip his army. Such an asset had never been available to Braddock.

From Philadelphia, Forbes had two prospective routes available to him. Initially, he would utilize existing commercial roads to Carlisle, where he would establish his first forward position, and then to Fort Loudon, a small frontier fort at the foot of the Allegheny Mountains. From here he would follow a road that had been constructed during the Braddock Campaign, but never finished, to Ray's Town, where he would establish his major advanced depot.[16] This portion of the route was predetermined by the presence of the Philadelphia merchant center and the network of extant roads, and would not be altered.

From Ray's Town, the first possibility was to construct a new road nearly due west across the Allegheny Mountains to Fort Duquesne, while continuing to draw his supplies and transportation assets directly from Philadelphia. The alternative route was to finish completing the road between Ray's Town and Fort Cumberland, and then follow Braddock's Road from Cumberland to Fort Duquesne, finishing the last few miles from the site of Braddock's defeat to the French fort.

Regardless of which route he selected, once past Fort Loudon, Forbes intended to construct a series of fortified positions to protect magazines and storehouses along his supply road. In this manner, even if a reverse occurred, either due to French action or the vagaries of nature, Forbes could simply withdraw to an established, protected supply depot immediately to his rear, and then resume his advance at his leisure. The small defensive positions contained garrisons that could offer a safe overnight haven to supply convoys, patrol the countryside for hostile Indians, and repair the road in the immediate vicinity of their post, thus further stabilizing Forbes's connection to his base. Unlike Braddock, once Forbes captured Fort Duquesne he would have a well-established supply line connecting him to the great mercantile center of Philadelphia. Forbes described in great detail to Pitt:

> As my offensive operations are clogged with many Difficultys, owing to the great distance & badness of the roads, through an almost impenetrable wood, uninhabited for more than 200 Miles, our back inhabitants being all drove into Carlisle. I am therefore lay'd under the Necessity of having a stockaded Camp, with a Blockhouse & cover for our Provisions, at every forty Miles distance. By which means, altho' I advance but gradually, yet I shall go more surely by Lessening the Number, and immoderate long train of provisions Waggons &c, For I can set out with a fortnight's provisions from my first deposite, in order to make my second, which being finished in a few days, and another fortnight's provisions brought up from the first to the second, I directly advance to make my third, and so proceed forward, by which I shall have a constant Supply [and] security for my provisions, by moving them forward from Deposite, to Deposite as I advance, and lastly if not thought convenient to settle upon the Ohio, or in that Country, I shall have a sure retreat, leaving a road always practicable to penetrate into those back Countrys.... I need not point out to you, Sir, my reasons for these precautions, when you consider that had our last Attempt upon Fort DuQuesne succeeded, we must have retired directly, for want of provisions, and at that time our back Settlements were much nearer advanced to Fort DuQuesne and the Ohio, than they are at present, having properly speaking none to the Westward of Carlisle.[17]

Forbes's strategy would be considerably slower, and more tedious, than Braddock's rapid advance across the endless ridges. Unlike Braddock, who had in large part sacrificed the quality of road building and establishment of a logistical tail in his haste to maintain his schedule, Forbes intended to establish an adequate road that could sustain a garrison at Fort Duquesne once that post fell to British arms. The construction of storehouses, depots, and magazines along his line of march, along with entrenched positions to defend them, would necessarily occupy many months and occasion much effort.

Forbes had been considering such a campaign in America for some time, for an undated memorandum in his headquarters papers responded to a request from Lord Loudon for Forbes's thoughts on just such an enterprise:

> As all interprises in warr ought to be sensibly considered before they are entered upon, and that your Army Artillery Magazines &c. ought ale [all] to be proportioned with regard to the Enemys Strength, The forts to be attacked, and the roads that you have to pass, I therefore beg leave to represent to your Excellency that as a scheme had been formed by the Earl of Loudon, for the march of a Body of Troops under the Command of Major General Webb to the Ohio and Fort DuQuesne, I therefore refer to the Instructions to have been given to that general for what after mature deliberation and the best intelligence that could be gott, was thought absolutely necessary to have carried their Enterprise into execution.
>
> 1st 2,000 of the Regular troops compleat consisting of Mr. Webb's own Regiment and either the First or Second Battalion Royal Americans. The Provincial Troops of Pennsylvania, Maryland & Virginia, which by their quota ought to amount to 4,000 men, but by turning away the riff raff or leaving them to serve as convoys and to repair the roads. The remainder was supposed to be 3,000 good men with a body of Cherokee Indians—which it was supposed might amount to 700. And the Virginia Regiment [i.e. the 1st Virginia Regiment under Colonel George Washington that was already formed].
>
> The Artillery was proportioned to this body and was to have consisted of—
> 12 pounders
> 6 pounders
> 2: 8 Inch Howitzers
> Coehorns, &c.
>
> The ammunition was proportioned to those and as there was a great deal of work to be done, in building of blockhouses at proper distances. Making of flatts, battoes &c and repairing and making of roads—the working tools were to be augmented accordingly.[18]

Upon his assumption of the actual command of this expedition, Forbes organized and directed it along these lines.

At the commencement of his campaign, Forbes had not committed to a definite route. One of the shortcomings of the Braddock Campaign was that Virginia was poorly supplied with wagons, horses, fodder and provisions. In fact, the overwhelming majority of Braddock's wagons and horses had come from the colony of Pennsylvania. Forbes clearly intended that his campaign's logistical base would be Pennsylvania. Initially, it appears that Forbes considered Conococheague Creek as the site of his first advanced depot, which suggested that he intended to use Braddock's Road to advance upon Duquesne.

However, shortly after his arrival in Philadelphia, Forbes became aware of the presence of what was known in Pennsylvania as the "Old Trading Path." Essentially a long-established Indian trading route across the Allegheny Mountains, this path had been substantially improved by Pennsylvanian James Burd in 1755 in support of the Braddock Campaign. It was now popularly known as "Burd's Road." Recognizing that he would eventually have to draw supplies and equipment from Pennsylvania, Braddock had ordered Burd to cut this road from Carlisle west to Ray's Town, then southwest to the Great Crossing of the Youghougany River to join Braddock's Road to Fort Duquesne.

This trading path had been used for centuries as the overland route by the Native Americans, traveling between the Atlantic coast and the Ohio Valley. Before Burd had worked on the road in 1755, the only Europeans who had used it were a few Indian traders, leading strings of pack horses across the mountains. Burd had reached the top of Allegheny Mountain when the news reached him on July 17, 1755, that Braddock had been defeated. Accordingly, Burd and his party had retreated east, burying their work tools at the top of the ridge.[19] From this point, nothing more had been done on this road, but at least an option now existed for Forbes of a more direct route than Braddock's Road, a route which was likely to save considerable miles in distance to be traversed, and was closer to the logistical base of Philadelphia.

Accordingly, Forbes determined to make Burd's Road to Ray's Town his solitary supply route. By the end of May, Forbes had abandoned any intent of using Conococheague, or any other forward base, for he instructed St. Clair on May 30 from Philadelphia: "I think that for the future all things going or coming from Winchester here, ought to go one route by Carlisle, Shippensburgh, &c. which will prevent confusion, and that road will always have escorts."[20]

A critical component of Forbes's planning was timing. He intended to conclude his advance in October or November, "because of the trees losing their leaves, by which one can see a little thro' the woods, and prevent the Enemy's surprizes, which is their only strength, and likewise, that in those two Months the Indians leave the French as it is their chief hunting Season, in which they provide for their familys during the winter."[21]

By late fall, Indian warriors were impatiently planning their departure for their annual winter hunt, which was absolutely necessary for them to gather furs for trade, and food for their families. The Cayuga Nation of the Iroquois Confederation traditionally celebrated their harvest ceremony early in November, which provided a thanksgiving for the crops that they had received at that year's harvest.[22] All Iroquois nations had a similar ceremony. This was the last major celebration of the year, and was very important to the Mingos, formed from the various nations of the Iroquois Confederacy who had migrated into the Ohio country.[23] The Mingo warriors of western Pennsylvania annually returned to their home villages to participate in this ceremony, for this ritual also signaled the time to begin preparations for and travel to their winter hunting grounds.

With the imminent arrival of winter, the Native American warriors traditionally lost interest in further warfare for the year. Winter was a time for hunting, not war. The Ojibway nation of the western Great Lakes, some of whom had fought with the French at Fort Duquesne, would remark, "The winter is the season of consultation, for war is rarely carried on then, partly because the canoe could not be employed on the frozen lakes, and partly because the snow would betray their trail and the direction of their march too easily."[24]

Edmond Atkin, a South Carolina merchant with expansive experience with the Natives through the Indian trade, was appointed British Southern Indian Superintendent in 1756. Atkin, when devising a plan in 1755 for British control of the Southern Indians including the Cherokees and Catawbas that participated in Forbes's campaign, specifically instructed, "That the [British Indian] Commissioners and Provincial Deputies, do visit all the Nations ... Yearly.... These Annual Visitations to be made at such a time as shall not interfere with the planting Season of the Indians in the Spring; or with their Hunting Season in the Winter."[25] With the approach of winter the Algonkian tribes of New England, some remnants and survivors of which had moved into the Ohio country, traditionally withdrew from their settlements on the seacoast into the interior country, "where they settled into their seasonal winter encampments."[26]

An Indian captive named James Smith, who had been taken during one of the many Indian raids on the Pennsylvania frontier in 1755, provided the most definitive discussion of the timing of the annual winter hunt in the Ohio country. Smith reported of the beginning of the hunt in 1756: "Some time in October, another adopted brother ... asked me to take a hunt with him on Cayahaga." Smith reported of the next year's winter hunt: "About the first of November [1757] a number of families were preparing to go on their winter hunt, and we all agreed to cross the lake together."[27] Thus, given Forbes's military skills and acumen, he had always planned a late fall advance on Fort Duquesne to assure him that either none, or a mere handful, of Indian warriors would remain with the French to oppose him. This is documented in an undated memorandum that Forbes prepared for Lord Loudon in the fall of 1757: "Therefore while their Indians are set upon their hunting and their defence at home small, one is naturally led to believe that any attempt made upon Fort DuQuesne and the other settlements might be attended with success."[28] An unidentified correspondent familiar with the Braddock Campaign, possibly St. Clair, had also suggested to Forbes, "The beginning of the fall appears to be the best season for making an attack upon the Ohio."[29] Bouquet similarly suggested to Forbes "not to hurry our advance, but allow the enemy time to use up their presents and their provisions, which would make them lose their Indians, and much more certainly because they will be led to believe that we only intend to make a diversion; marching at the beginning of September with our troops somewhat trained and in good order...."[30]

In fact, on August 9 Forbes would write Bouquet, "Betwixt you and I be it said, as wee are now so late, wee are yet to[o] soon. There is a parable that I shall soon explain."[31] Forbes's parable was that he did not want to arrive too early before Fort Duquesne, when the Indians were in considerable strength, and when concealment provided by vegetation was at its full thickness. Rather, he wanted to delay his ultimate movement until both the leaves, and the Indians, were departed.[32]

Forbes developed a particularly robust campaign plan. He first established a sound logistical base, at the largest commercial and mercantile center in North America. He meticulously planned a deliberate advance, which would construct two major advanced supply depots, and connect them with a number of small intermediate posts. The intermediate posts provided Forbes's supply convoys with local security, and facilitated the maintenance and repair of the road that would be his logistical lifeline. The larger supply depots enabled Forbes to stockpile sufficient supplies to account for any reverse that might occur due to enemy action or the forces of nature, and to fully implement each successive move forward without concerns of running short on supplies. The final element in his campaign plan was that of timing, arriving when not natural conditions most favored his advance, but at a time when the Indians' annual cycle would be most likely to denude the French of necessary manpower just as Forbes reached the Forks of the Ohio. It was a brilliant campaign plan, extremely well suited to the conditions of the Ohio country, but it would require considerable skill and exertion to successfully implement it.

FOUR

"It is now time to form our Magazines"

Forbes's First Parallel Advances to
the Foot of Allegheny Mountain

The campaign had begun as early as February 14, 1758, when Lord Loudon ordered Bouquet to sail with five companies of his Royal Americans from Charleston, South Carolina, to New York City, so that they could participate in the spring's campaign. Bouquet received these orders on March 10, and immediately complied with them. Bouquet acted with promptness, a character trait that he would shortly and repeatedly demonstrate to Forbes's complete satisfaction. Bouquet arrived in New York City with the five companies of the Royal Americans on April 23, 1758, although only four of these companies would advance with him upon the Ohio.[1]

Bouquet and Forbes met in Philadelphia in early May. Although no record of these meetings survives, they were among the most important of the campaign, for at these conferences Forbes and Bouquet established the working relationship that they would maintain throughout the remainder of the campaign. Bouquet shortly departed to take command of the forces at Lancaster, and he arrived "here this morning" on May 20.[2]

On that same date Forbes formally began the campaign, instructing Bouquet:

As it is now time to form our Magazines I must therefore give you the trouble to Contract for 120 Waggons to be ready to enter into the Kings pay at Carlisle by the first of June in order to transport the provisions from thence backwards to Ray's Town, where it will be necessary to have storehouses erected for the covering of the same, and a good large spott of Ground Capable of Containing a body of Troops for the protection of the stores. For this purpose ane Engineer must chose a proper Spott of Ground for this fort, and all the Carpenters belonging to the troops may be ordered up there to gett it execute as soon as possible. By which all our route will be in safety for our Convoys, and the head of ane army formed at Raes Town....[3]

With this missive, Forbes began the first phase of the campaign, or to use the vocabulary established by Count Turpin, Forbes began to establish the first parallel of his siege of Fort Duquesne. Forbes had the following objectives for this initial component of his advance:

- Movement of the four companies of Royal Americans, and three newly raised companies of the 77th Foot, from Philadelphia to Ray's Town;
- Movement of the ten companies of the 77th Foot by water from Charleston to Philadelphia, and marching them from Philadelphia to Ray's Town;
- Improving the condition of the Royal Americans and Highlanders, who were in poor health following their service in South Carolina, or as a result of the long sea voyage across the Atlantic;
- Receipt of the store ship from England containing the Royal Artillery, and other ordnance and quartermaster equipment for the campaign, and moving these supplies from Philadelphia to Ray's Town;

41

- Recruiting, organizing, equipping, and training the newly raised provincial forces from Pennsylvania, Virginia, and the Lower Counties;
- Moving the newly raised Pennsylvania provincial forces forward to Ray's Town, and the Virginia provincial forces forward to Fort Cumberland;
- Retaining the Maryland provincials in Royal service, relieving them of garrison duties at Fort Cumberland and Fort Frederick, and moving them forward to Ray's Town;
- Establishing the logistical and transportation requirements of the army, so that the supply base at Philadelphia could support the campaign;
- Establishing his first two encampments at Carlisle and Ray's Town, constructing sufficient storehouses to enable him to stockpile and safeguard supplies, and constructing adequate earthworks to defend these encampments against French and Indian raiding parties;
- Retain the Cherokee and Catawba warriors, launch them on raids against Fort Duquesne, and join them with British and/or provincial scouts to garner intelligence on the French defenses;
- Initiate negotiations with Native Americans to either gain their support for the advance on Fort Duquesne, or else obtain their neutrality; and
- Have the engineers perform reconnaissances and feasibility assessments to ascertain if a viable route could be constructed due west from Ray's Town across the Allegheny Mountains; and at the same time evaluate the viability of using Braddock's Road from Fort Cumberland as the principal avenue of advance.

At this early stage in his campaign, Forbes was not pressed for time, as recruiting, organizing, and moving his army and attendant logistics forward would occupy at least a couple of months' time. Until he sorted out his army and marched it to his first major supply base at Ray's Town, he had not reached the critical decision point for the campaign. The time necessarily occupied in these activities would provide Forbes with sufficient opportunity to adequately evaluate the two alternative routes, so that he could make an informed decision on the course that he would take to the Forks. Before he could even contemplate making this determination, Forbes had to obtain better information on the strength and composition of the French defensive force at Fort Duquesne, and had to ascertain which of the two avenues was tactically, technically and logistically the more feasible. In any event, Forbes planned for his campaign to be a deliberate movement forward, and he possessed absolutely no intention of attacking Fort Duquesne until the Native Americans' winter hunting season.

The distances involved at this stage of the campaign were not formidable, and according to Forbes's calculations were[4]:

From Philadelphia to Lancaster	66
From Lancaster to the crossing of the Susquehanna River at Harris's Ferry	40
From Harris's Ferry to Carlisle	17
From Carlisle to Shippensburg	21
From Shippensburg to Fort Loudon	24
From Fort Loudon to Fort Littleton	18
From Fort Littleton to the crossing of the Juniata River	18
From Juniata River to Ray's Town	14
Subtotal, Philadelphia to Carlisle	123
Subtotal, Carlisle to Ray's Town	94
Total, Philadelphia to Ray's Town	217

Forbes's concept of operations was described to Bouquet:

As I will suppose you will march Colonel Armstrong's Regiment to Fort Littleton and Loudon, upon Mr. Burd's people coming to Carlisle so I fancy you will push both those regiments forward to Raestown, leaving at proper distances, escorts for the provision waggons, and carrying forward the 3 additional Companys of Highlanders to join the 4 [Royal] American Companys at Carlisle whenever any of the provincialls are able to form a body at Lancaster. By which all our route will be in safety for our Convoys and the head of ane army formed at Raestown. Covered towards the Alegany mountain and west branch of the Susquehannah by the Cherokees, who you will Contrive to keep constantly employed sending always provincialls with them when a Scouting.[5]

The movement of Forbes's long columns began on April 29, 1758, when Captain McLean dispatched his three companies of Highlanders from Philadelphia to Lancaster. They continued their journey forward from Lancaster on June 12 and arrived at Carlisle on June 14, having traversed no less than 57 miles in three solid days' worth of marching.[6] This effort alone should put to rest the widely held and frequently disseminated viewpoint that British regulars were not capable of expeditious road marches. On May 29 Burd's Pennsylvania provincial Battalion became the first of the Provincial forces to begin the long trip west, proceeding from Carlisle to Fort Loudon and then Fort Littleton.[7] On May 30 the Lower Counties Battalion followed Burd with two companies of Mercer's Third Pennsylvania Battalion.[8] Bouquet reported that Armstrong's Battalion would in turn proceed on May 31. Bouquet himself departed Carlisle on June 8.[9] Constructing the road as he went along, and supervising the movement of convoys that were always escorted by small detachments of soldiers, Bouquet only reached Ray's Town on June 24. Bouquet would spend the next two months here, constructing Forbes's advanced depot, first scouting and then constructing a route across the Allegheny Mountains, accumulating supplies, and organizing and drilling his command.

Bouquet was appalled during these early marches to observe the Pennsylvania provincials using their muskets as carrying poles, loading them with various implements of their camp and personal equipage. It was not an uncommon soldier's solution to carrying his load, and various historic prints from the middle of the 18th century depict troopers carrying their equipment in just such a manner. But it was not a good idea, either in Europe, where alert cavalry patrols could sweep down upon a column that had for all practical purposes rendered themselves defenseless, or in the Pennsylvania woods, where marauding hostile Native American warriors would be more than willing to do the same. Captain Thomas Sims, an experienced British officer who issued a wealth of military treatises on various subjects, had once described just such a debacle:

A battalion consisting of five hundred men (Commanded by a Colonel whose time in service did not exceed twelve years) being ordered to march from one quarter to another, and imagined, from the distance of the enemy's frontier garrisons, which was at thirty miles distance, that he had nothing to apprehend from the enemy, therefore neglected the common precautions taken by an old officer, in ordering his advanced guard to reconnoiter all suspected places, where men might lay concealed, beside which, he took no care in keeping up his files, but permitted them to run into a rear of a mile long. A large brush wood stood alongside of the road, close by which they was to march, and in this a complete company of light infantry lay concealed, divided into two divisions, the advanced guard passed by without examining it, and as soon as the center of the battalion came opposite to the interval between the two divisions, they rushed out, fired upon them and charged bayonets. One division attacking the right of colours, and the other the left, and after killing and wounding about three hundred of them, the rest surrendering themselves prisoners, for the men having their tent poles fastened to their firelocks could make no resistance, and by marching in this straggling manner could not form in time.[10]

In short order the professional Swiss soldier, who had doubtless both viewed and disapproved of similar sights in his many years of campaigning in Europe, issued peremptory orders: "Upon a March the Soldiers are not to hang to their Firelocks any Bundle or Kettle, but are to carry them on their Back tied with good strong Straps, the Six Men of each Mess Carrying their Kettles by Turns, as likewise their Tent Poles in their Hands and Tent Pins tied to a String."[11]

Once at Ray's Town, Bouquet also initiated construction of a road connecting this post with Fort Cumberland. Fort Cumberland, which had served as the logistical advanced post for Braddock's Campaign, would also serve as the concentration point for the Virginia regiments and detached companies. Regardless of whether the Virginians would march north to join Forbes at Ray's Town, or Forbes's army would march south to join the Virginians at Fort Cumberland, this road was essential. Bouquet sent orders to Washington on June 30 to employ three hundred of his Virginians to begin cutting the road north from Fort Cumberland.[12] Forbes ensured that Bouquet was working on this route, ordering him on July 6: "Let the road to Fort Cumberland from Raes Town be finished with all Deligence."[13] Bouquet ordered additional soldiers to work on the road from Ray's Town, and soon had five hundred men at work on it. This portion of the road was completed, as much as any portion of a hastily constructed dirt trail would ever be finished, by July 20.[14]

Once this road was functional, Forbes's army would have two points of concentration, that of the Virginians and Maryland Battalion at Fort Cumberland, and that of the Pennsylvanians, Lower County Battalion and regulars at Ray's Town. This offered advantages to Forbes, as he could make a careful selection of his two possible routes, and advance along either axis almost immediately with his forces thus deployed. Additionally, by having his army at two separate locations, he would reduce his logistical demands at any individual point, and would also reduce wear and tear on a single segment of road. Besides this, if his army were under observation by the French (a likely proposition), such a concentration would deceive them as to his real intentions.

In addition to the road from Carlisle to Ray's Town, and the road between Fort Cumberland and Ray's Town, Forbes also authorized the construction of a road between Fort Frederick and Fort Cumberland in Maryland. The purpose for this road is challenging to ascertain. Apparently it provided an enhanced line of communications between the two forts, and particularly to Fort Cumberland from the more densely populated and agrarian coastal region of Maryland. Bouquet, acting under Forbes's orders in this as in nearly all cases, asked Governor Sharpe of Maryland to reconnoiter the route of this road on June 13.[15] Sharpe in turn gave the assignment to Captain Evan Shelby on June 15. Shelby was an experienced member of the Maryland Battalion, and was described as "possessing a strong mind and an iron constitution of body with great perserverence and unshaken courage."[16] Shelby performed his reconnaissance rapidly, and provided Sharpe with an evaluation on June 25. The report is a case study in a concise, comprehensive military engineering evaluation. The types of soils, topographical grades, construction methods, and number of days and men required for each particular stretch of the road were all meticulously presented. Without such a road, communications between the two forts were by water using the Potomac River, which was entirely dependent upon the depth of the river. A road between the two posts would offer advantages to the future growth of Maryland, regardless of which route Forbes eventually chose. Accordingly, on his own volition Sharpe ordered his men to start work on this road.[17] This road was never completed during this campaign, and played no significant role in Forbes's advance. Forbes himself wrote Bouquet regarding it on July 14 that "[we] have all along thought the road from F. Frederick to Cumberland Superfluous, if we could have done without it, which I am glad to understand wee can do by Raes Town."[18] Still, the planning for this road is interesting, in that it indicates that Forbes was continuously striving to keep all options available to him, until a final decision had to be made.

Amidst all of this road construction and planning, Forbes's army continued to garner strength. Montgomery's battalion arrived at Philadelphia on June 7, was disembarked June

8, then briefly encamped for two days to enable his soldiers to regain their land legs, and the Highlanders began their march forward as early as Sunday, June 11.[19] Although Forbes was not pressed for time at this point in the campaign, still it is evident that he was not dallying, for this was an extremely aggressive schedule. The 77th Foot apparently had a relatively easy voyage from South Carolina, for they reached Philadelphia in good health. The *Pennsylvania Gazette* reported of their arrival:

> Colonel Montgomery's Battalion of Highlanders was reviewed by the honourable Brigadier General John Forbes, in the Presence of a great Number of People, whose highest Expectations were fully gratified. The Novelty of their dress, and the manly and warlike Deportment of both Officers and Men, was really a fine Sight; and the Time, Order and Activity with which they performed their Exercise, was not inferior, we presume, to any thing of the Kind ever seen among us. In short, the Behavior of this Battalion has hitherto been so remarkably regular here, and their Appearance so promising, that People in general seem highly pleased with their Appointment to the important Service they are going upon.[20]

With their departure from Philadelphia, the second element of Forbes's first parallel was completed.

Perhaps the single most important logistical event in the campaign occurred when the store ship with ordnance supplies arrived in Philadelphia. Forbes gave various dates for the arrival of the artillery. In a letter to Pitt dated June 17 he stated that the store ship had arrived on June 11. However, a letter to Abercromby on June 15 stated that the store ship had arrived "Tuesday morning," or June 13. In a letter to St. Clair dated June 16 Forbes noted the arrival of the artillery "two days ago," or June 14, 1758.[21] Regardless of the exact date, the store ship was filled with large quantities of military supplies. Not only did Forbes receive such typical items as artillery pieces, muskets, and ammunition, but of perhaps greatest importance the ship's hold disgorged large quantities of entrenching tools, ammunition wagons, forge carts, rope, block and tackles, and triangular gins to winch heavy objects. These supplies were, in fact, the most valuable cargo aboard this store ship. A complete inventory of these stores is provided in Appendix B. Forbes shortly began moving them forward from Philadelphia, in trains of thirty and forty wagons, escorted by one or two companies of Montgomery's Highlanders. This far to the east there was little chance of French or Indian attack, but the soldiers were necessary to relieve the wagons if they became stuck along the roads, and to prevent the local inhabitants from plundering them at will.

With his regulars now arrived, Forbes and Bouquet turned their attention to completing the formation of the provincial forces. Merely equipping the provincial soldiers proved an immense undertaking. Apparently the Lower County Battalion arrived in good order, and was ready to take the field immediately. However, the Virginia, North Carolina and Pennsylvania Provincials were another matter altogether. Bouquet received a typical missive from a Pennsylvania officer on May 31:

> [They] have not ten Firelocks, they have no Ammunition, Canteens, Knapsacks, Blankets or Tents, nor in short any Acoutraments whatsoever: They have no Regimentals, and many of them little Cloathing of any Kind; half of em have not rec[eived] their Bounty, and not a Farthing of Advance to purchase Cloathing. There are no Orders what their Uniform shall be.[22]

Bouquet would report to Forbes:

> I find their [Pennsylvania] battalions in the utmost confusion. Their guns are entirely unfit for use, more than three fourths unfit to fire, the wood in pieces, and the screw-plates attached to the barrels with strings. They have no tents, neither the officers nor the soldiers. Not a single kettle, axe or tomahawk. No ammunition or provisions, and no one to furnish them.[23]

Alarming letters continued to be received from all quarters with tales of woe and misery regarding the situation of the provincials. Representative was that written by Captain Jonathan Blackwood of the Pennsylvania Provincials to the governor's office on May 29: "[O]ur Canteens are so leaky that they are worse than none…. Napsacks are much wanted, if the Commissioner would allow a few Axes I think they would be very Serviceable."[24]

Even such a mundane item as shoes would require a strenuous effort to supply. Bouquet wrote on May 30: "Experience makes me feel the necessity of having a good supply of shoes for the army, besides the three pairs which each soldier ought to carry including the ones on his feet. The dew in the woods makes the leather as supple as old linen, and as the roads are stony, a pair of shoes is in pieces in a week."[25] Since three pairs of shoes per soldier meant that 18,000 pairs of shoes would be required, this in and of itself was a logistical demand of staggering import. Forbes promptly responded, "[T]hey will be provided by sending to New York or elsewhere—1000 pair will be sent directly."[26] Probably the 1,000 pairs that Forbes was sending from Philadelphia were every single pair of affordable and appropriate shoes available in the city.[27] Forbes immediately contracted for another 1,000 pair in Philadelphia, doubtless the maximum number that the city's cobblers could realistically be expected to produce on short order, but even then his army would still be short 16,000 sets of shoes![28] To partially offset these shortages, when hunters could be safely dispatched, deerskins were gathered, and turned into moccasins for the use of the soldiers.[29]

Every single article required that a reputable merchant or artificer be located in Philadelphia; the terms of contract negotiated; a prototype produced and accepted; production/fabrication/assembly performed; delivery made; the articles inspected and accepted; then packaged, safeguarded from weather and theft until they could be transported; and finally loaded onto a wagon for the long and tedious trip west. This was an intricately detailed and frustrating process that required Forbes's personal involvement. Even in Philadelphia, the largest commercial center in the colonies and the major port on the American side of the Atlantic Ocean, there were numerous shortages that could not be filled.

It shortly became clear to Forbes that he would have to personally supervise all of these various acquisitions in Philadelphia, or the necessary and indeed absolutely critical logistical arrangements to move the campaign forward would never happen. Forbes informed Bouquet on June 16, "I find I must absolutely see every thing sett out before I can stirr from this."[30] Forbes wrote Bouquet on June 10, "I assure you for my own part no Serjeant or Quarter Master of a Regiment is obliged to look into the small detail more than I am, and find that if I did not see the execution of things myself, we should never gett out of this town."[31] He would inform St. Clair on June 16, "I see an absolute necessity of being the last man here myself, otherwise all I leave undone will remain so."[32] Forbes similarly told Bouquet on June 27, "I hope to gett every thing out of this town by Thursday morning [June 29, 1758] and shall follow the same day myself being resolved to be the last man."[33]

Arming the provincials was a particularly daunting task. At times it must have seemed to Forbes that he had entered into a truly strange and different land, where normal English laws and procedures had no rule of force. On April 20, Governor Denny ordered Thomas Janvier, Pennsylvania Provincial armorer, to issue 218 light fusils to General Forbes. These light muskets, or muskets of reduced size, were perfectly suited to Native Americans. These fusils were urgently needed for issue to the Cherokees and Catawbas already gathering to join Forbes, in order to retain their services. Janvier demurred to issue these weapons, on authority of the Pennsylvania Provincial Assembly. Forbes remonstrated, "Such a refusal of what is the undoubted Right of the King to demand, or the Officer Commanding his

Majesty's subjects under Arms in the Province, is what I am astonished at." Governor Denny summoned the armorer, and "he was ordered peremptorily to deliver the Fusees directly." Even such a simple task as the delivery of the King's arms to the King's command-ing officer required Forbes's personal involvement and force of will to have executed![34]

Colonel Byrd explained to Forbes the machinations that he had to go through to sup-ply his Virginia Regiment with muskets:

> I have been a good deal puzzld about arming my men, but have at last done it compleately by pick-ing the muskets &c. which came from Williamsburgh & Maryland. Sir John St. Clair has ordered me to return the Maryland arms & to take the remainder of the Williamsburgh arms in the room of them. I have [consulted] the armorer who says he does not think the old guns (about 320) are fit for service, for they have been in the magazeen ever since the reign of King William. I hope Sir you will not think I do [amiss] in not returning all the Maryland arms, as in that [case I should] either be obliged to march to Fort Cumberland without that [number] of guns, or dissobey Col. Bouquet's orders & wait till I could get those you mention'd from Carlisle [from the ordnance store ship] which would take up a fortnight. I think it best to replace Lord Baltimores arms out of those at Carlisle.[35]

Captain Joseph Shippen of the Pennsylvania Provincials chronicled his own personal manipulations necessary to arm and equip the new soldiers of his state. Shippen left Philadelphia on Tuesday, June 6, with orders from Forbes to facilitate the organization of the three new Pennsylvania battalions. Shippen met with Colonel Armstrong in Lancaster the next day, and sent Forbes information regarding what his battalion required. Shippen then proceeded to Carlisle on June 8, and ensured that arms and blankets intended for the 1st and 2nd Battalions safely arrived and were stored there. In order to catch up with Col-onel Bouquet, Shippen left Carlisle at 2:00 A.M. on June 9 and reached Shippensburg "at sun rise." Armed with Bouquet's guidance, Shippen then returned to Carlisle on June 10 and Lancaster on June 11. On June 15 Shippen had to deal with a particularly unruly gang of free-minded Pennsylvanians:

> Ordered Capt. Boyd's with half of Capt. McClung's Company to march for Carlisle this afternoon. But Boyd's people being without Blankets & Accoutrements & their Capt. absent, refused to march so that it was with great difficulty that we got all of them (except 12 who would not & dispersed themselves) to march by 7 O'Clock P.M. Two of the 12 were found this Evening & confined them. Lancaster, Friday 16th June 1758. Found 8 more of the Men who refused to march Yesterday agree-able to Orders, & therefore confined them in the Guard House.

On June 17 four wagons containing 371 additional "musquets, Bayonets[,] Cartrouch Boxes & Slings &c." arrived at Lancaster. With companies and portions of companies indis-criminately arriving, Shippen found himself micro-managing detachments as he organized them to march for Carlisle, at one point holding 93 muskets with him for direct issue, while forwarding the remainder on to Carlisle, where the Pennsylvanians were being for-mally organized, armed and equipped. Shippen's concise diary entries mask the incessant labor that his efforts entailed.[36]

In order to supply enough hatchets, a piece of equipment absolutely critical to clear-ing roads and campgrounds, constructing fortifications, and building fires to clean mus-kets, cook and launder with, Bouquet ordered blacksmiths at Carlisle to manufacture numbers of them as the army gathered there in early June.[37] Blankets were another recur-ring problem. Forbes was forced to tell Bouquet on May 29: "Blanketts are scarcely to be gott, unless wee take a kind of French Blanketts made [of] owl &c. hair which we must take rather as want."[38] "Owl hair" was a decidedly inferior type of wool, of a quality and density similar to felt. The situation was so severe that Bouquet asked Pennsylvania recruiting officers to have new recruits "furnish themselves with Blankets, by bringing them off their own beds, or otherways if they can find none to Purchase, for they can get none from us, and there is no going Thro' the Campaign without."[39] Still more blankets were ordered from Philadelphia by Colonel Armstrong, probably from a merchant with whom he had a personal relationship. Meanwhile, Forbes requested Governor Sharpe of Maryland to purchase blankets in Baltimore, and Sharpe on his own initiative purchased seventy blankets available in Annapolis.[40] Captain Joseph Shippen of the Pennsylvania Provincials used his own connections to obtain 150 blankets from Lancaster County that were provided to Forbes late in June.[41] When Armstrong's battalion of Pennsylvania Provincials marched from Carlisle on July 20 he specifically noted a shortage of blankets, three of his companies "have Only ten Blankets, which the General has purchas'd of a Pedlar."[42] The blanket situation remained a continuous problem throughout the campaign, the Reverend Barton noting that he had presided at the interment of a soldier at Ray's Town on August 19:

> Buried a Virginian Soldier this Day. He was launch'd into a little Hole out of a Blanket & there left naked.—And when I remonstrated against the Inhumanity as well as Indecency of it, a Serjeant inform'd me that he had Orders not to return without the Blanket.—Upon which I got some small Bushes cut & thrown over him, till I perform'd the Service.[43]

The sheer quantity of necessary supplies was staggering. Forbes initially shipped Bouquet 271 tents on May 20, then dispatched another three hundred soldiers' tents and twenty horsemen's tents (a larger size of tent) on June 1, and he followed these up with another two hundred tents on June 8, and yet two hundred more on June 17.[44] And not only large tents but the smallest of items were in demand, and had to be located and purchased. Forbes lamented on August 28 to a correspondent in Philadelphia: "I am in want of spying Glasses to send out with my partys so pray buy for me two or three good ones, and sent up by the very first Express.... I have broke my little Barometer, I wish you could purchase me another and sent it up safe."[45]

Forbes, Bouquet, the officers of the Pennsylvania battalions, and the civic leaders of the colony of Pennsylvania all worked urgently and furiously to reverse these conditions. Bouquet remarked to Forbes on June 3, "You have performed a miracle in obtaining the means to equip their troops from the commissioners."[46]

The Pennsylvania Provincials were apparently supplied with both shot pouches and powder horns, and the more familiar cartridge boxes that the 77th Foot and Royal Americans carried. On June 5 Governor Denny of Pennsylvania ordered that 265 muskets with bayonets and cartridge boxes be sent to Lancaster, and 424 muskets with bayonets and cartridge boxes be dispatched to Carlisle, to equip the new Pennsylvania battalions. At nearly the same time, Forbes forwarded 48 dozen (576) powder horns from Philadelphia to Carlisle to completely equip these three battalions.[47]

Although there were established uniform specifications, the hasty and haphazard manner in which all of the provincials were established, equipped, clothed, armed and sent forward strongly intimates that they presented nothing like a uniform appearance. Forbes regularly inspected the provincial soldiers and their equipment, and following such a review at Carlisle on July 9 he remonstrated to Secretary Peters of Pennsylvania in a letter written by Major Halkett for him:

> The General Reviewed the [Pennsylvania] Light horse yesterday & tho' he never expected that the Commissioners [of Pennsylvania] would discharge their duty to the service as they ought to have done, yet he could not have believed that they would have impos'd upon it so much as they have done, by providing such trash for the Light horse, most of their accoutrements being rendered useless already.[48]

Little definitive is known regarding the uniforms of the various provincial organizations on this campaign. The Pennsylvania Provincials were ordered to wear "short green Coats, lappell'd with the same." "Spatter dashes," or short gaiters that covered the tops of shoes, along with haversacks, were sent to Carlisle in May for the use of the "light troops" of the Pennsylvania Provincials.[49] However, Bouquet also noted, "The General chuses that the several Captains in the back counties, should by all means use their utmost Endeavours to provide Cloathing for their Companies, for which purpose he will allow them a fortnight's time."[50]

With clothing and blankets brought from home, still more blankets purchased in at least five separate locales, a combination of cartridge boxes and powder horns, hatchets manufactured at one location and purchased in another, and a mixture of shoes from numerous cobblers interspersed with some few pair of moccasins, the Pennsylvania Provincials on the march must have presented an alarmingly haphazard appearance on their best day. The end result could not have been a particularly regular-appearing body of infantry, but Forbes and Bouquet were still pleased that they were equipped at all.

Washington suggested to Bouquet regarding the clothing for his own 1st Virginia Regiment:

> My Men are very bare of Cloaths /Regimentals I mean/ and I have no prospect of a Supply — this want, so far from regretting during this Campaigne, that were I left to pursue my own Inclinations I would not only cause the Men to adopt the Indian Dress but Officers also, and set the example myself.[51]

Washington proceeded with his plans, for on May 1st he ordered from David Franks, a merchant in Philadelphia, "As much green half-thick as will make indian-leggings for 1,000 men."[52] Franks promptly fulfilled this order, and Washington paid for these leggings on June 18, 1758.[53]

What Washington intended by "Indian Dress" is not precisely known; likely this uniform consisted of these green Indian leggings, wool breechclouts, and linen hunting shirts. When Washington dispatched Major Andrew Lewis and two hundred of his men to join Bouquet at Ray's Town on July 9, they were dressed in this manner. Bouquet approved, writing Washington two days later, "Their dress should be our pattern in this expedition."[54] Washington would subsequently write to Lieutenant Colonel Adam Stephen, "The Quarter Master brings you all the stuff he has for Breech Clouts: if the quantity falls short you must purchase more, and charge the Publick with the cost.... It gives me great pleasure to find this Dress — or undress as you justly remark — so pleasing to Col. Bouquet and that therein I seem to have anticipated the General Orders. If my orders shoud be a little unintelligable in any Instance you will make the dress of the Officers and Soldiers of Majr Lewis's Company a guide to come at my meaning; that we may even in this trim, have some regard to uniformity."[55] To complete this "undress" they were also equipped with powder horns and shot pouches.[56] To conserve scarce leather, Washington's shot pouches were constructed out of raven duck, a fine quality of sailcloth.[57]

Byrd apparently thought along similar lines, for he told Forbes as early as May 29: "We are in great want of blankets or match-coats for I intend to dress them after the Indian fashion."[58] On June 3 he reiterated: "If you have no objection I propose to dress my Soldiers after the Indian fashion."[59] Forbes approved this approach, supporting Bouquet on June 27: "I have been long in your Opinion of equiping Numbers of our men like the Savages, and I fancy Col: Byrd of Virginia has most of his best people equipt in that manner."[60] Byrd's regiment was also more formally issued with "French Prize cloaths" or eight hundred French uniforms that had been captured at sea and purchased by the colony of Virginia, although the specifics of the colors, facings, and compositions of these uniforms in unknown. Still, Byrd apparently at the same time kept his soldiers in a coarser uniform, for on the same date he was advised "there is materials for the leggings" available for his regiment at Williamsburg.[61]

Even with such an irregular and relatively simplistic dress, the provincials still had to be provided with canteens, blankets, mess kettles, haversacks, hatchets, powder horns, shot pouches, gunpowder, bar lead or musket balls, and muskets. In short, equipping an 18th century army was a major industrial effort, and the fact that so many soldiers were raised and equipped in such a comparatively short time strongly intimates that Philadelphia was a more than suitable logistical base for Forbes's campaign.

As if providing for the material comforts of his soldiers was not sufficient labor, Forbes was also concerned for the spiritual well-being of his soldiers. Although the assignment of chaplains in the British Army by this time had become little more than a post of preferment for material gain, Forbes ensured that active chaplains were assigned to his command and accompanied his soldiers on their march.[62] Chaplain Charles Beatty, a Presbyterian minister and "a Gentleman of Strict piety," was appointed to Armstrong's Pennsylvania Battalion on June 9.[63] The Rev. John Steel, another Presbyterian, was assigned as the Chaplain for the 2nd Pennsylvania Battalion.[64] Montgomery's 77th Foot was accompanied by its own Chaplain, the Rev. Henry Munro, presumably a Presbyterian minister given the religious proclivities of the Highlanders. Forbes also directly appointed the Rev. Thomas Barton, chaplain of Mercer's 3rd Pennsylvania Battalion, as Chief Clergyman for the Church of England to the army:

> I am sorry to find that the Troops of the Communion of the Church of England are not properly provided with a Clergyman of their own Profession. In consequence therefore, of your laudable zeal for the Service of your King & Country.... You are hereby invited & authorized to the Discharge of all Minesterial functions belonging to a Clergyman of the Church of England, amongst the Troops under Command.... And be assured, Sir, that in all places & at all times, the Clergymen, & those of the Church of England, shall always be properly encouraged & protected.[65]

The chaplains preached regularly to the troops, apparently as often as opportunity and the exigencies of duty permitted. The Reverend Barton, an Anglican, carefully recorded his sermons, and the selections that he made revealed much about how he viewed the campaign: "Sunday July 30th 1758 — Preach'd from 2 Chron: 14.11 — to about 3000 Men — in the Presence of Col. Bouquet — Governor Glen & all the Officers." In the fourteenth chapter of 2 Chronicles, King Asa of Judah commanded an army that was outnumbered by an invading Cushite (Ethiopian) army of "thousands upon thousands." This verse is Asa's prayer of reliance upon God to "help the powerless against the mighty." Asa's army was victorious. Barton's sermon conveyed to Forbes's soldiers that the "underdog" could be victorious if God ordained their cause. Barton probably perceived this as a good message for men in a hostile wilderness.[66] On August 20, the good chaplain recorded that he had: "Preach'd before the Commanding Officer & all the Troops from these Words in Jeremiah-23–10 — Because of Swearing the land mourneth." Profanity in any army is a universal problem, and Forbes's army was doubtless much the same. In this chapter the prophet Jeremiah is stating that because of lying prophets and adulterers (in this context, those who worship other gods), the land is withered. Barton doubtless interpreted this verse as a warning to soldiers not to use profanity.

He continued his ministrations to the soldiers later in the month: "Sunday, August

27th. A dark Morning, but a very sultry Day. Preach'd at 11 O'Clock P.M. from the 144th Psalm & the 3ᵈ Verse, to all the Troops." The psalmist expresses the transient nature of humanity and the fact that God still cares for them. Men are like a "breath" or a "fleeting shadow." Thus, Barton preached a sermon on the fact that death is always imminent, especially on the battlefield, and no one is immortal. Barton was encouraging the soldiers to embrace eternal salvation through worship. He maintained a regular schedule: "Sunday September 3ᵈ. Preach'd from these Words in Nehemiah-4–14. "Be ye not afraid of them: Remember the Lord which is great & terrible, & fight for your Brethren, your Sons, & your Daughters, your Wives & your Houses. Present the Commanding Officer, Governor Glen, Sir Allen MacClain, & the whole Troops." On Sunday, September 10, at Fort Cumberland, Virginia, "I preach'd at 7 O'Clock on Sunday Morning by Desire of Col Washington from Nehemiah 4–14." Nehemiah, an Israelite who had been taken away in exile by the Babylonians along with the rest of his people, received permission from the Persian King Cyrus, who had conquered Babylon, to return to Jerusalem and rebuild the city walls. During Nehemiah's exile, pagan neighbors (the Ammonites and various other ilk) had taken over the surrounding area. With the return of the Jews, they perceived a threat to their livelihood and threatened the workers who were trying to rebuild the defensive walls of Jerusalem. Nehemiah urged his followers not to be afraid — to "remember the Lord, who is great and awesome" — in other words, remember that God is on your side, so they should "fight for your people, your sons and your daughters, your wives and your homes." Barton thus preached an excellent motivator for troops far from home — remain firm under adversity because everything you do here is God-ordained and will protect your loved ones. Certainly this was a particularly valid sermon to preach at a fort under construction.

Barton continued his efforts into September: "Sunday September 17th. By Order of the General preach'd to all the troops at 11 O'Clock P.M.—from St. John's Revelation 2ᵈ Chap & 5th Verse." Revelation 2:5 is an admonition from Christ to the church in Ephesus calling them to repent for turning away from their "first love." The Reverend Barton's sermon probably focused on eschewing soldierly vices. Thus, since this sermon was preached "by Order of the General," Forbes had asked the Chaplain to employ religious guilt and judgment to maintain and where necessary restore good order and discipline within the ranks. Finally, the chaplain recorded, "Sunday September 24th. Mʳ. Monro Chaplain to the Highland Regiment preach'd to all the Troops from 2 Sam 10 Chap: & 12 Verse." Joab, King David's military commander, was surrounded by superior numbers of Arameans and Ammonites. He split his force in two to break out of the trap. If one side of the enemy were too strong for one Israelite wing, the other wing pledged to come and reinforce them to secure the breakout. The verse is an exhortation to "be strong" and "fight bravely for our people and the cities of our God." A Scottish chaplain preaching such a sermon in a wilderness surrounded by French and Indians must have been a particularly resounding performance.

Among the chaplains' other duties were to baptize children born to soldiers and their wives, a service that Barton regularly performed. At Ray's Town in August the Reverend Barton was particularly busy, for on August 7 he "Baptiz'd a Child" and then six days later "Baptiz'd a little Girl of 10 Years of Age, the Daughter of a Soldier." On Sunday, August 20, following his sermons he again baptized "the Child of a Soldier." The Chaplains also regularly visited the hospitals, ministered to the sick, assisted with the interment of the dead, and were present at the relatively rare executions of deserters and other military criminals.

It was not always easy going for the chaplains. Soldiers tend to be a particularly hard-living, cynical, dissolute bunch, and certainly Forbes's men were no different, and no better. One Pennsylvanian remembered:

> We had for our chaplain a zealous Presbyterian Minister, Mr. Beatty, who complained to me that the men did not generally attend his prayers and exhortations. When they enlisted they were promised, besides pay and provisions, a gill of rum a day, which was punctually served out to them, half in the morning and the other half in the evening and I observed that they were punctual in attending to receive it; upon which I said to Mr. Beatty: "It is, perhaps, below the dignity of your profession to act as steward of the rum; but if you were only to distribute it out after prayers, you have them all about you." He liked the thought, undertook the task and, with the help of a few hands to measure out the liquour, executed it to satisfaction; and never were prayers more generally and more punctually attended.[67]

In addition to the infantry battalions, artillery, chaplains and Indians, Bouquet and Forbes also had to make arrangements for a bevy of skilled craftsmen who were absolutely critical to facilitating the movement of the army. Bouquet provided a partial list of the skills that were needed: "Sadlers, Wheel-Rights[,] Black-smiths, Gun Smiths, Oven Markers &c."[68] Besides this partial list would be counted joiners and carpenters to repair wagons and carriages, "white-smiths" to repair items of tin such as mess kettles and canteens, sailmakers to manufacture or repair wagon covers and meal bags for the pack horses, harness makers to repair wagon and artillery harness and leather items such as cartridge boxes, coopers to repair the casks that carried provisions, saddlers and collar-makers who would repair horse collars and pack saddles, tanners who would preserve deerskins and cowhides to manufacture moccasins, armorers to repair weapons, bakers to prepare bread and biscuits, and tailors who would sew and repair uniforms. These men were obtained by three principal means. The Virginian companies of artificers would have specifically recruited such men. Calls were regularly made to the battalions to identify men with these skills, and they would then be permanently detached to practice their trades. For example, on July 2, Bouquet issued orders at Ray's Town that:

> A List of Names is to be given in by Companies in the Morning from each Battalion to the Brigade major of all the Tradesmen, as Carpenters, Joyners, Bricklayers, Masons, Oven Makers, Sadlers, Millrights, Coalmakers, Coopers, Tin Men, Sawyers, Mealmakers, and they are to know That they are to receive nine pence Pennsylvania currency and a Jill of Rum or Whiskey per day.

Men that knew how to pack or drive pack horses were also recruited on July 31, once the decision had been made by Bouquet to begin utilizing such horses: "A Number of Horse Drivers are wanted for the Service, All Soldiers who Understand packing and Driving are to give in their Names to Day, they will be Paid when Imploy'd." [69]

For trades that were particularly difficult to locate, or for which more men were needed than could be identified, civilians were hired on a contractual basis. All of these various skills were to be placed under the Quartermaster Department, although it appears that Forbes and Bouquet mistrusted St. Clair so much that they personally supervised the employment of these highly skilled and irreplaceable soldiers and civilians.

Besides the men providing these trained skills, women accompanying the army provided laundresses, and were detailed to assist in the hospitals. In the British Army of the time, women were specifically authorized to accompany the army, normally a set number per company that would intermittently be adjusted. These women, required to be married to a soldier, drew half rations, and were considered to be part of the army.[70] On August 20, Bouquet ordered at Ray's Town, "Six Women from the Line to be sent to the Hospital immediately to attend the Sick to be relieved weekly, they will receive Provisions & 6 pence Sterling Per Day." Presumably, this order meant that women working in the hospital would draw full rations. One week later, Bouquet again instructed, this time slightly altering his original order:

> Six Women to be sent to the Hospital immediately — they are to be relieved every Fortnight. The Highland Regt are to send 2 Women. The Pennsylvania Regiment are to send 2 Women. The Maryland Companies are to send 1 Woman. The Lower County Companies are to send 1 Woman.[71]

These "Regimental Women," as they were known, only infrequently appear in official records of the campaign, but they accompanied Forbes's army as it hacked and chopped its way into the wilderness.

Once Forbes had raised and equipped an army, and turned it over to Bouquet to push across the mountains, it still had to be prepared for combat. Military training in the middle of the 18th century, although regularly practiced, remained in its infancy.[72] Efforts were made to ensure that the provincials were ready for the campaign. The Pennsylvania Provincials in particular required considerable training, as without a previous military tradition in the colony there was not a corps of trained, experienced soldiers to draw upon to serve as noncommissioned officers and instructors. Captain Jameson of the Pennsylvania Provincials typically informed Bouquet on June 5: "I find it very difficult to keep the recruits in order as there is no Sergeants among them the least acquainted with duty nor so much as a Single Drum."[73]

To correct these deficiencies once Forbes's fledgling army had been organized, equipped, armed and marched to Ray's Town, and provided with suitable liquid refreshments clearly blessed by the hand of God, Bouquet instituted a regimen of drill. Instruction had already begun at Carlisle, for a young German sergeant named Johann Michael Lindenmuth with the 2nd Battalion of Pennsylvania Provincials recorded, "The 26th [May] we marched to Carlisle.... We stayed almost 4 weeks at Carlisle and were drilled daily in exercises."[74]

At Ray's Town Boqueut established a large drill field to the south of the main stockade, "Where Colonel Bouquet Exercises the Troops, Marching in Columns, and Forming in Line of Battle."[75] All elements of the army were first formally ordered to drill on August 2 and 3 by Bouquet; presumably this consisted of battalion- or brigade-level maneuvers personally supervised by him. By August 6 this had become a regular activity, as Bouquet's Orderly Book directed, "All the Troops not upon Duty to be under Arms Tomorrow at 3 P.M. and to march out as usual." On August 8, Bouquet reported to Forbes, "I am having the troops drill, but they are very raw, and I cannot give it all the time necessary."[76] Firing exercises with blank cartridges were performed on August 10: "All the Troops not on Duty to be under Arms at 3 oClock ... the Arms to be unloaded and no Cartridges with Balls or any loose Balls left to the soldier, every Man to have ten Cartridges without Balls." Barton simply recorded, "This Afternoon spent in the field as Yesterday." The next day they were ordered to have "Nine Cartridges without Balls." On this date Barton recalled, "This Afternoon was spent in exercising the Troops, in running & firing in the Indian manner." The next day he noted that "the arms [are] to be cleaned and put in good order" following these firing exercises. Yet, they still drilled on this date also, Barton again documenting, "The Troops are led to the Field as Yesterday & exercis'd in the same Manner." Again on August 13 the army was back to firing ten rounds of "Cartridges without Balls."

Forbes also ensured that his army was to regularly perform marksmanship training, or "firing at marks" as it was then referred to. Forbes was of course well familiar with a previous order issued by Lord Loudon: "The men are to be taught to load and fire, lying on the Ground and kneeling."[77] Forbes himself stressed that his soldiers were to: "Practise firing at Marks, and of taking their stations behind trees." Forbes specified to Bouquet on June 1 that "if any of the Provincials want powder to practice," he was "to drop them a Barrel."[78] Since a barrel contained 233 pounds, this was a substantial amount of gunpowder allocated to marksmanship training. Shortages of lead ball initially limited these efforts, but the arrival of the ordnance store ship in mid–June alleviated this issue, and permitted Forbes and Bouquet to allow their men to regularly "fire at marks." Captain Allan McLean with the Highlanders wrote to Forbes as early as May 10:

> [A]greeable to your orders by Major Hacket, I keep the men constantly at the Exercise in the Mornings they are regularly drilled by the Sergeants and Corporals and in the afternoons are kept close at the marks. I am sorry to inform your Excellency that in the last of these they make but a sorry proficiency[.] Its easy to perceive the difficulty of bringing them to any kind of perfection at marking; when the major part of them have been even thoroughly ignorant of the method of charging a piece. Whatever my opinion has been formerly, I seek it my duty now to inform you that our men cannot make any decent appearance in the field, till they are more in the practice of the marks. Three weeks I think will make a great alteration upon them....[79]

Most of July and early August was spent in perfecting individual and company drill and marksmanship, and by the middle of the month this training had progressed to the point that more advanced maneuvers could be performed. Forbes stressed that their tactics, drill, and firing exercises must be adapted to the conditions of the frontier: "[I]n this Country wee must comply and learn the Art of Warr, from Ennemy Indians or any thing else who have seen the Country and Warr carried on inn itt."[80] Bouquet took these instructions to heart, for during his advance from Juniata Crossing to Ray's Town, and during all subsequent movements, he specified the addition of "two flanking Parties to the Head & to the Rear of the Collumn."[81] The incorporation of such additional protective measures into his marching formations would protect against surprise by hostile Indians in ambuscade. Joseph Shippen with the Pennsylvania Provincials also observed from Ray's Town on August 15: "Every afternoon he [Bouquet] exercised his men in the woods and bushes in a particular manner of his own invention which will be of great service in an engagement with the Indians."[82] On August 8, Chaplain Barton recorded in his diary, "The Commanding Officer led out the Troops this Afternoon a Mile into the Woods & there exercis'd them in Marching & Counter Marching, &c." By August 13, Bouquet had already worked miracles with his small army, for Barton recorded a particularly complex drill on this date:

> At 3 o'Clock the Troops are led to the Field as usual & exercis'd in this Manner — Viz. — They are form'd into 4 Columns 2 Men deep, parallel to, and distant from each other about 50 Yards, After marching some Distance in this Position, they fall into one Rank in forming a Line of Battle with great Ease & Expedition. The 2 Front Men of each Column stand fast, & the 2 next split equally to Right & Left & so continue alternately till the whole Line is form'd. — They are then divided into Platoons, each Platoon consisting of 20 Men & fire 3 Rounds; the right Hand Man of each Platoon beginning the Fire, & then the left hand Man & so on Right & Left alternately till the Fire ends in the Center: Before it reaches this Place, the Right & Left are ready again — And by this Means an incessant Fire kept up. — When they fir'd six Rounds in this Manner, they make a sham Pursuit with Shrieks & Halloos in the Indian Way, but falling into much Confusion; they are again drawn up into Line of Battle & fire 3 Rounds as before; After this each Battalion marches in Order to Camp.

Their ability to perform such complicated evolutions after less than a fortnight's training is indicative of Bouquet's military acumen, and the capabilities of the army.[83]

These maneuvers were representative of the evolutions that the army would have to execute in combat in the woods of western Pennsylvania Colony. By marching in columns and files of two, the army could easily pass through the trees and obstacles of the wilderness. The use of alternate firing ensured that a continuous, rolling musketry would be maintained; rather than a single volley that the Indians could readily evade, and then rush into the British ranks while the muskets were unloaded.[84] Bouquet observed to Forbes, after that General instructed him to open paths for the critical flanking parties parallel to the main road:

> Your idea to have paths opened for flanking parties is excellent, and I shall have it carried out at once. I have always drawn up the troops and had them march in double file, and I have found by experience that seven columns in this order have penetrated the densest thickets, and at a drum signal they have spread out and formed line of battle in two minutes, holding a very long front — with light troops and cavalry off to the side keeping up a continual fire, and the same all along the line. In all the encounters in the field or in the woods, I notice that the enemy — especially the Indians — attack our flanks first and try to surround us. This will be impossible for them through this plan; we should outflank them every time, and if they detach parties to turn our position, they must encounter our light troops advanced at least 200 paces; but more about it at meeting.[85]

But although drill and tactics were important, stockpiling of three months' supplies at Ray's Town was the predominant focus of Forbes and Bouquet during the army's sojourn at this post. Merely obtaining and moving the necessary supplies was a major endeavor. Forbes estimated that the following provisions would be necessary to support the initial movement of his army of six thousand men from Philadelphia for the first three months:

Flour	Pounds	504,000
Pork	Pounds	144,000
Live Cattle	Number	420
Rice	Pounds	36,000
Peas	Bushels	3,375
Butter	Pounds	27,000[86]

The integral component of all of Forbes's calculations was the soldier's daily ration, or the amount of food that he was issued each day. This constituted the single largest supply requirement of the army. Although the ration was modified intermittently in response to overages or shortages of specific food items, Forbes established the following ration as his army's standard:

- Eight Pounds of Beef or Five Pounds of Pork per week;
- Seven Pounds of Flour [or previously cooked biscuit] per week;
- One Pint Rice in lieu of one pound more flour per week.[87]

Forbes later noted on July 14, "As the troops are now mostly supplyed with fresh Beef, they are to receive it at the rate of seven pounds per week. And if they gett pork, they are only to have four pounds of pork."[88]

Pork placed into wooden barrels full of heavily salted brine was regularly employed by Forbes during this campaign, since this technique preserved it for a relatively lengthy period of time. However, the bulky and heavy barrels that weighed 233 pounds apiece required transportation and storage. Additionally, sometimes the pork spoiled, a particular problem when the pork was pickled during warm weather. During the campaign, frequent complaints were lodged concerning pork from the southern colonies that had to be condemned. Draper S. Woods, Deputy Commissioner of Stores, expressed his concerns along these lines to Forbes early in May: "I am inform'd by the Contractors Agents that chief of their salt provisions are or will be purchased at Norfolk in Virginia for the use of this Campaign I thought it my duty to inform your Excellency that there are large quantitys of pork imported into that place [Norfolk] from Carolinas, &c. the Eastern Shore of Chesapeake Bay which is bad in its kind, and should they purchase any of that commodity it might be greatly prejudicial to his Majesty's Service as it will not answer the end its design'd for it being both of a fishy & oily nature, therefore very liable to throw persons into fluxes &c."[89] A Board of Officers condemned 27 barrels of salt pork at Carlisle in early June: "[W]e have found upon inspection twenty seven barrels of pork not fit for men to eat, and we are [of the] opinion that the badness of said pork did not proceed from the insufficienty of his Majesty's stores at Carlisle but from the nature of it."[90] Woods elaborated to Forbes about one week later, "I have examined chief of the pork & have found most of it extream bad nay worse than I expected, some was entirely rotten & stunk & the most of it Carolina Pork."[91]

When not rancid, this brine-preserved pork also carried a reputation as being extremely salty. Lieutenant Colonel Stephen of Virginia, an experienced campaigner, recounted to Bouquet on August 12: "[T]he Salt Pork, has very near dryd up your Spring, at this Encampment."[92] Still, although the quality of the pork may have been poor at times, it appears that Forbes's commissary agents were meticulous in their duties. At Carlisle Encampment on August 4 the provisions were inventoried, and it was noted: "Pork at Ray's Town, Carlisle and on the Road from Philadelphia — 350 Barrels, weight 82,682 [pounds]." This means that each barrel contained an average of 236 pounds per barrel, which were barrels of true weight.[93]

When feasible, based upon the availability of forage, live cattle were preferred to provide fresh beef. Bouquet noted from Ray's Town on August 11, "The cattle which we have been expecting every day have not arrived, and we have no more than 64, which can furnish only eight days' subsistence to the army."[94] Since Bouquet calculated his army's strength at 6,000 men at this time, this meant that the butchered cattle would provide approximately 48,000 pounds of meat. Thus, each beef dressed out to 750 pounds, markedly smaller than beef cattle today (modern yearling beeves are typically marketed at 1,100 to 1,200 pounds). These were probably Red Devon or Galloway cattle, two sturdy breeds of horned cattle well developed by the 18th century and known to be imported to the American colonies by that time. Both breeds survive today, although they are considered to be threatened minor breeds.

This established ration was supplemented with peas and oatmeal, and beer as it was available. The army brewed the beer as it marched forward, either small beer or spruce beer. At least one brewer is known to have accompanied the army, Captain John Hambright of the 3rd Pennsylvania Battalion.[95] Small beer was brewed with molasses as the primary ingredient; other spices and flavorings were added as they were available. Spruce beer was brewed with molasses and water boiled with fresh spruce tips. Both were relatively low in alcoholic content, served as an anti-scorbutic for the soldiers living on a restricted diet, and were considered to be healthier than water. The simple truth, of course unknown in the 18th century, was that because the water had to be boiled for a considerable length of time to become beer, it was thus sterilized, and it would be considerably safer and more sanitary than drinking filthy water contaminated with bacteria by several thousand men and animals of the army. Both small beer and spruce beer were finished with hops, which raised the alcoholic content, and served to preserve the beer once brewed. For this purpose, Bouquet requested that "400 weight of Hops" be provided him on June 3.[96]

When feasible, hunters were also dispatched into the woods, primarily to supplement the soldiers' and officers' diets. Obviously, there would never be enough hunters to feed an army of six thousand men, and such a large force would certainly raise enough noise and commotion to frighten most game well away from any large encampment. Still, evidence

of their success is well documented by the archaeological record at Fort Ligonier, for fau-
nal remains found at the fort included turkeys, passenger pigeons, deer, bear, raccoon, fox,
bobcat, beaver, woodchuck, squirrels, rabbits, turtles, and rattlesnakes.[97] Although doubtless welcomed for its variety when available, such augmentation never constituted a
significant food source, and the army had to rely upon the provisions that the overworked
wagons and horses drew across the ridges to them.

Bouquet regretfully informed Forbes from Ray's Town on August 8: "Instead of three
months' provisions, we have only two here, and little or no pork, which renders the subsistence of the army very precarious. Before we can go beyond Loyal Hannon, another
month will have elapsed.... We should need some for at least two months in advance when
leaving Loyal Hannon."[98] Forbes's headquarters papers are positively stuffed with statements on the precise quantities and number of supplies as they trickled into his newly constructed storehouses in fits and spurts.[99] Numerous detailed accounts from both Bouquet's
and Forbes's papers are typical of the meticulous record keeping necessary to continuously
monitor the status of these critical supplies. To accumulate enough rations, even remnants
from Braddock's 1755 campaign that had been stored in Alexandria, Virginia, were located
and moved forward. On May 15 Forbes was told:

> Inclosed you have the quantity of stores & provisions under the care of Mr. John Carlyle Store-
> keeper which are 83 barrels of beef, 17 barrels of flour, 229 firkins of butter, the Beef is extremely
> good considering the time it has laid in stores and great part of the butter might be used the Flour
> entirely spoiled.[100]

The culinary qualities of three-year-old pickled beef and butter can only be imagined, or
perhaps shuddered at.

At one point in August the acquisition of supplies was slowed by problems with the
payment of contractors. Forbes once again displayed his strength of character, writing a
blistering reproach on August 15 to Mr. Joshua Howell, one of the contracting agents for
the campaign.

> I am quite astounded that the Contractors business of furnishing provisions (such as I should see
> necessary from time [to] time) for this Army should meet with any hinderance or stop from you
> or the Contractor Agents either for purchase or transport of the provisions for want of money. You
> know as well as I that Mr. Kelly [Kilby] and I at Philadelphia settled matters so that whatever
> money advanced by the Contractor for the above services should upon examination be repaid by
> the Crown if the expense belonged to the Crown, but that in the meantime there was to be no stop
> whatever upon this Account as that was a matter to be settled afterwards. I therefore think it very
> strange that Mr. Hoops is not furnished sufficiently with money for the carrying on the extraordi-
> nary charge of the Contract.
> As salt provisions is the sole and real dependence of an army, I therefore never doubted but you
> had always 3 months of that species for 6000 men upon hands— Live cattle does very well where
> you can feed them, or keep them along with you with safety but where both those means fail salt
> provisions is our only dependence, and therefore I insist upon that being particularly looked into
> without delay or hesitation and that the Quantitys you have upon hand may be sent up the Coun-
> try to Ray's Town without loss of time, and that not only by such Contract waggons as we can send
> from this, but likewise by applying to the magistracy for their aid & assistance in procuring you
> good and sufficient waggons for the transport of the provisions to Raystown where they shall
> receive orders for their money according to the Number of Hundred Weight they have transported
> and then sent back to their homes. The Crown indemnifying them for their loss of Horses or Wag-
> gons by the Enemy in that Service.
> I fancy I need urge this subject no more, because you ought to know that the wants of one days
> provisions to an Army is of more consequence than the value of 3 months. I have already advanced
> Mr. Hoops money on account but as I brought no more with me than to defray the necessary con-
> tingencies attending an army cannot supply him at present, and therefore you will take care that he

don't want what is necessary because there must be no stop in any one article for the want of money. If at any time a sum of money is wanted upon account of the Countractor's Convenient time must be given for warrants to be drawn upon the paymasters down the country for that purpose.

I beg for the future there may not be so much as a seeming stop or hinderance in anything belonging to your Department because all may be made easy by a little foresight in not delaying of things to the last.[101]

As noted in this missive, at one point, Forbes's money chest began to run low, and his deputy paymaster was obliged to borrow 50,000 pounds (probably in paper money) from the colony of Pennsylvania.[102]

But while Forbes was concerned about salt pork and money, his independent-minded provincials had other worries. Perhaps the most important element of the soldiers' rations was their regular issue of spirits, intended to keep them healthy during the incessant bouts of bad weather in western Pennsylvania, and to serve as compensation for the hard manual labor of constructing roads and fortifications and hauling supplies forward. In the British army of the time, rum was the traditional spirits. Bouquet, a European gentleman with refined tastes, must have been appalled to discover that the inhabitants of the North American frontiers were particularly fond of "their Distilled liquor called *Visky* [which] will cost about 2 shillings a gallon." Shortly he ordered twenty hogsheads or 1,260 gallons of what was almost certainly Pennsylvania locally distilled rye whiskey.[103]

Having grown up in an extremely rural portion of western Pennsylvania, the author suspects that the Pennsylvania provincials must have been concerned that Forbes and Bouquet had purchased so little whiskey, and wondered just what they intended to do with all that flour. Washington, an experienced frontier officer, recognized the importance of spiritous beverages to the army, sending the alarming missive to Bouquet, "Rum too I fear, will be a scarce Article with us."[104] By the time that Bouquet had reached Fort Loudon, he realized that his initial estimates of whiskey were woefully inadequate, and he informed Forbes, "About 50 [hogsheads of whiskey] will be needed for the expedition, and as much rum."[105] Bouquet had become better acquainted with the provincials' actual or perceived needs, and from this point on he began ordering whiskey in quantities of fifty hogsheads, or 3,150 gallons. By the middle of June he was telling Forbes, "We shall want about 100 Hogsheads of Rum and Whiskey for the Expedition."[106] St. Clair, well experienced on a previous campaign with the wicked and thirsty ways of the provincials, assured Forbes on June 17: "I have directed all the whiskey I can get to be brought up."[107] The Pennsylvanians must have figured that this was more like it, and that these foreign officers were now serious about crossing the mountains.

To move this superfluous flour, and invaluable whiskey, the British army had to contract with private wagon owners for the wagons, horses and/or oxen to pull them, and drovers to guide them. In Europe this was normally not a difficulty, but in North America, where such commodities were in relatively short supply, it was considerably more challenging. Crippling shortages of wagons in Virginia and Maryland had seriously hampered Braddock's campaign. Only the intervention of Benjamin Franklin, who delivered wagons from Pennsylvania to Braddock, enabled the campaign to move forward.[108] Forbes had known from the beginning that the acquisition of wagons would be a critical element, writing Pennsylvania's Governor Denny on March 23: "[T]here will be a Number of Waggons and Carriages wanted in the Province of Pennsylvania."[109] Forbes had run advertisements in the *Pennsylvania Gazette* to solicit wagons, teams and drivers almost immediately upon his arrival in Philadelphia, the first notices being printed as early as May 11.[110] Yet, as he had foreseen, Forbes had problems with wagons, attesting to Bouquet on June 10: "I have been very ill used with regard to Waggons in this Country, and scarcely believe those Contracted for will be able to go further than Carlisle."[111] Compounding Forbes's problems was the interference of his bumbling quartermaster, who already at this early point in the campaign was working hard to validate his reputation for incompetence. On May 25, George Stevenson of York, Pennsylvania Colony, wrote, "Sir John said when here that 70 [wagons] was enough, or there might have been more." [112] Forbes and Bouquet's blood must have fairly boiled when they read this particular letter. For, as with the others supplies that Forbes's army required, the sheer number of wagons was staggering. The artillery train alone required 120 wagons, which Forbes contracted for in Philadelphia in early June, along with an additional ninety horses to move the artillery carriages and wagons that had been brought from England.[113] Forbes believed that a total of 360 wagons would be "sufficient," meaning that he believed that he would have to haul 360,000 pounds of supplies in one direction at any given time (assuming that half the wagons would be empty on a return journey, and that each wagon could carry two thousand pounds).[114]

To avoid damaging the roads or causing obstructions in the case of a wreck of some sort, small wagon trains of ten to twenty wagons escorted by fifty to one hundred soldiers were typically dispatched. A representative convoy was sent by Adam Hoops from Carlisle to Ray's Town on June 17: "I have Sent of 34 Waggons this Day 10 of which is Loaded with Rice, 2 with 100 Bushels of Oats, two with 10 Barrels Whiskey[,] the remainder with flour Chiefly in Baggs & 20 waggon Cloths [wagon covers]."[115] Another typical wagon train was dispatched from Carlisle on July 19: "[W]e have this day sent off for Ray's Town Eighteen Waggons, Seven of which are loaded with Powder, Eight with Rum, two with Eighty Tents & tent Poles compleat to be sent for Colonel Washington & Colonel Byrds Regiments to Fort Cumberland, and three Chests of Light Arms for the Indians ... and one for the Baggage of the party that Escorts them. You will receive in the Waggons loaded with Rum four hundred & Sixty odd weight of Iron."[116]

Obtaining these wagons from Pennsylvania proved time-consuming, expensive, and challenging. Fair wages for their hire, regulated not by the Crown but by the Pennsylvania Assembly, were being offered in hard money. If farmers needed money to equip or repair their wagons, it was made available. Forbes established a system to ensure that the farmers' wagons and horses would be inspected and appraised before they entered service, so that they would be adequately compensated in the event of their loss.[117] Still, the Pennsylvanians' record was a poor one. Bouquet, in a tired but all too typical complaint, wrote to Forbes on June 21:

> Of the 73 wagons I had at [Fort] Littleton, there are 33 to be repaired, which have been broken or put out of condition to travel since Fort Loudon. Most of these wagons are old and the horses worn out. The bad faith of the farmers, as far as their unwillingness is concerned, is due to the people in authority.[118]

In a similar tone nearly a month later, Bouquet repeated on July 11:

> We were very shamefully supplied with wagons. Some who had good horses when they were appraised, kept them and sent nags who were unable to drag themselves along. The roads are strewn with broken wagons. The wagon masters for the most part are good for nothing.[119]

St. Clair's management did little to facilitate the matter, for on June 6 Forbes reported to Bouquet that he had arrived at Carlisle "night before last and did not find things quite so well as I could have wished particularly the Waggons, which by mixing of Brigades and employing Waggon masters promiscuously, have fallen into the greatest Confusion."[120]

When the Pennsylvanians proved recalcitrant, Forbes and Bouquet finally turned to impressment. Certainly impressment sounds to modern ears, used to stringent property rights and limitations of government authority, to be a measure both draconian and autocratic. Indeed, two modern historians have jumped to this conclusion.[121] Impressment simply meant that if insufficient numbers of wagons were contracted for, and if the King's business absolutely required it, then wagons would be essentially "drafted" into military service. Yet for all the seeming harshness of this measure, the Crown was still required to pay the established daily rate for the wagons, and provide compensation if the wagons or horses were lost or damaged, the same as if they had been regularly contracted.[122] Thus, although the farmers had the wagons forcibly removed from their use until the end of the campaign, they would still be properly and completely reimbursed. Bouquet informed the sheriff of Cumberland County on May 28 that press warrants would be issued for his county.[123] However, it should be noted that Bouquet resorted to this measure only after every other approach had been exhausted, yielding only eight wagons from a county that certainly contained the twenty-five wagons that Bouquet required, the inhabitants consistently ignoring orders of the sheriff and Constables. The situation was absolutely pressing; as Bouquet justified these measures to Forbes, "I am hoping to get at last the 25 wagons I have asked for, and that I will be able to furnish provisions to the Cherokees and the garrison of Fort Littleton, where they have had nothing but flour for two days."[124] Forbes had warned Denny as early as March that press warrants would be necessary if wagons were not forthcoming, so the inhabitants certainly could not complain that they had not been provided ample warning.

Nearly every county proved troublesome to some degree. Bouquet noted to Pennsylvanian Edward Shippen on June 3:

> I expected to meet with Some difficultys in getting Waggons from Berks & York County, but never imagined to be disappointed in Lancaster. Every thing is ready for us to march & take Post at Raes Town, but by want of a Sufficient number of Carriages, I am obliged to Stay here, and to loose precious time, that I could employ in Securing our frontiers.... I must have Waggons without delay & Either by Contracts, or impressing.... They will ... be paid ready Cash. ... if they want money on Account, I will advance it.... I never knew better Conditions nor worse Subjects.

On this date, Shippen noted that Lancaster County had provided only three wagons, instead of the sixty that were required. Following up with another letter to York County on the same date, Bouquet neatly summarized the problems that he and Forbes would have throughout the campaign:

> Having received the Generals Orders to take Post at Reas Town, I required Sixty Waggons from your County.... These 60 Waggons, with the same number from Lancaster, and as many from Berks County, are to be paid 15/ [shillings] per day for all the time they shall be employed in Transporting said Magazines to Reas Town. Tho' Your County has at least four or five hundred Waggons, yet I find by your Letter, that they make Difficultys of supplying me with the small Number I require, under Pretence that they have formerly received unfair wages from some officers, I know of none except, perhaps, one horse that was drowned last year & not paid for. I hope that for a Dead Horse, the People of York County will not Distress the Service ... with the Consequences of such undutiful Behaviour towards their King and Country.[125]

Still, eventually, one way or another, sufficient wagons were finally acquired to permit the service to go forward.

The wagons that the British army contracted for, or when necessary impressed, in eastern Pennsylvania were essentially smaller versions of the famous "Conestoga" wagons that are so well known from their frequent and often romantic portrayal during the 19th century in the movement west across the North American continent. This Conestoga wagon was essentially the Pennsylvania farm wagon in general use at the time, also known as a "Dutch wagon" to distinguish it from the more traditional English farm wagon. This distinctive style of Conestoga wagons was derived from both German and English wagon designs. A mid–18th-century painting by English landscape and portrait artist Thomas Gainsborough depicts a Suffolk farm wagon very similar to the early American Conestoga wagons. These Conestoga wagons always had smaller front wheels than rear wheels, so that in turning the wagon the tires would be less likely to rub the sides of the wagon box (only the front wheels turned; the rear wheels were fixed). These wagons would generally have been smaller and simpler in design and ornamentation than the fancier and more familiar Conestoga wagons of the 19th century. It is believed that a typical early wagon would have had a bed higher at either end than the middle, with the ends angled slightly out; this served to create a stronger and more resilient wagon than a simple straight frame would have provided. Additionally, this upward-swept front and rear would have been helpful in locations, such as those promiscuously located throughout Pennsylvania, where steep ascents and descents are regularly encountered. Accordingly, the bed would have varied in length, typically about twelve feet long on the bottom, and fourteen feet long on the top. A typical wagon bed was 32 inches deep, and width may have varied from 42 to 46 inches. A number of bows, usually eight, supported a linen or oilcloth cover. The diameter of the front wheels might vary from 40 to 45 inches, while the rear wheels would have been 10 to 20 inches larger. A wagon wheel recovered from the Forbes Road in Edmunds Swamp had a wheel diameter of 64 inches, consistent with a larger-sized rear wheel, and the tire was two inches in width.[126] A standard team of four horses typically pulled the wagons on this campaign. The teamster had no seat on the wagon and generally walked alongside, or rode the left (near) wheel horse. These wagons were heavily constructed, with the liberal use of iron and reinforcing boards to strengthen them. The wagons had a simple friction braking mechanism, and were usually equipped with toolboxes, and feed troughs for the horses.

The standard contract between the British Army and the wagon owners called for each wagon to be well equipped with tools and spare parts, based upon the experience of the Braddock campaign:

> That each Waggon is to be furnished with four good strong Horses, properly harnessed, the Waggon to [be] compleat in every Thing, large and strong, having a Drag Chain, eleven Feet in Length, with a Hook at each End, a Knife for cutting Grass, Falling-Axe, and Shovel, two Setts of Clouts, and five Setts of Nails, and Iron Hoop to the End of every Axle-tree, a Linen Mantoe, a two Gallon Kegg of Tar and Oil mixed together; a Slip, Bell, Hopples, two setts of Shoes, and four Setts of Shoe Nails for each Horse; two settts of spare Hames, and five Setts of Hame-strings; a Bag to receive their Provisions; a spare Sett of Linch Pins, and a Hand Screw for every six Waggons. The drivers to be able bodied Men, capable of Loading and Unloading, and assisting each other in case of Accidents. The Owners to receive, for a Driver, Waggon, and four Horses, Fifteen Shillings per Day. For every four Horses, after they leave the inhabited Parts of the Province, will be allowed Six Gallons of Oats per Day, or Indian Corn in proportion. It is expected each Waggoner will bring his Gun along with him.[127]

The "Linen Mantoe" referred to was actually a "mantle" or covering over the wagon. The "Tar and Oil mixed together" was used as grease for the moving parts, as petroleum-based lubricants did not yet exist. The "Slip, Bell, Hopples" were actually a slip rope and hobbles used to keep the horse from straying while grazing during evenings, while the bells could be used to help locate the horse if it did succeed in wandering away. A linch pin was used to secure the wheel of the carriage onto the axle. The "Hand Screw" was a wagon jack, to enable the bed of a wagon to be raised and held in place if the wheel or axle had to be repaired. The other items were various pieces of horse harness and hardware that could not be readily replaced on the frontier and could expect to be worn in regular service. Even this meticulous loading list turned out to be inadequate, as it became apparent that "Hemp Ropes with Strong Iron Hooks fix'd to them will be necessary to assist the waggons where they may Stall in miery places." And still this was not enough, for this was later doubled by hard experience such that "Each wagon should have two ropes with two strong iron hooks at the ends, so that the soldiers can pull them out of the mudholes, and help them to climb the mountains."[128]

Forbes's artillery train brought twenty-four artillery wagons, two powder carts, and two forge carts with them from England.[129] According to a 1757 *Treatise on Artillery* prepared by John Muller, a professor of artillery, fortification and engineeering at the Woolwich Royal Academy that trained artillery and engineer officers, these English carriages were of the following sizes. The powder cart was a two-wheeled cart, twelve feet six inches long and about six feet six inches or 78 total inches in overall width, thus it was nearly twice as wide as one of the Pennsylvania wagons. It contained a set of single shafts, such that either a single horse, or a team of horses in line, could pull it. The powder cart held an enclosed bed with two-foot-tall standing sides, and was about five feet long by 3 feet six inches in width. Muller noted: "The roof is covered with oil cloth to prevent dampness from coming to the powder, and each shot locker is divided into four parts by boards of an inch thick, which enter about an inch into the shafts. Each of these carts can stow

Reproduction British Army artillery wagons at Fort Ligonier Museum, Ligonier, Pennsylvania. The artillery wagons were the largest carriages on the Forbes Campaign, and the roads and bridges had to be constructed specifically to accommodate them.

four barrels of powder only." It should be noted that four barrels of powder would weigh 932 pounds. The ammunition wagon was a long, four-wheeled wagon, with larger rear wheels than front. It was 25 feet in length, and seven feet or 84 inches wide. It contained an open bed about fourteen feet long by three feet six inches wide that was lined with wicker (woven basket) work. The ammunition wagon, as the name implies, carried ammunition for the artillery. According to Muller: "This waggon serves likewise to carry bread, it being lined round in the inside with basket work." The travelling forge was a two-wheeled carriage, fourteen feet in overall length by six feet six inches in overall width, the same width as the powder cart. These forges contained a bellows, an iron-plated fireplace, a wood trough to hold water, an iron hearth, and boxes to hold the anvil and blacksmith's tools. It was an extremely important piece of equipment, necessary to keep all of the artillery carriages functional and in good working order. The tires on all these carriages were a consistent three inches wide. As can be garnered from a simple comparison, the English artillery wagons were considerably wider, heavier and longer than the Pennsylvania Conestoga farm wagons.[130]

Forbes had anticipated that these Conestoga wagons would be able to transport two thousand pounds during his campaign. This weight was still markedly less than Forbes would have expected his wagons to carry in Flanders or Germany during his previous campaigns. Even after reducing his calculations, he was stunned when "I found the Waggons in place of carrying 2000 weight were only able to carry 12 or 1400 weight."[131] Bouquet had independently discovered that the wagons were only capable of carrying 1,400 or 1,500 pounds.[132] The whiskey wagon load of June 17 is an important source, as it tells us that a typical wagon's load was five barrels of whiskey, or approximately 1,165 pounds. This verifies Forbes's statements, and other sources, that noted that the wagons were carrying relatively light loads. This reduction in weight capacity meant that the original estimate of the number of wagons required was insufficient, and this shortfall caused Forbes and Bouquet challenges throughout the campaign.

Silent partners to the Forbes's campaign were the horses used to pull these wagons. Almost nothing is documented regarding the size, strength, colors, or appearance of these horses. Because only four horses were contracted to pull each wagon, these had to be powerful draft horses. A typical breed of this type of draft horse peculiar to eastern Pennsylvania of the late 18th century was the Conestoga horse. Unfortunately, this breed is no longer in existence, having been absorbed into the general horse stock early in the 19th century. Predominantly black in color, the Conestoga draft horse was a large and powerful horse. It typically stood seventeen hands (about five feet) high, was well muscled, and weighed about eighteen hundred pounds. Its dark color and large size strongly suggest that it was a cross breed with the Percheron draft horse, the descendant of the French knight's massive war horse that still survives today. In an age when horses were practically viewed as an expendable commodity, unfortunately almost no written records survive of their contributions to this campaign. Yet these Conestoga draft horses were every bit as important to the successful outcome of the campaign as the leaders and soldiers, for without their hard work and struggles nothing would ever have moved forward across the Allegheny Mountains.

Because of the problems with the wagons, Bouquet proposed the use of pack horses to alternately replace or augment them. The use of pack horses was routine in the British Army. Such horses were formally referred to as "bat horses" from the French "cheval de bât" which literally means "horses of baggage," a "bât" being a pack saddle. In the British

Army of the Seven Years' War their use was authorized by officers to transport their personal gear, and officers were provided with an allowance to pay for bat horses when on campaign. Certainly it was no great leap of logic to realize that bat horses could also be used to transport the equipment and supplies of the army, and Bouquet may have seen them used or actually employed them in his previous military operations in the mountains of Italy.

Bouquet believed that each pack horse could carry two hundred pounds, using specially constructed pack saddles. The advantage was that pack horses could move faster than wagons, would require fewer drovers since they could be roped together into larger teams, and would cause less damage to the roads. Forbes partially concurred with this plan, stating to Bouquet in response:

> As to your Scheme of getting quitt of most of the waggons for Bats horses, I have ever been of opinion that the Advanced part of the Army in order to make the deposites, &c. ought to have nothing else with them but then I thought that after taking post, and making of the roads that Waggons would be the most expeditious method of bringing forward the provisions, but as you are upon the spott and see the nature of the roads, you must certainly be the best judge of what is properest to be done. However Sir John St. Clair and Colonel Armstrong are now engaging so many Pack Horses 200, and they may engage more.[133]

Possibly anticipating this need, John St. Clair had already begun to purchase pack saddles and stout bags to carry loads, informing Forbes in mid–May: "I have got ... 1000 bags for Oats, and 600 carrying Saddles. If you think the number of pack saddles is not sufficient please to order more."[134] Forbes was not pleased with St. Clair's efforts in these regards. He wrote Abercromby on July 4: "Sir John having served me as he did General Braddock, promising every thing and doing no one Individual thing in the world, except confusing what he undertakes. There are 700 Bats horses and Bats saddles provided by him, the first days tryal of the sadles gauled all the Horses into the bone, so they must every one be refitted & new stuffed."[135] Forbes continued his complaints to Abercromby five weeks later, "I mentioned ... the Scandolous imposition of the 700 Packsaddles, which after ruining a number of Horses are now useless until I can get fresh Stuffing up from Lancaster."[136]

Still, once the saddles were adequately repaired, Forbes depended upon a combination of pack horses and wagons to carry his supplies forward. In addition to the pack horses that hauled the army's supplies, pack horses were also distributed to his soldiers to assist them with transporting baggage:

> The General's Intention in sending pack horses without appointed drivers is, that upon their arrival at Ray's Town you should distribute them amongst the Troops at the Rate of four horses to such Companies as Consist of hundreds, and three to the others, which is the allowance to be made for carrying their Baggage during the Campaign. Each Company is to find a Batt man for the horses alloted them.[137]

In large part, Forbes and Bouquet found this necessary for no other reason than to reduce the wear and tear on the roads, which were rapidly becoming the bane of their existence, for as Bouquet had lamented on July 11, "The roads are strewn with broken wagons."[138]

On paper, the road from Philadelphia to Carlisle was a well-established line of communications, in good maintenance, and from Carlisle to Ray's Town it was known to be frequently and regularly traveled. These roads were in fact completely adequate for an occasional farm wagon's load of supplies, or convoy of Indian trade goods on pack horses. However, they were far from capable of accommodating the continuous flow of numerous, heavily laden wagon convoys; the larger British ammunition wagons and extremely ponderous artillery pieces; and the thousands of soldiers that the Forbes campaign placed upon them. Accordingly, Bouquet would consistently have to dispatch large work parties to repair the roads before he could even reach Ray's Town. For example, on June 2, Bouquet reported from Fort Loudon, "I arriv'd here yesterday Evening after a fatigueing March Occasion'd by the heavy Rain and the badness of the Road, which I had to repair in Several places, this Morming I sent a command of Twenty four Men with an officer to mend the road towards Shippensburg, and to Morrow I purpose sending a detachment of as many more to repair the Road to Littleton which is very much wanting."[139] Neither Forbes or Bouquet had planned upon having to make such major and recurring repairs on a road that was already extant.

At Harris's Ferry on the Susquehanna River, Bouquet stationed one hundred Pennsylvania Provincials, along with bateaux to augment the three flat boats that were already there.[140] To maintain these boats, oakum, pitch and caulking was acquired and positioned at the ferry. This longstanding and well-established river crossing was fully capable of supporting the campaign, for no complaints were lodged regarding it. After the Susquehenna River had been crossed, it was a short journey to Carlisle.

In 1758, Carlisle was the last settled town in what was considered to be eastern Pennsylvania, and civilization. To the west was the frontier, with all that that entailed — empire and conquest, opportunity and death. Beginning in May 1757, Colonel John Stanwix had constructed an entrenched camp at Carlisle along Le Tort Springs Run, to provide a "camp of continuance, either now or hereafter."[141] Essentially, this camp was intended to provide a secure encampment, with room for several storehouses and at least one barracks. Three storehouses are known to have been planned, one ninety feet long by thirty feet wide intended to store almost 2,500 barrels of flour; two more forty feet long by thirty feet wide for the storage of salt pork and rice; with a fourth building twenty feet square intended to issue these provisions.[142]

The approach taken by Stanwix was to erect a massive, crudely star-shaped encampment, consisting of a number of salient and reentrant angles, 630 feet by 375 feet in size. It was constructed by the simple expedient of digging a dry ditch to the front, and throwing the excavated dirt to the rear to form a protective parapet. Sod would have been cut away during construction, and then secured by wooden pegs atop the parapet to protect it from erosion. A plan of the encampment prepared by Lieutenant Basset, the engineer in charge of its construction, showed the ditch to be eighteen feet wide and seven feet deep. A berm was located between the ditch and the parapet, essentially a flat spot designed to prevent the defensive wall from sliding into the ditch. The parapet provided protection to the soldiers from enemy fire, and was eight feet thick by 7½ feet high, sufficient to enable a man to walk behind it with impunity. An eight-foot-thick wall provided complete protection against musket and rifle fire, and against small field cannon up to about six-pounders. To the rear of the parapet was a second flat spot, four feet wide according to Basset, known as a "firing step" in English, or "banquette" in French, which provided soldiers with a raised step to fire over the top of the parapet. Basset's plans show no indication that any logs, wood or stone were to be incorporated into this work. A good well was located within the encampment, although the adjacent run provided a continuous source of clear water. No designated sally port, essentially a well-defended entry or exit from which the garrison could easily sortie, was included in the plans. Simply, a gap in the parapet was noted.[143] This was the most rudimentary type of fortification possible, but the ditch and parapet did provide a well-defined encampment with easily controlled access. This entrenched camp essentially defined the limits of a rigidly disciplined military encampment, where valuable supplies could be stockpiled and readily protected, and from which soldiers would have a difficult time leaving or deserting. It was intended more to keep the new recruits in, rather than any possible French raiders out, Forbes himself noting, "otherwise the soldiers cannot be so well governed, and may be absent without the gates at a time of greatest necessity."[144]

This encampment was strengthened by Bouquet and then again by Forbes, to include an upgrade that turned it into a more regular fort. One of Forbes's engineers, Lieutenant Dudgeon, evaluated the condition of this fort in July 1758:

> Pursuant to an Order Received from General Forbes I have inspected the state of Carlisle Fort & am of opinion the place will be in a sufficient state of defence when the following repairs are made — vizt.
> - The stockadoes in many places are too open & loose & consequently will require to be better fastened & new stockadoes to cover intervals which in some places are too wide
> - It will also [be] necessary to open loopholes in the curtains, four feet & an half high from the ground
> - The upper platforms of the bastions are greatly out of repair & require flooring in several places as well as stairs to go up to them
> - The planks which form the faces & flanks of some of the bastions are so badly joyned & so open that it will be necessary to take them up & new close them
> - The faces & flanks in general are too low & require to be rais'd one plank higher in order to cover them from being enfladed & I look'd into upon the Reverse
> - The gates & sally ports are in good repair
> - There is a barrack & house for stores & a well (at present a little out of repair) plentifully supplied with water.[145]

This report clearly notes that pickets, or a stockade fence constructed of vertical logs carefully set into a deep ditch and interlocked then sharpened at the tops, was constructed at Carlisle; that wood was incorporated into the works to stabilize them and provide additional defensive protection; and that a formal gate and sally port were now present. All of this was beyond what Stanwix had constructed the previous year. The fact that the gate and sally port were in good repair lends credence to the idea that the encampment was really intended to maintain the soldiers within its boundaries. This camp was located on the site of the modern Carlisle Barracks, U.S. Army installation.[146]

Between July 10 and 25, Forbes's entire army departed Carlisle for points west, except for a small garrison that remained behind in accordance with Forbes's overall campaign plan.[147] From Carlisle, the Forbes Road followed a previously established and relatively well-maintained road, generally southwest, approximately twenty miles to Shippensburg. The Rev. Thomas Barton, chaplain to the 3rd Battalion of the Pennsylvania Provincials, would record his journey along this trail on July 20: "A good Road through shallow barren land much broken with Stones & little Hills led us to Shippensburg a small poor Town about 20 Miles from Carlisle, where we arriv'd the same Evening."[148]

In Shippensburg the army regularly encamped at what was known as Dunbar's Encampment, a campground located on "low ground" east of town. This camp site had originally been established by Colonel William Dunbar, Commander of the 48th Regiment of Foot and successor to Braddock, during his retreat in August 1755. In Shippensburg the Pennsylvania Provincials had erected a small fort, Fort Morris, apparently without any professional supervision or guidance, sometime after Dunbar's departure, between 1755 and 1756.[149] Barton would note of it: "At a little Distance from the Centre of the Town, is Fort Morris, a trifling Piece of Work with 4 Bastions, & about 120 Feet Square. It does not appear that a Vauban had any Hand in laying it out." Marshal Vauban of France was the greatest designer of military fortifications, and the allusion implies that the fort was designed without any skills. Colonel William Eyre, a British military engineer who visited this fort in 1762, remarked upon "A Well within side seventy feet deep, and very good Water."[150] Forbes also had this fort surveyed by engineer Dudgeon in August 1758:

> The fort is a regular square with four bastions and one gate in that curtain which fronts due east towards the town. There are three swivel guns in the salient angles of the S.E. S.W. & N.W. bastions, but none on the N.E. These guns are so fix'd that they can't be pointed to any object, but in a horizontal line. Loopholes are in many places entirely wanting, and where they are, are badly and irregularly cut, being only about four feet from the ground in the bastion, the more in some places on the inside. There are nine huts and houses within the fort sufficient for barracks, magazine & storehouse for about 150 or 200 men; a good draw-well, and an oven.

Dimensions of the Fort	Feet
Diameter from Curtain to Curtain	Abo^t 113
Curtain	Abo^t 63
Faces of Bastion	Abo^t 45
Flanks	Abo^t 21
Line of Defense	Abo^t 117
Height of the Stockade	Abo^t 10

> Amendments Proposed — There there sho^d be a ditch cut round on the outside of Abo^t 3 feet deep; or that a banquette sho^d be made on the inside of Abo^t 3 feet height; In which last case, the loopholes sho^d be cut at about 6 feet height from the outside & the present ones filled up. That loopholes should be cut all round within three feet of each other, and the logs on the salient angles of the bastions cut; so as to make it possible for the guns to be pointed at any object.[151]

From Dunbar's Encampment at Shippensburg, the road continued generally southwest until it passed west of modern Chambersburg, then it looped around and ran north to Fort Loudon, fourteen miles from Shippensburg. Although this was a well-established road in 1758, this section still caused problems early in the campaign. Bouquet reported to Forbes on June 7: "In spite of all the repairs made on the roads, they are almost impassable beyond Shippensburg because of the continuing rains on the clay soil. Several wagons have stuck in the mud, and several have been three days in going from Shippensburg to Fort Loudon. I am having them worked on continually, but they must be given time to become hard. This is an obstacle that cannot be overcome."[152]

Fort Loudon was a crudely constructed frontier post built by the Pennsylvania Provincials in 1756, poorly sited, and of decidedly limited utility.[153] The Reverend Barton would note of this fort:

> The Fort is a poor Piece of Work, irregularly built & badly situated at the Bottom of a Hill subject to Damps & noxious Vapours. It has something like Bastions supported by Props, which if an Enemy should cut away, down tumbles Men & all. — At a little Distance from the Fort appears Parnel's Nob, a round Hill of great Height. — The Fort is properly a square Ridout of 120 Feet. Here I found Captain Harding with 380 Royal Americans. — camp'd there all Night, & was well treated by the Officers.[154]

From Fort Loudon the route as originally proposed followed the road constructed in 1755 by James Burd to connect Pennsylvania to the Braddock Road. Burd's Road proceeded roughly due north, skirted Parnell's Knob, and crossed the initial major ridge of the Allegheny Mountains, the Tuscarora Mountain, at Cowan's Gap. This was the first real test for Forbes's army of a major terrain obstacle that had to be traversed. It was approximately eighteen miles from Fort Loudon to Fort Littleton, another small frontier fort erected by Pennsylvania Provincials. Reverend Barton described this difficult journey, which was undertaken after the road had been improved and placed into relatively good order: "[We] pursued our

Reconstructed Fort Loudon, on site of original Fort Loudon, at base of Tuscarora Mountain and Cowan's Gap.

Journey to Fort Littleton — The Road between these two Places is extremely bad — And Nothing to be seen but Mountains & Hills, & wrecks of waggons & Flower Casks &c." Bouquet absolutely railed about the condition of this stretch of the road to Forbes on June 11:

> We were deceived, my dear general, about the road I am taking. It is almost impassable from Loudon to Littleton. Of all the road where it is possible for a wagon to go, this is the worst, and it cannot be repaired. It is of rock, partly solid, partly loose and sharp stones. The rains have carried away all the earth, and there is none in the vicinity to cover them again, not even wood for making fascines. Our wagons are breaking down; our horses are losing their shoes. It is a wretched state of affairs.[155]

Bouquet accordingly had this stretch entirely resurveyed. He initially determined, "After a careful consideration of our route to Fort Littleton, it was found that the old road could be made passable rather than open a new one." However, Bouquet remained displeased with the road, and again reconsidered. He reported to Forbes on June 21: "[T]he road from Loudon to Littleton, after hard work, has been almost entirely changed and is now passable."[156] Burd's Road was abandoned at this time, and no longer served as Forbes's route.[157]

Bouquet's new road followed high ground on the western bank of the West Branch of Conococheague Creek. Although Bouquet would not have known this, the new path followed a course of weathered sandstone that was considerably more stable and better drained than the marshy conditions of the Ordovician Reedsville Shale that Burd had unknowingly built his road upon.[158] These new grades were fairly mild, although the last mile up Cowan's Gap that followed the hollow of Stumpy Run was quite steep, and remains an extremely difficult ascent even paved and improved today. Having ascended Tuscarora Mountain at Cowan's Gap, the trail turned right and continued north along the South Branch of the Little Aughwick Creek to Burnt Cabins, the location where an illegal settlement had been forcibly evacuated and burned several years before hostilities had commenced. The route then turned left and continued due west for Ray's Town. The road here followed high ground on the south bank of Aughwick Creek until Fort Littleton was reached.

Little information is known regarding this fortification. As with the other posts along this portion of Forbes Road, it was constructed by Pennsylvania Provincials to provide frontier defense in 1756. It was probably quite similar to Fort Loudon in size and construction.[159] The Reverend Barton remarked, "This Fort is a regular & well plac'd Square Stockade of 126 Feet."[160]

Once Fort Loudon's rude stockades had been left behind, the Forbes Road would have to negotiate the endless ridges of the Allegheny Mountains. Nine miles beyond Fort Littleton, the Forbes Road had to ascend Sideling Hill; the road was a piece of construction that required seven reverse curves and two 90-degree turns to climb this long, steep slope. Barton reported a "good Road to Sideling hill, to the Top of which you ascend after many Windings & Turnings."[161] Bouquet also reported this section of the road to be in good condition, although he noted with despair, "The [road] from Littleton to Juniata is so hilly that it will never be good."[162] After another nine miles of road that Barton reported as bad, then better, the crossing of the Juniata River was reached.

The Juniata River constituted the only significant body of water that Forbes's army would have to traverse, with the exception of the Susquehanna River that was crossed by the long-established Harris's Ferry. The Juniata River was relatively wide at this point, and pontoons or flat bottomed boats were constructed to carry wagons, horses, and soldiers across the river when the water was too deep to be forded. Obviously, this crossing would be a vulnerable location to attacks or raids, and accordingly Bouquet made the decision to construct a fortified position on both sides of the Juniata, directly at a bend of the river. Barton dismissed this work as: "A small Fort just erected & the Ford of Juniata picqueted in, in order to protect Waggons &c. in passing."[163] The fortification was designed by Captain Harry Gordon and constructed under Bouquet's supervision. He reported on June 22, "Our fort will be almost finished tomorrow."[164]

This fort was extremely odd, indeed. The eastern segment of the position was a small, classic four-bastioned fortification with four small log storehouses inside, 200 feet by 100 feet with the long side parallel to the river. The three exterior curtain walls were formed by one long barracks, and two smaller log buildings. The fourth curtain wall, facing the river, contained a covered way, or protected route, leading down to the Juniata River. A sally port led from the building on the eastern curtain wall to the river, probably to provide the fort's garrison with a secure access to drinking water at all times. The four bastions and the river curtain of the fort were constructed of simple palisades, as noted by Bouquet. Two exterior rectangular redoubts provided additional protection when necessary, probably when large numbers of soldiers or wagons that could not be contained within the fort might be delayed in crossing. On the west (opposite) side of the Juniata River a large, sprawling post was established in an odd L-shaped design, with the long side of the "L" parallel to the river. Apparently the purpose of this oddly shaped fortification, which bears no relationship to any established system of contemporary military field engineering, was to protect and secure encampments of wagons and soldiers within the boundaries of the "L" shape. Two "reservoirs of water" were excavated into the bank of the Juniata River, believed by historical architect Charles Morse Stotz to either provide livestock with a secure watering spot, or a location for boats to be protected from the current of the river.[165] A rectangular redoubt secured the open end of the "L." Its rather bizarre configuration notwithstanding, this was a relatively strong position, and the river crossing was well secured by it. Given its position miles to the east of Ray's Town, it appears to have been overdesigned and overconstructed for the minimal threat that it faced. Bouquet was clearly following Forbes's intent to apply Count Turpin's principles to the campaign: "[T]he general should have the right or left of it towards some advantageous post, which he should take possession of. ... this parallel should be strongly supported by taking possession of the rivers and town in the direction of it." With the construction of this substantial post, Bouquet had definitely taken possession of the Juniata River crossing.

As this is the first location on the Forbes Road where redoubts were prepared, a discussion of this type of military structure is appropriate.[166] Numerous redoubts were constructed by Forbes and Bouquet, from the crossing at the Juniata River nearly to Fort Duquesne. These redoubts provided simple defensive features that could be easily and speedily constructed with means readily at hand, could be secured with relatively small numbers of soldiers, but still comprised a defensive locale sufficiently robust that a French attack would be unable to seize it. In order to understand the military application and utility of redoubts, and the procedures and materials used to construct them along the Forbes Road, an evaluation of their design, configurations, and materials is necessary. For this purpose, four military engineering manuals from the middle of the 18th century were consulted.[167]

By 1758 the "redoubt" was a well-established type of military fortification. Nearly every contemporary engineering manual described their construction and defensive utilization. Lewis Lochee of the British Royal Military Academy compiled one of the most succinct descriptions of a redoubt:

> The Redoubt is a work generally enclosed on all sides. It serves to secure a post, a grand guard, or communications; to defend a defile, a bridge, a ford, etc., and is of various dimensions, that is, of different plans and profiles. The extent of it is proportioned to the number of men who are to defend it, and the parapet is generally of sufficient height to cover them. The redoubt has no precise or common form. ... the form, indeed, is determined by the spot of ground on which it is raised, and the purposes for which it is constructed.... By redoubt ... is understood a work enclosed on all sides, and formed wholly of salient angles.

When used in conjunction with the extensive masonry military fortifications designed and constructed in Europe, redoubts were placed within the outer-works to command critical angles, or to support other portions of the outer-works.[168] During sieges, the great French military engineer and field marshal Vauban noted that redoubts could be used to secure the siege lines against attack from the besieged garrison, or a relieving force.[169] More typically in America, redoubts were built as the stand-alone fortifications described by Lochee.

As designed and constructed in the middle of the 18th century, redoubts were designed with certain common features, which will be defined and described as appropriate:

- Parapet;
- Banquette;
- Embrasures;
- Ditch (with Berm, Scarp and Counterscarp);

- Palisades;
- Fraizes;
- Abbatis; and
- Entrance.

Parapet— According to Lochee, "the parapet is the bank of earth surrounding the post to be defended, and serves to cover the troops and artillery employed for its defense." As regards its thickness, this was based upon the size of weapons that it was anticipated to defend against: "When 2 feet broad at the top, it is capable only of resisting musket shot. When the parapet is 3 or 4 feet broad at the top, it can resist a three-pounder, when 4 or 5 feet a six-pounder; and when 7 feet, a twelve-pounder. When 18 feet, it is capable of resisting the shot of the larger cannon." British engineer Lieutenant J.C. Pleydell provided similar recommendations: "It should therefore be known, that a ball from three to six pounds weight, will enter three or four feet into earth newly cast up; and a twelve-pounder eight feet. This, at once, determines the thickness of the breastwork. The height of the parapet within, to form a complete covering for the men, should at least be 6 feet."

Regarding the size of the redoubt, this was based upon the strength of the detachment assigned for its defense; according to Pleydell: "Allowing an ordinary pace, or two feet, to each file [of soldiers], two deep. When cannon are intended to be placed in a field work, six paces are allowed to a field-piece, and eight paces to a twelve-pounder." However, Pleydell also noted: "The least interior circumference that can be allowed to a square redoubt is eighty paces."

Banquette (or as referred to in English, the "firing step")— Again, according to Lochee, "the design of the banquette is to elevate the men, that they may see over the parapet to fire upon the enemy. As the design of the banquette is to elevate the men, it necessarily follows, that the banquette must be raised within 4 feet of the summit of the parapet. The space of 4 feet allowed for the breadth of the banquette is absolutely necessary for forming upon it the men who are to defend the parapet. This space allows the parapet to be lined two deep." French military engineer LeCointe suggested a somewhat higher banquette: "You must make the parapet four feet higher than the banquette." Pleydell recommended a slightly narrower banquette of four feet.

Embrasures— These were openings incorporated into a work when it was equipped with artillery pieces. Rarely, artillery pieces were installed to fire directly over the top of the parapet, this circumstance being referred to as "en barbette." Most commonly, embrasures were cut through the parapet to enable the artillery to fire from behind the protection of the parapet. "The dimensions of the embrasure depend not only upon the nature of the soil, and the height and thickness of the parapet, but also on the caliber of the piece, the height of the wheels, and the construction of the carriage."

Ditch— Because the height of a redoubt's parapet was specified as a minimum of six feet, this could theoretically be climbed by determined troops. Accordingly, a ditch was incorporated to raise the vertical face of the parapet, making it more difficult to be scaled. Again, from Lochee: "The trench dug up at the exterior foot of the parapet, is called ditch. At the same time that it serves to furnish the earth necessary for raising the parapet and banquette, it contributes to increase the difficulty of approach. The dimensions of it depend on the dimensions of the parapet and banquette; its depth should, if possible never be less than 6 feet. The slope nearest to the parapet is called scarp, and that opposite to the parapet, is called counterscarp." A small level space between the ditch and the parapet, which served to keep the parapet from sliding into the ditch, was referred to as the berm. Pleydell noted, "two feet are sufficient for the breadth of the berm."

Palisades— Lochee suggested the use of vertical poles to add an additional defense to a redoubt: "Palisades are stakes of strong split wood, of about 7 or 8 inches broad, 3 or 4 inches thick, and 8 or 9 feet long, of which 3 or 4 feet are sunk into the earth. They are pointed both at the top and bottom, and that they may be of greater strength, they are fastened to a horizontal rail within two feet from the top, and are generally placed so close to each other, as only to admit the muzzle of a piece between them. Their greatest distance from each other is never so great as to afford room enough to creep through them." Palisades could be erected around a post for protection from surprise, or installed at the bottom of the ditch. LeCointe succinctly added regarding their positioning: "[F]ix pickets quite round [the] post." Pleydell added: "Palisades, used in fortifying the ditches, are nine or ten feet long, and six inches broad, pointed at one end, but if a sufficient number of these dimensions cannot be had, smaller may be made use of, provided they are properly intermixed with the large."

Fraizes— These were often referred to in historic documents as "fraizing." Lochee recorded: "Palisades fixed in the parapet are called fraizes. When the stakes are 9 feet long, 4 feet lie within the body of the parapet, and the remainder leans over, inclining a little towards the ditch. The stakes are sufficiently close to each other; they do not afford room enough to creep through them. To strengthen the fraize, the stakes are fastened to two sleepers, one of which lies upon the level ground, and the other lies within the body of the parapet." This inclination was to permit hand grenades thrown from within the redoubt to bound off them into the ditch, and to make it more difficult to throw hand grenades from the ditch into the redoubt's interior. Pleydell provided some elaborating information: "Fraises are made eight feet long, and five inches broad, sharp at one end. The beams, or sleepers of wood, laid along the parapet, are twelve feet long, and six inches thick, to which the fraises are fastened with nails seven inches thick."

Abbatis— Essentially, an abbatis was constructed as an obstacle to an attacking force, to delay it while exposed to fire from the redoubt. Lochee recommended: "It consists of hewn trees with the points of their branches turned towards the enemy, and to increase the danger and difficulty of forcing it, the trees are not only placed close to each other, but the branches are stripped of their leaves and twigs, sharpened at their extremities, and interwoven one in another. The trunks of the trees are generally sunk 3 or 4 feet into the earth, and the principal branches that lie on the ground are fastened down by stakes." LeCointe added: "Surround your post with a breast work of trees, with their trunks buried about three or four feet in a ditch made on purpose. You may sharpen their points, and take off all the leaves, place the trees as near each other as you can, so that the branches may twist into one another, and see that they point a little towards the enemy."

Entrance— Lochee noted: "[T]he entrance, which is made in the side or face least exposed, has no greater breadth than is absolutely necessary for passing and re-passing, and is commonly defended from within by a traverse." Pleydell echoed Lochee: "The entrance should always be made in the face least exposed to an attack. It is five paces wide to give room for the cannon to pass, but if none are to be put into it, three or four paces are sufficient." The renowned French engineer Vauban gave nearly identical measurements for a redoubt entrance: "The bridge for entrance into the redoubt ought to be ten or twelve feet broad, when you would bring the cannon into it; otherwise five or six feet of breadth will suffice." Pleydell provided some distinctive commentary regarding defense of the entrance to a redoubt: "The entrance of the redoubt ought likewise to be secured with a good barrier, a kind of open gate, made of cross-bars about seven feet long, and six inches thick, which troops may fire through with small arms, or with two or three chevaux-de-friese."

Although a redoubt could be constructed of masonry, in North America they were almost always constructed of earth. Frequently, the earth would be placed within a framework of wood. The wood consisted of either interlocked hewn trees (similar to a log cabin), fascines (tightly bound bundles of sticks about six feet in length staked into position), gabions (small open woven baskets typically 3–4 feet in diameter, staked into position and filled with dirt), or hurdles (essentially woven mats, secured vertically into the ground). Once this framework of wood was in place, it would be filled with earth from the ditch, and other available rubble, which was pounded firmly into position. Sometimes, earth was simply used, then covered with cut squares of sod spiked into place to hold the dirt. In cases of extremity, the dirt was simply piled up and tamped down. Lochee noted, "In a stony or gravelly soil, the banquette and lower part of the parapet are to be raised with whatever earth can be got, but the upper part of the parapet is to be raised with fine mould [soil], that the troops may not suffer more from the stones flying about, than from the bullets of the enemy."

One of the most important aspects of a redoubt is that although the classic configuration was square or rectangular, they were specifically intended to be adapted to the terrain that they were defending. Lochee, who exhaustively addressed how different redoubt shapes could be laid out and utilized, specified: "The redoubt has no precise or common form, but may be a square, a rhombus, a trapezium, a trapezoid, a pentagon either regular or irregular, a circle, or any other form. The form, indeed, is determined by the spot of ground on which it is raised, and the purposes for which it is constructed. When there is no essential reason to the contrary, the form is commonly a square." Pleydell, who devoted nearly his entire work to an examination of how the shape of a redoubt was adapted to the terrain, dictated: "It is not at all necessary redoubts should be traced exactly square, they are full as serviceable made in the figure of a rhomb, or with one side longer than another. This method, so far from being defective, becomes absolutely necessary when the ground neither allows, nor indeed requires, works to be exactly regular. Generally speaking, it is the spot redoubts are to be constructed on, as well as the lying of the ground near them, which should determine their figure." Both Lochee and Pleydell discussed at great length how redoubts were integrated with each other, and with other types of field works such as fleches, batteries and breastworks, to command important ground.

When properly sited, designed and constructed, these small fortifications constituted strong positions that could only be seized by a determined enemy conducting a deliberately planned attack with sturdy troops. Such troops were almost never available to the French in western Pennsylvania, and none of these redoubts were ever successfully assailed during this campaign.

From the Juniata Crossing on, Bouquet established a fairly regular routine for road construction. The main body of the army would remain at the advanced post, improving its fortifications, handling supplies and unloading wagons as they arrived, and drilling to improve their military proficiency. At the same time, large working parties would be dispatched ahead on the road, while smaller parties were sent ahead of them to explore future routes. Bouquet reported on June 21 from Juniata Crossing, "I shall leave 100 men here after 200 have marched today to cut the road ahead of us, and Colonel Burd sets out tomorrow morning with 200 others to establish a post at Raystown, where I shall join him day after tomorrow with the rest if the road is open. When I have been at Raystown a couple of days, I shall have the road across the Alleghenies reconnoitered by two detachments."[170] Until the roads were completed, nothing would move forward.

In 1758, roads were not constructed to any recurring standard.[171] The widest documented carriage on the Forbes campaign was the British Board of Ordnance's ammunition wagon, which was seven feet or eighty-four inches wide. Accordingly, the absolute minimum width that the road could have been would be eight feet. More likely, it was significantly wider. Typical roads of the period were one rod, or 16½ feet, wide.[172] A road constructed to this width would have permitted even two large ammunition wagons to pass each other, with their teams in harness. A road associated with the Thomas Ellison Grist Mill, New Windsor, Orange County, New York (in the Hudson Highlands), constructed in 1741, was "at least seventeen" feet wide when archaeologically excavated.[173]

Contemporary American and European drivers are used to carefully paved, meticulously graded, well-engineered roads constructed for automobiles and trucks and optimized to achieve high speeds, gentle turns, consistent inclines and long sight lines. To modern eyes, a typical 18th century road would appear as little more than a farm lane, adequate only for farm machinery to operate upon. Such roads typically followed high ground, to avoid the inevitable mud and water from low-lying locations. Wherever possible, roads went around ridges or hills, instead of over the top of them. Alignments were adjusted as necessary to achieve the gentlest possible slope. Roads were also aligned to minimize stream or swamp crossings. Additionally, it was anticipated that the precise road course would be regularly altered, as segments of the roadway became churned up or damaged by animal hooves and iron wagon wheels. Thus, road alignments were normally quite wide, to permit the actual pathways to meander around seasonally or temporarily impassable sections. Precise routes that were permanent are only the features of modern paved highways, and were unknown when Bouquet and Forbes constructed their road. Thus, an erroneous tendency of many amateur historians is to identify a particular historic road trace as "*the* Forbes Road." More properly, an individual road trace might in fact have been the Forbes Road only for certain months out of the year, perhaps only on those occasions when a summer was dry enough to make that particular road segment passable. When the weather was wet, that particular road section might have been easily and regularly bypassed.

Other factors were also considered. The construction of bridges would have been absolutely minimized, as bridge construction was time-consuming, required the services of an engineer to supervise, and demanded large quantities of materials. When low-lying ground or small streams had to be crossed, a causeway or corduroyed road was most typically constructed. A causeway was a raised roadway, with its boundaries laid out with stones or timber, and then filled with dirt and rocks. A corduroyed road was constructed from cut brush, small trees, or (in those rare cases when available) fence rails or salvaged building materials, that was laid perpendicular to the direction of travel. This type of construction, usually only seen on hiking trails today, would have been the preferred method.

A military solution was to use fascines to construct either a causeway or corduroyed road. As previously described, a fascine was essentially a large bundle of brush, twigs, sticks and small trees up to about wrist size, very tightly bound together with vines, green saplings, or rope. Soldiers were trained to manufacture fascines using a simple wooden cradle, and a small team of soldiers could produce large numbers of fascines extremely rapidly. The author has supervised living historians in the production of fascines on numerous occasions at various historical sites, and can attest that they can be created within a matter of minutes. The most time-consuming step in the process is the cutting and gathering of raw materials. On the Forbes campaign this would not have been an issue, as opening a road through the heavy woods of western Pennsylvania would have created all of the raw materials that could ever have been required. Fascines could be manufactured in various lengths, although six or eight feet in length were typical. Once constructed, they would be used to form the face of a causeway, to fill in a causeway, or to become corduroys.

If these techniques could not be utilized to cross a stream, a ford was the next preferred approach. The roadbed would be cut through the stream bank, to form a consistent slope into and out of the stream. If the footing of the ford was particularly bad, rocks, stones, or fascines might be used to stabilize the bottom of the watercourse. Similarly, the roadbed leading down to or out of the ford might have to be improved to enhance trafficability.

Only if none of these approaches were feasible would a bridge actually be constructed.[174] Most frequently on the Forbes campaign the bridges were simple squared trees of large dimensions, laid in place to form stringers directly across the stream, with other, smaller squared trees forming the cross members of the bridge. If the span to be bridged was too wide for a single long tree, simple stone piers would be constructed to hold additional stringers. Governor Sharpe of Maryland, while supervising the construction of the road between Fort Frederick and Fort Cumberland in Maryland to support Forbes, would document that he constructed "triangular piers made with logs and filled with stones" similar to those previously used on the Braddock campaign in Maryland.[175] Such a bridge would have been treacherous to cross, particularly in the absence of any railings or clearly defined edge, with an extremely rough and unleveled flooring, and liable to be swept aside by any heavy rain or flood. During archaeological investigations at Fort Ligonier, what were believed to be two stringers to a bridge across a small stream were located. These logs were two feet square and thirteen feet long. They were placed 7½ feet apart, and were not hewed, squared or finished in any manner.[176] This constituted the absolutely crudest, most basic bridge that could possibly have been constructed. Such a narrow width suggests that bridges were constructed to the minimum conceivable size, just barely wide enough to permit the large ammunition wagons to cross. Thus, these bridges also constituted certain choke points on the road.

More elaborate bridges were almost certainly not built during this campaign, although they would certainly have been added as rapidly as possible thereafter to make them safer, easier to cross, and more likely to survive freshets. For an example of this, late in 1759, Captain Lewis Ourry, then commandant at Fort Bedford, constructed just such a bridge near his post. Although Ourry created this structure well after the campaign of immediate interest was concluded, his description of his engineering feat is demonstrative of the time and techniques that were used to construct this road:

> I have finished what every body calls a very good Bridge, over the Creek about two miles above this Place, where there was an exceeding bad Ford. I have laid it about 60 or 80 Yards above the Ford & cut a Road in the side of a Rocky Hill to the Old Road. I began it the first of December, and a Waggon went over it on Christmas Day.[177]

When a road was built into or along a slope, a typical approach was to take fascines, large rocks or stones, place them down slope to form the bottom edge of the road, then excavate up slope and throw the removed soil down slope or against those rocks or stones. Thus, a level roadway could be created, with a minimum of labor, and with a relatively stable down slope wall formed from fascines or large rocks so that the road would not shift or collapse. The author has observed several military roads from the late 18th or early 19th century in the Hudson Highlands near West Point constructed to these specifications, and historian Edward G. Williams observed evidence of the same construction techniques along the Forbes Road.[178]

Alternatively, boggy or wet sections might have been filled in with pebbles or small stones to create "French drains." The stones permitted the water to move down slope, while at the same time providing relatively good footing for animals and soldiers. An advantage to the use of stones or pebbles is that the water is still permitted to flow naturally, while preserving the road with a minimum of maintenance. The use of French drains is typical for any construction, including commercial structures such as furnaces, residential houses, and walking paths, during the 18th and 19th centuries. Fascines could also be used for this purpose, as they are loose enough to permit water to flow through them.

Ruts or holes, where they developed, would have been filled in with earth, stones or rocks that were excavated, fascines, or common debris. A typical practice was to use relatively stable garbage such as broken dishes, cutlery, glasses, coal cinders, and ashes from fires for just such a purpose.[179] A major effort of the construction of the Forbes Road was removal of brush and trees, which would have been cut as low as possible, then pushed to the side of the road beds so that a wagon could have been driven over or around the stumps, which would not have been removed from the roadbed, as such work required considerable time and effort. Rather, they would have been cut low to the ground and permitted to naturally rot.

Large boulders would usually have been simply driven around. When that was not possible, smaller rocks would have been pried or levered out of the ground by brute force using "crows" (crowbars in today's verbiage) which were carried specifically for that purpose by Forbes's army. When a rock formation could not be avoided, but needed a minimum of removal to achieve necessary clearances or slopes, hand chisels and sledge hammers would have been used to carve away the edges of the rock. When complete removal was mandated, blasting holes would have been drilled into the rocks again using hand chisels and hammers, and gunpowder would have then been employed to demolish the entire rock formation. Among the plethora of Ordnance supplies carried by Forbes's army to support road building and other construction operations were:

• 4 iron drills;	• 89 hand bills;	• 25 whip saws;
• 11 sledgehammers;	• 25 spare helves for pickaxes;	• 16 cross cut saws;
• 562 pickaxes;	• 25 ballast baskets;	• 12 broad chisels;
• 39 mattocks;	• 3 earth rammers;	• 4 scribing chisels;
• 341 felling axes;	• 3 large wood mauls;	• 1 pairing chisel;
• 646 spades;	• 75 wheel barrows;	• 2 crows of iron;
• 327 shovels;	• 13 hand barrows;	• 2 sets of miner's tools[180]
• 1,321 hand hatchets;	• 132 wheel barrow wheels;	

The result of literally tens of thousands of man-days of arduous manual labor performed with this panoply of tools was a road that by modern standards would be judged fit to be negotiated only by a particularly courageous operator of a farm tractor, but by 18th century standards was an easily traveled, completely passable highway. In fact, almost immediately following the capture of Fort Duquesne and the removal of the immediate French and Indian threat, commercial traffic began to utilize the Forbes Road.[181]

Once across the Juniata River, the road essentially followed high ground north of the river, roughly due west for twelve miles until Ray's Town was reached.[182] Bouquet told Forbes, "The road beyond Juniatta is very good, and all the woods are full of excellent forage."[183] The Reverend Barton left a fine description of the journey that he took on July 24 from the crossing to Ray's Town, following a night in which he had been "without a bed, or any covering at all but a single blanket":

> The Road good — Some extraordinary land & rich Bottoms, with here & there a little Hill — Met with fine Grass about 4 Miles from the Crossing — turn'd out our Horses to feed upon it — After resting 2 Hours — purs'd our Journey to Snake Spring, where we cut Locust Bushes for the Horses, & refresh'd ourselves with Punch, Bread, Cheese & dry Venison — After a Stay of about an Hour, set out again for Ray's Town distant from the Crossing 12 Miles — Where we arriv'd in good Health about 4 Oclock in the Evening — Waited on the Commanding Officer by whom I was receiv'd in a very friendly Manner — All the other Officers treated me likewise with much Respect.— Here I found about 1,800 Men — a fine Fort & Store Houses — with two Encampments surrounded by Breast Works.-[184]

The "punch" that the good Reverend consumed was an extremely popular and common drink of the 18th century. It was a mixture of water, lemons or limes, a large quantity of sugar, and an even larger amount of rum mixed together. It was considered to be a refreshing repast, and its liberal consumption can indeed alleviate the effects of hard labor or extreme fatigue, at least temporarily. On the Pennsylvania frontier, even the ministers imbibed strong spirits.

The encampment that the Reverend Barton reached on July 24 had been in existence for precisely one month. Bouquet had marched for Ray's Town from the crossing on June 24, 1758. Because Ray's Town was intended to serve as the advanced depot for the campaign, Bouquet immediately initiated construction of a fortification here. First, however, he faced the challenge of properly siting the fort, as he described to Forbes:

> Since my arrival I have been almost constantly on horseback, searching with Captain Gordon for a terrain suitable for the proposed plan. We have searched without avail, and have found only high ground without water, or water in low and vulnerable places. Of the two inconveniences we finally chose the least and decided on the location which seemed least objectionable. The fort intended to contain our supplies will be on a height, and will have a communication with a water supply which cannot be cut off. Work has begun this morning, and will be pushed with all possible dispatch.[185]

In addition to the fort itself, Bouquet also constructed storehouses for provisions and equipment, and magazines for ammunition. While at Carlisle, Bouquet calculated the size and number of storehouses required, and drafted specifications for their construction detailed enough to provide the sizes and capacities for individual rooms. According to Bouquet's preparations, the following storehouses would be necessary:

> For 2,349 barrels of flour (enough for 6,000 men for three months), a single storehouse 90 feet long and 30 feet wide, high enough for the barrels to be stored five high;
> For 608 barrels of salt pork (enough for 6,000 men for three months), a single storehouse 40 feet long and 30 feet wide, high enough for the barrels to be stored five high;
> For Rice, a single store house 40 feet long and 30 feet wide;
> A single house 20 feet square to issue provisions.[186]

These or similar storehouses were constructed at both Carlisle and Ray's Town. This meticulous and painstaking attention to detail is typical of both Forbes and Bouquet throughout the entire campaign, for even the most inconsequential segment of the campaign required forethought and careful planning.

The fort itself was an irregular five-bastioned stockade constructed of palisades, with three storehouses and a headquarters or guard building contained inside. The most distinctive feature of this fort was a protected gallery that projected out from one bastion to extend over the Juniata River, to provide the safe water source that Bouquet was concerned about. Chaplain Barton observed regarding the construction of this fort on August 22:

> Large Parties are still kept busy at work, in digging a Trench round the Fort; covering such Parts of it as are expos'd; & making a Covert [Covered] Way to command the water, which runs in a pleasant Stream under the Fort &c.[187]

Captain Joseph Shippen with the Pennsylvania Provincials similarly described the fort as it appeared by September 19: "We have a good Stockade Fort built here with Several convenient Store Houses—And our camps are all secured with a good Breastwork & a small ditch on the outside."[188]

A hospital complex with an accompanying storehouse was located outside of the fort, a typical approach to prevent infection from the sick. A storehouse for hay was also constructed nearby. Two redoubts were located to the south and west of the main fort, in the direction of the most likely French or Indian attack. A large parade ground was located south of the main fort to drill ("exercise" in the verbiage of the times) the soldiers, most of whom were little more than raw recruits. The artillery park for the train of Royal Artillery was located just southwest of the fort. A location for sutlers, or private businessmen licensed to sell to the soldiers, was also provided outside of the main fort. To complete this massive establishment, eighteen bake ovens were also constructed nearby.[189] On the night of August 10, "Through the negligence of the bakers, who were baking biscuit, twelve of our ovens were burned last night." Bouquet promptly had them rebuilt, specifying this time: "All the Hatchet men, Masons and those who understand building Ovens; are to rebuild the Ovens directly of green wood."[190]

As if all this design and construction were not sufficient labor, Bouquet also understood that these posts were destined to become permanent garrisons to support the road and more important fortifications to the west. Accordingly, he took measures to ensure that the posts could become self-sufficient in the future, and began planting turnips in a garden at Ray's Town as early as the middle of July. The Reverend Barton noted, "A large Piece of Ground sow'd with Turnip Seed & harrow'd in this Day."[191] Bouquet also requested that additional garden seeds be sent to him to plant a full garrison garden.[192]

As units poured into the encampment, they each constructed additional entrenched square or diamond-shaped encampments with salient (or projecting) angles, that Bouquet properly referred to as ravelins. As defined by John Muller from Woolwich Arsenal in 1746, "Ravelin, is a work placed before the curtain to cover it, and prevent the flanks from being discovered sideways; it is made of two faces meeting in an outward angle."[193] Bouquet specified that guards would camp inside these ravelins, to provide protection for the camps, for they could immediately place enfilading fire around the entire circumference of each encampment in the event of any attack.[194] Bouquet realized that it was unlikely that Ray's Town would be attacked, but he wanted the provincials to gain experience in the construction of fortifications that would be essential as the campaign progressed. He specifically instructed on July 15: "Every Regt to incamp in a Square which they are to Intrench Separately to learn how to do it when alone."[195]

Eventually, four of these large encampments would be constructed. The first, approximately three hundred feet square, contained the thirteen companies of Montgomery's 77th Highlanders, with a small "General's House" intended for Forbes located within it. Governor Glen of South Carolina described this particular encampment to his cousin, Forbes, on July 22:

> I found here Sir Alex. McLane and Captain Cameron, since which arrived Captain McKenzie and yesterday Monroe and Robertson, they are situated upon a hill (Montegrand) with a wooden pavillion in the middle for the General which you will find necessary, and from which you will see the whole line, it is square of three hundred feet, secured from a surprise by a breastwork, with small bastions in the middle of each side, at which I would minutely describe to you but I suppose Bouquet does, whose words and actions you may safely act upon, one great good is that the men are kept from straggling, the Indians Suttlers &c &c. are excluded at night and in case of any alarm every man who steps out of his tent finds himself at his post.[196]

The second, also three hundred feet square, contained the Maryland battalion, the North Carolina battalion, and Mercer's 3rd Pennsylvania Battalion. The third and largest at 450 square feet contained Washington's 1st Virginia Regiment, the 1st and 2nd Pennsylvania Battalions, and the Royal Artillery. The fourth and smallest, approximately two hundred feet square, contained the Royal Americans, and immediately adjacent to this was another entrenchment with the Pennsylvania Provincial Artillery. Just above this camp was a star-shaped redoubt. These entrenchments were constructed from the same materials, and using similar techniques, as the redoubts at Juniata Crossing and the large entrenched camp at Carlisle.[197] Brigade Major Joseph Shippen with the Pennsylvania Provincials recorded of these fortifications: "We have a good Stockade Fort built here with several convenient Store Houses, and our Camps are all secured with a good Breast-work & a small Ditch on the outside."[198]

With all of these men and animals jammed into a relatively small area, Bouquet recognized that illness would soon result if measures were not taken to control common filth, and to maintain a clean water supply. Bouquet ordered on June 24, immediately after arriving, "Necessary Houses to be Built, Cleanlyness of the Camp Recommended." In the language of the 18th century, latrines were referred to as "necessary houses." They were sometimes also alluded to as "houses of office." Two days later Bouquet ordered that: "The Hatchet men ... are to make necessary Houses.... The Camp Colour Men are ... to Assist in Making the Camp and keeping it Clean as likewise to throw Earth into the Necessary Houses every two Days." Bouquet also cautioned on July 3: "The Quarter Guard is to mind that no Body wash either Meat or Linnen in the Springs About the Camp, they are to be kept Clean for the use of the soldiers. All Cloaths are to be wash'd in the River." Necessary houses were regularly filled with earth and routinely moved, to prevent them from contaminating the camp. Certainly, their rough appearance scattered throughout camp did little to improve the sights, smells and sounds of the encampment (and, interestingly enough, not a single recreated fort contains a period "Necessary House"). Some soldiers apparently considered their use to be optional, for Bouquet reminded his command on July 3: "The men are to go to the Necessary House, and no Dirt or Dung to be left in the Camp."[199]

Bouquet would begin constructing this fortification with eight hundred men, and the army would spend approximately sixty days at Ray's Town while the road and additional advanced posts were constructed towards Fort Duquesne. These two months would be absolutely critical to the campaign, for it was during this time frame that the supplies necessary to support the next movement forward would have to be acquired, moved to Ray's Town, and secured in storehouses.

To augment previously salted meat, live cattle (sheep, hogs or cows) were also driven along. This obviously made sense, as the animals moved themselves, didn't require packaging and transportation, and could be driven with fewer soldiers than were needed to manage an appreciable number of pack horses or wagons. When needed, the animals were simply butchered on the spot and fresh meat issued to the soldiers. Adam Hoops sent two hundred cows to Bouquet in the middle of June, which was a typical herd of live animals.[200] Later in the campaign, in response to Forbes's concerns regarding the sufficiency of grass, a smokehouse would be constructed at Loyalhanna to enable the live animals to be butchered and preserved on the spot. Forbes would note in late August, "[A]s the grass will now fail or in a short time I fancy the live cattle we have must be killed and salted it would not be amiss if a good deal of it could be smoaked."[201]

To ensure that the live animals destined to become rations, and the draught horses pulling the wagons and artillery train, were adequately fed, Bouquet established meadows or grazing pastures at various locations along the road. Bouquet mentioned from Carlisle in early June, "I have spoken for all the meadows in this vicinity, and have had them appraised by jurors named by the magistrates, so that they may be paid for if they are used."[202] Bouquet was also pleased to inform Forbes on August 3 from Ray's Town: "I have found, four or five miles from the camp, on the western side enough grass to feed the artillery horses and our cattle for two weeks, and I shall have them guarded by a strong detachment."[203]

To supplement these regular rations, Forbes also ordered that "Six or Seven Waggon Loads of Bacon" be purchased, presumably about 12,000 pounds.[204] Although this appears to be a large quantity, since bacon was considered to be pork for ration purposes this was only enough meat for the full army of 6,000 men for four days at half a pound per man per day. Forbes probably ordered this bacon as a reserve ration for a forced march or emergency, as it could be consumed without having to be cooked.

Significantly complicating the entire logistical effort were the inadequate preparations made by Quartermaster St. Clair, which contributed their full share to what would become the eternal saga of wagon, horse and forage problems that Forbes and Bouquet struggled with nearly until the end of the campaign. Forbes was extremely displeased with St. Clair's conduct, almost from the onset of the campaign. St. Clair did little to help his cause, as he wrote Forbes an airy missive on May 21 from Winchester in which he essentially stated that he was serving on this campaign as an independent commander. In fact, under the British Army system the quartermaster had no authority to command or issue orders to any troops or officers, except in the performance of his official duties. St. Clair would complain to Forbes:

> I am concerned that you should put me under his Orders [Colonel Bouquet] /after giving me yours in writing/ as if he were able and in a condition to relieve me from the many difficulties I labour under, nor do I apprehend it is in your Power at the distance you are, so as to remedy the Evils, I must now lay before you. I shall correspond with Colonel Bouquett and advise him of every motion I make, and you may depend on my never assuming to order anything when I am in his Neighborhood. Until I have your answers I shall act as my Honour directs me, and consult the good of the Service, in following your Intentions, but if I am totally to act under Colonel Bouquett's Orders please to let me know it, and your commands shall be punctually obey'd and with pleasure.[205]

Forbes responded in a blistering reproach to St. Clair on May 25:

> I did not understand your *paragraph with regard to your acting under Colonel Bouquet's orders totally: when you have any orders in writing; or at your being concerned for being put under his orders* [emphasis in original]. You know very well that Colonel Bouquet is named by the Government the second in this command, and consequently commands ever where in my absence; And

you may easily believe I shall give no orders without acquainting of him, and therefore fancy he knows the service too well, and will have better manners, than to alter any of my orders in my absence; without very good cause; and what fresh orders he gives according to circumstances in my absence, are most certainly as valid, as if they came from me. And as you very well observed that one at a distance cannot judge of circumstances, so well as those present, I have therefore always thought that affairs of moment trusted to proper officers ought in most cases to have discretionary power in the execution, according to the exigencies of things. So I cannot see that you will find any difficulty in carrying on the service, as it is scarce to be supposed that I am to order one thing, and Colonel Bouquet another, or that he present is to order one thing, and I absent to order the contrary.[206]

St. Clair shortly began to demonstrate his propensity for argument and controversy. Colonel John Armstrong, the experienced commander of the 1st Battalion of the Pennsylvania Provincials, would report:

You desire the reasons of [his brother, Major George Armstrong] George's sending down his Commission; it was owing to Sir John St. Clair's ordering him in Arrest, on the Complaint of a Serjeant (to whom George had given a Box on the Side of the head for Some neglect or other) without hearing George, together with sundry blustering threats out of the Usual mode of treating an Officer — this, tho' a matter which Sir John Shou'd not have trouble have troubled him Self before I had heard it, I put up with, but found that Gentleman's rash and extraordinary manner of treating the new Levys under my particular Care & Command, together with his ingrossing the detail of the Troops which belongs to every Colonel or Commander of a Core [corps], that I was Oblig'd to resent the Conduct, upon which a Quarrel ensu'd betwixt us.... I hear the General has made all this matter Square.... Sir John is now very Polite.[207]

In addition to having to deal with St. Clair's interfering with other officers' commands and getting into quarrels with provincial officers, Forbes was furious that his quartermaster had done such a poor job in his preparations for the campaign. Forbes angrily fumed to Bouquet on July 10 from Carlisle:

The Waggons have been the plague of my life, as I found them here in the greatest degree of Confusion, nor indeed had Sir John taken the smallest pains, or had made the least inquiry how to sett those matters to rights. I hope however to gett to the bottom of it, when the empty waggons now at Raes town return. You will give orders that each Convoy as they arrive be examined, and those Waggons or horses found unsufficient to be marked down and turned out of the service giving them passes and marking the days that they were discharged. Wee likewise have been and were like to be at ane Intire stop for want of provender for our horses as Sir John has only made ane Imagineary provision, for in reality wee have not one pound of Hay.[208]

Forbes remained incensed regarding St. Clair's performance, as he further described to Bouquet on July 23:

The Provincials are all gone from this [Carlisle], and I proposed to have left it yesterday with the four remaining Companies of the Highlanders, but not to crowd you or distress you [at Ray's Town] in Provendor, the providing of which has been most terribly neglected, the troops now shall move slowly on, and in place of allowing the Waggon Horses, and Bat horses to make their halting days of refreshment at Raestown, you will order their Waggon Masters to conduct them backwards, and you will give them days of refreshment anywhere else, otherwise we might be drove to the necessity of quiting Raestown before we choose it for want of forage and provendor for our horses. I have spoke very roundly upon this subject to Sir John, who was sent up the Country from Philadelphia for no other purpose than to fix the roads and provide forage, both of which I am sorry to say it, are yet to begin.[209]

Forbes also began at this time a struggle that would occupy much of his energies throughout this campaign, attempting to supply and equip, keep happy, and gainfully employ the various numbers of southern Indians that had joined his army. The first problem, of course, was that the Indians had arrived from the south too early in Forbes's estimation, but at precisely the right time according to the Native Americans' methods of making war. These Indians were Cherokees and Catawbas from the southern colonies. In 1755, Governor Arthur Dobbs of North Carolina estimated that the two major Indian tribes in the southern colonies had the following total strength:

- 240 Catawba warriors under King Hagler; and
- 2,390 Cherokee warriors.[210]

Of these, by May 1, 1758, no fewer than 650 Cherokees had marched north to join Forbes. Forbes was completely unprepared to receive these Indians, and at this early point in the year's campaign he didn't even have an army to accompany them. Accordingly, Forbes had to move fast to attempt to placate the Indians, and he had to do it without any assistance from the two English Superintendents for Indians in North America, Sir William Johnson and Edmond Atkin. Forbes, who had initially intended to work through Johnson and Atkin, had been bitterly disappointed in that regard. He complained to Brigadier General Stanwix on May 29, "It is amazing to me that neither Sir William Johnson nor Mr. Atkins [sic] have either come themselves, nor have they sent any one person to look after those Indians, altho repeated applications have been made to both those gentlemen." To Pitt he wrote on May 19, "Sir William continued at his Settlement 500 Miles North of this, and Mr. Atkins remained at Charleston 700 Miles to the South, I found myself obliged either to act as I have done or must have seen those Indians return to their own Country disgusted, and probably ready to join the Enemy against us."[211]

Forbes must therefore have been pleased to receive the following suggestions on May 2 from Captain Abraham Bosomworth of the Royal Americans, who had spent time with the Natives and gained experience with the demands of Indian management:

For the better regulation and management of a body of Indians going to War and acting in Conjunction with His Majestys Forces it is highly necesssary. That a proper person be appointed by the Commander In Chief to have the sole command and direction of the said Indians during the Campaign. That a Certain number of white People be appointed as officers to attend the Indians on their march and go on their scouting and other parties proportionate to the number of Indians employed in our Service who are to be under the direction of the head Warrior of the said Indians. That all the Interpreters that can be procured to attend the Indians who with the Conductors and the other necessary officers appointed for this service are to be subordinate to the person whom the General shall think fit to give the sole command of our Indian allies. That the Indian Camp be detached at some distance from the Army and formed in different parts round their incampment for the better security of the same. That a proper quantity and assortment of goods be carried with the army to be occasionally distributed to the Indians to encourage them in the service and others lodged on the road with the military stores in such magazines as shall be thought fit to be erected for that purpose. That the Deputy Agent for Indian Affairs and his assistants do attend the Army and make the distribution of the said goods and give out such presents from time to time as the sole commander of the said Indians shall direct. That no soldier be suffered to go to the Indian Camp or have any traffick or communication with them whatever and no sutler be permitted to give them strong Liquors under the highest pains and penalties. That some particular signals be settled & agreed upon between our Indian allies and the English and certain conspicuous marks be affixed to the said Indians the easier and plainer to distinguish them from the Enemy and to prevent the ill effects of killing one another which might prove highly injurious to the Service.[212]

Forbes eagerly accepted Bosomworth's recommendations, and appointed him to be responsible for the management of the Cherokees and Catawbas, in orders dated May 12:

You are hereby directed and required to sett out from this Place with such Indian Presents as have been bought up for the Cherokees in this Town, and have them safely conducted to Carlisle, Fort Loudon, Fort Littleton, as you shall see occasion. And when efforts appear necessary, the Commanding Officers of the different troops are hereby ordered to furnish you with such a number of

Men as may be wanted for that purpose. You are also directed to take out of the presents sent to Lancaster such an aportionment as you shall judge proper to send to Capt. Thomson at Fort Loudon to be distributed amongst the Cherokees in such manner as you shall judge most expedient for the Service. And you are further injoined, with the advice of Sir John St. Clair, Col. Washington, Col. Armstrong, or any of the Commanding Officers of the troops until Col. Bouquet's arrival, to take the most effectual measures to preserve the Indians employed in our Service in good temper & to direct their ranging and scouting in such manner as shall be judged most advantagious to the security of the back settlements, covering the frontiers and distressing the enemy. On your arrival at Winchester or also when you are to obtain me an exact and true state of the Indian stores by whom the goods are furnished, to whom distributed, and the quantity still remaining, distinguishing such prices, particularly, and who has the care and charge of said stores are hereby directed to give your signed account of the same which you are to transmit to me further. And all Agents, Conductors, Interpreters and others employed amongst the Cherokees and Catawbas, are hereby ordered and required to give you all the assistance in their power towards forwarding the service and if a greater number of interpreters & conductors may be found necessary than are already employed you are then in conjunction with Mr. Gist to appoint such as are most useful upon the occasion. And you may employ Mr. Trent and Mr. Gist to assist in managing and regulating the Indians going to War if you should find the exigency of the Service requires it. I have nothing further to add, but that you from time to time send me an account of your proceedings & give me the earliest intelligence of the Motions of the Enemy.[213]

The Indians initially assembled at Winchester, Virginia, where in short order they made a nuisance of themselves. John St. Clair found it necessary to issue the following "Proclamation at Virginia," as he haughtily called it, from that town on May 16:

As several very great abuses have been committed by the Selling of Rum and Spirituous Liquors to the Indians. These are therefore to give notice to every inhabitant in & about this place that if any person is found selling or giving strong Liquors to the Indians or buying their Provision they shall incur Military Execution, that is to say they shall have their houses razed as unworthy to live under His Majesty's Government. And further notice is given that from this day if any Indian is seen drunk every cask of Rum in Town shall be stove.[214]

Even this early in the campaign, having just arrived at the theater of war, the Indians complained about their treatment, clamored for presents, and talked of heading home, although most of them must have just barely left their villages.[215] Still, Forbes clearly valued their participation, and he was determined to do everything in his power to keep them with the army, and employ them ahead of his marching columns. He called upon every officer that had prior dealings with the Indians to assist, including his two Virginia colonels who were both experienced in their management. He purchased large quantities of Indian goods in Philadelphia, and appointed Bosomworth as his primary Indian agent with the assistance of experienced traders such as Christopher Gist. He ordered the gratuitous distribution of prodigious quantities of these gifts to the Indians. He also hastened forward the movement of the organizations that he had immediately available such as McLean's four additional Highlander companies and Bouquet's four Royal American companies. On May 25 Quartermaster St. Clair sent the Indians forward to Shippensburg to join Forbes's main column, so that they could cover the front of Bouquet's wagons and supplies, which were then moving forward to Ray's Town.[216] This feat was eventually accomplished, but not without considerable trouble and cajoling.

Upon their appearance at Shippensburg, Forbes initiated a generous issue of provisions from the King's stores to the Indians. His orders on this account, passed through St. Clair, were acknowledged by Adam Hoops on May 29: "Sir John St. Clair wrote me of 500 Indians he sent to Shippensbourg and I have sent them fresh provisions according to his Directions. The Indians at Carlisle get 2 pounds beef per day besides rice & flour, and the same is ordered to be given them at Shippensbourg."[217] It is revealing that this was a greater amount of meat per day than Forbes's own soldiers were receiving!

Once Bosomworth and Forbes managed to get the Natives maneuvered to where they could cooperate with the army, almost immediately another issue surfaced. Specifically, the problem was keeping his poorly trained provincials and trigger-happy regulars, who likely would have been unable to discriminate between friendly and hostile Indians by either inclination or knowledge, from engaging his own Native allies. Forbes adopted various methods of signals, ordering: "That they may be distinguished and the particulars of each Command known each party ought to have some Union Flags and the particular Indians or Soldiers dress'd as such the Yellow Shallown or Buntin upon their head or remarkable part of their body."[218] Forbes consistently ordered that his friendly Indians were to utilize yellow fabric that was provided to them, along with "Union Flags" that they were to carry.[219]

It appears that the Cherokees were reluctant to fully support Forbes in the campaign, but the evidence is that the Catawbas were more dependable and responsive to the British officers, although not consistently so.[220] Still, Bouquet and Bosomworth were persuasive, and shortly after the Native warriors' arrival in Shippensburg and the massive distribution of gifts, they began launching scouts and raids to the west. In late May raids were launched by the Indians against Fort LeBouef at the southern terminus of the portage from Lake Erie and French Creek, and Fort Machault at the intersection of French Creek and the Allegheny River, both key posts on the French line of communications and supply to Fort Duquesne. Raiding parties were also dispatched against Fort Duquesne itself in early and mid–June, and early July.[221]

Attempting to ascertain precise numbers of Indians with Forbes at any given point and time is an almost impossible task, as individual war bands came and went incessantly and indiscriminately throughout the campaign.[222] In early May, somewhat more than six hundred Cherokees and Catawbas initially appeared at Winchester. From that point on, numbers steadily decreased, but several hundred appear to have remained throughout the summer, and several score participated with Forbes on the final movement upon Pittsburgh in November. The precise numbers are not particularly relevant. Rather, the fact that Forbes managed to retain meaningful numbers of Native warriors with him throughout the entire campaign was in fact astounding. This indicated that Forbes's efforts at keeping the Cherokees and Catawbas well-supplied, properly employed according to their own estimation, adequately supervised by Captain Bosomworth and other officers, respected by members of his army, and appreciated by his leadership were successful. Bouquet specifically mentioned on June 16, "I must give justice to Bosomworth. It is to him principally that this success [two hundred Indians continuing to support Forbes's Army] is due." Bosomworth "continues to manage his Indians very well," Forbes noted on July 11.[223]

The Native warriors doubtless appreciated these measures, although due to a lack of written accounts by their own hands they must remain silent participants in the campaign. Forbes's army was the first British army in North America — aside from those directly under the management of William Johnson, who enjoyed a close and personal relationship with the Mohawk Nation of the Iroquois Confederation — that had ever managed to retain Native Americans throughout an entire campaign. Forbes put them to good use scouting and harassing the French at Fort Duquesne, and performing security patrolling in the vicinity of his own army. As a result, Forbes's army sustained relatively minor annoyances by the French and hostile Indians, and managed to completely deceive the French and Indians as to the location of his army until Grant's advance upon Fort Duquesne in September. These were important contributions to the conduct of Forbes's operations, and the absence of first-person written records documenting the accomplishments of the Cherokee and Catawba warriors with Forbes should not permit them to be trivialized. This relative handful of Native American warriors made a substantial commitment to the eventually successful outcome of Forbes's campaign.

While Bouquet struggled with his numerous tasks at Ray's Town, Forbes also initiated diplomacy with the Native Americans, particularly the Delaware, Shawnee and Mingoes of western Pennsylvania, who had heretofore supported the French. Shortly after Forbes arrived in Philadelphia he was approached by Israel Pemberton, a prominent Quaker politician and businessman, who fervently desired a diplomatic approach to the Indian problem. Following discussions with Pemberton, Forbes summoned a meeting at Philadelphia in early June and issued peremptory directions that official messages be sent from the colony of Pennsylvania under his name to Teedyuscung, a Delaware chief. This Delaware representative was deeply resentful of the treatment of his people but had proven himself to be open to rational discussions. The Pennsylvanian's message, sent at Forbes's direct and insistent orders, requested that a council be held with Teedyuscung to discuss how the current situation could be resolved.

On June 6 a Moravian missionary, Christian Frederick Post, who had lived among the Delaware and could speak their language, was dispatched to carry this official message from Forbes and other Pennsylvania representatives to Teedyuscung. Forbes explained to Bouquet on June 16, "I am in hopes of bringing about a treaty with the Delawares &c. by which we may gett them to make their Brethren abandon the Ohio."[224] To support this initiative Forbes instructed St. Clair, "[P]ray establish your marks of distinction that the scouting partys may know one another, and all our Indians must be told to keep to the westward of the Susquehanna, and not to molest our friendly Delawares for the present, as by this means I am soon in hopes of bringing back their brethren from the French upon the Ohio."[225] With these actions, Forbes and Pemberton began the first serious negotiations with the western Pennsylvania Indians since the commencement of hostilities upon Braddock's arrival in 1755.[226]

Finally, as if all of this activity were not enough to exhaust any mere mortal, Forbes also ordered Bouquet on June 16, "I wish the road on the other side of the Allegany mountains was reconnoitred, so as to form a judgement whether we can go that way or not."[227] And Forbes at all times had to be looking forward to the second stage of his operation. He initiated conversations with Bouquet regarding his "second parallel" of advance upon Fort Duquesne as early as July 14: "If the road be found convenient across the Laurell Hill leaving the Yohageny to the left hand, why should not A Detachment of 500 Men or more if necessary be sent directly to Laurel Hill or some where there; to take post there, and make a Stockade and place for the reception of our Ammunition & provisions."[228]

Individually, any single aspect of the first parallel of Forbes's campaign would have been a dauntless task. Amazingly, Bouquet and Forbes accomplished all of these tasks simultaneously and concurrently. Of perhaps greatest import, a strong working relationship between these two men that had been born in Philadelphia in early May was being well nurtured. A careful perusal of their correspondence supports the premise that their ability to cooperate effectively, not only as a well-functioning military command team but as seasoned professionals who mutually respected each other's skills and talents, and as close personal friends, was being created. Perhaps more than any single factor, the forging of these bonds would see this campaign through to fruition.

FIVE

Allegheny Mountain
Becomes Forbes's Rubicon

Forbes Chooses His Route

The single most critical decision point of the campaign was the route that Forbes's army would follow, whether by the Braddock Road, or by a new road across the Allegheny Mountains. Forbes knew from the beginning that upon this selection the whole course of the campaign would turn.[1]

Forbes's initial inclination was to proceed along Braddock's Road. However, regardless of whether he would finally employ it, he wished to maintain every appearance that he *was* going to use this road. Early in the advance Forbes accordingly ordered Bouquet to have Braddock's Road explored and cleared of brush, and Bouquet concurred, commenting, "at all events it may serve to deceive the Enemy."[2]

Without question Forbes did not have a preconceived route chosen, for on June 19 he had written Bouquet, "I suppose you will reconnoitre the road across the Allegany mountains from Raes town and if found impracticable, that the Fort Cumberland Garrison, should open the old road [Braddock's Road] forward towards the Crossing of the Yohagani."[3] As late as July 11 Forbes was still contemplating either road, as he wrote to Bouquet on that date, "I shall hurry up the troops directly so pray see for a road across the Allegany or by Fort Cumberland, which garrison may if necessary be clearing Braddocks old road."[4]

Forbes and Bouquet recognized that there were distinct advantages to opening a direct road from Ray's Town to the Forks. Bouquet wrote to Forbes on June 21:

> When I have been at Raystown a couple of days, I shall have the road across the Alleghenies reconnoitered by two detachments, one going directly toward the heights above the forks of the Youghiogheny and the other to the right to try to find a passage across Laurel Hill. The advantage of this latter route would be that it is shorter, avoiding all the rivers, having only small creeks to be crossed; and that it would confuse the enemy who naturally would not expect us from that direction.[5]

Once established at Ray's Town, Forbes immediately had Bouquet begin to scout a possible route across the mountains. It very shortly became obvious to Forbes that not only was such a route feasible, but it was in fact desirable. Forbes wrote Pitt on July 10:

> I am in hopes of finding a better way over the Allegany Mountains, than that from Fort Cumberland which Genl Braddock took, if so I shall shorten both my March, and my labour of cutting the road about 40 miles, which is a great consideration. For were I to pursue Mr. Braddocks route, I should save but little labour, as that road is now a brushwood, by the sprouts from the old stumps, which must be cut down and made proper for Carriages, as well as any other Passage that we must attempt.[6]

Bouquet had informed Forbes in a letter written July 11, "From all the disintereted persons who have gone from here to Fort du Quesne, I learn that it is possible to have a wagon road across Lawrell Hill, and that on the other side there is nothing but some small mountains which cannot stop us, with forage and water all the way." By July 31, Bouquet was becoming increasingly confident that the road across the Allegheny Mountain was feasible:

You will see by the enclosed Extract from Major Armstrong's letters what report he has made. Everything seems practicable, and even easy, but I distrust the observation of a young and inexperienced man too much to act on his advice. I have therefore sent Colonel Burd, Rhor, and Captain Ward to reconnoiter the Allegheny, to make a survey of all the difficulties, and to put me in a position to determine what reliance should be given to the rest of the explorations. Unfortunately, they found things very different, and that the mountain over which these gentlemen crossed so easily is worse than Sideling Hill and the climb much longer. As they did not think a wagon road could be cut in this escarpment without an immense amount of work, they searched along the mountain for another pass, and found about two miles to the north a gap of which no one here had the slightest knowledge.... It appears that with a great deal of work a road much more satisfactory than the other could be built there; it remains to be seen what obstacles are left as far as Loyal Hannon.[7]

The following report of Rhor's was absolutely critical, for Allegheny Mountain had to be crossed for the direct route from Ray's Town to be utilized:

The Distance from Ray's Town to the Top of the Alleghany by the Old Trading path is Fifteen Miles & one half. There is a Number of Hills all along the path passes over several, which are quite practicable.— The Ridge of the Alleghany Mountains where the trading path crosses cou'd not be cut for waggons without an immence Labour and is full three quarters of a mile in length and very steep — About two miles ENE there is a Gap in the Top very narrow with a gradual ascent & stony, but with a good deal of Labour a Road might be cut.[8]

This discovery by Ensign Rohr established the direction of the Forbes campaign. Rohr's contributions can hardly be overestimated.

But Bouquet was not trusting simply to Rohr, for he had dispatched three separate scouting parties to reconnoitre a possible route across the Allegheny Mountains. These parties were under the Command of Lieutenant Colby Chew of Washington's 1st Virginia Regiment, Captain Asher Clayton of the 2nd Pennsylvania Battalion and Captain Edward Ward of the 1st Pennsylvania Battalion. Forbes, through Bouquet, issued them extremely detailed instructions[9]:

Camp near Reas Town 7th July 1758
Instructions for Captains Ward & Clayton

1st They are to march from the Camp Saturday Morning 8th July with a party of 4 subalterns, 4 Serjeants, 6 Corporals and 90 Privates towards the Alleghany, taking the old path, observing the Road & the bearings.—
2d From the top of the Alleghany they are to take the Bearings of Laurel Hill and observe the Gap; then take to the right & go some miles towards the beginning of Laurel Hill —
3d When they are arrived at the foot of Laurel Hill they are to march along the ridge to the southward observing where a waggon road cou'd be practicable.—
4th They are to consider attentively the place where the old Path crosses the Laurel Hill and judge whether a Road cou'd be made ther for Waggons—
5th They will also be very particular in viewing the large gap which lies about [blank space] Miles south of the old Path.
6th They are to goe over the Mountain in the place that will appear to them most convenient for the intended purpose, to see what descent they find on the other side —
7th If they find a proper place, they are to mark it in such a manner as they may find it again.—
8th They are likewise to consider what course wou'd be most proper to take for the Road from the Camp to the place of the crossing of Laurel Hill —
9th They are then to continue to range that Mountain till they come to the three Forks, where they are to examine whether the new Road cou'd pass that way —

10th After they have reconnoitred the River & Crossing of Yioghiogeny, they are to return to the new Road & load their horses with as many falling axes & tools as they can conveniently carry down to the Camp —

11th They are to take every day the Bearings of the Mountains and Creeks, and observe likewise the Course they keep by their pocket Compass. —

12th They are to keep a minute Journal of everything they see, and not trust to their Memory —

Regulations for the March —

1st They are to march in the Indian file, observing a good distance between the men, with an advanc'd party and flankers, who are to be reliev'd often in bad roads—

2nd Before they arrive to the place where they intend to incamp, they must divide themselves to make several intricated tracks up and down. —

3rd Before they lay down their Arms the ground is to be reconnoitered all around —

4th One Corporal and six men to be advanced before them, the same number behind, and on their right & left.

5th Each of these four posts is to keep a Centry & when the Centries are either tired or sleepy they are to put another in their place —

6th The Victuals are to be dress'd in the middle of the day and no fire is to be made afterwards—

7th The Greatest Care is to be taken to keep the arms, ammunition & provisions dry —

8th They are not to permit any of their men (except the Indians) to go hunting, and not even them on the other side of the Alleghany —

9th The most exact silence is to be observed, and no noise suffer'd during the whole Expedition —

10th In case of an Attack, their Journal is to be thrown away, to prevent its falling in the Hands of the Enemies in Case of Accident —

11th They are to prevent the Enemy from surrounding them by extending their Wings; But if notwithstanding it shou'd happen so; They are then to make immediately a general push through their center, and get possession of another ground —

12th The horses are to be hoppled [hobbled] every night to prevent losing of time to hunt them in the morning; the worse Horse to be unloaded first —

The above and foregoing instructions are not binding, but liable to all such alterations as the circumstances and the judgement of the commanding Officer may suggest.

These instructions are also quite intriguing in that they provide very detailed tactical guidance to the two officers, instructions which are strikingly similar to the better known "Rules of Rogers Rangers" that the famous partisan warrior had taught to English officers in 1757 at Fort Edward, New York. It is extremely unlikely that Forbes was aware of these instructions, as they were not published until 1765. Rather, Forbes developed his own set of scouting procedures based upon his own experiences and contemporary military manuals. They are every bit as relevant, carefully considered, and tactically sound as any of Rogers's rules.

As each patrolling party returned, a detailed report was provided to Forbes and Bouquet, detailing the detachment's route, discoveries, and any accomplishments. Forbes would greatly depend upon these reports to provide him with detailed information on the route across the mountains, which had never been satisfactorily scouted, and were certainly not well enough known to propel a military force across them without adequate reconnaissance. Forbes would find Captain Ward's report to be particularly relevant, and frequently referred to it when describing his decision-making process. His report provided a particularly detailed accounting of the Laurel Ridge and Alleghany Mountain, which gave Forbes the information that he needed to ascertain that this was in fact a viable route.[10]

The factors that would influence the final selection between the Braddock's Road and the now scouted Allegheny Route were:

- Raw road distance from Ray's Town to Fort Duquesne;
- Amount of work necessary to complete the road from Ray's Town to Fort Duquesne;

- Obstacles that had to be traversed between Ray's Town and Fort Duquesne;
- Logistical considerations; and
- Tactical considerations.

According to Forbes, from Ray's Town to Fort Duquesne using Braddock's Road required a march of approximately 160 miles. From Ray's Town to Fort Duquesne by way of Loyalhanna was about ninety miles. To use the Braddock Road required detouring almost due south about 35 miles, then proceeding generally northwest. In effect, the army would have to traverse two sides of a triangle. However, the Allegheny Road could proceed nearly due west from Ray's Town, without having to divert. Thus, the first decision factor clearly favored the shorter route, directly over the Allegheny Mountains and almost due west.

The second decision factor appeared to favor the Braddock Road, as that road was finished almost to the Forks of the Ohio, except for those last critical eight miles that Braddock had never reached. To connect the Virginians with Forbes, the road between Fort Cumberland and Ray's Town was going to be built in any event. The entire length of the Allegheny Mountains road would have to be newly constructed past Ray's Town to Fort Duquesene. Only the last few miles of Braddock's Road had to be completed. However, the condition of the Braddock Road could easily be overstated. The road had never been particularly well engineered; rather, it had been hastily established so that Braddock could maintain his aggressive timetable. Although the Virginians who obviously favored its use were quick to ignore this fact, the road would require numerous improvements before it could handle the six thousand men, artillery train, packhorses, and three hundred wagons that Forbes intended to take across it. Braddock's Road had not been maintained since his defeat in July 1755, or in fact used at all since that time except by small parties on foot. Although Washington suggested that only light brush needed to be cleared from the road, a more accurate appraisal would be that it was nearly impassable except by these small parties.[11] The road would have to be widened throughout its entire length, as it was quite narrow in places, and in any event the edges of a road are always the first to disintegrate. Three years' growth of brush and saplings would have to be cleared; along with the other inevitable repairs to washed-out road sections, missing bridges, damaged fords, collapsed retaining walls, fallen trees and boulders, and similar acts of nature. Not to mention that it would be necessary to remove several obstructions that the French had placed to deliberately obstruct it. Bouquet noted on August 8 that the French had placed an "abatis" or obstruction of felled trees and brush, across the Braddock Road at at least one location.[12] Finally, the last eight miles of the road remained to be finished, and these were the most difficult and dangerous eight miles closest to the French fort. So although the second decision factor appeared to favor the Braddock Road, this was not an absolute advantage.

Regarding topographical and water obstacles, the Loyalhanna route would have to negotiate Allegheny Mountain, Laurel Ridge and Chestnut Ridge. Allegheny Mountain and Laurel Ridge were particularly feared; Chestnut Ridge was considerably less challenging. On the other hand, the Braddock Road had to traverse numerous and major water courses. These were the Potomac River or Wills Creek before Fort Cumberland could even be reached from Ray's Town, the Youghiogheny River twice, and the Monongahela River twice. Using Braddock's Road would add five major water crossings that had to be executed, and high water at any one of these locations could seriously delay the entire army. A direct route across the Allegheny Mountains west from Ray's Town had no major water crossings to execute. If a route could be identified across Allegheny Mountain and Laurel Ridge, the advantage would definitely go to the cross–Allegheny route.

Regarding logistical factors, one critical portion of the equation, which outweighed all other considerations, was that the Virginia economy simply could not support an army of the size of either Braddock or Forbes at Fort Cumberland.[13] Before Forbes would select this route, he had to be convinced that the campaign could be supported through Fort Cumberland, and this was by no means obvious, for it would add extra distance from his supply base at Philadelphia, and his advanced depot at Ray's Town. Quartermaster John St. Clair had reached the same conclusion following the Braddock campaign in 1755:

> Experience convinces us now that this Country was not well Chosen for carrying on our Expedition, the Representations that have been made at home with regard to the Advantage of water Carriage and so much much [sic] Waggon Road, have either been very partial or extremely injudicious; the water Carriage at the best of time is very tedious and liable to abundance of Accidents, through the smallness of the bottoms and Scarcity, unskillfulness, and Villany of the water men, in dry Weather it is quite impracticable. The Land Carriage is long, the Country very mountainous, many of the Mountains high, Steep, Rocky and Stony, the Plains between are Swampy, generally full of Close thick woods, and troublesome runns of water. The best of years there is a scarcity of Forrage, Cattle and Carriages, and the Country People are the least Adapted for Military Service of any that I have seen, they are both delicate and Timirous, we shou'd have avoided most of the disadvantages to the northward, where the Country is plentiful the roads much better and the people of a bold Warlike Genious [genius, i.e., spirit] besides that Road wou'd lead us thro a Country well peopled with Indians that would be ready to Join us if we made any Shew [show] amongst them.[14]

Another consideration was the availability of fodder for the animals. There was limited natural grass along the Braddock route, which in fact had caused Braddock considerable difficulties. The situation was better along the proposed Allegheny Route, which also had never had an entire army previously pass over it. In particular, there were expansive meadows available at Loyalhanna that could support Forbes's entire army for an extended period of time. The direct route west from Ray's Town had a decided advantage.

An entirely human, but not inconsiderable factor regarding the use of Braddock's Road was the association of that route with Braddock's crushing defeat.[15] If he utilized Braddock's Road, Forbes's army would have to march along the same route that led Braddock to his slaughter. At the most dangerous portion of the entire campaign, the final advance on Fort Duquesne that had proven so fatal to Braddock's fortunes, Forbes's army would have to pass directly through the killing fields where Braddock's men had been killed en masse. Their bones still lay scattered and rotting in the woods. Captain James Patterson reported on August 1 during a scout that he had led towards Fort Duquesne, "Cross'd Turtle Creek ... and came up opposite to the place of Braddocks Engagement and stayed there till Sunsett — Marched then down to the Road, and saw the Bones of the Men who were killed at the Battle laying very thick."[16] The demoralizing effect that this would have upon Forbes's soldiers could not be discounted. This was an important tactical factor, for soldiers are human beings, and if they are depressed or upset they don't follow orders with the same vitality, and are not inspired to make the exhaustive efforts that separate a successful from an unsuccessful army. Forbes had to take this into account in his decision-making process, and it was a huge factor that considerably weighed against the employment of Braddock's Road.

Finally, there was the principle of surprise, quite possibly the single most important factor in warfare. The French anticipated that Forbes would use the existing Braddock Road. The French themselves had been using it for three years to launch raids into Pennsylvania, Maryland and Virginia. The French were quite familiar with it, and were known to be regularly monitoring and patrolling it. The French had deliberately obstructed it in at least one location. By not using the Braddock Road, Forbes could quite possibly surprise the French. Lt. Colonel Adam Stephen of Virginia would state to Bouquet on August 10: "I Question if the Enemy dreams of your Opening a Communication this way, and what a glorious thing it would be, to have a Lodgement on the Loyal-hannon before they ever suspected your Intentions."[17] This was a legitimate and realistic assumption, for Major James Grant would completely surprise the French at Fort Duquesne in September, by approaching from the Loyalhanna Encampment rather than along the Braddock Road. It was not until the French interrogated several of Grant's men taken prisoner that they learned that Forbes was coming by a different route than the Braddock Road. Forbes wrote in August to Abercromby:

> The Enemy has as yet given us no disturbance nor do I believe that they suspect my coming this way whereas along Mr. Braddock's route from the Great Meadows to the Great Crossing of the Yoghegenny, they have reconoitred every pass and Defile, and have proceeded so far already to have a *Batis de Bois* [abatis of wood] where of necessity we must have passed had we been Confined to that road intirely.[18]

Forbes still believed this to be the case in September, "...nor had the Enemy ever suspected my attempting such a road till very lately, they having been all along securing the strong passes, and fords of the rivers, upon General Braddocks' route."[19] In fact, the commandant of Fort Niagara, when he wrote his *Memoirs* of the Seven Years' War in North America in 1781, still believed that Forbes had used Braddock's Road, for he recorded, "In his march to the Belle-Riviere [Ohio River], Braddock blazed a trail every day as he advanced. But the English remade it in 1758 and improved it in 1759."[20] The Allegheny Route provided Forbes with operational surprise. Again, the new approach through Pennsylvania had much in its favor.

Washington, a loyal Virginian with a vested interest in seeing a road constructed from the colony of Virginia to the Forks of the Ohio, lobbied hard for the Braddock Road route. Washington practically bombarded Bouquet with letters in which he meticulously documented his reasons why that road should be followed. In a prolific lobbying effort, Washington wrote two letters on July 24, one letter on July 25, and two letters on August 2.[21] Bouquet and Washington met in person, but Bouquet was not particularly impressed with Washington's argument: "I had an interview with Colonel Washington to find out how he imagines these difficulties can be overcome. I learned nothing satisfactory. Most of these gentlemen do not know the difference between a party and an army, and find everything easy which agrees with their ideas, jumping over all the difficulties."[22] Washington vigorously resisted any suggestions for a new road, fanatically boosting Braddock's Road at every opportunity. Desperate to maintain the interests of his colony and the Ohio Company, Washington wrote two strong letters towards the end of the debate. The strongest in tenor was written on August 2 to Francis Halkett, Forbes's brigade major, with whom Washington had become friends during Braddock's campaign:

> My dear Halkett — I am just returned from a Conference held with Colo. Bouquet. I find him fixd — I think I may say fix'd, upon leading you a New way to the Ohio; thro. a Road, every Inch of it to be cut, at this advanced Season, when we have scarce time left to tread the beaten Tract; universally confessed to be the best Passage through the Mountains. If Colo. Bouquet succeeds in this point with the General — all is lost! All is lost by Heavens! Our Enterprize Ruind & We stopd at the Laurel Hill for this Winter — not to gather Laurels by the by, desirable in (their effects) — The Southern Indians turn against Us — and these Colonies become desolate by such an Acquisition to the Enemy's Strength.[23]

Washington also wrote to Virginia Governor Francis Fauquier on August 5:

I am just returnd from a Conference held with Colo. Bouquet on this occasion.... In the conference I urgd, in the most persuasive terms I was Master of, the advanced Season as an argument against new discoveries. I pressd also—the difficulties of cutting a [erasure] over these Mountains—the length of time it must require to do it—the little time left for that Service—the moral certainty of its obstructing our March—and the miscarriage of the Expedition from that cause.... In fine, I said, and did everything to avert a [erasure] that seemd to forebode our manifest ruin—this is the light it appeared in—I pray Heaven my Fears may prove imaginary only—but the thoughts of opening a Road 100 Miles in length—over Mountains almost inaccessible, at this advanced Season, when there is already a good Road made—a Road universally confessed to be the best that either is, or can be found any where thro these Mountains....[24]

Forbes was given a copy of one of these letters of Washington's, for he wrote Bouquet on August 9: "By a very unguarded letter of Col: Washington that Accidentally fell into my hands, I am now at the bottom, of their Scheme against this new road, a Scheme that I think was a shame for any officer to be Concerned in, but more of this at meeting." Apparently Forbes remained displeased with Washington, for he would obliquely mention this incident to Bouquet again on September 4: "Therefore would consult C: Washington, altho perhaps not follow his advice, as his Behavior about the roads, was no ways like a Soldier."[25]

Historians have speculated regarding which specific letter of Washington's this might have been. Archer Butler Hulbert exhaustively analyzed the incident and concluded, "What letter this was of Washington's I do not know, it could not have been the letter written to Halkett, it hardly seems possible that it could have been the ... letter which Washington wrote to Governor Fauquier."[26] Dr. Alfred Proctor James believed that the letter was the one written to Halkett on August 2.[27] The editors of the *The Papers of Henry Bouquet* felt that this letter was "Possibly Washington's letter to Halkett, August 2, 1758, although it does not disclose any scheme against the new road. A letter to Fauquier, August 5, would meet the specifications, but how that letter could have fallen into Forbes's hands is open to question."[28] Certainly it appears unlikely that Washington's letter to Governor Fauquier could have reached Williamsburg, been opened and copied, and then been forwarded to Forbes, within four days. No other extant letters written by Washington appear to conform to Forbes's description, except the one to Halkett dated August 2.

Forbes himself resolved the mystery, for he wrote to Abercromby on August 11:

A Jealousy arising amongst the Virginians that I was to direct my march by another route, than by Fort Cumberland, came such a length as to be most Singularly Impertinent nor Could I Discover the bottom, or cause from whence this sprung untill that Colonel Washington in a letter to Major Halkett fairly shows the leader and adviser of their foolish suggestions upon this Head.[29]

It should not be surprising that Forbes became aware of this letter, although it is most unlikely that it "accidentally" fell into his hands. Halkett's father and Forbes were close and lifelong friends, and both families were from the same community in Scotland. The relationship between Forbes and Major Halkett was more like that of uncle and nephew than of general and aide. Upon the death of Colonel Sir Peter Halkett, Forbes had apparently assumed responsibility for the patronage of his friend's son, Captain Francis Halkett. This explains the presence of Halkett's memorandum previously cited in Forbes's headquarters papers, as most likely Forbes had sent this on with his personal endorsement. Whether Washington comprehended Halkett's relationship with Forbes or not is unknown. Washington may have deliberately written the letter to Halkett expecting the major to show it to Forbes, or he may have written the letter hoping that his friend Halkett would thus influence the General. If the first case, it was a particularly poorly considered course of action. If the second case, Washington had clearly misread both Halkett and Forbes, and he certainly did not comprehend the importance of patronage in the British Army. Washington's letter of August 2 did nothing to influence Forbes's decision, which in any case had already been made, but it did much to erode Washington's standing in Forbes's estimation. Colonel John Armstrong of Pennsylvania would report on October 3 from Ray's Town: "The Virginians are much chagrin'd at the Opening of the Road thro' this Government & Colonel Washington has been a great deal Sanguine & Obstinate upon the Occasion, but the presence of the General has been of great Use on this as well as other Accounts."[30]

Forbes did not make this decision quickly, or without considerable reflection. By late in July he was clearly leaning towards the route due west across the Allegheny Mountains rather than the Braddock route:

> As I disclaim all parties myself, should be sorry that they were to Creep in amongst us. I therefore cannot Conceive what the Virginia folks would be att, for to me it appears to be them, and them only, that want to drive us into the road by Fort Cumberland, no doubt in opposition to the Pennsylvanians who by Raestown would have a nigher Communication to the Ohio.

To assist him in making his determination, Forbes questioned St. Clair closely — "I showed him Captain Ward's Journal" — and then attempted to determine how much he actually knew regarding this route. St. Clair stumbled around the question, telling Forbes that "there were many Indian Traders that knew these roads very well." In exasperation, Forbes "Stopt him short by saying if that was the case, that I was sorry he had never found them out, or never thought it worth his while to examine them. In short he knows nothing of the matter." Thus, having determined that his bumbling quartermaster had failed to adequately survey and evaluate the different routes, an integral component of his professional responsibilities, Forbes continued:

> The difference at present in the length of the road the one way and the other Stands thus. From Raestown to Fort Cumberland 34 miles or upwards from Fort Cumberland to Fort Duquesne by General Braddocks 125 Miles in all 160 to which add the passage of rivers &c. and the last 8 Miles not cut. The other road from Raestown to the top of the Laurell Hill 46 miles from thence to Fort Duquesne suppose 40 or 50 miles in all 90, with no rivers to obstruct you and nothing to stop you that I can see, except that Bugbear, or tremendious pass of the Laurel Hill. If what I say is true and those two roads are compaired, I don't see that I am to Hesitate one moment which to take.[31]

Bouquet carefully examined the situation from his forward position, and wrote Forbes on July 26:

> Colonel Washington has had the beginning of Braddock's Road cut, which I have fixed at ten miles from Fort Cumberland. From the guides I have sent you, you will have learned the advantages of this route, which is open and requires few repairs; and its inconveniences, which are the lack of forage, its length, its narrow passes, and the river crossings.[32]

In the midst of all this contrivance, Forbes revealed on two separate occasions that even though he was seriously ill, he in fact possessed an absolute spine of steel, and was clearly not a man to be trifled with under any circumstances:

> Colonel Byrd in a paragraph of his letter from Fort Cumberland, amongst other things, writes, that he has upwards of sixty Indians waiting my arrival, and ready to accompany me, but they will not follow me unless I go by Fort Cumberland. This is a new system of military Discipline truly; and shows that my good friend Byrd is either made the Cats Foot of himself, or he little knows me, if he imagines that Sixty scoundrels are to direct me in my measures.[33]

In writing to Abercromby regarding Washington's attempts to sway the road route from Pennsylvania to Virginia's favor, Forbes stated:

I believe I have now got the better of the whole by letting them Very roundly know, that their Judging and determining of my actions and intentions before that I had communicated my opinion to them, was so premature, and was taking the lead in so ridiculous a way that I could by no means suffer it.[34]

Forbes received an important letter on this subject from a man that he deeply trusted, as he had known him his entire life: his cousin Governor James Glen with Bouquet at Ray's Town. Glen would tell Forbes on July 26:

I presume by your sending for the guides that one of the present objects of your attention is the roads and a most material one it is both as it may affect the King's Service and your own reputation, and as both are dear to me (I speak with sincerity) permit me to make some observations.

You are to consider that the Provincial part of your Army is divided upon this point and tho' Washington is a cool sensible modest young man yet he and all the Virginians espouse Braddocks Road with warmth and should you meet with any difficulties in your march on any other path it will be said why did you not take the well known tried and beaten road. But as I have heard all that could be said in favour of Braddocks Road when I was at Cumberland and as Colonel Bouquet has called me to several private examinations here I think I am pretty well qualified the advantages and disadvantages of both.

What I wrote is not the sense of one or two but it is what I have collected as the concurring testimony of the directest most knowing and most credible.

From this Camp to Fort Cumberland it is thirty five long miles from thence to Fort DuQuesne a hundred and fifteen in all hundred and fifty. From hence by the Allegeny Mountains it is not ninety consequently sixty miles will be saved.

From Cumberland to the Great Meadows is sixty four miles in all that way there is no food for horses or cattle. Mr. Frazer told me that the creatures might pick a little on the mountains. Lieutenant Colonel Mercer of Byrd's Virginians says that there is pretty good grass at one place of that sixty four miles. The Alligany Road all agree abound every where with fine rich pastures where thousands will find plenty interspersed with springs, and brooks every three or four miles.

Gen. Braddocks Road the Army must cross the Yahiageni [Youghaghanie River] three times and Monongahela twice and tho when he passed, it was low, reaching only mid thigh as Captain Gordon the Ingenier [Engineer] informs me yet the banks he says are both high and steep from which I conclude that it is sometimes deep. I have heard that it rises to fifteen or eighteen feet. In all events should the French attack you in the River, the difficulty of climbing steep banks ought prove of fatal consequence. Along this road there is no river the whole way.

Gen. Braddocks Road there are many dangerous defiles (such as I wrote you I had passed though where two hundred men could stop 5000) one of them is described to be a narrow bottom a very few yards wide but near seven miles in length betwixt two extreamly steep rocks and the men at their leisure may clamber up and post themselves to advantage behind stones yet it is mortally impossible to march on the face of all the fire of these men, neither can I learn that by going round, you can get behind them. In this road there is no dangerous pass the whole way.

Perhaps I might add that the French undoubtedly and [illegible] expects us by Braddocks Road and that the memory of two victories there [Washington's surrender at Fort Necessity at the Great Meadows and Braddock's defeat at the Monongahela] may animate them and give sport to their Indians, but most certainly as they are now perfectly acquainted with that road and have critically examined every inch of it and you may lay your account with opposition at many places where he passed unmolested.

Weight all these circumstances and you will find nothing in Braddock's scale, this must preponderate with every disinterested person.

But on the other hand the Alligany Mountains require your serious thoughts. You must apply a good deal of Hannibal's vinegar to these alps, that is some time and much acidity [sic]. They described them to be near two miles and a half high and that is in particular one pinch (I give at you in their own words) is exceeding bad rather worse than Sideline Hill & about half a mile in length that it is very stony and rocky, but that immediately under the stones there is plenty of earth. The Colonel had sent a very expert waggoner a distinct sensible man to view it who told me that every step he went he seed himself as driving his waggon and he is clear and positive that there is obstructions that cannot be removed, and he is sure that he can carry the loaded waggons all the way. That he thinks it might be adviseable in one or two places to blow up a part of the rock tho' by what he said it did not seem to be absolutely necessary.

Some say that there a few stony ridges between that and Laurel Hill but all agree that the Laurel Hill is nothing difficult and after that no obstructions.

A person who has travelled that road fifty times says that there are several small swamps which however may easily be made good as there is great plenty of wood. But as it is he has often brought gangs of pack horses loaded with 200 weight from the French fort in four days.[35]

A rational, unbiased comparison of the various decision factors clearly indicates that there was no real advantage to using Braddock's Road, and many disadvantages. It appears that Glen's analysis, which was as impartial as any that Forbes could hope to find, was the final impetus that Forbes required to make up his mind. On July 31, Forbes published his decision to construct a new road due west from Ray's Town, across the steep green Pennsylvania ridges. Although he was extremely ill at Carlisle, Forbes instructed Major Halkett to write to Bouquet:

[A]s he thinks that no time should be lost in making of the new Road, he has directed me to inform you, that you are immediately to begin the opening of it agreeable to the manner he wrote to you in his last letter, as he sees all the advantages he can propose by going that Route, and will avoid innumerable Inconveniencys he would encounter was he to go the other.[36]

The "decision point" of Forbes's campaign, or the "Schwerpunkt" as the great Prussian commander Frederick the Great would have referred to it, had been reached. The army would go directly west across the mountains, blazing a new road as it went. Allegheny Mountain would become Forbes's Rubicon.

· SIX ·

"The Waggons have been the plague of my life"

Forbes's Second Parallel Crosses Allegheny Mountain

Once Forbes had selected the course upon which his army would focus its labors to traverse the endless ridges of the Allegheny Mountains, he could initiate the second phase of the campaign. To use the vocabulary established by Count Turpin, Forbes began to establish the second parallel of his siege of Fort Duquesne.

During the formal conduct of a siege, the first parallel was intended to begin the approach the enemy's works, and to establish initial firing positions only. With the second parallel, the works were pushed aggressively forward, and serious firing batteries were established, and all preparations made for the final parallel to batter a gap through the enemy's fortifications and prepare for the ultimate assault that would defeat the foe. Thus, this second parallel of Forbes campaign was intended to push the work forward, and establish the base from which the final movement upon Fort Duquesne could be conducted.

Forbes had the following objectives for this second parallel of his advance:

- Construct the road from Ray's Town, across Allegheny Mountain and Laurel Ridge, to Loyalhanna Creek;
- Establish a strong advanced encampment at Loyalhanna Creek, with sufficient storehouses and logistical facilities to enable him to stockpile and safeguard supplies, and adequate earthworks to defend these facilities against French and Indian raiding parties;
- Move his army forward from Ray's Town and Fort Cumberland and concentrate it at the Loyalhanna encampment;
- Continue to organize and train the newly raised provincial forces from Pennsylvania, Maryland, Virginia, North Carolina and the Lower Counties;
- Form his army into a cohesive unit ready to serve and fight together;
- Continue regular scouts to Fort Duquesne to obtain intelligence upon the condition of that post and its garrison;
- Make all necessary preparations for an October or November advance upon Fort Duquesne;
- Retain the Cherokee and Catawba warriors, launch them on raids against Fort Duquesne, and join them with British and/or provincial scouts to garner intelligence on the French defenses; and
- Continue negotiations with Native Americans to either gain their support for the advance on Fort Duquesne, or else obtain their neutrality.

This second portion of the campaign essentially stretched from Forbes's decision on the route that he made on July 31, through the establishment of the Loyalhanna entrenched camp in September and October, and until the decision regarding the final assault on Fort Duquesne was made late in the evening of November 12. Throughout the late summer and early fall months, Forbes's health continued to deteriorate. He suffered a severe reverse in his physical condition in early August and again in early September, and may have almost succumbed to illness at this stage in the campaign.[1]

As Forbes struggled to make his decision regarding the course of the campaign, he was already seriously ill. Halkett wrote to Bouquet from Carlisle on July 23, "General Forbes is so extreamly Reduc'd & low in Spirits with the Flux, and other afflications, that he is not able to write you."[2] Halkett continued to write for Forbes, telling Bouquet on July 31, "The General is so much indispos'd this day by taking Phisick, that he is not able to acknowledge the Receipt of your letter himself."[3] It appears that by August 2 that Forbes was in desperate circumstances, for on this date Halkett wrote an alarming note to Bouquet: "As the General recovers but slowley, & has frequent Returns of his most painful simptoms, he desired that you will order Lieut. James Grant of the Highland Regiment, whom the General has a confidence in as a surgeon, to set out immediately for this place...."[4]

An undated note, presumably from this timeframe, provided Forbes with the following medical advice of somewhat dubious utility: "At eight in the morning let him take a Gill of Milk warm from the Cow with as much Pyrmont Water and a little Nutmeg and Sugar —...." "Pyrmont Water" refers to naturally carbonated water from the German Mineral Springs and Royal Spa of Bad Pyrmont, Lower Saxony. In 1758, contemporary medical beliefs were that the introduction of fixed air (now known as carbon dioxide) into the body, through the naturally carbonated medium of Pyrmont Water, would prevent the putrefaction of flesh from disease. It was also believed to prevent, arrest, and treat scurvy. This mineral water almost certainly did nothing to cure Forbes, although it possibly assisted by keeping him hydrated.[5]

> At Ten O'Clock let him repeat the same with a little Mush, Biscuit or well baked Bread & Marmalade; or a Jelly, a little Chocalate [*sic*], or the white of an Egg beat up with Barley Water and any pleasant aromatick [*sic*] to make it palatable.
> At Eleven let him take two or three of the Stomach Sick Pills and ride out in his Chariot —
> For Dinner he may take Broths made of the Flesh of young Animals the fat being first taken off, and eat the meat boiled therein, or these meats cooked to his Liking. He should not eat to Fulness, but rather take a morsal of any light thing in the afternoon a Jelly or such like. He may drink a few glasses of generous Wine alone or diluted with Pyrmont Water. He should avoid all high seasoned salted and smoak dryed meats, Fat meats, fat fish, water fowls, and flatulent Plants.
> His Supper should be light, with a few glasses of wine.
> He should continue his frictions and fumigations, and by degrees lessen the opiate, both at Bed time and in his Glyster —[6]

Presumably, such a regimen would have either healed Forbes, or killed him off all the faster.

Forbes complained on August 2 to Bouquet, "I have been tormented day and night these 14 Days with what they [the surgeons] call a Flux, and what I call a Violent Constipation. I hope I shall now gett the better of it altho I neither eat nor sleep." Forbes told much the same story to Abercromby, "I have been very much out of order by what Dr. Bassett will call the flux, which is a most violent constipation attended with Inflamation in the Rectum, violent pain & total suppression of the Urine, in short I have been most miserable."[7] Forbes followed up by writing Bouquet on August 9, "I am now able to write, after 3 weeks of a most violent and tormenting Distemper, which thank God now seems much abated as to pain, but has left me as weak as a new born Infant."[8]

Forbes seemed to be better by August 10, for Major Halkett wrote Bouquet on that date from Carlisle, "The General is so much Recover'd, that he proposes to begin his March to morrow after noon...."[9] However, Forbes only made it as far as Shippensburg before he experienced a relapse, writing Bouquet on August 15 from Shippensburg: "[M]y journey here from Carlisle raised my flux & pains to so intollerable a degree Yesterday morning, that I was obliged to stop here...."[10]

As he had at Carlisle, Forbes suffered terribly at Shippensburg. The flux, or constipation in modern terms, that Forbes had previously complained of had returned. He wrote to Philadelphia on August 28, "I stand greatly in need of a few prunes by way of Laxative, if any fresh are lately arrived a few pounds will be a great blessing, or a pound 2 or 3 of such fine raisins as Mr. Allen's were, as I eat nothing." Forbes in turn would write Bouquet, clearly with deep regret, from that place on September 2: "I really can not describe how I have suffer'd both in body and Mind of Late. And the relapsis have been worse as the dissapointment was greater however I comfort my self in thinking that I have retarded nothing by my infirmity...."[11]

It was not until late in August that Forbes was finally recovered, as the Reverend Barton reported on August 30: "It is said that the General unable to ride, and determin'd to proceed at all Events, had order'd a Litter to be made to carry him with the more Ease." Forbes himself would write to Governor Sharpe of Maryland on September 3, "I propose leaving this place [Shippensburg] tomorrow morning, in a kind of Horse litter, being so weakened by my distemper that I can neither ride nor bear the roughness of my slopwaggon [here Forbes is writing dispargingly of his carriage]."[12]

Forbes's health was so precarious that in addition to ordering this special litter to be constructed, he also instructed that log cabins with chimneys be constructed for his use along the newly cut highway. Captain Ourry reported from Fort Loudon as early as July 13: "I have cover'd, clean'd out, & fitted up the Summer house near the River Side, in which you had the talk with the Indians, as the most agreeable & Commodious Place for the General, to refresh himself in at his arrival here."[13] Forbes himself requested on July 17 that Bouquet at Ray's Town "make the best Hutt you can for me, if it is not too much trouble."[14]

Forbes finally reached Ray's Town on September 15, after a long and terrible journey. His reception at that settlement, as reported by the good Reverend Barton, must have done much to cheer him:

> Friday September 15th 1758 — General Forbes arriv'd in Camp [Ray's Town] this Day, carried in a Sort of a Sedan Litter between 2 Horses & guarded by Captain Thompson's Troop of Light Horse, & Colonel Montgomery with 100 Highlanders. He was in a low State, yet a great Satisfaction & Pleasure appear'd in his Contenance upon finding himself at Ray's Town with his Troops. The Roads were crowded with People to see him, whom he saluted with a Smile as he pass'd along — And they in their Turn discovered a Secret Joy upon seeing him. He was conducted to the Highland Camp by a Number of Gentlemen who went 5 or 6 Miles to meet him, where a pretty little Tent with a good Chimney, lin'd within with Boards, & without with Oil Cloths, was prepar'd for him. The Troops seem to inspir'd [sic] with fresh Spirits upon the General's Arrival, & a Chearfulness appears in every Face.[15]

As Forbes suffered on his progress from Carlisle to Ray's Town, Bouquet directed the efforts of his army in constructing the new route that Forbes had selected. The distance from Ray's Town to Loyalhanna is fifty measured, modern miles. The course that Forbes had determined to follow left Bouquet's stockade at Ray's Town and ran generally due west for two miles before crossing the Raystown Branch of the Juniata River at "an exceeding bad Ford" where Lieutenant Ourry would construct his bridge following the campaign. A mile and half further west, the road for Fort Cumberland turned to the south, while Forbes's new road continued due west. About four miles past this the road crossed Shawnee Creek near a location known as "Shawnee Cabins" for a long since abandoned Shawnee village. Shawnee Cabins is frequently mentioned as a campground on the road. However, as it is only eight comparatively level miles from Ray's Town, it served as a resting and watering spot rather than a formal campground. This area was quite large, with as much as fifty acres available, and provided a well-watered, level location with good forage for the army's convenience.[16]

The road then ran up Keg Run (possibly named for the voluminous amounts of Bouquet's "Viskey" that the Pennsylvania Provincials must have been imbibing by this point) for about three miles. The low ground around Keg Run provided luxuriant grass for Forbes's valuable animals, and the route ran on the south side of the Run.[17]

The route then ascended higher ground to the north to avoid the marshy narrows of Negro Hollow Run (a 19th-century name, not in use in 1758). Once past this point, the road begins to ascend to cross the dreaded height of Allegheny Mountain. The modern Lincoln Highway (US Route #30) follows the historic track of the Forbes Road at this point, as topography dictates the course of both roads. At the historic "Shot Factory" (a late 18th-century home, not in existence in 1758), a natural platform offered a resting spot for both horse and man. From this resting spot, a mile's prodigious work nearly due north up an extremely steep ravine is required to reach the top of the ridge at Rhor's Gap. The road up Rhor's Gap ascends 600 feet in ¾ of a mile, an average grade of 15 percent.[18] This was the single most difficult portion of Forbes's Road, longer and more precipitous than the challenging climb up Cowan's Gap. As discussed, even locating this route had required considerable effort, and until Rhor had determined this draw to be usable, the entire route west was in jeopardy. Thus, in addition to being the most difficult, it was also the single most important topographic location along Forbes's Road.

Once out of the ravine and atop the summit, the road turned hard left, to south-southwest, and half a mile further along was constructed "Fort Dewart." Actually this was a simple sixty-foot-square earth redoubt rather than a true fort. Fort Dewart offered convoys a protected encampment where they could safely rest their soldiers and animals, while repairing whatever damage to men's shoes and accouterments, horseshoes, harness and wagons had been incurred on the rigorous ascent up Rhor's Gap. This fort was frequently referred to as McLean's Encampment, for Captain *Allan* McLean of Montgomery's 77th Highlanders had constructed it. Fort Dewart was more properly spelled "Fort Duart," as it was named for Duart Castle, the ancestral Scottish home of Clan Maclean overlooking the Sound of the Isle of Mull.

A respite at this location would have been critical, as after about three miles the road now entered a difficult and dangerous marsh first known as the "Shades of Death" and then "Edmunds Swamp." Here a long corduroy road was constructed, and the road cut through a dense tangle of mountain laurel, brush, saplings and briars over soft ground where daylight rarely reached, and which travelers found extremely depressing. At Edmunds Swamp another redoubt was constructed. Lieutenant Colonel Adam Stephen had his Virginians at work near Edmunds Swamp by the first week in August, reporting to Bouquet on the Shades of Death:

> This morning has set the men to work about bridging the Swamp, and goes my Self with a party to reconnoitre the Shades of Death, a dismal Place! And wants only a Cerberus [mythical three-headed dog that guarded the Gates of Hades] to represent Virgils gloomy description of Aeneas's entering the Infernal Regions.[19]

Once clear of this dismal obstacle, the road gradually descended to the north about two miles down the valley of Oven Run to the site of yet another redoubt, this one known as

Jameson's Redoubt for Captain David Jameson of the 1st Pennsylvania Battalion, who supervised its construction. Eventually lending their name to the adjacent watercourse, at this location Bouquet ordered ovens to be constructed to bake bread for the army. These would have been relatively simple ovens built out of clay and green wood, could have been readily fabricated, and just as easily abandoned. From here, the road turned west another 2½ miles to the Stony Creek Crossing, which was frequently mentioned by participants of the campaign.

At Stony Creek, Bouquet ordered a more substantial fortification constructed, to guard the important ford. A strong redoubt, with associated storage sheds, and rudimentary barracks for a small permanent garrison, was placed here. When Forbes passed across the mountains, a small hut (probably a simple log cabin) with a fireplace was constructed for him at Stony Creek.[20] From Stony Creek, there were actually two Forbes's Roads. The first was the initial construction, that followed a ridge top nearly due north for about 3½ miles, then turned at a right angle to the west to follow another ridge line another two miles to the crossing of Quemahoning Creek, then continued on high ground nearly two more miles. Here, Fort Dudgeon (named for the engineer Captain Dudgeon who located and designed it) was constructed. This area was known as "Old Clear Fields," for it was a rich meadow across extensive bottom lands. Apparently this route was not well considered. Bouquet remarked that it was "absolutely impracticable" as it had been "opened in such great haste."[21] Accordingly, a new road was built almost immediately, for it was open and operating by late October. This new segment was "four miles shorter and eight miles better" according to Bouquet.[22] This new road ran nearly due west from Stony Creek, along generally better surface conditions. Near Fort Dudgeon the two roads converged, and continued nearly due west as they gradually climbed for the top of Laurel Ridge, descended it, then followed ridge tops until Loyalhanna was reached.

Constructing this segment of the road, from Ray's Town to Loyalhanna, would be the most challenging proposition of the campaign. The ascent across Allegheny Mountain was the key to the entire route, and this stretch not only entailed the most road construction, but it also traversed the most challenging terrain. Even before Forbes had made his final decision regarding the route, Bouquet had an advanced detachment sent west from Ray's Town to initiate preliminary construction and perform a comprehensive evaluation of the path across Allegheny Mountain. A younger brother of Colonel Armstrong, Major George Armstrong of the same battalion, directed this party. Young Major Armstrong's correspondence throughout the campaign suggests that he was rather hotheaded and impetuous, which was probably just the sort of man Bouquet wanted commanding a vulnerable advanced party working on the road. Armstrong reported to Bouquet on July 27 and 29:

I marched from this [Drounding Creek, atop Allegheny Mountain] toward Loyalhanning and returned here last night. Lawrel Hill is about 2½ Miles over the top of it a little stoney and the West side more so, however they are but loos and can be pretty easie removed it is about 18 Miles from this place to Loyalhanng the latter is a very pretty place; well wattered and Grass in abundence. The Situation is undoubtedly Good for nature has supplyed it with all conveniencies, and what makes it more desirable is the Western breeses carrying with them the Small [smell] of the French Brandy.... The road indeed will take a Good deal of Labour to make it fit for Wagons, not from its hillyness but also from the stoneyness & swampey places, however where bridges are to be made there will be no difficulty to find Timber for that purpose and the stones, which are in many places of the road, are in general loose and pretty easie removed.[23]

Based upon Armstrong's reports Bouquet dispatched Quartermaster St. Clair, Colonel Burd, and Chief Engineer Ensign Rhor to perform a detailed reconnaissance of the route from

Ray's Town to Loyalhanna. Bouquet noted, "Everything seems practicable, and even easy, but I distrust the observation of a young and inexperienced man too much to act on his advice."[24]

By early in August, Bouquet had parties at work on various places of the road, covered by a larger command to their front. The use of small detachments was the favored approach, as it had been discovered that large parties working at a single site served more to obstruct each other than to forward the work. Major George Armstrong had written regarding this to Forbes from Edmunds Swamp on July 25:

> There is about two miles of the Allighany Hill that is pretty stony, but they can be removed without much difficulty, and in that two miles there is two hills where all the hardship in crossing the Allighany lays & even there when the road is cut to advantage [Wagon Master William] White is of oppinion, he can bring 20 weight [20 hundredweight, or just over 2,000 pounds] up it in his own Waggon, so that it is without doubt practicable to find a wagon road through this Mountain. There is a small pinch above where we now lay, and I can't [learn] that there is any more in this mountain, therefore am inclined to think the road cutters may be employed as soon as you please. I wou'd offer a thought with regard to the disposition of the road cutters if I cou'd hope it woud be agreeable to you, and that is a party to begin at Colonel Burd's Road where the old Road strikes off, a party at Nelsons, a party at the foot of Allighany Hill, a party about two miles up the hill where the two pinches ends, a party at Edmonds Swamp, and a party at Stoney Creek &c. If you think this impertinent I hope you'll be kind enough to excuse the freedom, as it is well intended, and a great number of men at one time and at one place wou'd only be an incumberance to themselves.[25]

Captain Allen McLean of the Highlanders was located near the Shawnee Cabins, observing to Bouquet on August 7: "I thought it no more than my duty to make the Roads as passable for Carriages as possible. And shall endeavour to finish them so as to give Satisfaction, but at the same time shall comply with your Orders by going on with all possible dispatch. ... there are more difficulties in making a Road here than was represented, as I have two miles of a new Road to cut, and Several Bridges to make."[26] Lt. Colonel Adam Stephen had his Virginians hard at work near Edmunds Swamp early in August:

> I design to give you as Easy a passage through them [the Shades of Death] as possible but it will be a Herculean Labour; and the few men I can employ after a days hard working, will Scarcely leave their marks at Night. I want about 400 more men to employ on this Side the [Allegheny] mountain.... I will then Answer your Expectations— Hurl mountains out of their Seat — Shortly have a Waggon Road to the Top of Lawrel Hill....[27]

Stephen repeated on August 10:

> In my last I took Leave of you, to enter the Shades of Death, and now I have the pleasure to inform you of my Easy passage ... make my way good with the Tomhawk. Near thirty of us Spread & wandered through those Shades, perplexed with Lawrels, Logs & Rocks, coverd with weeds, or Brambles interwoven with Young Locust; and were so lucky in our researches, that had it not been for this days Rain, before night a Coach & Six might have easily past through the place.[28]

Quartermaster St. Clair advised Bouquet on August 12 from the foot of Allegheny Mountain, "The work to be done on this Road is immence. ... the work I have to do is all digging, pick Axes Crows & Shovells is what is most wanted. Likewise more Whiskey." St. Clair repeated the ominous concern that whiskey was running low with the hard-working road building parties in the mountains: "Send me as many men as you can with digging Tools, this is a most diabolical work, and whiskey must be had."[29] Lt. Colonel Stephen reinforced St. Clair's concerns: "There is nothing would have a greater Effect upon these Rocks, than the Essence of Fat Beef gradually mixt with a Puncheon of Rum, This would add weight to every stroke given them. Please to send us three or four Cros Cut saws to Separate the numberless, damned, petryfyd old Logs hard as Iron & Breaks our Axes to pieces."[30] Bouquet himself was by now well into the spirit of how things were accomplished on the mountainous western frontier of His Majesty's American colonies, for he wrote to Forbes from Ray's Town on September 4, "It will be absolutely necessary for the health of the troops to give them a little liquor beyond the mountains. A soldier will work cheerfully to earn his gill, and that is one of all our supplies we are sadly lacking."[31]

The work continued on at a feverish pace, St. Clair again writing to Bouquet on September 16 from "Allegany Mountain":

> The labour is immense, the road from the top of this Ridge or gap will be finished this day, and Sir Allan's [McLean's] party will work with me to morrow. I shall send Colonel Armstrong to Camp on the 2d rising at the spring and work backwards. Captain Field is encamped with 200 Men at Stephen's Spring half way between Edmunds Swamp and the Spring where Armstrong is to encamp & Colonel Stephens is encamped at Edmunds Swamp where he is working forwards. All I can say is that no Man of the partys on this Road shall have any rest till it is finished.[32]

Still, St. Clair had time to ask Bouquet on this date, "Send me turnup Seed to sow my Garden." Bouquet must have wondered just why, where and when St. Clair intended to plant a garden in the middle of a campaign atop one of the highest peaks of the Allegheny Mountains. Such an odd requisition strongly intimates that St. Clair may not have been entirely mentally balanced. The nature of this exceedingly bizarre request, as with so much else about the man, must remain a mystery.[33]

Lt. Colonel Stephen provided Bouquet with an excellent report of how these small parties worked together, from "Camp near Quemahony [Quemahoning Creek]" on August 26:

> August 16 ... I sent him [Quartermaster St. Clair] a Report of our progress on the Road, by a Serjeant who went with 16 men for Liquor for the Workers who returned without it, tho' we had been now Eight days at Work;
> [August] 17. Captain Field, McClughans & Boyles with 2 Companies & a Detachment of 40 men continued at the first spring to the westward of the Allegany [Mountain] employed in Opening eastward. Visited all the Posts & different Parties on the Road, and Cleared two miles towards Quemahony from our Camp at Edmund Swamp. Being advised that Colonel Bouquet had sent up Liquor for the Workmen sent a serjeant & party with Canteens to bring some for them, who Carryed on the work with chearfulness & dispatch.
> 18. Received Orders in a very Odd manner from the Quarter Master General about erecting Shades for Provisions at Edmunds Swamp. Visited the different Partes at work ... reconnoitred with Mr. Rhor. The Road being Opened very near the Top of the Mountain [by other work parties directly under St. Clair], orderd up Captain Boyles with his Detachment & 20 men of Captain McClughans Company. Leaving Orders with Captain Fields & McClughan to join me next day, after finishing their Share of the Road....
> 19. ...marchd & Encamp'd at Lawrel Run. Was Obligd to Leave an Officer & 30 men at Edmund swamp to take Care of the sick of them two Companies.
> August 20th. The Road about Lawrel Run difficult & Stony, employed every man at work in four different divisions. In the evening movd to Stony Creek Leaving Captain Stewart to finish the Road about Lawrel Run....
> 21. ...The Road Opend this evening all the way Quemahony except about an hours Work....[34]

Bouquet provided a summary of the magnitude of this construction effort in a long report to Forbes from Ray's Town on August 8:

> There are 700 men, in four divisions, employed in cutting the road from here to Armstrong's post [Kickenpauling, on Quemahoning Creek] including the detachment which protects the workers. And as there is much to do, and the time is short, I shall reinforce them in two days with the rest of the first battalion of Pennsylvania, in order to make a new entrenchment at the Major's post and some bark covering for a temporary storehouse there. The rest of the Virginia detachment will set

to work with Colonel Stephens, who is cutting on the mountain, and Byrd's second company of workmen will join Major Lewis to open the gap. This makes in all more than 1200 men in these 37 miles. After that, if you approve, I shall march to Loyal Hannon before the road is open from Kickeny Pawlins—with 1500 men of whatever troops you find suitable. I shall construct a post and storehouses there, and shall protect our workers cutting the way behind me. It will be easy to get supplies to this corps by means of the depot above, and with our pack horses, until the wagons can get through; and I will be able to push small parties ahead to get news [of Fort Duquesne].[35]

Besides the road itself and redoubts at various important locations, and logistical installations such as ovens, other structures had to be constructed along the way. These structures were most typically intended to serve as storehouses to protect the important provisions and ammunition as they were conveyed towards Loyalhanna. The irrepressible Major George Armstrong reported to Bouquet regarding both the length of road that a small work party could construct in a single day, and the specifics of the construction of just such a structure at "Drownding Creek" (now modern Beaver Dam Creek west of Stony Creek crossing):

Sir John St. Clair gave me orders to Clear the road to a Certain Spring about 3 Miles from hence towards the Lawrell Hill, and this night will have it half done, and tomorrow will set every body upon the road towards Colonel Stevens, except a sufficient party for the breast Work.... I have sent down all the bags that come formerly up. I have finished a large Shade for Provisions within the breast Work which is covered with bark as I had no frow to make Clapboards.[36]

A froe is a long, sharpened cleaving tool attached at right angles to a wooden handle and used to split out shingles or staves from blocks of wood, or puncheons from logs. Without this tool, shingles cannot be manufactured. Thus, bark had been peeled from trees to construct crude siding, although this is more effective than it might appear. The Iroquois Indians, known as Mingos in western Pennsylvania, regularly used elm bark to construct their longhouses as this bark is waterproof.

Even with the expenditure of this arduous labor, the roads were not constructed to Bouquet's satisfaction, for he reported to Forbes from Loyalhanna on September 11: "After the fine description which had been given of the roads, I was greatly surprised to find them abominable. The way has been opened by cutting down trees, but that is all. No trouble has been taken to go around the hills, to remove or break the stones, and the bridges are worthless[s]. To my great regret it is a job which must be done over."[37]

With all of this intensive labor underway at the critical moment in the campaign, a casual observer would perhaps think that even John St. Clair would have been able to maintain a sense of harmony, and work with his fellow officers towards reaching the Forks of the Ohio. However, they would be mistaken, for at this critical juncture in the movement west John St. Clair singlehandedly managed to almost scuttle the campaign.

By this point, both Forbes and Bouquet were completely frustrated with St. Clair's incompetency as quartermaster. Among the greatest of St. Clair's myriad of responsibilities was providing forage for the wagon and packhorses. Without food, the animals could not move their loads, and an old Army adage still in use today and that probably dates to the time of the Pharaohs holds that "until something moves, nothing happens." Bouquet recognized early in the campaign that St. Clair had utterly failed to take adequate measures to locate, obtain, safeguard and stockpile forage. On July 27 Bouquet wrote to Forbes on this topic:

It was a great Neglect in the Quarter Master General [St. Clair] not to have given directions in time, to make [a] magazine of Hay at Cumberland, having Such facility, and so many Hands to employ. That omission is Sufficient to ruin the Expedition, as I hear that grass is very Scarce in

Several Places upon the Road, and we Shall be unable to Support Several Places upon the Road, and we can not carry the whole at once....[38]

Forbes, in exasperation, reported to Abercromby on August 4, "Sir John having served me as he did General Braddock, promising every thing and doing no one Individual thing in the world, except confusing what he undertakes."[39] Forbes complained to Governor Sharpe on September 3, "I foresee I shall be in great distress for want of waggons, the Horses of those with me being ruined as they say for want of forage, a neglect that Sir John St. Clair can never answer for, who was sent from Philadelphia by me to make magazines of Forage all along the march route and to have a great Quantity in store at Raestown."[40]

During the construction of the road across the Allegheny and Laurel Mountains during this timeframe, Bouquet had specifically ordered that only small guards of 25 men were to be left at each post along the road, to safeguard convoys overnight, provide local security, and perform immediate road repairs. St. Clair, on his own volition, had countermanded those orders and instructed Colonel Armstrong of Pennsylvania to leave sixty soldiers at each of these locations. Armstrong chose to disobey these orders, as he had been fortuitously provided with a copy of the overruling instructions from Bouquet.[41] Unfortunately, this incident was not an isolated one.

Besides Bouquet and Forbes, other officers were becoming well aware of St. Clair's idiosyncrasies. Forbes's cousin, Governor Glen, recounted from Ray's Town in early August that St. Clair had "returned yesterday from Loyal Hanning, his appearance was somewhat grotesque, a long beard, a blanket coat, and trousers to the ground. A masterly hand would have found matter sufficient for a curious caricature...."[42] Chaplain Barton at Ray's Town recorded in his diary for September 4, "Sir John St. Clair arriv'd in Camp from Loyal Hannan & seems much dissatisfied with some Field Officers there, who contended with him about Rank."[43]

St. Clair had already antagonized one of the principal Pennyslvania Provincial officers, Major George Armstrong, and through him his brother Colonel Armstrong, as previously described. Now, he would similarly anger the other major component of the army, the Virginia Provincials. St. Clair exploded his personal bomb in a note to Bouquet written on August 27:

Lt. Col. Stephen's behaviour is the most extraordinary, I ever saw or hear'd of, I have confined him for Mutiny in the camp, so that the Virginians are now under Major Lewis.... As I had not sufficient Strength to take him by the neck from amongst his own Men, I was obliged to let him have his own way, that I might not be the Occasion of Blood Shed. The Reason I confined that Lt. Col. was that he told me he had given out his Parole and that rather than receive any Orders from me he would break his sword in pieces.[44]

St. Clair had earlier tangled with Colonel Burd, who reported to Bouquet late in August following the dispute between St. Clair and Stephen:

I am sorry to see matters here in such state as Cannot Conduce to the good of the service. Sir John St. Clair & Colonel Stephens has no doubt inform'd you of their Affairs & disputes, something of the same Nature had like to have happen'd to me, but I have Carefully avoided every thing that should have the least tendency to Retard the service, Sir John & I form Different camps & I Command in my own to prevent disputes.[45]

As can well be imagined, Lieutenant Colonel Stephen had a rather different view of the affair, as he had already reported to Bouquet one day earlier, in a letter that in retrospect appears considerably calmer and more reasoned. Stephen claimed St. Clair had previously insulted him by intimating:

...that the Road [that Stephen was building] was impassable which I had pretented to Open, after Waggons had pass'd it, because he had no hand in Making it. His imperious & insulting manner of communicating his Intention making no difference; giving the Same orders to ensign under my Command as my Self. His assuming the Authority of Ordering troops or Work in an arbitrary manner without regard to Detail. Upon receiving a genteel Letter from me Informing him of the officers Sentiments of that Affair — He bellow'd out Mutiny & appearing to be in the greatest dilemma roard out what shall I do; shall I fire upon them!

Stephen then went on to describe the incident that occurred late in the evening of August 24:

I walked up to him in a respectful manner with my hat off, and Whispered softly to him that as I had sent over the Serjeant for Orders, and likewise spoke to him myself I thought that he had a mind to leave us to Order our selves; and According I had given out the Parole. Upon Which he flew in a passion & ordered me in an imperious manner To Alter it! Alter it! I told him that He had Usd me extreamly ill in Not sending his Orders by the Serjeant in a proper maner & Seasonable hour, nor mentioned any thing of them to me when I arrived on the Road ... and as I looked upon him as Quarter Master general then I imagin'd I should not be Obliged to Alter the Parole. As to the Number of men he wanted, or where they were to be employed &c. If he would inform us of it, They should be ready at any hour; but as to any Other Orders I would not receive them from him; untill I was better informed & that the Gentlemen under my Command thought themselves so ill Used, that they complained to me of the Affair & that I could not bear his insults nor would I allow them under my Command to be emposed upon. He asked me if I bullied him in my Own Camp, I told him I was the same at any place & upon roaring out some thing about his Orders he Orderd me in Arrest.... I had no Orders & Saw no Order about obeying him other than as Quarter Master General about the Roads....

Most damning to the hard-working Virginia Provincials, Stephen also noted "His not supplying my Detachment with Rum."

Bouquet's response indicated that he was not amused in the least with St. Clair's antics, for he dispatched a stinging rebuke to St. Clair on August 28, immediately upon receipt of St. Clair's report:

I am afraid, My dear Sir, that there has been Some heat in this affair, and that you will have a good deal to do to justify the necessity of Such a violent measure against an officer of his Rank, Commanding a Corps. I am not So thoroughly informed of all the Rules of the English army.... But I know that in all other Services, They have no right to command as such: You do not act in this Expedition as Colonel, but as Q.M.G. only, and the Parole being the Ensign [symbol] of Command, I doubt that you can pretend to give it and if by usage you have exerted [exercised] that right it was left to you by the Commanding Officers as a Compliment and not an obligation.... His [General Forbes's] Intentions and repeated order to me are to establish and preserve a good harmony with the Provincial Troops, and you may be Sure that he will find this measure & you both precipitate and unseasonable. If you think proper to have him informed of it I think you should State the Case to him your Self.[46]

Bouquet reinstated Stephen in command on September 13, following a careful investigation of the actual circumstances that entirely vindicated Stephen.[47]

Certainly Bouquet was well justified in censuring St. Clair, for a British military manual of the time specifically noted the duties of the quartermaster general:

- ...he works with the General on whatever regards the marches of the army;
- ...he has no direct authority over the troops;
- ...he goes to receive the parole from the Major General of the day; but when necessarily employed, he sends one of his assistants to fetch it to him.[48]

Succinctly, St. Clair was entirely in the wrong, had fully exceeded his authority as quartermaster, and violated the orders and instructions of his commanding general. But he was contending with the will of a fellow Scotsman, and Forbes would shortly be able to take advantage of even St. Clair's temperament, and work it to his own advantage.

Throughout the entirety of the campaign, the simplest of logistical considerations threatened to impose delay upon the army. At one point, the supply of heavy bags used to carry flour and other supplies, and which were particularly necessary for baggage horses, began to run low. As the old military adage "for want of a nail" conveys, the shortage of even the most basic and simple item could derail the forward momentum of the entire expedition. Bouquet wrote to Colonel Burd on August 25:

> I Send you number of Horses and Baggs of flour, and desire you will make Shift to lodge Safely the flour and Send us with the horses all the Baggs back. You could take a number of oild Cloath [oil-cloth, essentially linen that had been impregnated with substances such as linseed oil or beeswax to make it waterproof] to cover the ground, Empty the Baggs upon them, and cover the whole with a frame and the rest of the Waggon Cloaths untill you can make Granarys: We have no more Baggs and the whole Supply would be Stopped.[49]

The seriousness of this situation is neatly masked by Bouquet's matter-of-fact instructions. Such a rickety, makeshift structure could not have been adequate to protect the flour from damage in the case of a storm or heavy wind, although it might have been sufficient against morning dews or light rain. The fact that Bouquet was willing to run the risk of damage or destruction of the valuable flour that had just been transported across Allegheny Mountain at such great effort, suggests that the shortfall of bags was considered to be the worse of the two evils.

Even with the Herculean efforts that Forbes, Bouquet, and their soldiers and contractors were performing, other shortages regularly surfaced. Bouquet wrote to Forbes on October 20, almost apologetically in a postscript:

> Our best woodsmen, accustomed to moccasins, cannot be used for lack of footwear. If it were possible to send 500 prepared skins from Philadelphia, there would be the means of providing them; and without moccasins, these men do not like to go into the woods. Besides, we have no shoes.[50]

In addition to the construction of the road, and movement of the main army, there was a continual traffic of convoys traveling in both directions, with the wagons and horses fully laden heading for the sunset, and returning empty in the direction of the sunrise. Because of the omnipresent danger of Indian raiding parties, these convoys were always escorted by a small detachment. Colonel Burd issued typical instructions to Ensign Joseph Armstrong of the 1st Pennsylvania Provincials, commander of one of these escorts from Loyalhanna on September 9:

> You'll proceed Directly with your party of 20 men to Stony Creek and you'll take all the Waggons & Teams under Your Escorts[.] That's under the Care of Mr. Robert Javier the Waggon Master. Upon your arrival at Quimahong, you'll put all the Flour, tools, or any thing else you find in that Breast Work, with Mr. Javier's Waggons, and Deliver the same to Col. Armstrong at Stony Creek. You'll March with you the small party that is on the Breast Work at Quimahony — and evacuate that place[.] You, with your party, are to Remain at Stony Creek, and Colonel Armstrong will find a fresh party to Escort the Waggons &c. to Ray's Town. You will observe that Mr. Javier is to March and Halt when and where he thinks proper, and that you are to have nothing further to do with him or his teams, but to cover them from the Enemy on their March from hence to Stony Creek.[51]

These instructions are revealing, as they clearly place the convoy under the command of the wagon master, and not the escort commander. The escort commander was not permitted to direct the convoy to optimize the tactical requirements of the escort, or halt at the most defensible or safest locations. Rather, the wagon master was permitted to dictate the rate of march and halting places for the convenience of the wagons, and presumably based upon the need to rest or recruit the teams, or repair the wagons and harness. Thus, these simple instructions intimate that Forbes's focus was to preserve the wagons and teams from the overwork and exhaustion which were certain to occur, with the convoy's protection from the occasional and isolated Indian raider being rated a secondary consideration.

Wagons and horses were never far from Forbes and Bouquet's thoughts, for they remained a consistent inhibiting factor upon the army. It was not until early in September that Forbes finally broke the equine jam. On September 9 Forbes wrote to Governor Denny of Pennsylvania:

> I have the Honour of laying before you the Situation of His Majesty's Affairs under my Direction ... at this Critical Juncture.... The laying in Provisions for the Support of the Army I attempted to do without even being obliged to impres any Carriages. The Quantity of Provisions to have been Collected at our principal Magazine has fallen greatly short of what I had reason to expect, because most of the Waggons were not Loaded with more than Fourteen Hundred Weight and took a Third more time in the Carriage than what they ought to have done, which obliged us to break in upon the Stock of Provisions laid in at Ray's Town, while the troops were opening a Road over the Mountains, and Securing its Communication, which is now effectually done to within Forty Miles of the French Fort, so that if the Inhabitants who have Waggons are not obliged to furnish a Sufficient number of them ... the Expedition cannot go forward, nor can I maintain the Ground I am already Master of, but shall be Obliged to draw off my Master's Forces to the Inhabited Parts of the Country, and take Provisions and Carriages wherever they may be found. The Evil which will attend this Procedure is, that the Innocent must suffer with the Guilty, and the Exigence of the Case is so pressing as to admit of no delay....[52]

Having laid out the criticality of his situation in regards to transportation, Forbes continued by presenting what must have been a truly hideous and horrifying threat to the inhabitants of the colony of Pennsylvania. Only intimidation of this magnitude would be sufficient to separate the recalcitrant Pennsylvanians from their valuable wagons and horses. John Forbes threatened to turn Quartermaster John St. Clair loose upon them:

> I have sent to Philadelphia the Quarter Master General, who will explain to you fully the Situation of the Army. I should be sorry to employ him in executing any Violent Measures, which the Exigency of Affairs I am in at present must Compel me to do, if I am not relieved by a Speedy Law for the Providing the Army with Carriages, or a general Concurrence of Magistrates and People of power in those Provinces in assisting, to their utmost, to provide the Same, and that with the greatest Diligence. Everything is ready for the Army's Advancing, but that I cannot do unless I have a Sufficient Quantity of Provisions in the Magazines at Ray's Town. The Road that Leads from the advanced Posts to the French Fort may be opened as fast as a Convoy can march it. Therefore my movement depends on his Majesty's Subjects entering cheerfully in carrying up the necessary Provisions.[53]

The vision of Quartermaster John St. Clair, who may well have been one of the most argumentative and hotheaded men in North America, along with being one of the most incompetent and disorganized, being unleashed with uninhibited martial powers in their countryside was enough to break even the vacillating Pennsylvania politicians loose from their lethargy. Shortly, large numbers of Pennsylvania wagons and horses would begin to reach Forbes at Ray's Town and Loyalhanna.

Forbes had indeed proven himself to be a shrewd and calculating Scotsman. As the Reverend Barton recorded on September 5:

> Sir John acquaints me this Morning that he is going into the Inhabitants to look for Waggons in which if he should not succeed, the Expedition must go to the D____ [Devil] he strongly solicited me to accompany him, and at last Desir'd me to write to a Gentleman of my Acquaintance who had a great Influence over the Dutch, & might be of much Service to him in getting Waggons. I wrote to the Gentleman, & am in Hopes Sir John will find him very useful. Governor Glen, Sir John S^t. Clair, & Captain Young set off together towards the Inhabitants escorted by 30 Light Horse.[54]

Forbes had delicately removed St. Clair from his army to avoid future controversies and arguments with the provincial field grade officers, while at the same time he had stroked St. Clair's ego by telling him that he was on an important and crucial mission. Forbes had then succesfully employed St. Clair as a "stick" to encourage the Pennsylvania Assembly and Proprietory Governor, and thus cleverly manipulated some of the most accomplished politicians in the British Empire. It was, simply put, a brilliant solution.

But Forbes was not willing to be entirely dependent upon Pennsylvania, and he ensured that additional sources of supply were in place. When he heard from Governor Sharpe of Maryland at Fort Cumberland that "Shannando [Shenadoah] Waggons being 41 in number are just arrived with 28 Days Flour" at that location on October 1, Forbes immediately ordered Sharpe to "engage as many of them as possible, upon the same terms as the Pennsylvania Waggons, to go upon our Expedition." At the same time Sharpe was instructed to locate any spare wheels or carriage parts that might be at that fort and send them on to Forbes. Sharpe couldn't locate any "spare Carriages or wheels for Howitzers or Cannon" but he did make the remarkable discovery "there are in an out Store House about fifteen or sixteen compleat Military Waggons."[55] Presumably remnants from the Braddock campaign, these wagons must have made a fine complement to Forbes's wagon train. With Pennsylvania, Virginia, Maryland and even John St. Clair working together, Forbes had ensured that he would have enough wagon transportation and horses when he needed them.

Forbes and Bouquet also continued, when feasible, the military exercises of their diverse command. Although the exigencies of constructing the road and the encampment at Loyalhanna resulted in the necessary dispersal of the army, every opportunity was taken to continue the instruction of the provincial battalions. The Reverend Barton noted on September 22: "The Officers of the 3[d] Battalion [Pennsylvania Provincials] practise the manuel [sic] Exercise under the Direction of the Serjeant Major."[56] Whenever possible, Bouquet maintained his regimen of regular drill. The soldiers at Ray's Town practiced marksmanship on both August 13 and 14.[57]

One of the greatest problems faced by Bouquet and Forbes was that of desertion from the battalions. Desertion, or simply departing the army without permission or authorization, without any intent to return either sooner or later, was a consistent problem in all 18th century armies. Forbes and Bouquet well recognized the importance that discipline played in any effective military organization, particularly one composed of so many soldiers recently raised, from so many different locations. Forbes and Bouquet both went to great efforts to display leniency whenever possible, but not to the point of permitting anarchy to reign within the camps. Given the already small size of his army, Forbes could absolutely not tolerate desertion of soldiers. Although the magnitude of this problem can only be guessed at, by late September it appears that it may have begun to reach epidemic proportions.

On September 24 a general court-martial was held at Ray's Town that sentenced several soldiers from different corps to death for desertion. The fact that soldiers were condemned from various regiments suggests that the problem was rampant, and also that Forbes wanted to make a universal impact upon his army. The Reverend Barton was assigned a particularly difficult task, but one which he would have considered to be extremely important:

Sunday September 24th. Receiv'd Orders from Major Halkett to attend John Hannah Soldier in the 1st Virginia Reg[t], Thomas Williams Soldier in the Maryland Companies, Benjamin Murphy & Salathiel Nixon of the N Carolina Companies, & John Doyle of the Pennsylvania Regiment, who are all adjudg'd to suffer Death by the general Court Martial, whereof Col. Mercer was President, & order'd by the General to be shot at 7 OClock on Tuesday Morning next.—

Monday September 25th. At 6 O'Clock this Morning visited & pray'd with the Prisoners, who have not yet receiv'd their Sentence.

After having condemned the prisoners to death, Forbes pardoned several of them. By doing this Forbes was able to demonstrate his great leniency to the army, knowing that the mere threat would be communicated throughout the various regiments, and that the relieved soldiers would serve as a living reminder to other potential malcontents that they could be both apprehended and punished for their misdeeds. But at the same time, one firm example had to be made. Barton continued his ministrations:

Monday September 25th. Visited the Prisoners in the Evening, who I found in Tears under terrible Apprehensions of approaching Death. I pray'd with them; & examin'd into the State of their Souls & their Preparations for Eternity; but to my great Mortification found very little Sense of Religion in any of them. Before I left them an Officer came in with the General's Order [of pardon] to John Hannah, Thomas Williams, Benjamin Murphy & Salathial Nixon, who seem'd more affected and more penitent at the thought of Living than the thought of dying. They were immediately discharg'd.

Tuesday September 26th. Very early this Morning visited & pray'd with John Doyle, who is to be shot to Death at 7 OClock P.M.—He told me he was brought up a Papist; & as his Conscience never supply'd him with sufficient Reason to renounce that Profession he was resolv'd to dye one—yet as he made no Doubt but the Prayers of good men would avail much, he beg'd of me to stay with him the few Minutes he had to live, & attend him to the Place of Execution; to which I agreed.—In a little Time came in the Provost & pin'd a Paper to his Breast with these dreadful Words—Viz—"Camp at Ray's Town September the 26th 1758

John Doyle, a Soldier in Captain Patterson's Company in the Pennsylvania Regt, is to be Shot to Death for Desertion."

I walk'd with him to the Place of Execution, surrounded by a strong Guard.—He behav'd with uncommon Resolution;—exhorted his Brother Soldiers to take Example by his Misfortunes:—To live sober lives;—to beware of bad Company;—to shun pretended Friends, & loose wicked Companions, "who, says he, will treat you with Civility & great Kindness over a Bottle, but will deceive & ruin you behind your Backs.—" But above all he charg'd them never to desert.—When he saw the Six Men that were to shoot him, he enquir'd if they were good Marks Men; and immediately strip'd off his Coat, open'd his Breast, kneel'd down, & said—"Come, Fellow Soldiers, advance near me—do your Office well, point at my Heart—for God's Sake do not miss me, & take Care not to disfigure me." He would suffer no Handkerchief to be ty'd over his Face, but look'd at his Executioners to the last, who advanc'd so near him that the Muzzles of their Guns were within a Foot of his Body.—Upon a Signal from the Serjeant Major they fir'd, but shot so low that his Bowels fell out—his shirt & Breeches were all on Fire & he tumbled upon his Side;—rais'd one Arm 2 or 3 Times & soon expired. A shocking Spectacle to all around him & a striking Example to his Fellow Soldiers![58]

Forbes had demonstrated the terrible might of military justice, and he hoped that his disorderly provincials were suitably impressed by the spectacle.

For all of his occasional grumblings about provincial soldiers and officers, and intermittent problems with desertion, Forbes made it a priority to develop and maintain good relations between the regulars and the provincials. Even with his severe illness weighing upon him, Forbes still contributed his full share to fostering and maintaining good relations within the army. On September 25 he invited Anglican Chaplain Barton to dine with him, as the good Reverend dutifully recorded in his journal:

Receiv'd an Invitation from Major Halket, Aid du Camp, to dine this Day with the General, who was very factious [factitious, suggesting that Forbes was joking or engaging in word play] & in high Spirits at Table, tho' extremely weak & in a low State of Health: He enquir'd much into the Moral State of the Army; declar'd he was concern'd at not being able to attend Divine Service; & that he was sorry I had so disagreeable an Office upon my Hands at present, as that of attending Persons under Sentence of Death. Much was also said about the Expedition, which is not proper to mention.[59]

Clearly Forbes was sympathetic to the difficult task that he had assigned Barton of ministering to the condemned prisoners.

Bouquet in particular made great efforts to develop an effective, cooperative and mutually beneficial relationship between the multifaceted components of the army. His views on the subject have already been documented, as Bouquet lectured St. Clair during his disagreement with Colonel Stephen. A measure of Bouquet's success was noted by the Reverend Barton on August 24: "A perfect Harmony & Union subsists thro' the whole Camp: and Colonel Bouquet gains more & more upon the Affections of the People."[60] Bouquet reported to Forbes on August 20 from Ray's Town:

I assure you that, whatever our fate, you will never experience the indignities suffered by General Abercromby through the laxness of his provincials. I have established harmony between the different corps which will prevent any accident of that nature, and by holding the balance even, encouraging these, and restraining the overbearing spirit of the others, chiefly of your countrymen, I can truly assure you that you will find no fault other than ignorance and inexperience, which I cannot remedy — but they are loyal and will not abandon you.[61]

Among the measures that Bouquet implemented was to ensure that courts-martial were composed of equitable numbers of both regular and provincial officers. For example, a "Court Martial of the Line" (regimental court-martial) sat on August 16 to "try Swan the Sutler for disobedience of orders." The 2nd Pennsylvania provided a captain as president, and subalterns were provided from the Royal Americans, Highlanders, North Carolina Battalion, and Maryland Battalion, thus achieving an almost perfectly balanced court as regards to both assigned duties and experience of officers.[62] Courts-martial were regularly held, and consistently maintained to this equal representation.

Bouquet also ensured that the soldiers were treated fairly. The measures that he took to reimburse a soldier for a stolen rifle were previously documented. Bouquet ordered at Ray's Town that "all Prisoners not Confin'd for Capital Crimes be tried within 24 hours by a Court Martial & released."[63] Bouquet ensured that soldiers were not held in a guardhouse under confinement for an unreasonable length of time, but instead that they received a rapid trial and resolution of their case, by either appropriate punishment or acquittal. Bouquet also implemented what today's military or business world would be referred to as an "open-door policy," although such leniency was almost unheard-of in the regular British army of the age. Bouquet announced to his army at Ray's Town on August 7: "...any Soldiers in the Line who have any Complaints to make, or any Pretension are to apply immediately to the Commanding Officers of their Corps, who will see Justice done to them."[64]

With the army in as good order as Bouquet could reasonably hope to establish, given the limited duration that it had been in existence, it was time to begin the forward push. Bouquet had written to Forbes as early as August 8, stating:

Sir John [St. Clair] has returned and is giving you an account of his observations as far as Loyal Hannon. It seems that the road will be very practicable. ... if you approve, I shall march to Loyal Hannon ... with 1500 men of whatever troops you shall find suitable. I shall construct a post and storehouses there, and shall protect our workers cutting the way behind me.... Along the creeks there is grass all winter beyond the mountains, which would facilitate this expedition.[65]

The location of the post at Loyalhanna Creek was ordained by the presence of abundant pastures and meadows, which could feed the horses and live animals upon which Forbes and Bouquet depended for transportation and fresh meat for their soldiers. Bouquet noted on August 20 to Forbes, "We shall not lack for pasturage here, and we shall find it in abundance, they say, at Loyalhanna."[66]

Bouquet dispatched Colonel James Burd of Pennsylvania with the Royal Americans, five companies of Highlanders, his own Battalion of Pennsylvania Provincials, Stephen's battalion from the 1st Virginia, artillery, entrenching tools and provisions from Ray's Town on August 23 to move ahead to Loyalhanna. Bouquet issued Burd with very precise instructions, including:

- You are to proceed to Loyal Hannon.
- As Soon as you arrive at Loyal Hannon Mr. Basset is to lay out your Incampment at the Place assigned by Mr. Rhor, with two Small Redoubts at 200 yards; All hands are then to be employed in entrenching the Camp;
- A Store house of 120 foot long, and at least 25 wide is to be built immediately to lodge your Provisions and Ammunition, in the Place where the Fort is to be erected, and covered with Shingles;
- An Hospital is to be built near the Fort, and Ovens. Mr. Rhor is to give the direction for the Fort;
- If there is any possibility of making Hay, no time is to be lost;
- The houses of office to be kept clean and covered every day;
- Keep a Journal of Your Proceedings.

After being given such comprehensive instructions, Burd may have breathed a sigh of relief when Bouquet finished by telling him: "I give you the above instructions by way of Memorandum, and you are at Liberty to make any alterations that your judgement and the Circumstances may direct."[67]

Burd reached Loyalhanna Creek with 2,500 men on the evening of September 2 and immediately began to familiarize himself with the ground, as he wrote to Bouquet on September 3: "I arriv'd here last night all the Detachment except 200 left at the Clear Fields with the Train [of artillery] & I expect the Train here Tomorrow Evening.... I can say very little about this Place, but shall Soon be Acquainted with it, and if possible will make Hay...."[68] There was some early discussion regarding the precise location for the encampment. Ensign Rhor had selected another location, somewhat to the west of where Burd would finally entrench. Burd wrote a detailed account of the situation to Bouquet on September 6, along with a sketch of his proposed new entrenchment site:

The Troops here are all Employed on the Breast work & hope they will finish tonight. We have been Extremely interrupted & disconfeted with Continuall hard Rains & the weather does not appear Altogether settled yet.... Sunday [September 3] the Troops were employed upon the Encampment Mr. Rohr had formerly seen but upon reconnoitering we found a very fine piece of Ground naturally strong being high & having the Creek on one side, and a fine spring on the other, just under our works, we evacuated the old ground & began our breast work on the New, on Monday Morning [September 4]. I will have the troops in the breast work at 10 A:M today; when Mr. Rohr returns I will send you a draught of this (I really will say) fine place. I have had the ground Reconnoitered & can find no place to make Hay....[69]

Burd's subsequent sketch survives at the Western Pennsylvania Historical Society, and confirms that the site that Burd finally selected would become Fort Ligonier.[70]

Bouquet's initial plans for the entrenched camp at Loyalhanna were delineated in a letter to Forbes on August 20:

...as there is no one more energetic, and at the same time receptive to advice, than Colonel Burd, I shall send him with ... 1500 men will begin by making entrenchments for their camp, as protection against a surprise attack. Then they will go to work building storehouses for our provisions, and will shield them by a fort built of stockades or logs; and this fort may, if necessary, be reinforced by another exterior line, and the interval of fifteen to eighteen feet filled with earth from the ditch. For the present they will make only the interior enclosure. They will keep advanced posts all around them....[71]

Based upon the sketch that Burd sent Bouquet on September 6, Burd followed Bouquet's instructions and began constructing what would eventually become the outerworks of "Fort Ligonier."[72] Although this term is most commonly used by modern historians, the camp was not named Fort Ligonier until early in December, and for nearly all of the campaign was simply referred to as the encampment at Loyalhanna. Accordingly, the more accurate (and less commonly utilized) "Loyalhanna Encampment" will be employed in this study. These works were built on a prominent elevation immediately north of Loyalhanna Creek, where water was readily available. The site was not perfect, as high ground commanded it to the southwest and west. Still, the encampment was out of musket range from these two other pieces of high ground, and unless the French carried artillery from Fort Duquesne the location was quite well selected to resist any infantry attack.

The outer works were constructed of "logs fraized at top." Historical architect Charles Morse Stotz interpreted this as a stacked log barricade approximately four feet high, although it is possible that the outer works were faced or outlined with logs and then filled with earth and fraizing inserted.

Beyond these outer works, Burd established four redoubts, a classic square redoubt to the west, a second square redoubt to the northwest, an arrowhead-shaped redoubt nearly due north, and a second arrowhead-shaped redoubt to the east. Although these arrowhead-shaped redoubts are somewhat unusual, contemporary engineering manuals specified that the configuration of redoubts was to be adjusted however necessary to utilize the natural topography of the ground to be defended. These four redoubts served as the "advanced posts all around" that Bouquet had called for. The redoubts were apparently assigned numerical designations, for Burd specifically informed Bouquet during an attack in October that "the Enemy Attacked Redoubt No. 3." None of the surviving plans assign such numerical designations to the redoubts, although Burd's journal states that the road remained open to Bouquet located at Laurel Ridge to the east, suggesting that the redoubts were numbered counterclockwise starting with the furthest east redoubt. If this interpretation is accurate, this implies that Redoubt #1 would have been the first redoubt encountered when marching from Ray's Town.

Burd also constructed the specified storehouse facilities at the center of the breastworks. Bouquet had called for a single storehouse "120 feet long and 25 feet wide," or three thousand square feet. Because of the vagaries of the terrain, Burd instead constructed three storehouses, two of which were approximately seventy feet long by sixteen feet wide, and a third approximately sixty feet long by twenty feet wide. Thus, Burd fulfilled the square footage requirements that Bouquet had called for.

To protect these storehouses, a classic square bastioned fort was designed. Possibly Engineer Rohr might have assisted with the initial layout of the fort, although he was only at Loyalhanna a couple of days before he proceeded on an expedition with Major Grant to Fort Duquesne. Most likely, Captain Gordon designed the construction of this fort. Bouquet reported to Forbes on September 11: "I am having a small fort marked out around our storehouses in the center of the enclosure of the entrenched camp."[73] Forbes stated his concerns regarding the extent of fortification at Loyalhanna to Bouquet on October 10: "I was told this day to my great surprize that Captain Gordon was building at Loyalhanna fitt to stand a siege, you know we want nothing but a strong post. So for Gods sake think of both time money and Labour and put a Stop to all superfluitys...."[74]

As determined by archaeology performed at Fort Ligonier in the 1960s and a later drawing made by an English officer who was commandant there, the eastern portion of the fort is constructed of log cribs, filled with rocks and soil. These walls were ten feet thick, which would have been sufficient against field artillery up to the size of 12-pounders, or "fitt to stand a siege," as Forbes remonstrated against. The remainder of the fort is constructed of pickets, and is a simple stockade wall. As Stotz correctly discussed, typically the most exposed portion of a fort contained the heaviest construction.[75] However, with the encampment at Loyalhanna commanded by rising terrain to the southwest and west, ground located closest to the French at Fort Duquesne, this would have suggested that the western portion of the fort should have contained this type of construction. The author believes that Captain Gordon initially intended for the entire inner fort to consist of the more robust earth-filled log walls, but Forbes's unequivocal instructions put an immediate cessation to the heavier fortifications. Thus, the fort was built from the east to the west, so the more solid parapets were accidentally located to the east. This also supports the counterclockwise numbering system for the redoubts, as they were identified in the sequence in which they were constructed.

The interior or "parade ground" of the fort was only one hundred feet by sixty feet, barely large enough to form a company of infantry. Most likely, it was only intended to be sufficient in size to form the daily guard force in the morning. The outside of the fort is quite small, only 180 feet from the corner of one bastion to another. A fascine battery, added to the western portion of the fort along with a substantial ditch to supplement the defense in the direction of a likely French assault, extended another one hundred feet to the west in a roughly "U"-shaped appendage. This ditch was a considerable obstacle, measuring twelve feet wide at the top, and seven feet wide at the bottom. However, archaeologists measured its depth at only 52 inches, which would not have been a sufficient depth according to military engineering manuals of the time. It is possible that some of the surface was removed by erosion, agriculture, or domestic construction before the archaeologists performed their work. The fort enclosed the two longer storehouses, while the third, shorter storehouse was located just north and outside of the east gate of the fort.

As Bouquet intended for this to be major advanced post for the eventual advance upon Fort Duquesne, a large number of logistical and support structures were built here. Within Gordon's small fortress two additional log cabins were constructed. One served as a magazine to protect ammunition. The other is identified on contemporary maps as an "Officer's Barracks," although it seems more likely that this would have served as a guardhouse for the daily perimeter guard force. These structures were relatively ornate, included shingled and hipped roofs, and were clearly intended to be permanent.

One additional officers' house was located immediately southeast of the east gate, and two more officers' houses were located just north of the north sally port that led to one of the springs. One of these buildings was specifically constructed for Forbes; as Bouquet wrote to Burd at Loyalhanna on October 12, "I hope the General's hut is ready, as he will soon be with us. He mends apace."[76]

A hospital consisting of three log buildings was constructed within the redoubts, but outside of the outer works, presumably for health reasons. Additional small batteries and earthworks were built, particularly to guard the east gate. Overlooking Loyalhanna Creek and constructed as part of the outer works were still two more batteries, the "East Battery" and "West Battery." Presumably, other such batteries were originally planned by Gordon around the entire position, but were canceled by Forbes. At least one smokehouse and several latrines were also constructed, along with a designated location for the Indian camp outside of the redoubts' perimeter. Presumably, the Indian camp may have contained some simple lean-tos or similar structures. A blacksmith shop previously existed at Loyalhanna, to support the Indian trade. This smithy consistently appears on contemporary maps, suggesting that it was maintained once the army arrived, most likely to provide a location to repair the Indians' weapons.

Bouquet continued to issue instructions to Burd to improve the fort. On September 25 he ordered:

> A Fort of Logs is to be built round the Store Houses. The Timber to be prepared in the Woods and haul'd by the Waggons that shall come from Ray's Town. One Hundred and fifty fit Men of the Line are to be appointed for that Work with Officers who are to do no other Duty, as as they are to be constantly employ'd, they are to receive one Jil of Rum per Day.
> The Road is to be cut to the advanced post by Two Hundred Men, and two Hundred more to cover the Cutters. Captain Shilby will attend in cutting and marking the Rout....[77]

Thus, even with the entrenched camp still under construction, work was already in progress to cut the road to the next advanced post, on the Chestnut Ridge to the west of Loyalhanna. The "Captain Shilby" mentioned was Captain Evan Shelby of the "Royal" Maryland Battalion, the same man who had so skillfully surveyed the road between Fort Frederick and Fort Cumberland earlier in the campaign. From this point on he was regularly employed, effectually as an "Assistant Engineer," and his principal responsibility was selecting the route from Loyalhanna to Fort Duquesne.

Bouquet ordered a large patrol of the Maryland Battalion, who were experienced frontier fighters, with forty rangers of the 1st Battalion of Pennsylvania, the whole under Lieutenant Colonel Dagworthy, to regularly scout around the camp. Among their duties were to recover any horses that they found in the woods. By now Bouquet was an old hand at dealing with the provincials, and he instructed Burd "for which they will receive a Dram [of liquor]."

The Loyalhanna Encampment was a sturdy, heavily fortified, relatively large entrenchment capable of protecting the army's camps, storehouses, and additional logistical facilities such as blacksmith shops, hospitals, bullock pens, and smokehouses. It would serve Forbes well as his advanced depot, and with its construction Forbes's second parallel was ready to support the final movement on Fort Duquesne.

Unlike Bouquet's movement to Ray's Town from Carlisle, there was never any general advance from Ray's Town to Loyalhanna. Primarily to avoid damaging the newly constructed road, Bouquet ensured that the army advanced in segments. Most commonly, battalions or companies advanced individually, either escorting convoys to safeguard them, or else working to improve specific portions of the road. On August 23 Bouquet ordered the Royal Americans, five companies of the Highlanders under Major Grant, the 2nd Pennsylvania Battalion, and the Virginia companies at Ray's Town to begin the march forward. After the road was completed, the 1st Pennsylvania Battalion and Lower Counties Battalion followed, along with the train of artillery.[78] However, as Bouquet complained to Burd on August 26, completion of the road was mandated before any substantial numbers of forces could be transferred to Loyalhanna, for they could not be sustained at that advanced post until the line of communications had been opened.[79]

As Forbes's columns had begun to close in on Fort Duquesne, he instructed Bouquet to initiate an aggressive schedule of scouting parties to be sent against the French. Forbes desperately required accurate intelligence regarding the strength of the French fort. Specifically, he demanded the specifics of Fort Duquesne's construction, the number and type of cannon, the quantity of ammunition and provisions in the fort's storehouses and magazines, the number and composition of the garrison, how alert and aggressive the garrison was, the morale of the soldiers, the quality of the leadership of the French command, and the nature and interests of the Natives at and around the Forks. This had always been a priority of Forbes's, but now that he was nearing the Ohio country it had become an urgency. From the beginning of the campaign, Forbes had taken measures specifically to facilitate such scouting parties. Draper Woods, deputy commissary, had discussed with Forbes as early as May:

> As Biscuit will be wanted on the march for the use of ranging or scouting partys it would be necessary that the Contractors Agents shou'd order Biscuit to be baked for the above purpose at Lancaster York Town Carlisle &c and by so doing great expence will be saved to the Crown in regard to Carriage of the same, all of which I leave to your Excellency's wise consideration.[80]

Even as Bouquet's column approached Ray's Town in late May, Forbes was already imploring St. Clair: "Try all means to get intelligence of Fort DuQuesne and the road from Raestown, and send always provincials with the Cherokee scouting partys, and don't trust them with too much ammunition."[81] Forbes reiterated in mid–June:

> I beg that every scheme may be try'd to get intelligence from Fort DuQuesne, and the Ohio, by getting some good officers to go a Scouting, and pray establish your marks of distinction that the scouting partys may know one another, and all our Indians must be told to keep to the westward of the Susquehanna, and not to molest our friendly Delawares for the present, as by this means I am soon in hopes of bringing back their brethern from the French upon the Ohio.[82]

A party of fourteen Cherokee Indians and two white men had gone from Ray's Town to Fort Duquesne in mid–July, and provided Forbes information that the French were constructing new works at the Forks.

Bouquet received news from another party of five Cherokees who scouted from Fort Cumberland to Fort Duquesne, returning to Ray's Town early in August: "[T]he day they left the fort, they saw about a hundred Indians arrive there, a part in canoes, but they did not see any tents or troops around the fort. The French do not venture out any more, and they saw outside the place only a woman who was washing in the river and too near the fort for them to kill her."[83] Another party of 24 Cherokees accompanied by two Virginia officers also scouted Fort Duquesne about the same time, without providing Forbes any reputable intelligence.[84]

Governor Glen reported to Forbes that several small mixed scouting parties had set out from Ray's Town on August 7 and 8, destined for Fort Duquesne.[85] Forbes received detailed reports of these two scouts. These reports are reproduced in their entirety, as they provide a fascinating rendition of the daily distances that could be covered by such a party, the length of time necessary to stealthily traverse the mountains, the interactions of the Cherokee and Catawba Indians and the provincial officers and men that made up the parties, and the difficulties and challenges that were faced by these reconnaissance patrols.

Intelligence from Ensign Colby Chew of the First Virginia Regiment

Monday the 7th of August 1758. Set out from Reas Town by order of Colonel Henry Bouquet with a Party of Indians and white men to make discoveries of the strength and situation of Fort Duquesne. I proceeded accordingly as far this night as the Shawnee Cabbins, about 8 Miles S. 80 degrees W.

Tuesday the 8th, we proceeded on course along the Old Trading Path; Cross'd the Allegheny Ridge, and encamped at Edmond's Swamp, 12 Miles N 70 Degrees W.

Wednesday 9th we marched about 9 miles N 60 degrees W to Quamchong Creek, at which place we continued Thursday the 10th.

Fryday the 11th we proceeded early in the morning; Cross'd the Laurel Ridge and came to an old encampment at the Loyal Hanan Old town 15 Miles N 55 degrees West.

Saturday the 12th We continued on our way along the Old trading path which kept for 10 or 12 Miles for the most part along the low ground of the Loyal Hannon [tho' it sometimes] turned off the River and cross'd [some Ridges and the high points] of Hills [. The High Ground is] a well timbered [the Ridges not high, the] low ground [of the river] and in general [of all the creeks] and [very thick and bushy this] day discovered [some very late] and signs of Indians 15 Miles N 60 degrees West.

Sunday the 13th we marched very early and continued till 10 o'Clock when the Indians halted to Conjoin [in other words, "conjure" or make magic] as they had all the day seen fresh signs of the Enemy (the low ground very thick and busy) we sent out scouts who continued out till near dark, which occasioned us to encamp there that night when the scouts returned they informed that the Enemy had gone on directly towards Fort Duquesne this afternoon when the sun was about an hour high heard the report of 12 cannon as we immagined at Fort Duquesne 5 miles N 20 degrees West.

Monday the 14th we continued our march and sent out scouts who discovered no sign, unless those that went along the path; but heard seviral guns firing, the path went over several Ridges well timbered 7 Miles Course near West.

Tuesday the 15th we marched very easily and came in about eight miles from our camp to a large path that comes from the northward into the Old Trading Path which we saw the tracks of a great many Indians going both ways we imagined the guns that our scouts heard yesterday was fired by a party going along the Road. Several horses, some of which was shod, had been along this path the day before towards Fort Duquesne. The way was good, the ridges low and well timbered: but all the branches very thick with brush trees and white thorns. 12 miles West. As the provisions was near spent, the Indians this night held a Council of War, in which it was determined that all except myself, Sergeant Vaughan, and five Indians, should return.

Wednesday the 16th. We sent back those that was to return, and I proceeded on our way, being only seven in number we came where a large party of Indians had been about 10 days ago. I imagine from the size of this Encampment about 100, they had cleared about 5 or 6 feet squared very clean and had left in it five pieces of bark with two or three pipes full of tobacco in each piece; it was about six miles from our last camp to this place, the path but indifferent, crossing many ridges, and coursed about N 80 degrees West.

The hills end at this place, and it is a plain Country from here to the Fort. We here left the Old trading path and went about 3 miles N.W. then turned [S.W. crossed the path] and kept a course till we were [within two miles of the] French Fort [then went to the] N. of W. [and came to an old Indian] Town on [the Ohio about 1½ miles above the Fort where I had a] good view up [and down the] the River [we see some Cattle grassing] on an island [down] the River and hid ourselves in a thicket till the Indians conjured and Painted; after which we went down the River within ¾ of a mile of the Fort, then turned S.E. and went upon a stoney ridge where the Chief Warrior with his Conjuring implements and tyd there about the neck of those Indians, and told them they could not be hurt, round my neck he tyed an otter's skin, in which his conjuring implements had been kept, and round the Serjeant he tyed a bagg of paint, that had been left with the rest of his conjuring things he then told us that none of us could be hurt for those things hid from the balls & from us. They then made us strip all our clothes except our breech clouts [and] mokesons, shook hands with us, and told us to go and fight like men, for nothing could hurt us, the first view I had of the Fort was from the banks of the Ohio, but at a great distances we saw a battoe and 2 cannoes, there were Indians in them fishing, we were then in a pasture filled in with trees fell one on the other we saw by the tracks that this pastured & the farthest part which is not above ¾ of a mile from the Fort was much frequented by Indians, we continued down the pasture from which place I could make no great [blotted; illegible] the number of troops, till almost sun setting, at which time I let the Indians know that I wanted them to accompany me to the top of a ridge, that ran directly towards the fort, but they disliked the proposal and refused, as they were in great expectations of getting a scalp. However when they saw that I was determined to go and had proceeded on towards the place, they followed me. From the top of this ridge I had an extraordinary good view of the

Fort, as it over lookt it, and scarce half a mile from the Fort. There were 50 or 60 tents pitched on the river Ohio, and about 100 yards from the Fort: and there was several houses on Monongahela: there was nither cannoes nor Battoes in this River; that I could perceive, nor could I discern any new works about the Fort. I imagine the men parade in the Fort, as I saw them going in at Retreat beating, and from what I saw Do not imagine there is above 300 French men. The Indians kept a continual hooping and hallooing, but could not see their Camp, unless the Tents I mentioned were pitched for them; which I judged were from the first; and the appearance of the people at them by their looks noise &c. imagined them to be Indians as I could see no sign of a camp or building of either side of the River. After dark the Indians got to singing and dancing, and by their noise judged them to be about 50 in number all which the Cherokees told me was Shawnees.

As I have taken a plan of Fort Duquesne as well as I could upon a separate paper, [I shall make no mention] of it here [see page 118].

This days march [had we kept the path] would have been about [42] miles, the course [about N. 80 W. The Ohio runs about 20 S.W. The] Monongahela at the mouth [runs from] near E from the top of this ridge I moved to another place nearer to the Monongahela, but could make no further discoveries.

From this place we went back to the head warrior, and after some consultations agreed to return home; upon which we came about a mile, and near the old trading path encamped. We heard the Indians singing and Dancing all night.

Thursday the 17th as soon as day broke we began our march, which we continued very fast till one O'Clock in which time we came near 30 miles, and over took our party which we ordered back we then called a halt to refresh ourselves; after which we continued our march together, and came about 12 miles further and halted for that night, about 2 miles before we encamped we came up fresh tracks coming from the Eastward.

Fryday the 18th. We continued on our march pursuing the tracks that we came on last night, the low ground and branches which I mentioned in my Journal as I went towards Fort Duquesene is very low and liable to over flowed, and consequently very moist and soft, so that I am afraid a road thro them will be but [indifferent for Carriages].

We followed the tracks till night, when we camped [about 4] miles from the camp and Quanahong Creek.

Saturday the 19th we marched early in the morning and came to the camp [at Ray's Town], where we found it was Ensign Allens Party that we had tracked, and that they had arrived at camp but the night before.

A report of Lieut. Allen of the Virginia Reg[t].

Tuesday August 8th 1758[.] Having obtain'd permission & I received orders from Col[o] Sir John S[t]. Clair to reconnoitre towards Fort DuQuesne and gain what Intelligence I cou'd of the strength of it—I this Day sett out from the Camp at Qumakaghock (in Company with Lieu[t] Patterson who with a party of thirty men was ordered to way lay the path if possible to retake some waggonsers that had fallen in with the Enemies hands) & marched to the Cabins near the Loyallhanning—13 Miles

Wednesday the 9th We continued our ways along the old trading path with M[r]. Patterson, march'd ab[t] 14 miles [& encamped]

Thursday ye 10th We proceeded on our way ab[t] 1½ miles when we came on the tracks of a small party of Indians it appeared as if they [had been] gone ab[t] 3 hours—we supposed the Indians to be those L[t]. Patterson was ordered [to waylay.] We slowly pursued the enemy's party about a mile, at which time Lieut Patterson being asked why he did not follow faster [if he intended to overtake] then answered I will be damned if I go farther than the top of the Hill I am now. When I found that he had stop't being chagrine'd that so fine an opportunity of retaking the wagonners & killing some of the Indians shou'd be lost I pass'd by him without taking leave of him and march'd along the road about half a mile in which space I had a good opportunity on moist ground of counting [their] tracks which were about 12. Having but 40 men with me I left the Road on the right & went ab[t] 9 Miles.

Friday the 11th[.] We continued our march between the old trading Path and the River Monongahela 15 Miles—

Saturday 12th[.] We march'd very early ab[t] Nine oClock cross'd an Indian path which was towards Ft. Cumberland, we heard several guns fired on each hand some near & some at a great distance I imagine they were fired by a hunting party of Indians—came to Monongahela ab[t] 2

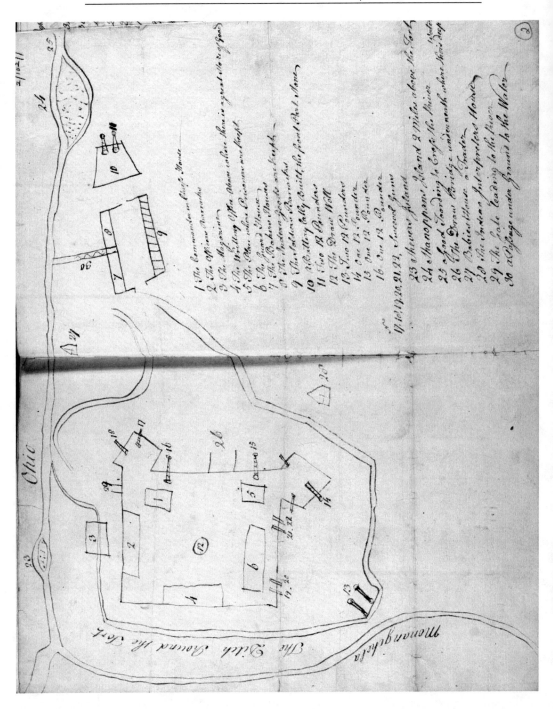

Plan of Fort Duquesne, probably prepared by Lieutenant Chew on his scouting party, August 1758 (National Archives of Scotland, GD45/2/102).

miles above the mouth of turtle Creek. The Cty from Loyalhanning to this place is in general very full of ridges and broken Hills, march'd this day 12 Miles—

Tuesday 13th[.] We cross'd Monongahela at Braddocks's Ford and marched on the River on the S Side marching ab^t 8 miles[.] 3 O'clock in the afternoon came on a hill that overlook'd Ft DuQuesne about ¼ of a mile distant from it—I had a good view from the top of this hill but thinking I could make a better discovery by going nearer. I left my men and went to the River [about a Quarter of a mile] from the Fort—The Fort appeared to be a a wall made of wood and clay ab^t 9 feet high—I think there was an Entrenchment on the Banks of the Monongahela I could discern no tents or Indian incampments, but on the N side of the Fort towards the Ohio I saw smoak arise and heard Indians singing, so that I judge the Indian camp to be there—I cou'd discern no new works. I cou'd [not see] the men parade at retreat beating so that time gine [probably means "join"] the parade in the front or on the N side, from the appearance of them I judge there are ab^t 400 French from the noise and firing near five hundred Indians—Ab^t an hour before sunset they begin to fire cannon, a couple of minute guns, which they repeated every quarter of an Hour till they fired ten which is answered by some arms fired in an Indian manner some near to the fort & others at a distance of a mile on the N side of the Ohio which I judge to be a large party of Indians coming to the Fort as I heard the Indians hooping whenever the small arms were fired—At Dark I went to my party & marched ab^t ½ a mile from the Hill and I heard the Indians singing & Dancing till I fell asleep.

Monday the 14th[.] We marched ab^t 7 miles So. & then turned by the ford we had cross'd the Monogahila and came to the River about 3 miles above and found that the River had risen so considerably that we could not cross it, I went up the River ab^t a mile further and camped.

Tuesday 15th[.] We marched up the River ab^t 10 Miles & finding [it too Deep to ford we made a Raft & crossed it & encamped]

Wednesday 16th[.] We marched ab^t 9 miles to cross Yeaghaogeny ab^t miles on this side cross'd Braddocks Road & very near it an Indian path much beaten & some fresh tracks in it just gone towards Fort DuQuesne, we this night incamp'd ab^t 2 miles within Braddocks Road

Thursday & Friday ye 17th & 18th[.] We continued our march without any remarkable occurrances & in the evening of the 18th having marched very fast these last days we arrived at the camp at Quimahong Creek.[86]

Colonel Byrd dispatched additional scouting parties from Fort Cumberland in late August.[87] Bouquet dispatched another party under Captain Patterson from Ray's Town to Fort Duquesne, between July 27 and August 2, which was not able to garner any appreciable information because of heavy fog in the vicinity of Fort Duquesne.[88] On August 8, Bouquet noted to Forbes that he had no fewer than four scouting parties dispatched from Ray's Town, with Washington at Fort Cumberland directed to send forth another from that installation.[89] Bouquet instructed Washington in mid–August to "continue sending Strong Partys along, with orders to reconoitre.... Every one of your Partys (who are to succeed one another constantly) are to detach Small Partys to reconnoitre the Ennemys, take if possible a View of their Works, and if they could get a Prisoner, know what Reinforcements they either have received, or do expect."[90] And Bouquet continued to discuss "all the Partys I have continually Sent out." Forbes dispatched a large party under Major George Armstrong in late August, which greatly disappointed Forbes by performing particularly poorly.[91] Burd sent two small parties from the encampment at Loyalhanna on September 1.[92]

It was not until late in September that one of these scouts finally achieved success at Fort Duquesne, Colonel Burd reporting that on September 29, "Captain [William] Trent [of the Pennsylvania Provincials] and the Indians are return'd from Fort DuQuesne they have brought in a scalp which they took nigh to the Fort."[93]

Forbes and Bouquet maintained this tempo of scouting parties nearly continuously as they began to plan their final advance from the camp at Loyalhanna. Following a French attack at Loyalhanna, on October 18 Burd dispatched a number of scouting parties in an attempt to capture any wounded, sick or stragglers from the French column:

I have this Evening sent out towards Fort DuQuesne four partys of 2 officers and 25 men each. One to go down the Kiskiminitas and reconnoitre about the advanced post, one to go between that and the Road the French Army marched to this place, another to go along the French road and then to go between the French road and the Youghagany examining Braddocks Road. I likewise send a Sergeant and 6 men to Fort DuQuesne with orders to cross the Monongahela and get upon the hill opposite the Fort in order to view their battoes and to endeavour if possible to bring me a Prisoner promising the former Reward of 20 Guineas.[94]

Forbes, Bouquet and Burd were all disappointed in their hopes to obtain a prisoner, for none was taken until a skirmish at Loyalhanna in early November.

Forbes was never completely satisfied with the quality of information that these scouts obtained for him regarding the status of the French garrison at Duquesne, and barely any of the intelligence questions that he asked were answered. From their surviving reports, few of these parties appear to have accomplished much, and they seem to have been hesitant to engage with the French, unlike the famous and more combative Major Robert Rogers and his Rangers of Lake George and Lake Champlain renown. However, it should be noted that Forbes's scouting parties had a considerably greater distance to traverse than the mere 35 miles between Fort William Henry on Lake George and Fort Carillon on Lake Champlain. Forbes's scouts had to cross an entire series of formidable mountain ridges, whilst Rogers' Rangers could utilize water routes for much of the distance they wished to travel. Furthermore, Rogers Rangers could pick and choose between two French targets—Carillon and Fort St. Frederick at Crown Point. The French at Fort Duquesne occupied only a single point, and it was considerably easier for them to maintain local security at this solitary location. Interestingly enough, the number of expeditions that Forbes and Bouquet dispatched were greater than the number of scouts that the renowned Rogers Rangers launched in a similar timeframe.

With the assistance of these numerous parties, Forbes was able to slowly but surely gain a picture of conditions at Fort Duquesne, and unlike Braddock three summers earlier, he was wresting the initiative from the French by sending his own raiding parties regularly forward against their fort. These efforts also kept the Cherokees and Catawbas remaining with Forbes gainfully, and apparently quite happily, engaged. At the same time, at least some of his soldiers were gaining valuable experience in wilderness procedures and actions. Forbes would note in early September, "My Highlanders here are vastly mended and ten times more steady and Cautious, by the Chacing of Indians these 10 days, and lying out at nights."[95] By the use of these small parties, although their accomplishments appear to have been distinctly limited, Forbes had seized the momentum from the French, aggressively patrolled to control the ground in front of his army, and obtained as much information as possible regarding the French opposition. Overall, these numerous small scouting parties made no appreciable impact upon the campaign, but their very presence indicated that that the tide was clearly turning in favor of Forbes.

Other events were also in progress that would combine with all of the great efforts of Forbes and Bouquet and their soldiers to convert this tide of success into an irresistible force. On August 27, 1758, one of these events occurred far to the northeast of Fort Duquesne, that would have a great effect upon Forbes's campaign. On this date, British Lieutenant Colonel John Bradstreet captured the French Fort Frontenac, on the Catarqui River and Lake Ontario.[96] Bradstreet was an experienced British officer whose colonial birth and heritage had inhibited his promotion. An extremely ambitious officer, Bradstreet had proven particularly adept at managing bateaux and bateauxmen, and at unraveling the normally convoluted logistics of a frontier campaign. There is some evidence that Forbes had attempted to obtain the services of Bradstreet as his quartermaster general rather than St. Clair, but the latter officer's previous service with the Braddock Campaign had decided the issue in his favor. Bradstreet would soon prove that Forbes had not misjudged his man, as he would still provide an invaluable service to Forbes.

After Abercromby's movement upon French Fort Carillon at Ticonderoga had ended in disaster in July, Bradstreet requested permission from Abercromby to launch a raid on Fort Frontenac. Abercromby, desperate to regain his reputation with a succesful operation under almost any circumstances, approved Bradstreet's request, and provided him with a powerful task force consisting of several thousand soldiers and a small train of artillery, predominantly provincials with a few Royal Artillerymen and some Iroquois warriors. Bradstreet used bateaux to proceed up the Mohawk River, crossed Oneida Lake, continued on the Onondaga River to Lake Ontario, rowed furiously along the shores of Lake Ontario to Sackets Harbor, continued their rapid advance up the lake, and landed at Fort Frontenac on August 26. Fort Frontenac was a critical link on the French supply chain between their bases of Montreal and Quebec, and the French positions further west including Fort Duquesne. Frontenac was also the harbor for the French Lake Ontario fleet.

However, Frontenac was a weak link indeed. The French were apparently counting upon its isolation and separation from the English, it was garrisoned by only 110 soldiers commanded by a 63-year-old officer. It was constructed of stone, but its walls were only thick enough to resist musket fire, and not artillery. Bradsteet pushed forward an aggressive advance, mounted artillery batteries close to Fort Frontenac, and with these guns soon blasted impressive holes through the thin stone walls. Desperately outnumbered, under heavy fire, their defenses breached, and with no real hope of succor from other French forces that were too far away to intervene, the desperately outnumbered French defenders surrendered the next day.

Bradstreet had inflicted a blow of staggering proportions upon the French logistics west of Fort La Presentation. He destroyed the entire French Lake Ontario fleet of nine sloops. He destroyed or carried away every single piece of French trade goods, presents for the Natives, provisions, and ammunition at the post, estimated at a value of 2,000,000 French livres. He captured and demolished nearly sixty pieces of artillery that had been stored at the fort. Pouchot would state that as a result of this operation, "goods & provisions continued in short supply. The loss of Frontenac increased all this disarray, and that caused the loss of Fort du Quesne, which had cost so many millions."[97] In a single raid, Bradstreet had decimated the ability of the French military to adequately supply their western garrisons, Fort Duquesne among them.

• SEVEN •

"My heart is broke"
Grant's Defeat

Even with all of this significant progress, Forbes's army and its commanders were becoming impatient to strike a blow directly against Fort Duquesne. As early as July 16, Washington and Bouquet had corresponded regarding "making an Irruption into the Enemys Country with a strong Party," intimating that Bouquet had long contemplated such a maneuver. Washington, highly experienced with fighting the Indians on their own terms, had recommended against such a project.[1] Other officers pressed Bouquet and Forbes with the same idea. Major James Grant had without success discussed a similar operation with Forbes while he was at Carlisle, "soliciting to command a party, which I [Forbes] would not agree to."[2] Major George Armstrong of the 1st Pennsylvania Battalion had written to Forbes on July 12 to propose:

> I had the hint from yourself a few days ago with regard of obtaining intelligence from Fort Duquesne. I wou'd think my self highly Honoured in the Command of one hundred men for that purpose, to be chosen out of the first and second Battalions of the Pennsylvania Regiment, or from any choir [corps] the General wou'd think fit for that service. Perhaps the General wou'd think a less party might answer as good an end, but upon our aproach to Fort Duquesne it might be expedient to make Small Detachments as reason at that time and place wou'd require, and if it did not at that time appear necessary to make such distributions, perhaps one hundred men would not be too large a party in case we should chance to fall in with the Enemy upon their way to distress the Inhabitants of this Province. If the General wou'd please to show his approbation, the execution of the scheme is at any moment to be endeavoured.[3]

Bouquet recalled that he had "a project about which I had spoken several times with Major Grant at Raystown which was to attack during the night the Indians camping in huts around the fort." Such maneuvers were not unknown in the middle of the 18th century; the use of raiding parties of various sizes to launch "surprises" upon an enemy post was a well understood and regularly conducted military stratagem. In fact, entire books had been written upon the subject, such as the French work *The Partisan*, that were readily available and widely read by experienced European officers such as Forbes, Bouquet and Grant.[4]

Forbes had held discussions with Bouquet that suggested his interest in just such an endeavour. Forbes had written on August 15, "I have never seen any Good yet come from those small scouting parties or any Good Intelligence receiv'd from the Indians, am therefore still of opinion that a strong party such as I proposed ... capable of supporting and bringing itself off, and when nigh the Enemy sending small partys for Intelligence, might be of considerable Service by always taking care of having a proper retreat."[5] However, Forbes had also issued a clear caution to Bouquet on August 2: "I would not be understood that as things are circumstanced, wee ought to Run the risque of meeting with a severe repulse, by any precipitate march of Coming immediately to blows with the Ennemy."[6]

Grant had arrived at the camp at Loyalhanna previous to September 5. Bouquet told Forbes that he had arrived at Loyalhanna on September 7.[7] Shortly after Bouquet's arrival, two Pennsylvanian provincials and a Highlander who had left the camp without permission to hunt were attacked by four Indians, and two Virginian provincials who had embarked upon a similar errand were assailed by nine Indians. Sergeant Lindenmuth, in the encampment with Burd's battalion of Pennsylvania Provincials, recorded: "25 Indians and Frenchmen came and attacked the Oxen guard. They killed a Highlander, and took George Mayer prisoner and stole three or four horses from us and returned home, namely to Ohio. In the meantime several skirmishes had occurred between us and the French and Indians."[8] Particularly disconcerting was that the surviving Provincials had thrown away their arms in order to flee more expeditiously. Bouquet was apparently concerned that "he was surrounded by Indian parties." He immediately ordered out two parties of about one hundred men each to secure the approaches to the camp.[9]

As these parties were being prepared, Major Grant approached Bouquet with a scheme to take "a large party to go straight to the source." Bouquet recalled:

> ...that he was surprised that I should take such a measure, after so many repeated proofs that these small parties never accomplished anything, and served only to make us lose men and discourage our people; but if I was willing to give him 500 men, he would go to the fort; reconnoiter the roads and the forces of the enemy, which — according to all our intelligence — did not exceed 600 men, including Frenchmen and Indians. This was confirmed by a party returning the previous day. Whatever detachments they were able to send out, they could not send more men than he would have; and by setting an ambush on their retreat he would be able to take some prisoners. I raised some difficulties about letting him go, but as he insisted and I was impressed by his reasons and the circumstances in which we were placed, I consented to it....[10]

It is astonishing that Bouquet approved Grant's concept. His reasons for authorizing such an ambitious and audacious movement upon Fort Duquesne, clearly in contravention to Forbes's meticulous, disciplined approach, do not seem adequate to support such an undertaking. Bouquet later defended his authorization of "Major Grant's proposal which could procure trustworthy intelligences for us, and some advantage over the Indians who were insulting us with impunity every day; and that this would be the means of curing our men of the panic terror they had of them, for those who had escaped that day had thrown away their arms in order to flee more quickly." Bouquet was obviously aggravated by the success of the Indian attacks, and determined to do something effective regarding the Indian threat; and Grant proved to be a smooth and effective salesman who, like all successful marketers, presented precisely the right plan at exactly the right time. Bouquet justified his decision, "The step was absolutely necessary, and it will be a good lesson for the troops."[11]

Certainly both Bouquet and Grant were well aware of the presence of a high hill "within the Forks" from which a commanding view of the French fort could be obtained. A Cherokee raiding party dispatched in early July had gained this position, and provided Captain Bosomworth with a detailed account of their successful scout:

> The Yellow Birds party consisting of fourteen Cherokee Indians and two white men went from this camp on the 6th July and proceeded within ten miles of the french Fort where /the head man being sick/ they left the two white men and the rest of the party except five who marched to a small hill within the forks of the rivers and where they had a full view of the fort, they discovered no Indians but saw a number of Frenchmen employed in cutting fascines and throwing up dirt which I suppose was for intrenchments, there was some new works near the fort which I apprehend to be rav-

elins the ground is cleared for a considerable distance around the fort and the bottom or savanah is planted with corn, they heared a drum beat and guns fired some distance down the river on the other side. After they had finished their observations they waylaid a narrow path about 400 yards from the fort leading to the cornfield where soon after a party of six French men came along on whom they fired, killed & scalp'd the first and wounded two others supposed mortally as they staggered much after they shot & got into a small swamp where they did not choose to follow for fear of being surrounded. One of this party went down to the River side to drink where they saw three French Officers in a cannoe diverting themselves, who had liked to have come within gun shot. Another Indian arrived here from a different party who had been viewing the fort and confirms the above account exactly with this additional circumspection of seeing 16 Indian warriors & two women come in a cannoe with small packs on their back from an island in the main River.[12]

Bouquet hoped to obtain detailed information on Fort Duquesne from this elevation, for he sent Chief Engineer Ensign Rhor along to perform a reconnaissance of the fort.

Bouquet's instructions to Grant, as he later relayed them to Forbes, were:

• The Major would march with 300 Highlanders, 100 Royal Americans, 150 Virginians, 100 Marylanders, 100 Pennsylvanians and all the Indians in the direction of the fort, regulating his marches so as to be five miles from the fort at the beginning of night, with the precautions necessary to prevent a surprise; and from there he would send Indians and those of our officers who knew the environs of the place to reconnoiter;
• If he found from the enemy's dispositions that he had not been discovered, he would advance upon the height half a mile from the fort, where he himself would reonnoiter the fires of the Indians;
• In case he saw them around their fires, he would send part of his detachment with white shirts over their uniforms to go and attack them a little after midnight, with bayonets fixed in their rifles, not firing a shot except in extremity—for it was not difficult to surprise them as they never posted sentinels;
• When this stroke had been made or lost, he would have a retreat beaten from the height where he himself was to stay with the rest of the troops and the Indians; and as soon as his men, directed by the sound, should have joined him, he was immediately to retreat six miles from the fort before daybreak, and set up an ambush there with all his men and Indians, in case the enemy followed him;
• If he defeated them in the ambush, he could return in complete safety to the fort to have a plan of it made and reconnoiter the vicinity;
• But if through his spies or himself he considered that he had been discovered, he should think only of retreating.[13]

These are extremely restrictive orders, and are clear evidence that Bouquet wanted Grant to maintain positive control over the operation at all times, and that he was not to actually assault the fort or endanger his command.

Bouquet was so concerned that Grant fully comprehended these orders that he ensured that Colonel Burd was present as a witness when Grant was issued with them, doubtless to ensure that there was no ambiguity. Later in September, Bouquet specifically asked Burd to document these instructions. The colonel responded on September 16 from the "Camp at Loyal Hannon." His response is provided in full, as verification that Bouquet accurately reported these instructions to Forbes:

Last Night you asked me if I remembered your Instructions given to Major Grant as I was privy to them, and I have thought proper to deliver you the same in writing, Verbatim, which was as follows, Vizt.

You ordered the Major to march from hence towards Fort DuQuesne, his Party to consist I think, Seven Hundred & Fifty men, Officers Exclusive & fifty Indians; Lieut. Col. Dagworthy to march at the Same Time with two Hundred Men Ten Miles & there immediately to make a Breast Work[.] The Major to march his Detachment in seven Columns a Breast, keeping always Small Parties of the best Woodsmen before to bring Intelligence of any Approaches of the Enemy, to endeavour all in his Power to march undiscovered in Case He should be able to effect this[,] of which He could be pretty well ascertained by sending Parties in the Night, under skillfull Officers, Such as Mesrs. Baker & Shaw, Allen and Riley of the Virginia Regt particularly recommended for this Purpose, being all Good Woodsmen & having reconnoitred the Fort but a little Time before to observe if the Indians & Soldiers lay out of the Fort and made Fires as usual[.] If they did not, he might be sure He was discovered & consequently his Scheme must be at an End[.] But if they did He then was directed to march nigh to the Fort in the Night to the Top of the Hill a little on this Side the Fort, from whence He could discover the Indian Fires on the Outside of the Works & the Tents— He was to lay on the Hill, keeping a perfect Silence in his Party untill Midnight when the Enemy would be all asleep, he was to order a sufficient Party from his Detachment to creep silently up to each fire[.] That they were ordered The Soldiers all having clean white Shirts [word missing] their Clothes to distinguish one another [word missing] himself, with a Corps De Reserve and a [word missing] to remain on Top of the Hill, All at [word missing] Parties to surround the Fires and Tents & with Hand to cut off all the Enemy[.] No firing allowed except at the Ambrosures [embrasures] in Case the Cannon were fired & that only a few Rounds & just before the Retreat[.] As soon as Major Grant judged the Business done He was to beat a Retreat, the Troops previously particularly instructed to retreat instantly to the reserves left with the Major on the Top of the Hill. As Soon as the Troops were assembled the Major to retreat with his whole Detachment 6 Miles, there to form an Ambuscade, having Some Scouts on the Top of the Hill to watch the Motions of the Enemy in the Morning when they appeared & if they perceived them to pursue the detachment The Scouts to retreat precipitously & inform the Major[.] But in Case the Enemy did not pursue the Major to march his Detachment to Loyal Hannon.

This is a true State of Col. Bouquet's orders to Major Grant as near as I can recollect.[14]

Even with such constraining orders, this remained a "somewhat hazardous task," as Bouquet described it to Forbes.[15] Still, the plan did hold promise, for although relatively rare in the 18th century, night attacks were not unheard of, and promised considerable benefits, particularly against relatively undisciplined Indians. M. La Cointe of the French Royal Academy discussed this tactic:

Night attacks are almost always successful, and the reason is pretty evident. The assailants are informed of the position and the strength of the enemy; the latter are ignorant both of the numbers and of the maneuvers that are to be employed against them; the one knows where to strike, and is sure of his blow; the other hardly knows what part he is to defend: in these circumstances whole battalions have been beat and routed by moderate detachments.... These kind of enterprizes have always been looked upon as very bold and even rash, to dare to attack a body of six or seven hundred men, with a detachment of two or three hundred, yet it is not to be doubted but a true partisan, who is well acquainted with the country ... may easily form his attack in the dead of the night....[16]

It should be recalled that twenty years later, during the War for American Independence, the British would launch a devastating night assault at Paoli, Pennsylvania, during the Philadelphia Campaign of 1777; and American forces would launch similarly successful night attacks at Stony Point and Paulus Hook in 1779. Yet Bouquet and Grant's approach violated the procedures for such an effort as laid out by La Cointe, who strenuously recommended a complete reconnaissance by a small party before any such endeavor was initiated, for success was predicated upon being "well acquainted with the country," which Grant clearly was not.[17]

As finally formed, Grant's party consisted of:

- 60th Foot, Royal Americans— Detachment consisting of 6 Officers and 108 other ranks, including Ensign Rhor serving as Chief Engineer;
- 77th Foot, Montgomery's Highlanders— Detachment commanded by Major James Grant consisting of 16 Officers and 373 other ranks;
- 1st Virginia Regiment — Detachment commanded by Major Andrew Lewis, 8 Officers and 167 other ranks;
- North Carolina Battalion — Small detachment of 13 other ranks;

- "Royal" Battalion of Maryland — Small detachment of 4 officers and 77 other ranks;
- Lower County Battalion — Small detachment of 14 other ranks; and
- 2nd Battalion, Pennsylvania Provincials — Detachment of 4 officers and 108 other ranks.

Thus this total force consisted of 38 Officers and 860 other ranks.[18] It cannot be positively determined how carefully this force was selected. La Cointe recommended: "The choice of men who are to march to the attack of a post is a thing so essential, that the success of the enterprize depends upon it. Therefore none should be chosen but willing and bold soldiers, and who are not rash or heedless."[19] The fact that this force contained small detachments from various units suggests that soldiers were specifically selected, or volunteered, for the assignment. Large numbers of men were from the 1st Virginia including Major Lewis and Captain Thomas Bullitt, highly experienced soldiers whose frontier service dated to 1754; and the "Royal" Battalion of Maryland who had also spent considerable time in service battling Indian raiders. Typical of the Virginia Provincials was Ensign Thomas Gist, son of renowned scout Christopher Gist, who had grown up on the frontier among the Indians. The detachment was more than suitable for the work at hand, with one critical exception. That exception would prove devastating to the force's fortunes, for it was the officer in command, Major Grant, who would prove to be both "rash and heedless."

The destination and intention of the expedition was carefully safeguarded. Chaplain Barton would record in his diary, "Major Grant with 750 men consisting of Highlanders, Royal Americans & Virginians was gone upon a Secret Expedition towards the Ohio."[20] Bouquet would tell Forbes, "Nobody knows where he is going."[21] The secret was surprisingly well kept, for when Ensign Gist marched with this detachment, he would recall, "[W]e all paraded, with difrent opinions concerning our adventure. Some was of opinion that we was destined for some Indian town, other that we was to go to Bradocks road and perhaps to make some discoveries if posable."[22] When the inevitable and highly efficient army rumor mill has failed to obtain the details of the mission, then security has been well maintained indeed!

The command departed the camp at Loyalhanna on September 9, and proceeded to an advanced post called "Grant's Paradise" located about ten miles to the west. Along the way Grant exercised the men in "the art of bush fighting." Once at Grant's Paradise they "worked very hard all day making a breastwork of logs." Provisions, including live bullocks, were moved forward for the forced march, and Bouquet inspected the detachment on September 10 and "spent the night there." The fact that Bouquet spent the night with Grant suggests that he was nervous regarding the expedition, and he may have spent the additional time reviewing his instructions with Grant. Bouquet must have been reassured, for he saw Grant "leave on the 11th with his detachment in the best order." Additionally, the effort spent constructing the entrenchments was also time well spent, for Bouquet noted, "As this post was very nearly in condition for defense, I returned to the camp."[23]

In his personal papers, Grant retained a badly worn copy of his Orderly Book from this expedition, which describes in great detail his exhaustive efforts to maintain the integrity and secrecy of his approach march.[24]

[September 10, 1758 — the cover and the first page or pages are missing] The columns are to be equally divided amongst the officers appointed to command them, each officer is to march & encamp with the Platoon which is alloted to him that the men may know exactly under whose immediate orders they are, a Sergeant and Corporal is to be appointed to each Platoon and they are to continue constantly with their platoons in the same manner as the Officers are directed to do, when any Officer of a column is sent upon any duty he is at all times to carry his own Platoon with him and when a Captain commanding a column is sent he is to carry his own Platoon and the Platoons of the Officers he takes with him[,] and the Platoons to be numbered in the same manner as the Columns are from one to four and five according to the number of Officers, so that the men may immediately know when they are wanted by an officer going with head of a Column and calling No. 1, 2, 3, 4 of the 1st, 2nd, 3rd or 4th Column and so on.

The Officers are carefully to inspect into the state of the Arms & Ammunition of the men of their respective platoons exactly at daybreak so that every morning for the [last line of page totally illegible and mostly missing] future to expect that every officer & man of the Detachment are to be under Arms exactly at that time & if any Column is found dilatory it will be considered as a neglect of duty in the Officer appointed to the Command of that Column.

Ensign Gist recorded how Grant's instructions were implemented: "At night the Virginians were drawn up and devided into plattoons, by which we were to march and do other duties, and every officer to lay with his party. We likewise received orders to hold our selves in readiness to march at a minutes warning."[25]

Sept. 11th   The Parole Louisburg

The men to lie upon their Arms ready to form at a moment's warning. If an alarm should happen the Columns are immediately to stand to their Arms but not a man is to be allowed to move out of his Rank upon any Account and the Column are to remain upon the ground they encamped upon till they receive orders. Each column is to mount a Sergeant and 12 men to their front and they are to place two advanced centries [sentries] as appropriate to their lines & one upon each flank.

None of the Centries are to challenge but they are to continue silent & alert upon their posts.

September 12th   Parole Marlborough

The troops are immediately to receive two days flour, the four bullocks which are to be killed are to be equally divided amongst the troops. One fire is allowed to each Column & no more upon any accounts. The men are to make the two days bread and to dress the two days beef as they will have no fire tomorrow.

The troops are to lie upon their arms and to observe the orders of yesterday. The fires will be ordered to be put out this night. No cutting with hatchets and no noise of any kind in camp. The officers are desired to recommend this in the strongest terms to the men. The fires at the different grounds to be put out the moment it [last line of page totally illegible and mostly missing]

The 1st & 7th Columns to march immediately without horses or baggage under the command of Major Lewis. Each of these columns is to leave a Corporal & 6 men to bring up the Officers Horses & Bat. Horses when the rest of the troops march to join them.

Ensign Gist reported for this day: "Marched early this morning and arrived at a high hill ten miles from the Fort Duquesne about 2 oclock in the afternoon, where we received orders to kill our bullocks and have our provisions drest against the next morning."[26]

Grant would subsequently write to Forbes: "We were lucky enough not to be discovered in our March.... We got to an Advantageous Post the 12th about 3 in the afternoon which According to the information of all our Guides from Ten to Twelve Miles from the French Fort ... but I afterwards found that Our Guides were much mistaken about the distance for as near as I can judge the camp is about Sixteen Miles from the top of the Hill where we was to take Post."[27] However, there is a discrepancy between Grant's reporting of distances, and the fact that he sent out Ensign Allen of the 1st Virginia Regiment with ten men "to go near the fort and make what discoveries he could. He did not return till very late in the night and brought word that he had seen a number of fires on both sides the river."[28] Allen had previously performed other scouts to Fort Duquesne, and should have been familiar with distances and the amount of time necessary to cover the ground. Either Allen did not provide accurate information to Grant, Grant discounted the report that he provided, or Grant chose to ignore it and proceed anyway.

Sept. 13th Within Five Miles of Ft DuQuesne   Parole Forbes

The troops are immediately to put on a White Shirt without noise over their clothes which are to be loose about them, a knot put into their pouches [this means the tails of the shirt] that each man may take hold of the others shirt and direct the march accordingly — by this distinction no mistake can happen in the dark as every man in a white shirt is considered as a friend. To prevent noise every man is to leave his canteen and camp kettles is likewise to be left, they are to be put together by columns & each column is to leave a Lance Corporal with 3 men to take care of them, who are to be under the Command of Captain Bullock all those things are to be left at the Old Town. The Columns are to leave them as they come up without noise an Officer will be left to show them the place[.] All the officers horses, Bat & Pack Horses are to be left there. Captain Bullock to have the Command of the whole and to relieve the Maryland Column who are to fall into the rear of the Highlanders when we march from this ground. Captain Bullock's Column is to fall into the rear at the Baggage.

An officer of the Pennsylvania Column is to join Capt. Bullocks Column and is to be posted with the Detachment of that Column who have already joined that Column [i.e. he is to join Bullock's Column with the baggage].

Lt. Baker of the Virginians at the end of the thicket near the Fort, he is to march from this Ground betwixt the Americans and the Advanced Guard where Mr. Rhor will shew him his post.

The Officers Commanding Columns to wait of Major Grant as soon as they have received those Orders in the rear of the American Column in order to receive directions from him for their Conduct during this night [End of Orderly Book].

Thus, the momentous events of the night of September 13 and morning of September 14 began.[29]

At daybreak on September 13, Grant dispatched Major Lewis with two hundred men and the Indians, with "orders to post them in Ambuscade about five Miles from the Fort, which was all the Precaution I could take to prevent our being discovered in the [French] camp." Ensign Gist recalled, "This morning Major Lewis with about three hundred men marched very early [and] formed an ambuscade within five miles of the fort." There was nothing in Grant's instructions from Bouquet regarding forming a large ambush with a considerable portion of his force, so far in advance of his main body that the two detachments could not mutually support each other. Grant had not even reached Fort Duquesne, and he had already violated his orders.

The remainder of Grant's command spent most of September 13 resting in their transient camp, while Lewis's party performed its advanced ambuscade without enemy contact. Grant claimed, and Gist confirmed, that Ensign Chew of the Virginians was sent forward on a scouting expedition with "three Indians" which went astray. Grant moved forward about 3:00 P.M., each man carrying a white shirt as per the orders contained in Grant's Orderly Book, which would be used for purposes of visibility and recognition in the night. Knots were tied into the tails of the shirt, so soldiers could hold onto each other in the darkness. The wearing of white shirts over uniforms during night attacks was a standard tactic of the time, and the practice was formally called "camisades." In time, the attack itself became formally known as a camisade: "An attack by surprise, at night, or at break of day, when the enemy is supposed to be in bed. This word is said to have taken its rise from an attack of this kind, in which the soldiers, as a badge to distinguish each other by, bore a shirt over their arms."

Grant found Lewis about four miles from his main camp, "...which post I was assured was not seven Miles from the Fort, Tho' I found it was above twelve." The failure to send out adequate scouting parties before the expedition ever left Loyalhanna was becoming more apparent. Grant either had an inadequate understanding of the true distances involved, or else he did not comprehend the amount of time it would take a large party of men to cross wooded, unscouted terrain in the face of the enemy. Grant's failure to adequately interpret times and distances was to seriously and adversely effect the expedition before a single French or Indian was ever encountered. Unfortunately, the few surviving accounts of his march are inadequate to attempt to accurately interpret the true distances involved.

Once Grant reached Lewis, he was involved "giving orders to the Troops & Particular Instructions to the Captains." These are doubtless the Orderly Book orders published above. Here, each man donned his white shirt, the tails carefully knotted, over his uniform. Superfluous equipment was left behind in the care of Captain Bullitt, who remained with a detachment of about fifty men to safeguard the baggage.

Grant's column moved forward about 6:00 P.M. Even with his foolish detachment of Lewis, which fortunately had not gone astray, Grant had accomplished the first and second portions of his mission. He had successfully regulated his march to be within about five miles of the fort at the beginning of the night, and as he not been discovered he was now going to advance to the hill "half a mile" above the fort. During their approach march Lieutenant Chew, who had apparently become lost when his Indian scouts deserted him, revealed himself and rejoined the column about three miles from the fort. He "informed us that there was a number of Indians encamped about it." This confirmed intelligence obtained by Allen on the day before: "He ... imajined there was a great number of Indians and heard and saw them singing and dancing very merily."

Grant had intended to reach the top of the hill above Fort Duquesne "about 11 at Night" but "as the distance was so much greater than I imagined" his force did not gain this position until "after Two in the morning" according to Grant's watch. It was a challenging march, as remembered by Ensign Gist:

> The light of the sun being now gone we marched by the light of the moon, and was not the most agreeable sight that I ever saw[,] for the road being very crooked gave us in the rear an opportunity of seeing the glistening of the firelocks against the moon, and the white shirts appearing to dodge every way in a movement which made some of the soldiers observe that we look'd more like ghosts than soldiers.

Once Grant reached this vantage point he must have been discouraged not to see any fires, particularly since Ensign Allen had observed such fires just the day before. Grant surmised that "those Fires either had not been made, or were burnt out before we got to the Ground." Bouquet's orders were peremptory. Grant was to "advance upon the height half a mile from the fort, where he himself would reconnoiter the fires of the Indians; In case he saw them around their fires, he would send part of his detachment with white shirts over their uniforms to go and attack them." Grant's letter to Forbes is clear: he saw no fires, yet he proceeded to launch the attack anyway. Grant stated his rationale:

> ...as we had been misinformed by the Guides with regard to the distance & by that means had got there much later than we expected, it was impossible to make the projected disposition of a party of Men for the attack of each Fire, but that it was impossible to continue another Day without being discovered & that as the Night was far advanced there was no time to be lost. I therefore ordered him [Major Lewis] to march directly with 100 Americans 200 Highlanders & 100 Virginians & to Attack every thing that was found about the Fort.... Were not to fire a Shot, 'till they were close to the Enemy—& that after they discharged their pieces they were to Use their Bayonets without Loading a Second Time. I told the major that I would order all our Drums & Pipes to beat the retreat, when it was time for the Troops to retire, that I was indifferent what Order they came back in, for that it was the same thing to me if there was not three of them together, provided they did the Business they were sent upon. The Major had not half a Mile to march into the open plain where the Fort stands, the 400 Men under His Command had a white Shirt over His Cloaths, to prevent Mistakes & that they might even at a distance distinguish One another.

Again, Grant was in violation of his orders from Bouquet that the attack was to be launched "with bayonets fixed in their rifles, not firing a shot except in extremity," or unless cannon were fired upon them during their retreat.

Grant's decision to attack would prove to be disastrous. The fires would have provided Grant's soldiers with an easy bearing, but without the flames serving as points for their advance to guide upon they soon became disoriented. Ensign Gist reported:

> A party being ordered down towards the fort, the Royal Americans taking the front with Major Lewis at their head, the Virginians the rear, and the Highlanders, Marylanders and Pennsylvanians in the center, we marched down the hill, each holding his leaders shirt tail, and keeped the most profound silence. We had not gone far when there was a halt and soon after the Highlanders or Royal Americans began to cock their pieces and immediately after came back with such violence that we was obliged to give them the road and they keeped it till they joined Major Grant on the top of the hill from whence they came. A very thick fog arising prevented us from seeing the fort or anything about it.

The confusion that Ensign Gist observed was also described by Lieutenant Archibald Robertson, with the Highlanders in the rear:

> Major Lewis of the Virginians was ordered off with the Royal American Column, Captain Hugh McKenzie's Column, Captain McDonald's (I belonged to McDonald's Column) Column, and a column of Virginians— Major Lewis' orders was to attack briskly all around the Cabbins, Tents, and houses without the fort: When this business was going on our Pipes and Drums on the hill were to play (in order to let us know where our main body lay). When we got down to the bottom, about a musket short from the fort, we heard rustling in the woods above us: we all fronted the hill, the men cocked their pieces, as they observed people in the woods who they imagined were the enemy. The officers made them [hold] their fire; them in the woods in a little while called out friends ... proving to be the Royal Americans and 2 or 3 other platoons that had lost their way.[30]

It was not darkness but dense fog that had caused Major Lewis and his detachment so many problems. The full moon was on September 17, only four days away, and Gist mentioned marching by moonlight on the way to Grant's hill. However, Gist, Lieutenant Robinson with the Highlanders, and Grant all mentioned fog, which is typical of the low-lying ground in the triangle between three large rivers surrounded by towering hills, and can become extremely heavy at times. During a scout early in August to Fort Duquesne, Captain Patterson had noted that upon arriving at the same hill that Grant now occupied, "the Fogg was so thick that I cou'd not see fourty yards from me."[31]

Traversing unscouted ground in this heavy fog, without fires to guide their advance, the advancing columns became entirely disordered. The security of the French and Indians remained abysmal, for the raiding party still had not been discovered, even with four hundred men blundering about the woods, challenging each other, and cocking their muskets, an action which makes a very distinctive and clear sound at night. Most likely, the dense mists served to mask their noise.

In the fog and unfamiliar ground, Lewis's attack disintegrated. Lewis decided to bring his men back to Grant where he had remained on the hill with the main body. In this portion of the night's events alone Grant complied with Bouquet's orders regarding "the height where he [Grant] himself was to stay with the rest of the troops." Lewis informed Grant:

> ...That it was impossible to do anything, that the Night was dark, that the Road was bad, worse than anything I had ever seen, that there were Logs of wood across it, that their were fences to pass that the troops had fallen into Confusion & that it was a mercy they had not fired upon one another, that they had made so much noise he was sure they must be discovered & that it was impossible for the Men to find their way back thro' those Woods.

Here the absence of an adequate reconnaissance manifested itself again, for nearly six weeks previously Captain Patterson had noted that upon descending Grant's Hill, he "went along the Road towards the Fort where I found great Quantitys of fallen Trees, laid across the Bottom."[32] Somehow, this information had not been transmitted to Grant or his leaders, and apparently Grant's own scouts had similarly failed to take note of these obstacles.

Lewis's soldiers returned "in the greatest confusion I ever saw Men in." For some reason Grant seemed surprised at this, even though he had instructed Lewis to return in just such an order. Lewis and Grant's conversation became quite heated, and Grant stated that he intended to arrest Lewis upon their return to camp. Without question, the problems of operating in a dense fog were overwhelming to Lewis, but not so to Grant on top of the hill, presumably above the obscuring mists.

Bouquet's orders at this point remained valid and clear: "When this stroke had been made or lost, he [Grant] would have a retreat beaten from the height where he himself was to stay with the rest of the troops and the Indians; and as soon as his men, directed by the sound, should have joined him, he was immediately to retreat six miles from the fort before daybreak, and set up an ambush there with all his men and Indians, in case the enemy followed him." Thus, as Bouquet would subsequently tell Forbes, "The major ... had but to retreat, but he unfortunately got the notion that the garrison was too weak to dare risk a sortie, and consequently he remained on the height until daybreak." An anonymous letter in the *Pennsylvania Gazette* stated, "Major Grant had some reason to believe there were not above 200 men in the Fort, including Indians."[33] Grant apparently thought that the garrison was that weak based upon their lack of response to his night attack. Yet both Ensigns Allen and Chew had reported large numbers of Indians at the fort during their recent scouts. Grant apparently chose not to listen to mere provincials, or conveniently decided that they had been mistaken. Of greater import, Grant also chose not to adhere to his commanding officer's orders. Had Grant at this point reformed his command — which Lewis had clearly been able to do without needing any pipes or drums played to rally upon — and retreated, the expedition would have accomplished little, but his command could have returned to Loyalhanna intact and safe.

Yet Grant was determined to gain glory, and to linger and accomplish more than Bouquet's orders authorized. Grant sent "Lieutenant Robinson [Robertson] & McDonald w/50 Men to make an Attack.... I desired them to kill a Dozen of Indians if possible & I would be satisfied. They went directly to the place they were ordered & finding none of the Indians they set fire to the House, but it was daylight before they could return." Most likely, McDonald and Robinson launched their raid on the "hornwork" extending to the northeast of the main fort that had been constructed by the French that year to extend the size of the fortification, as it was closest to Grant's position on the hill.[34] Robinson reported, "[I]t was now very dark as the moon was down." They reached the exterior of the hornwork, entered two cabins filled with bales of goods, "heard the French Centinels talking to one another," and then set one of the cabins on fire and retreated. Lieutenant Alexander McDonald of Grant's Highlanders described his role in this incendiary incident:

> Was very Severely wounded at the affair of Major Grant now General Grant at Fort Du Quesne in the year 1758, that I ever did Execute the most Daring piece of Duty that ever an Officer was sent upon by Order of the same General Grant to Attack a log house within a pistol Shott of the Walls of Fort Duquesne[,] the Night before the Action Major Grant being informed that said house was full of Indians & Canadians. My orders were to save One or two white persons [i.e., to take one or two French prisoners] & to put all the rest to the Bayonet, that upon coming to the house I found it empty Contrary to expectation and tho' I was so near that I heard the French Centinels talking

to one another I waited till I Struck up a Fire [i.e., he used his flint and steel to start a fire] & set the house in Flame to Convince Major Grant that I had done my Duty.[35]

Most other British participants mention this log cabin's being burned.[36] The anonymous letter in the *Pennsylvania Gazette* recorded, "Major Grant sent two officers and fifty men to the fort, to attack all the Indians, &c they should find lying out of the Fort; they saw none, nor were they challenged by the sentries. As they returned, they set fire to a large store house, which was put out as soon as they left it." [37] Surprisingly, the French still did not react. Most likely, fires in wooden buildings with split wood shingles or simple bark roofs were not all that uncommon at Fort Duquesne, and the fire was put out without arousing the entire garrison or causing undue concern on the part of the French.

Having gathered Lewis's command, Grant ordered him to return to the baggage and Captain Bullitt's detachment in accordance with Bouquet's original instructions to "immediately to retreat six miles from the fort before daybreak, and set up an ambush there with all his men and Indians, in case the enemy followed him." That Major Lewis was able to reorganize his command in the predawn darkness and rapidly move them back to Bullitt's baggage suggests that Lewis's men were not nearly as disorganized as Grant later claimed. Ensign Gist remembered: "About sunrise Major Lewis was ordered from the top of the hill to the baggage where he placed his men on the most advantageous post in order to wait for Major Grant."

By now it was "about 7 in the Morning after the fog was gone & the day cleared up." Grant should have withdrawn his forces and joined Lewis's ambush, as his orders dictated. Instead, he finally and inexorably violated Bouquet's instructions. Grant dispatched Ensign Rhor, guarded by Captain McDonald and a hundred Highlanders, to move forward to prepare a plan of the fort, with the absolutely superfluous "directions not to expose himself or the Troops." Grant claimed that "it was found impossible to take a Plan of the Fort from the height where the Troops were posted." Even though downtown Pittsburgh now occupies the location of the engagement, and the top of Grant's Hill has been reduced, sight lines down the main and side streets from Grant's Hill to Point Park remain distinctly clear, suggesting that Grant's report to Forbes was an attempt to cover his errors. For, once again, sending Rhor to prepare a plan of the fort was directly in violation of Bouquet's definitive instructions: "If he defeated them in the ambush, he could return in complete safety to the fort to have a plan of it made and reconnoiter the vicinity; But if through his spies or himself he considered that he had been discovered, he should think only of retreating." Grant had not ambushed the enemy; in fact, he was close to being ambushed himself, and he also had been discovered. But Grant was not thinking of retreating.

Atop his hill, Major Grant was "about the same time being informed that some of the Enemy Indians had discovered Captain McKenzie who was posted upon the left almost facing the Monongahela. In order to put on a good Countenance & to Convince our Men they had no reason to be Afraid, I gave directions to our drums to beat the reveille." Washington, hearing the story of the engagement from the survivors of his regiment, would in disbelief report, "[H]e also ordered Major Lewis two miles back to their baggage guard where Captain Bullitt commanded, and while this was doing caused the Reveille to beat in different places, which caused the Enemy to Sallie upon them in very great numbers, hence ensued an obstinate Engagement." Washington added, "[T]he Major ... sent an Engineer with a covering party in full view of the fort, to take a plan of the works—at the same time causing the Reveille to beat in several different places. The enemy hereupon sallied out...."[38]

Why Grant chose to send Ensign Rhor forward to make a plan of the fort when his left flank had just been discovered is inexplicable, as is his decision to play reveille with his drums at that precise moment. Forbes would later suggest that Grant must have lost his senses, and this certainly appears to be valid, for Grant's actions by this time are in defiance of sound military tactics, and negate every logical explanation. When the French attack finally came, Grant had segmented his command into four detachments: the reconnaissance party of one hundred men with Engineer Rhor; the baggage detail under Captain Bullitt of fifty men; the two-hundred-man battalion under Major Lewis moving from his hill position to the baggage; and the main body, now reduced to 500 soldiers under his direct command. Bouquet later reported to Forbes, based upon survivors' accounts, that about eight hundred French and Indians had attacked Grant. None of Grant's individual detachments was strong enough to defeat the French and Indians, and in fact he was probably outnumbered about two to one where the blow fell upon him.

Grant aligned his forces atop the hill that would shortly bear his name with about 250 Highlanders under the command of Captain McDonald on the left (southern) flank. At this time and place, the Monongahela River had deep banks, which permitted the Indians to expeditiously move under cover from Fort Duquesne. Inexplicably, Grant did not ensure that his left flank was solidly anchored on the Monongahela River, so it was highly vulnerable to being turned. His right (northern) flank was defended by the one hundred soldiers of the 2nd Pennsylvania Battalion, and this flank was positioned "in the air" and not secured to any terrain feature. Although their precise alignment is not described in any primary sources, presumably the Royal Americans and other provincials, including the large number of "Royal" Marylanders and the few men from North Carolina and the Lower Counties, filled in his center between the Pennsylvanians and Highlanders.

Ensign Gist, well to the rear, recalled hearing "Major Grant's drums.... Immediately after we heard several guns and then platoons [firing]." Grant later recounted to Forbes, "For about half an Hour after the Enemy came from the Fort, in different parties, without much Order & getting behind Fences [i.e., behind trees and cover] they advanced briskly & Attacked our left where there were 250 Men. Captain McDonald & Lieutenant Campbell were soon killed Lieutenant McDonald was wounded at the same time & our people being overpowered gave way." Lieutenant Robertson also recorded that the fighting occurred "20 or 25 minutes without gaining or losing, we were at last obliged to retire from superior numbers."[39] Private Robert Kirk, with the Highlanders, recalled of his participation in the engagement at this time:

> ...two large parties of Indians ... when we least expected, attack'd us in the rear, and the whole strength of the garrison in our front. The three companies before mention'd stood firm a long time, and by their regular platoon firing annoyed the enemy greatly. But by their superiority and repeated attacks, this brave handful was at length broken and obliged to retreat in confusion to the main body. In this critical situation we exerted our utmost courage and kept the enemy at bay for a full hour, until we were in short almost all cut off.[40]

During this phase of the engagement, the Highlanders and presumably the Royal Americans employed platoon firing, which initially succeeded in keeping the Indians from advancing upon their front. Platoon firing was a new tactical development of the mid–1750s, and its employment by the 77th Foot supports the premise that Forbes's army was as well trained as possible, and was employing the most modern military tactics. Platoon firing employed alternate firing by platoons of each company. This was a preferred method of firing, as it maintained platoon integrity, command and control while ensuring that a battalion could employ continuous fire along its front.[41]

The anonymous *Pennsylvania Gazette* letter recounts, "The Highlanders exposed themselves without any cover, and were shot down in great numbers, and soon forced to retreat. The Carolinians, Marylanders, and Lower Countrymen, concealing themselves behind trees and the brush, made a good defence; but were overpowered by numbers, and not being supported, were obliged to follow the rest."[42] The only available Indian account is a secondhand account heard from a participating warrior by Pennsylvanian James Smith, a captive then living with an Indian family in the Ohio Country, "The French and Indians knew not that Grant and his men were there until they beat the drum and played the bagpipes, just at day-light. They then flew to arms ... and as he had his Highlanders in ranks, and in very close order, and the Indians scattered, and concealed behind trees, they defeated him with the loss only of a few warriors."[43] Both of these accounts correspond with the platoon firing by the Highlanders, for they would have had to remain in ordered ranks to fire such disciplined volleys.

Ensign Rhor and Captain McKenzie's company, ahead of Grant's main party attempting to prepare a plan of Fort Duquesne, never had a chance. In short order Rhor was killed, McKenzie was taken prisoner, and his two lieutenants were also slain. Captive Smith recounted the fate of McKenzie's company: "[T]he Indians ran up under covert of the banks of Allegheny and Monongahela, for some distance, and then sallied out from the banks of the rivers, and took possession of the hill above Grant; and as he was on the point of it in sight of the fort, they immediately surrounded him."[44] It was a sad fate for this gallant and talented engineering officer, who had contributed so much to Forbes's campaign. In fact, without Rhor's having discovered a gap across Allegheny Mountain, the entire campaign would likely have stopped at Ray's Town.

In his apologia to Forbes, Grant described the simultaneous collapse of his right flank: "I did all in my power to keep things in Order but to no purpose. The 100 Pennsylvanians who were posted upon the right at the greatest distance from the Enemy [actually, they were closest to Fort Duquesne's hornwork], went off without Orders & without firing a Shot, In short in less than half an hour all was Confusion & as soon as that happened we were fired upon from every Quarter." The account of the flight of the Pennsylvanians, under the command of Captain Clayton, who survived the action, was verified by Captain Daniel Clark, who would write Colonel James Burd from Ray's Town on September 21:

> It vexes my very soul to hear that your battalion in the late skirmish behaved inconsistent with Good Soldiers & Men of Spirit But by a late representation this conduct is ascribed to Captain Clayton only whom I flatter myself will be able to justify his Character to the Satisfaction of all his Friends & to avenge the injustice done him by so scandalous a report. I understand that those Storys derive their Birth from Capt. Dagworthy who without exception says that Pennsylvanians run at the first Fire.[45]

Washington also had reported to him by survivors from his regiment "the running away of the Pennsylvanians, who were just behind, and ought to have sustained the Highlanders."[46] An anonymous letter to the *Gentleman's Magazine* back in London similarly reported the same incident: "[T]he enterprise must have succeeded, but for an absolute disobedience of orders in a provincial officer. ... by this man's quitting his post next morning the party was in a manner cut to pieces."[47]

As they had done to Braddock three years earlier and but a few miles away, the Indians employed their favorite and well-practiced tactic of launching a double encirclement against Grant.[48] Once Grant's left and right flanks collapsed, his command was doomed. It appears that Grant never really understood how the French and Indians had defeated him.

Private Robert Kirk, with the Highlanders, remembered the collapse of the Highlanders' lines:

> It is impossible to describe the confusion and horror which ensued, when all hopes of victory was gone. We were dispersed here and there, for my part ... I was pursued by four Indians, who fired at me several times, and their shot went through my cloaths, one of them however made sure, and wounded me in the leg with a buck shot. I was immediately taken, but the Indian who laid hold of me would not allow the rest to scalp me.[49]

Lieutenant Alexander McDonald of Grant's Highlanders described his actions at this critical juncture: "I call upon Major Grant ... to Witness if he did not see me after being Severely Wounded rally the men & endeavor to make a Stand tho' almost fainted with the loss of Blood till at last all hopes were over[.] I made my escape I don't know how."[50]

Ensign Gist, with Major Lewis's battalion at the baggage, "observe[d] them retreat, the officers & soldiers all eager to go to Major Grant's assistance with all the men except Captain Bullett's party, which still remained with the baggage. We marched under the foot of the hill. We came opposite to the parties engaged and then took straight up the steep hill, and after a great deal of trouble and difficulty arrived at the top of the hill, almost out of breath and in the rear of the Indians." Gist recounts that the Indians had fully completed their encirclement by the time that Lewis could return from Bullet's position, and had completely surrounded Grant. Lewis's Battalion struck the Indians in their rear and apparently inflicted some casualties, but was soon routed in turn. By this point Grant's force had disintegrated, and the Indians simply turned their attentions to Lewis, who was badly outnumbered and somewhat disorganized from his hasty advance. Ensign Gist recorded of the engagement: "We attacted them before they knew we were at there heels. We stood and fought as long as they would let us be at arms length. By this time I could not see two white men together, so I took my leave in a very abrupt manner by turning my back upon them and making the best of my way down the hill." Grant managed to rally some survivors, and the battered remnants of his command fought their way back to Bullitt's baggage train.

Here, Grant's orders to leave a party behind with the baggage proved their worth, and in fact this might have been his solitary wise tactical decision of the expedition. Captain Bullitt and his company put up a stout resistance, which permitted many of Grant's men to flee the battlefield and reach eventual safety in the by now aptly named Grant's Paradise. The *Pennsylvania Gazette* account would state: "As soon as the enemy came up to Captain Bullet, he attacked them very furiously for some time, but not being supported, and most of his men killed, was obliged to give way. However, his attacking them stopped the pursuit, so as to give many an opportunity of escaping."[51] Washington claimed, "Captain Bullett's behavior is matter of great admiration.... Your Friend Bullett has acquired immense honour in this Action, defending himself with what Virginians were left against the whole Force of the Enemy while his Ammunition lasted, and then was the last Man that left the field."[52] Bouquet reported to Forbes, "They would probably have been cut to pieces but for Captain Bullet of the Virginians who with 100 men sustained the battle with all their forces until, having lost two-thirds of his men, he was pushed in the direction of the river, where he found the poor Major. He urged him to retreat, but he told him he would not leave the field of battle as long as there was a man who would fight. 'My heart is broke,' said he, 'I shall never outlive this day.'" Grant would recall seeing "Captain Bullet surrounded on all sides, by the Indians & when I expected every instant to be cut by pieces without a possibility of escaping, a Body of the French with a number of their Officers came up & offered me Quarters, which I accepted off." Surprisingly enough, even with conducting this last stand to cover the retreat of the survivors, Captain Bullitt survived the engagement.

Ensign Gist left a particularly detailed account of his frantic efforts to escape, which must have been representative of nearly every soldier in Grant's command that dismal morning:

> When I came almost to the bottom of the hill I overtook Lieutenant [James] Baker [of the 1st Virginia] with about 20 men. We stear'd now for the baggage and arrived there soon, but met with such a reception from a party of Indians who had posted themselves on purpose to receive us, that we was obliged to face about and march back toward the fort, till we got out of their sight. Then marched down to the [Monongahela] riverside, where we heared a party of the enemy firing at some of our straglers. They was coming very swift upon us. Lieut Baker took to the river with the men, then made for the hills [he was subsequently killed during the retreat]. I had not gone far when I saw two Indians at about a hundred yards distance, and believing they did not see me I stop'd behind a tree and stripped myself [i.e., he removed his knapsack and extra equipment] and should have stay'd some longer, but I discovered the party making down to the place where Baker took the water. I made for the hill which the two young fellows discovering, pursued me with all their speed and coming within twenty yards of me I expected they would fire so I turned quickly about and presented my piece at one of them, upon which both of them fired. Upon which I ran again but being almost spent, I could not get out of their sight before they had charged [their muskets with powder and ball] again. It was not long before they overtook me and came within fifteen steps of me, and calling as before, I turned about and fired at one, who fired at me at the same time, shot me across the forehead and knocked me down. I got up immediately and the other shot me through the right hand. I then had nothing left but my heels to depend on which I made as good use of as was in my power till fairly run down. I was obliged to surrender to a husky likely young Indian man, almost naked and painted all over. ... he took hold of my hand and look'd at it, then put it into my bosom and made signs to me to march towards the fort, which I agreed to without grumbling. We soon came to where they had killed Lieut: [John] Billings of the Royal Americans, which after stripping off his cloaths was cut almost to pieces by some young Indians who came up in the meantime.... I believe I wounded the one I shot at. When I was brought back to the place he could not be found; tho the other hallowed for him. I saw one at the fort wounded with two balls, and I shot two balls at that fellow I mentioned.

Both Private Kirk's and Ensign Gist's accounts suggest that those soldiers who escaped being wounded were able to successfully evade their Indian pursuers, but those that were injured were easily picked up. Only forty wounded men managed to reach Dagworthy at Grant's Paradise, while 485 unwounded men returned.

Realizing that the situation was desperate, early in the action Grant had dispatched Ensign Alexander Grant to Loyalhanna to request succor. Described as a "large, stout man," Ensign Grant would still reach Grant's Paradise in good time, but reinforcements could not possibly be dispatched to the battlefield in order to do Major Grant any good. Still, Ensign Grant would shortly be promoted to lieutenant for his efforts.[53]

The first intimation that Grant's expedition had gone amiss reached Bouquet at Loyalhanna Camp late on September 14, when Lieutenant Colonel Dagworthy, then commanding at Grant's Paradise, sent an obviously hurried dispatch:

> Ensign [Alexander] Grant of the Highland Regiment, a number of Indians & eight Soldiers are Just now come in here from Major Grants Party & report that this Morning they had an Ingagement with a Considerable Body of the Enemy in sight of Fort Du Quesne & that after some time, our Men were put to the Rout and he believes most if not The Whole are Cut off, he left Major Grant near two Miles on this side the Place they first Ingaged but the Enemy was then all Round him.[54]

Bouquet's blood must have run cold.

In response to Ensign Grant's pleas, Lieutenant Colonel Adam Stephen was dispatched with all the men that could be spared from Grant's Paradise and the Loyalhanna camp, to rescue those men who were exhausted, and recover all the wounded that he could. Stephen would eventually march thirty miles to the west, to a point that must have seemed dangerously close to Fort Duquesne, to render aid and assistance. It was a difficult and risky assignment for which Stephen deserved considerable credit. Sergeant Lindenmuth, from the encampment at Loyalhanna, reported:

> Sixteen wounded came back to Loyalhanna on the 18th with bloody heads. Adjutant Clayton commanded those remaining who were not scattered. Two days before, an attachment of 200 men under Captain [Jacob] Morgan's [of the 2nd Battalion, Pennsylvania Provincials] command had been sent to meet them to cover them, and they met some of them 15 miles this side of Pittsburgh in distressed circumstances.[55]

Stephen would not be attacked in his performance of his rescue mission, probably because the Indians were busy looting and plundering the massacre site.

French accounts of this action are scarce. Captain Pierre Pouchot, then commandant of Fort Niagara, who received an accounting of the campaign at first hand from the French participants, recorded one French perspective of their attack:

> On 14 September, 800 Scots & militiamen, under the command of two majors, approached at daybreak right up as far as the cleared ground created around Fort du Quesne, without being spotted. The militia major [Major Lewis] was hesitant to attack, but the Scotsman, Major Grant, reluctant to turn back without doing anything, had a small shed in an outlying area of the fort set on fire to provoke an engagement. The Canadians & a few Indians, who were lodged in huts around the fort, noted this unusual early morning fire and were curious enough to slide down into the brushwood in order to discover what was happening. They went one after the other. Since the Indians & Canadians wear nothing more than a shirt in fine weather, they were very soon ready for action. Those who arrived first saw the troops and began to fire on them. The English beat the retreat, causing the alert to be sounded in the fort from which assistance was sent to the first men who had sallied forth from it. The enemy corps was so vigorously attacked that 250 scalps resulted and 100 prisoners were taken, among them six officers & the two majors. The remainder were pursued into the forest, where most of them perished.[56]

Sergeant Lindenmuth had remained with the majority of his battalion at the entrenched camp at Loyalhanna, but his comrades in arms who survived the ensuing debacle recounted their stories to him, which he dutifully recorded in his journal:

> ...it was decided by Brigadier General [then Colonel] Bouquet that an attachment of 700 men with their officers and an engineer should search the place [Fort Duquesne] and the surroundings. Because Major Grant commanded the attachment [detachment], and because he was an inquisitive man, they ventured close to the fort with the engineer and with all the troops without firing a single shot on either side, until finally the enemy discovered how strong we were and sent an ambush party down the Monongalia to surround us, which also occurred. The firing both in front and in the rear became very heavy and our people found it necessary to fight their way through in distressed circumstances. Major Grant was captured by the French. The engineer lost his life and another 150 compatriots also.[57]

Stephen provided Bouquet with detailed lists of the officers and men that had returned.[58] The final casualties were determined to be:

- Killed or Taken Prisoner by Indians— Fourteen Officers and 335 other ranks (Lieutenant Billings and Ensign Rhor of the Royal Americans, Captains George Munro and William McDonald, Lieutenants Alexander McKenzie, Colin Campbell, William McKenzie, Roderick McKenzie and Alexander McDonald of the Highlanders, Lieutenants Baker and Campbell and Ensigns Allen and Chew of the 1st Virginia, and Lieutenant McCra of the "Royal" Maryland Battalion; 35 Royal Americans, 187 Highlanders, 62 Virginians, four Carolinians, 27 Royal Marylanders, two Lower County Battalion, and eighteen of the 2nd Pennsylvania)
- Survived— Sixteen Officers, 485 other ranks (not wounded), forty other ranks (wounded)
- Prisoners of the French— Six Officers (Major Grant; Lieutenant Ryder (Wounded and Prisoner)

and Ensign Jenkins of the Royal Americans, Captain Hugh McKenzie of the Highlanders, Major Lewis of the 1st Virginia, and Ensign Hollar of the 2nd Pennsylvania Battalion).[59]
  • Prisoners Taken by the Indians—Two Officers (Ensign John McDonald of the Highlanders, Ensign Thomas Gist of the 1st Virginia).[60]

These were devastating casualties. Of the 38 officers engaged, 22 would become casualties (nearly 58 percent). Of the 860 soldiers, 335 would be killed or captured (39 percent), and another forty (.046 percent) would return wounded. Over forty percent of Grant's expedition were lost. If a modern military unit were to sustain such casualties it would be considered *hors de combat* until it could be reconstituted. For the officers and soldiers of Forbes's army there was no such respite. By September 17 they were already back at work, strengthening the works at Loyalhanna in anticipation of a French counterattack that never came.[61] And even with such devastating losses, the army surprisingly remained in good morale. Captain Joseph Shippen of the Pennsylvania Provincials would report to his family in Philadelphia: "The Troops now breathe nothing but Revenge & are in high Spirits."[62]

The affair had been a disastrous reverse to British arms. From the very beginning, it had never been adequately planned, and the failure to perform a comprehensive reconnaissance before the expedition had been dispatched would doom it to failure before it had ever marched out of the camp at Loyalhanna. Why Bouquet approved the expedition is nearly inexplicable. It was directly against Forbes's intent, which otherwise Bouquet appeared to have absolutely understood and complied with throughout the entire campaign. Grant was a popular officer, and was well regarded throughout the army. Forbes and Bouquet both thought quite highly of him and depended upon his leadership and experience to help guide the campaign. It appears that Grant was a superlative salesman, and marketed his plan to Bouquet so smoothly and adeptly that Bouquet approved it, although his restrictive instructions suggest that he did so only with reservations.

Grant performed an extremely competent march to Fort Duquesne. In fact, he was able to guide a large force of eight hundred soldiers literally into the ditch of the French fort without being discovered. First, this suggests that the Loyalhanna Camp was not precisely "surrounded" by Indian parties, as Bouquet had told Forbes. Second, it suggests that French security around the fort was inadequate, and that the Indians were not properly patrolling the approaches to the fort. At this time, the French and Indians were still focusing their attentions upon the old Braddock's Road. That such a large party could reach the fort undetected is overwhelming evidence that the French command did not understand the route that Forbes's army was actually taking towards them. Grant, his officers, and his soldiers were well deserving of praise, for they performed a difficult and lengthy approach through enemy territory without being detected. Grant's surviving Orderly Book indicates that the march was carefully considered and meticulously supervised, and his soldiers performed superbly.

Grant's expedition to the point where it arrived at the Forks of the Ohio was well organized, well disciplined, carefully considered, and splendidly executed. However, once he arrived before the darkened wooden ramparts of Fort Duquesne, Grant completely violated Bouquet's instructions. His operations throughout the night of September 13 were directly in contravention to his orders, and are strong evidence that, as Forbes would note:

... my friend Grant had most certainly lost the *tra mon tane*, and by his thirst of fame, brought on his own perdition, and run a great risque of ours, which was far wide of the promises he made to me at Carlisle, when soliciting to command a party, which I would not agree to; and very contrary to his criticisms upon Gen. Abercromby's late affair, has fallen unhappily into the individual same error, by his inconsiderate and rash proceeding.[63]

It is remarkable that Forbes, from such a great distance, so well understood Grant's actions at Fort Duquesne. Of course, he was a fellow Scot! Grant's reward for failing to heed Bouquet's carefully considered course of action was the destruction of his command, and the loss of many valuable soldiers and officers. Most damaging to the campaign was the death of Chief Engineer Rhor, whom Forbes would greatly miss.

The blame for the defeat must rest entirely upon Major Grant. He had divided his command on numerous occasions both during the march and in front of the French fort. His segmentation of the command early in the morning exposed his command to being defeated in detail by the Indians' flanking parties, although he had as many soldiers available as the French, and was posted on a strong position. His tactical positioning atop what would become known as "Grant's Hill" was badly flawed. He placed his least reliable soldiers, the Pennsylvania Provincials, on his right flank, and failed to anchor his left flank on the Monongahela River. The result was that the wily Native warriors were able to employ their favorite tactics, turn both Grant's flanks, and then surround him from the rear. A more legitimate alignment would have positioned the Pennsylvania and other provincials on the left flank, carefully anchored on the river so that the Indians could not outflank him. Grant could then have placed his most dependable command, the Highlanders, in a refused position on the right flank. The result would have been a battle line with two secure flanks that positioned his individual detachments to take advantage of their respective strengths and weaknesses. The Pennsylvanians would have been considerably steadier in a more secure position, rather than exposed on the end of Grant's line as they found themselves. Not dividing his command would also have enabled him to mass sufficient firepower to repulse the Indians' attacks.

Grant's actions on the morning of September 14 were so incompetent as to be criminal, and that he was never court martialed for violating his orders is nearly incredible. Possibly, it was felt that having the stigma of so great a defeat placed upon his reputation was punishment enough. Yet, because of Forbes's carefully regulated advance, and the establishment of entrenched depots at frequent intervals connected by a well-constructed road, Grant's defeat did not terminate Forbes's advance. Certainly, Bouquet and Forbes were made of sterner stuff than Colonel Dunbar, who had commanded Braddock's rear column, and had fled all the way back to Philadelphia following Braddock's defeat. Rather, Grant's defeat does not appear to have constrained Forbes and his campaign in the least. Colonel John Armstrong wrote on October 3 from Ray's Town, "Since our Quixot [sic] Expedition, you will no doubt be greatly perplex'd about our fate, God know what it may be, but I assure you the better part of the Troops are not at all dismay'd, the General comes here at a Critical & Seasonable juncture. He is weak, but his Spririts good, and his head Clear, firmly determin'd to proceed as far as force & provisions will Admit, which, thro' divine favour, I hope will be far enough."[64]

In the event, Grant's massacre, although it was a tactical defeat, was an operational victory for Forbes. Many of the Indians at Fort Duquesne concluded that they had defeated Forbes as they had crushed Braddock three years earlier. They had garnered considerable scalps, prisoners, and plunder. They had validated their season as warriors on the war path. The mid–September date of Grant's defeat meant that the Indians would now begin planning their departure upon the winter hunt. Bouquet recognized this, noting to Forbes after Grant's debacle: "We have not seen an Indian for a week. It is believed that after this success it will be difficult for the French to keep them."[65] This is certainly supported by the experiences of the two prisoners, Ensign Gist and Private Kirk. Ensign Gist and his captors left Fort Duquesne on September 16, and "my lot was to carry about fifty pounds of plunder that they had got chiefly from the Highlanders." Gist would eventually reach the vicinity of Detroit, where he was adopted into an Indian tribe. Kirkwood would leave Fort Duquesne within five days of the engagement and be similarly taken into a Shawnee family. He specifically mentioned, "The Hunting season approaching we decamp'd, each seeking their game in the best manner they could. This took up a considerable time. ... upon this expedition I heard that the French had blown up their fortification at Fort Duquesne, abandoned it...."[66]

The only real result of Grant's defeat was an immediate depletion of manpower at Fort Duquesne, precisely when Forbes planned for this final advance to occur. It would prove to be a deadly combination to French fortunes. Grant had, inadvertently, sacrificed his soldiers to ensure the eventual success of Forbes's campaign.

EIGHT

"Immediately a regular Attack Insued"
French Resurgence at Loyalhanna

Even with Grant's debacle occurring so early in the life of the encampment, Burd rapidly pushed construction at Loyalhanna. By the middle of October, Bouquet could report to Forbes, "Be at ease about the post [Loyalhanna]. I left it in a condition to defend itself against any attack without cannon."[1]

Indeed, it would shortly sustain just such an attack "without cannon." The French, having finally ascertained the direction from where the English were coming courtesy of the incompetence of Major James Grant, determined to launch what could be variously referred to as either a spoiling attack, or a large raid, upon the camp at Loyalhanna. The objectives of either were the same, and only the scale differed. The French hoped to inflict another reverse upon English arms, and in particular they desired to ravage the English transportation and logistical assets including horses, wagons, stored provisions, live cattle such as sheep and beeves, Indian trade goods, ammunition, and the many other supplies upon which Forbes's army depended. Through their scouts, who had been hovering around Forbes's advanced columns since mid–September, they were well aware that the English army was too numerous and well entrenched to hope that they could defeat them in a general engagement. And without carrying a train of artillery from Fort Duquesne across Chestnut Ridge, which would require the construction of a road and occupy considerable time, they could not realistically hope to seize the English encampment. However, capturing and destroying the English supplies was feasible with a large enough raiding force, aggressively led, and executed with determination and vigor. The French commanders could legitimately believe that inflicting severe damage upon the English forward logistics this late in the season would effectively terminate the English advance for the campaign. Accordingly, the French dispatched a substantial force that comprised every available soldier and Native warrior at Fort Duquesne, approximately 440 French Marines and Canadian militia and 150 Native warriors, under the command of Captain Charles Philip Aubrey, an experienced French Marine officer from the French settlements in the Illinois country.[2]

On October 12 this French column closed in on Loyalhanna. The English, as usual, had "grass guards" out, which were small parties of guards positioned to protect animals that were grazing in the abundant meadows that surrounded the encampment. Although the size of the grass guard that was attacked this morning is not recorded, Captain Joseph Shippen of the Pennsylvania Provincials maintained a roster of camp guards at Ray's Town throughout August and September that is doubtless representative of the size of the Loyalhanna grass guards. Typical grass guards from this period consisted of:

- September 4, 1758—"Bullock Guard" 1 Captain, 2 Subalterns, 2 Sergeants, 2 Corporals, 48 Privates;
- September 4, 1758—"Artillery Horse Guard" 2 Subalterns, 2 Sergeants, 2 Corporals, 48 Privates;
- September 4, 1758—"Additional Horse Guard" 1 Sergeant, 1 Corporal, 12 Privates;
- September 5, 1758—"Grass Guard" 1 Captain, 3 Subalterns, 5 Sergeants, 6 Corporals, 89 Privates;
- September 6, 1758—"Bullock Guard" 1 Captain, 1 Subaltern, 2 Sergeants, 3 Corporals, 46 Privates;
- September 6, 1758—"Artillery Horse Guard" 2 Subalterns, 2 Sergeants, 2 Corporals, 30 Privates;
- September 6, 1758—"Additional Bullock Guard" 1 Sergeant, 1 Corporal, 12 Privates.[3]

And it should be noted that these grass guards were usually dispersed to protect the animals that would be grazing across a relatively large area. It was one of these grass guards that the French initially assailed.

Colonel Burd reported to Colonel Bouquet, who was supervising road work at Rhor's Gap on Allegheny Mountain well to the east:

> This day at 11 A:M the enemy fired 12 Guns to the South west of us upon which I sent out two partys to surround them but Instantly the firing increased, upon which I sent out a large party of 500 men they were forced to the Camp and Immediately a regular Attack Insued which lasted a long time I think above two hours....[4]

A grass guard of twenty to ninety men, that was necessarily scattered, would have had little opportunity to successfully defend itself against a large French force augmented with considerable numbers of skilled Native warriors. Certainly, these small guards were roughly handled, for one account noted, "Twenty-nine of the missing were upon Grass Guards when the Enemy attacked."[5] Burd's partial diary surviving from the encounter would note finding dead and wounded men scattered throughout the woods for the next three days.[6] The French and Indians descended from a prominent hill located southwest of the fort, outside of musket range, but that provided spectacular views of the British encampment. Why Burd did not guard this hill by placing a picket post upon it is not discussed in contemporary documents, but it certainly should have been, and this failure in fundamental security enabled the French to surprise the grass guards.

Accounts of the engagement are limited, but an account provided to Governor Sharpe of Maryland, probably by Colonel Dagworthy, provides some additional information on this initial contact:

> The Enemy being in Number about 1200 fired upon a Party of our Troops that had the Care of some Cattle which were feeding at the Distance of a Mile & half from the Camp, the Firing being heard at the Camp about 200 more of our men that were without the Breast Work ran out to the Assistance of them that were attacked but they were all soon obliged to retire by the superior Number of the Enemy who pursued them almost to the Breast Work within which near 2000 Men were by that time drawn up under Arms.[7]

Suspecting that this was only a relatively small French raid upon his livestock, Burd initially ordered out the Maryland Battalion of two hundred men to support the grass guards. Burd believed that this force would be sufficient to repel a typical Indian party, consisting of at most a dozen or so warriors. But instead, the Maryland Battalion was heavily outnumbered, probably by odds of no less than three to one, and were driven back in short order. Hearing the firing approaching the entrenchments, and probably realizing that this was an attack by a comparatively large force and not simply the raid that he had initially envisioned, Burd then ordered out five hundred men from the 1st Pennsylvania Battalion. The Pennsylvanians were in turn driven back towards the breastworks. The redoubtable Captain Pouchot provided a scarce French rendition of this assault:

M. Aubry, a captain of the Illinois, set out from Fort duQuesne with a detachment of about 600 men, Canadians & Loups Indians [Delaware Indians], in order to reconnoitre the English camped at LoyalAnnon. He found a small camp just beyond the retrenchments which was held by a corps of 2000 men. As soon as the vanguard of our detachment was discovered, the English sent out a captain & 50 men to reconnoitre it. They stumbled upon the entire detachment, which utterly destroyed them.

This is clearly a garbled version of the initial engagement with the grass guards.

By this time Burd had placed his entire garrison under arms, and the French must have been brought up short when they discovered nearly two thousand men behind fortifications, ably supported by a formidable train of artillery. The English gunners were extremely active. The guns poured out a veritable storm of fire that did much to demoralize the French and Indians. Stymied by the heavy volume of artillery fire, the alert and large garrison, and the substantial defenses, the French attack seems to have lost impetus and purpose. Burd reported in his diary:

...while writing my letter to Coll: Bouquet Attack'd twice, at 9 P.M. the Enemy Attacked Redoubt No. 3 were Repuls'd, kept hooping in the woods, fired Cohorn Shells at them which soon Silenced them[.] the Bullocks broke out of the Pen and run [word missing] the woods— All the Troops under Arms tonight[.] buried 4 French Sold[rs] [soldiers].[8]

The French raiders failed to interdict the critical road to the east, for Burd reported in the middle of the engagement on October 12 "at 4 P.M. Lieut. Cairy of the 2d Virginia Regt arrived with a small party and a few horses with cloathing belonging to the Virginia Regt — at 7 P.M. An Express arrived of two light horse from Coll: Bouquet...."

The French and Indians paused in their attack, waiting for the cover of night to approach the fort to continue their efforts at theft and destruction. Once darkness arrived the French and Indians attempted to close in around the fort. However, they were apparently disconcerted by the charge of the bullocks, and then diverted by attempting to catch said cattle. Lieutenant Robertson with Montgomery's Highlanders recalled that the Indians "hallowed and Hissed about us all night."[9] Throughout, the English artillery continued its heavy fire, which forced the French and Indians to respect a good distance from the works. An anonymous correspondent, possibly Burd, published a letter in the *Pennsylvania Gazette*: "The Enemy attempted in the Night to attack us a second time; but, in Return for their most melodious Indian Musick, we gave them a Number of Shells from our Mortars, which soon made them retreat."[10] Burd told Bouquet the next morning: "The Enemy has harassed me all night, they made some little faints [feints], but I think they were Cheefly Employed in Carrying off their Dead & wounded.... I played upon them with shels last night which soon stop their savage Tones.... Captain Gordon's Musick from the Great Guns farr Exceeded The Indian Solos."[11] Pouchot continued his account from the French perspective:

In pursuing those who had been put to flight, the French came across the small camp, took it by surprise & sent the garrison fleeing for the main retrenchment, which they only just reached in time. They pursued the enemy right up to their retrenchments, where they were fired upon by the cannon. For two days, M. Aubry formed a kind of blockade around it.[12]

Pouchot's rendering of the engagement is generally consistent with British accounts. However, because British parties and messengers were able to regularly enter and leave the eastern gate of the fort, the French "blockade" was clearly ineffectual, and it also only lasted for one afternoon and a portion of a single night.

Governor Sharpe's witness provided a realistic appraisal of what the French and Indians were up to: "They stayd about the Camp all night & being employed in killing or driving away near 200 Horses." Distrressed by the heavy artillery fire, and having picked up what scalps, plunder and horses they could locate in the night, the French and Indians departed under the cover of darkness. They had been at Loyalhanna less than twelve hours. Bouquet correctly told Forbes, "The enemy was around the entrenchments all night, and made several feigned attacks. The cannon and the coehorns intimidated them." [13] Burd reported "13th Friday, No appearance of the enemy." The French incursion was complete.

Not surprisingly, Forbes was able to make good sense of this affair, and provided two comprehensive reports that accurately described the engagement. The first went to General Abercromby:

> The 12th in the morning about eleven oclock the advanced post were alarmed by hearing some fireing about half a mile from them, which was succeeded by the Indian Halloo upon which 60 of the Marylanders run towards the place whence the noise came, and when they got up, the firing became brisk — whereupon Colonel Burd of the Pennsylvanians who commanded, ordered a party of the first Battalion of Pennsylvanians to go and support the Marylanders, who had not marched half a mile when they met with the Enemy who were surrounding the Marylanders, and gave them their fire for some time, but upon finding them too numerous begun to retreat, a third party was ordered out, but the fire encreasing and approaching the breast work, the rest of the troops were ordered to their posts in the breast work and to line the skirts of the wood to favour the retreat of the three partys, and the alarm Guns were fired to make the Cattle and horse Guards take care themselves. In about an hour from the beginning the Enemy had drove our people into the breastwork and appeared in numbers along the edge of the wood from whence they begun afresh a very brisk fire, but our Cannon & Cohorns kept them at a distance, and certainly did execution as they were well served, however after an hours firing and finding they could make no impression they began to retire leaving only two killed and one wounded where the fire was hottest.... We saved all our Bullocks but they have carried off the officers horses and Batts horses....

Forbes's second report went to Secretary Peters of Pennsylvania:

> Upon the 12th in the morning the French from Fort DuQuesne having a mind to repay Major Grants visit came to drive us away from our advanced post at Loyall Hannon destroy our Magazin, Bullocks, Carriages, &c. They consisted of a body of 900 French and Canadians and two Hundred of those Friends, you are now treating with [i.e., Indians] they had gott within five miles of the post, and proposed attacking all the out post and Guards next morning, but being discovered they resolutely attempted to storm the Breast work thrown up about the Camp — accordingly fell a firing and hallooing in order to bring out detachments, by which they proposed entering the Breastwork pellmell with them when routed. The 60 Maryland Volunteers [for Royal service] went out and attacked them with vigour and Courage, but [were] overpowered, Colonel Burd who commanded sent out a strong detachment of the 1st Pennsylvania regiment to sustain them, but they being likewise repulsed a third detachment of the Virginians &c. went out to bring the other off, which they did by retreating to the Breastwork. The Enemy followed close to the edge of the Wood where they were stopt by the Grape Shot from our Cannon and the shells of the Coehorns and Howitzers, however they continued firing upon the breast work from eleven to three in the afternoon without any considerable loss on our side, they retreated a little, and carried away their dead and wounded.... Wee saved all our live Cattle, but the officers horses are either carried away or a missing.... That [loss] of the Enemy we cannot ascertain, altho it must neads be Considerable considering the advantages wee fought with against them, a Breast work & Cannon. [14]

French casualties were unknown, but they must have been relatively light. Pouchot reported:

> He [Captain Aubry] had 200 [English] cattle or horses killed. Almost all of our men returned on horseback. They estimated enemy losses at 200 men while ours were one corporal and two soldiers. The French took about a hundred scalps & seven prisoners. [15]

Burd reported burying four French dead, and listed his own casualties as:

- Lt. Thomas Prater, "Royal" Maryland Battalion, killed
- Lt. James Duncanson, 1st Virginia Regiment, wounded
- Ensign Bell, Maryland Battalion, wounded
- Lt. Matthews, Maryland Battalion, missing
- Lt. Wright, Royal Artillery, "wounded slightly in the head"
- 1 Noncomissioned Officer, 1st Virginia Regiment, wounded
- 2 Noncommissiond Officers, Maryland and 1st Pennsylvania, missing
- 10 Rank and File killed
- 15 Rank and File wounded
- 29 Rank and File missing
- Total — 12 killed, 18 wounded, and 31 missing (61 total).[16]

The significant involvement by the Maryland Battalion is reflected in the comparatively heavy casualties that they suffered, three of the five officers, and eleven of the total 57 other rank casualties. The 1st Pennsylvania Battalion, sent to their relief, also lost twenty other rank casualties. These two units were those most heavily engaged, and sustained the majority of the British losses.

This relatively minor single-day affair, which would later be elevated to the lofty status of "The Battle of Fort Ligonier," bears little credit for either the British or French. From the French perspective, the spoiling attack failed to accomplish all but one of its objectives. Their solitary success was that some horses were captured or killed, but no live cattle had been taken. The British defenses were never penetrated. No buildings were burned. No trade goods, provisions, ammunition or other supplies were damaged or destroyed. None of the precious wagons were smashed or wrecked. The French and Indians failed to effectively isolate the garrison, for two very small parties reached the fort in the midst of the engagement. In retrospect, it appears that the French went to a great deal of effort, and marched a large body of men a considerable distance, simply to capture a few horses. A small Indian raiding party could have done just as much with considerably less effort and less risk to the Fort Duquesne garrison.

From the British standpoint, as Bouquet confessed to Forbes:

> The affair, between ourselves, appears humiliating to me. A thousand men keep more than 1500 blockaded, carry off all their horses, and retire undisturbed with all their wounded and perhaps ours, after burying their dead. This enterprise which should have cost the enemy dearly shows a great deal of contempt for us, and the behaviour of our troops in the woods justifies their idea only too well.[17]

Clearly, British patrols and local security measures were not adequate, for they had permitted a large French party to attack the fort without warning. Burd's failure to picket the hill overlooking the fort provided the French with a superb vantage to plan their assault. Burd possessed overwhelming strength at Loyalhanna. He had squandered this advantage at the onset of the French attack upon the grass guards, by the dispatch of two small relief parties, each individually weaker than the French and Indians. Although their combined numbers were greater, Burd's faulty deployment permitted them to be defeated in detail. Both the grass guards and the Maryland Battalion's two hundred men were heavily outnumbered, and they were easily driven back by the French and Indians. A larger force, which was readily available, would have precluded this early reverse. The second relief column of five hundred Pennsylvanians was nearly equal in number to the French and Indians. The Pennsylvania Provincials' performance at Grant's defeat had been dismal, and it does not seem that they did much better on October 12, sustaining heavier casualties than the smaller Maryland detachment. Once the grass guards, the Maryland Battalion and the

Pennsylvanians had been driven back to the breastworks, Colonel Burd was perfectly comfortable to remain safely ensconced behind his fortifications, and initiated no further offensive actions until the French withdrew. Burd's own words to Bouquet appear to tell the tale: "[W]e had the pleasure to do that Honor to His Majesties Arms to keep his Camp at Loyal Hennon...." Sharpe's correspondent confirmed Burd's deportment: "Colonel Byrd of the Pennsylvania Forces who happened to have the Chief Command did not think himself at Liberty to order any of them out to act offensively so that the Enemy's Loss was very inconsiderable."

This engagement is notable in that it was the only time during the campaign that the Royal Artillery would be fired in anger, and they performed superbly. Clearly the heavy guns' commanding presence went far in dashing the Native warriors' ardor for both battle and plunder, for they withdrew precipitously that night, having accomplished little. The artillery's performance was the only bright spot in the British actions on October 12.

Still, the *Gentleman's Magazine* back in London reported of the affair: "Advices from America, bring an account of a repulse, which the enemy met with, in an attack, which they made upon the advanced guard of Gen. Forbes at Loyal Hanning, in the road to Fort Duquesne, which has put the troops under that general in high spirits; and 'tis hoped will prove a happy omen of an entire conquest of the place."[18] John Forbes arrived at the Encampment at Loyalhanna on November 2, determined to accomplish just such a conquest.[19]

NINE

"Colonel Washington did not discover his usual activity and presence of mind"

Combat, Fratricide and a Prisoner at Loyalhanna

While Burd labored at fabricating the army's advanced depot, Forbes continued yet another aspect of the campaign. In addition to the myriad activities needed to move his army forward, including building roads, training and organizing his army, managing his wagons and horses, performing scouts, and stockpiling supplies, Forbes still had to attempt to keep the Indians remaining with his army in good humor, and retain the services of at least a few of them. Merely keeping track of the Indians was a nightmare. Captain Shippen of Pennsylvania would astutely observe from Ray's Town on August 16:

> It is very uncertain what Number of Indians we shall have with us; it seems little Dependance can be put on any of them; I believe there have been about 150 Cherokees at this Place since the Army first formed a Camp here, but these have all left us except about 25 of them, we have besides these, Habus & 3 Delaware Warriors who came 2 days ago from [Pennsylvania Fort] Augusta, & 2 or 3 of the Six Nations—And Colonel Bouquet expects Captain Bullen (a Catawba Captain) with 30 of his Warriors to join us very soon; I understand they are to come from Winchester by the way of Fort Cumberland.[1]

Forbes found dealing with the Indians to be extremely tiresome and frustrating. He complained to Abercromby from Carlisle on August 11, "I have no mortal about me that understands Indian affairs or their Genius, I therefore immediately Dispatched Major Grant and 200 Highlanders ... to represent to them in moderate terms...."[2] Grant reported upon his efforts in this direction from Fort Loudon five days later:

> I found the Indians encamped near this Fort, they committed no disorder, did not even ask for rum, but they were very impatient to receive their goods as they were pleased to call them, they had got those presents before, and kept them for some days, so as every man knew his own bundle, the distribution was easily made, I expected the morning that they would have apply'd to me for a talk, but finding they did not I sent Mr. Crawford about eleven oClock to acquaint them, that I was much fatigued but that I should be glad to see their chief men at any time they pleased the next day as I was sent by you for this purpose, this I did to gain time, but they could not bear the thoughts of a moments delay, and upon being informed that they were making themselves ready to go off without waiting for their presents, I was obliged to order them to be delivered to them in hopes to bring them into better temperance to prevent the consequences which might attend their bad humor in going home. When they were quite happy & pleased with getting possession of their presents, I told the Chief men that I desired to have a talk with them next day, which they readily agreed to and said they would hear every thing which I had to say to them as we were friends, brothers. Crawford informed them that I was to ask their whole party to dine with me and indeed I began to flatter myself that I should be able to keep them till you could come up but they were so anxious to get home, that they went off very quickly without waiting either for talk or dinner, they

had done no harm except carrying of a few horses, George the Indian went down with Crawford from Raes town went with them, he is more to blame than the others, and if I could have done it without quarreling with the rest I most certainly would have sent and made him prisoner, but that step could not be ventured upon, unless we had those gentlemen a little more in our power. I am sorry I have not succeeded better, but it certainly was impossible to keep them, they told the Delawars that they were always their Friends when they found them with their Brother the English, and they gave them a belt of wampum to deliver to the Chirokese at Raestown, who they said were going or gone to War.[3]

Both Forbes and Bouquet strived mightily to keep the Indians remaining with them contented, well cared for, and appropriately employed. Bouquet regularly issued orders regarding the Native warriors, such as those given to Indian Superintendent Captain Abraham Bosomworth on September 3:

> You are to march with all the Indians under your command the 4th Inst. And proceed with L. Col. Deyworthy [Dagworthy] to cover the head of the Army. You are to Send continually Small Partys out to Scout and reconnoitre the Ennemy and inform the Commanding Officer of all the Intelligences you may receive. In case the assistance of the Indians should be required for some Enterprise, you are then to march with them, following the orders that you shall receive from the Commanding Officer with you. As the Delaware and other Indians settled on the West Side of the Ohio Seemed disposed to conclude a Peace with us, You will prevent your Indians to go over the Ohio and disturb them, untill you receive further orders. You are not to permit any of our Indians to go out of the Camp without his Badge to prevent any accident. And you will repeat to them to Remember the Signal agreed with our Messengers sent to the Ohio of a Swinging Blankett.[4]

When the Indians did arrive, they inevitably required outfitting and equiping. Halkett wrote for Forbes to Governor Sharpe of Maryland, from Shippensburg on August 13 on this topic. "Last night General Forbes arriv'd here, where he met with an Express from Colonel Bouquet, informing him of fifty Catawbas and other Indians having come to our assistance at Winchester, they are in great want of every thing, particularly the artikle of Blankets, in which we ourselves are greatly distressed. The General therefore directs you will be so good to order three hundred pairs to be bought at Baltimore, or else where, as they most conveniently can, and immediately be sent up to Reas Town...."[5]

Considerable quantities of goods were expended upon the Indians, as presented in Appendix A. These Native American warriors were predominantly Cherokee and Catawba, although 27 Tuscaroras from the Six Nations were reported to have joined the army on August 11.[6] The Indians regularly came and went, but enough remained to constitute a viable scouting and reconnaissance force.

In addition to maintaining numbers of Indian warriors with his own army, Forbes was also determined to sunder the Native Americans from the French. On June 6, as previously described, Forbes had dispatched Christian Frederick Post to arrange for negotiations with the Delaware Chief Teedyuscung.[7] Before a meaningful conference could be conducted a number of obstacles would have to be removed, including contacting Indians further to the west who would have to participate, simultaneously involving and bypassing the Iroquois Confederation, addressing previous injustices that had been done to the various Native nations, and convincing adjacent colonial governments to participate in the process. Once Teedyuscung was contacted, he responded, "Let us press heartily on, I don't only press you on alone, but tell you let us press together." Teedyuscung recommended that messages be carried into the Ohio country, to Delaware leaders in their villages there. Post was again asked to carry Forbes's messages, this time in the guise of peace belts to these Indians on the Ohio that Forbes fervently desired to entice into negotiations. To ensure Post's survival on this difficult mission, a prominent Delaware sachem named Pisquetomen accompanied him, along with a small band of Pisquetomen's warriors. This was absolutely integral to Post's mission, and in fact to his existence. Within his Native American culture, by assuming responsibility for Post's safety, Pisquetomen had pledged his own honor and very survival to protect Post. After an arduous and dangerous journey across the Allegheny Mountains in the midst of an active military campaign, Post succeeded in delivering his belts, and summoning the various Native American nations of the Ohio to council with the English. Although Post received the credit for this accomplishment, it would not have been possible without the guarantees and efforts of Pisquetomen and his warriors.

Through the efforts of Pemberton and other Quaker apostles, the colony of New Jersey was also brought into the fold, and joined Pennsylvania in Indian negotiations. Historian Francis Jennings ably documented Iroquois interference with Forbes's peace process, obstructions which Forbes succeeded in removing through skilfully manipulating Abercromby, who in turn issued preemptive instructions to Northern Indian Superintendent William Johnson, who held considerable sway with the Confederation. Under pressure from Forbes and Abercromby, Johnson persuaded the leaders of the Iroquois Confederation that it was time to participate in a large and significant council. Throughout this convoluted and complicated process, Forbes adroitly moved events inexorably forward through an impressive assemblage of tactics ranging from subtle hints through brute force. Forbes's efforts were rewarded on October 7, 1758, at Easton, Pennsylvania, when Pennsylvania and New Jersey convened a great treaty council with representatives of fourteen Indian nations or separate bands present.

Forbes would record of the efforts necessary to light the Easton council fire, in a letter to Bouquet from Shippensburg on August 18:

> After many Intrigues with the Quakers, the Commisioners [and] the Governour [of Pennsylvania], the Governour and Government of New Jersey and by the downright Bullying of Sir William Johnson, I hope I have now brought a Convention with the Indians of whatever denomination or Tribe, pretty near to a Crisis, the Six Nations and all the Chief men of the Indians living to the eastward of the [Great] Lakes and upon the Ohio as far down as the Wabache and Illinois, have all accepted of our Belts of Invitation and friendship, and have promised to meet the Governours and Commissioners from all those different Provinces at East town in Pennsylvania by the 12th or middle of September, where I think nothing can prevent a solid peace being established with most of those Indian tribes, as the Indian Claims appear to me both Just and Moderate and what no man in their senses or in our situation with regard to the Indians would hesitate half an hour in granting them. I flatter myself great good may be drawn to the publick from this meeting as I hope that private Interest and provincial Picques will, and ought to be drove away from this meeting.[8]

After reading Forbes's letter, one has to believe that getting the Indians to agree to a Council was considerably less demanding than simply getting the colonial governments to cooperate and talk to the Indians.

The specifics of the great treaty council at Easton, although interesting and informative, are outside the bounds of this purely military study. Suffice to say that when the council concluded on October 26, a sweeping peace treaty had been signed between the British colonies of Pennylvania and New Jersey, and the Native American inhabitants of the Ohio country. The redoubtable duo of Christian Frederick Post and Pisquetomen again carried the message belts to the west, reaching Forbes at Loyalhanna on November 7, where Forbes inserted his personal assurances and messages to those already carried in their pouches. Their news reached the Ohio country about the same time that the French had suddenly found themselves running desperately low on supplies, thanks to Bradstreet's crushing success at Frontenac. Now, with the arrival of these belts, the French suddenly also found themselves without Native allies. And these two calamitous events occurred at precisely the moment when the French most needed both supplies and Indians, for events had conjoined to permit John Forbes to initiate his final march, the approach of his third and final parallel upon Fort Duquesne.

Forbes's first concern upon arriving at the entrenched camp at Loyalhanna was to ascertain just how effective the French raid had been. Forbes had been quite displeased with the performance of the Loyalhanna garrison during the action of October 12, grumbling that they had "neither made one *Sortie* or followed them half a yard, but shamefully allowed them to bury the few they had killed, Carry off their wounded with some Prisoners and all our horses."[9] Forbes rapidly determined that the only real result of their raid was the loss of some two hundred horses. Burd reported in a letter to Bouquet on October 14: "The Enemy have killed & carried off all our Horses except Twenty Six Waggon horses which I had ty'd up during the Action — My own [personal] Horses are all gone, but we have saved all our Bullocks."[10] Bouquet confirmed that "the enemy has carried off nearly all our horses...."[11] The precise number of horses with Forbes's columns cannot be ascertained from surviving sources. The percentage of horses stolen can be guessed at, for "James Couttas and Company" had contracted with Forbes to provide 124 horses for the campaign. One horse had died and one horse had been lost near Ray's Town early in August, and of the remaining 122 horses, "31 horses killed and taken by the Enemy at the Battle of Loyal Hannon at 11-11-0 p^r horse on an Average agreeable to the Valuation, 350-4-3" was paid to the firm for their loss.[12] This suggests a loss of approximately a third to a quarter of the horses with the campaign. This loss alone could have crippled the movement forward, had not Forbes expended such great efforts to obtain additional wagons and horses earlier in the fall. His exhaustive work now paid dividends, for large numbers of horses and wagons began arriving at this critical juncture.

The day after the raid on Loyalhanna, Captain James Sinclair, serving as assistant deputy quartermaster general at Ray's Town, told Bouquet, "I have this day sent off five & forty Waggons. ... there is a great number of Waggons on the road, I expect a hundred to morrow or next day. A division of the Artillery marches to morrow morning with 38 Teams [of four horses each]."[13] Sinclair reported five days later:

> The Waggons from below Crowd so fast upon us that I imagin we shall be able to send off at least one Brigade every day while the General stays here and the weather continues favourable. I sent off yesterday with John Morgan Waggon Master Nineteen Waggons.... I have this day sent off under Abraham Bar Waggon Master twenty Eight Waggons loaded with flower and one with whisky, they marched in the morning and Six and thirty more with Artillery Stores are followed this afternoon. I shall send off tomorrow between twenty & thirty loaded with flower & Pork.[14]

Forbes told Abercromby that "near 200 Waggons loaded from Philadelphia" would be arriving by mid–October. Colonel John Armstrong of Pennsylvania wrote from Ray's Town on October 3, "[W]e hear that three hundred Waggons are on the Road."[15]

With the arrival of these wagons and teams of horses by the end of October, Forbes had nearly 1,000 horses available to him at the encampment at Loyalhanna. If used as pack horses, they were capable of carrying no less than 200,000 pounds of stores at any given moment. Forbes told Bouquet on October 25, "The Waggon teams are extreamly good and I hope to be able to send up sufficient provendor to feed the horses and keep the Waggoners in good humour." Additionally, Forbes told Bouquet on October 30, "I have orderd sixty oxen to sett off from this [Stony Creek] to morrow and there still remains here 180 besides what is comeing up with the Last of the Waggons." This would have meant that Forbes had

180,000 pounds of meat on the hoof (assuming 750 pounds per beef), or 180,000 individual rations of fresh meat available to him. Forbes on October 24 told Abercromby, "I am now Master of provisions to the 20th of November." Upon his arrival at the Loyalhanna camp, Forbes had managed to accumulate sufficient food, wagons, and horses to support a November movement on Fort Duquesne.[16] Colonel John Armstrong of the Pennsylvania Provincials correctly assessed Forbes's situation when he wrote in early October, "About the last of this month will be the Critical hour."[17]

Forbes would be joined at Loyalhanna by Washington and the remainder of the Virginia troops from Fort Cumberland, that had marched by way of Ray's Town. Forbes had deliberately wanted to maintain "an appearance of troops at Fort Cumberland and of marching that way, In order to be a Blind that I may advance the easier by the other route."[18] With Grant's failed attack on Fort Duquesne in September there was no longer any chance of maintaining this charade, and Washington had almost immediately marched for Ray's Town, arriving there on September 21, and he reached Loyalhanna on October 23.[19]

Forbes had written Secretary Peters of Pennsylvania on October 16: "[Now that I have everything in readyness at Loyal Hannon, I only want a few dry days to carry me to the Ohio Banks."[20] Unfortunately for Forbes, the fall of 1758 proved to be an exceptionally wet one; the roads were all but ruined by a succession of heavy downpours, and Forbes's advance was seriously hindered. Forbes would write to Governor Denny of Pennsylvania on October 22, "The Heavy Rains that have fallen of late has rendered the Roads almost Impassable for Carriages."[21]

It was these heavy rains and ensuing damage to the roads that had caused Bouquet to be absent from Loyalhanna when the French attacked on October 12. Forbes similarly complained to Abercromby on October 24, "[T]he Extraordinary rains are quite unexpected & unusual, so that I have nothing to say, as I cannot stop the continued floods, nor repair the roads anew. I am now upon the very top of the Alleganey Mountain, and altho the best made road of the whole, The Waggons have taken one whole day to proceed 3 Miles and must halt a Day to refresh."[22]

Forbes was clearly discouraged upon his arrival at the camp at Loyalhanna, for he had reached there nearly a month later than he had intended, and the miserable weather had severely damaged his roads and accordingly delayed his plans. Among the challenges that Forbes discovered at Loyalhanna was that the severe weather, and arduous labors necessary to cut the road over Allegheny Mountain and to construct the advanced depot at Loyalhanna, had caused serious wear to the clothing of his army. An inspection of Bouquet's companies of Royal Americans on October 25 revealed that these four companies, consisting of about 350 soldiers, required 48 shirts, 120 pairs of stockings, 42 pairs of breeches, 144 pairs of shoes, 67 blankets, 37 hatchets and seven hats. Lt. Colonel Dagworthy of the Maryland forces simply reported on the same date, "The Whole wants Blankets.... The Whole wants Clothes."[23]

Accordingly, on November 11, Forbes convened a council of war at Loyalhanna, to discuss whether a final advance on Fort Duquesne was possible that season. According to contemporary military literature, a "council of war" occurred "when a commander in chief of an army, or governor of a garrison, assembles the principal officers for their advice, upon some affairs of importance." [24] Interestingly, this was the first, and would be the only, council of war that Forbes held during the entire campaign.

The council of war was presided over by General Forbes, with Colonels Bouquet, Montgomery, Washington, Byrd of Virginia, Armstrong, Mercer and Burd of Pennsylvania all present. Quartermaster St. Clair was also in attendance. Following debate, the council of war concluded that shortages of clothing and provisions, and the difficulty of carriage across the mountains in winter, rendered a further advance impossible. Bouquet recorded: "The risks being so obviously greater than the advantages, there is no doubt as to the sole course that prudence dictates."[25] Forbes's own correspondence is silent regarding the reasons why he chose this moment to hold a council of war, or his personal feelings regarding its findings. Presumably, he must have supported it, but must also have been deeply disappointed that the vagaries of weather had brought what he must have surely known was to be his last active military service to such an unsatisfactory close.

Events were to immediately transpire that would inexorably alter Forbes's plans. The very next day, on November 12, a small French and Indian raiding party moved against the camp at Loyalhanna. Improved security measures implemented by Forbes successfully detected their presence this time, and he responded aggressively. The result was a slight skirmish, inconsequential in scale, late that afternoon.

Five principal accounts exist of the engagement that occurred on November 12, a minor affair of no particular consequence in its own right, but whose results completely altered the course of the campaign. For military historians and soldiers, this small action serves as proof positive that even the most minor engagement, of no obvious tactical significance, can still be of strategic importance of the highest order.

The French raiding party consisted of forty French Marines from Fort Duquesne, and somewhere between one hundred and two hundred Native American allies. British scouts, whether Native American or provincials is unknown, detected the approach of this raiding party and alerted the main garrison at Loyalhanna.

Although a sizeable French detachment had been able to attack the fort without being spotted just one month earlier, after Forbes and Bouquet had arrived at Loyalhanna the English scouts successfully intercepted a much smaller French party. And not only had they done this before the French raiders could cause mischief, but in time to sortie parties from the encampment to aggressively maneuver against the French. Forbes's response to an approaching French attack was far different from what Colonel Burd's had been, as Forbes reported to Abercromby on November 17:

> Two hundred of the ennemy came to attack our live Cattle and horses on the 12th — I sent 500 men to give them chace [chase] with as many more to Surround them, there were some killed on both sides, but unfortunately our partys fired upon each other in the dark by which we lost two officers and 38 privates kill'd or missing. Wee made three prisoners from whom wee have had the only Intelligence of the Enemys strength, and which if true gives me great hopes, I shall in spite of every cross perverse accident still be able to give a good account of them. One of the Officers kill'd is Lieut [John] Evans of the Royall Americans.[26]

George Washington prepared the second account, although a considerable number of years had passed before he provided it to his biographer sometime between 1786 and 1789:

> The enemy sent out a large detachment to reconnoitre our Camp, and to ascertain our strength; in consequence of Intelligence that they were within 2 Miles of the Camp a party commanded by Lt. Colo. Mercer of the Virga line (a gallant & good Officer) was sent to dislodge them between whom a Severe conflict & hot firing ensued which lasting some time & appearing to approach the Camp it was conceived that our party was yielding the ground upon which G.W. with permission of the Genl called (for dispatch) for Volunteers and immediately marched at their head to sustain, as was conjectured the retiring troops, led on by the firing till he came within less than half a mile, & it ceasing, he detached Scouts to investigate the cause & to communicate his approach to his friend Colo. Mercer advancing slowly in the meantime — But it being near dusk and the intelligence not having been fully disseminated among Colo. Mercers Corps, and they taking us, for the enemy

who had retreated approaching in another direction commenced a heavy fire upon the relieving party which drew fire in return in spite of all the exertions of the Officers one of whom & several privates were killed and many wounded before a stop could be put to it. To accomplish which G.W. never was in more imminent danger by being between two fires, knocking up with his sword the presented pieces.[27]

The third account was provided by the redoubtable Captain Thomas Bullitt of Grant's defeat fame:

Two detachments from Colonel Washington's regiment (one commanded by himself) were out upon the frontiers endeavouring to surprise a detachment of French troops from Fort Duquesne, but instead of falling in with the French, they met themselves (the day being remarkably dark and foggy); each party mistook the other for the enemy, and a very warm fire was immediately commenced on both sides. Captain Bullitt was one of the first who discovered the mistake, and running between the two parties, waving his hat and calling to them, put a stop to the firing. It was thought and said by several of the officers, and among others by Captain Bullitt, that Colonel Washington did not discover his usual activity and presence of mind upon this occasion.[28]

A fourth account, although badly confused, was recorded by Sergeant Lindenmuth, the German soldier with Burd's Pennsylvania Provincials:

...about 1,100 French and Indians came to attack us. But they were discovered one mile from the Fort. Immediately 2,000 men were sent to meet them. ... to surround them in a valley behind a mountain. They however left their camp and our people ran into each other in the dark and killed 11 [of our] men and also wounded several of ours. They came back in several hours in a distressed state and our enemy sped quickly away [without] having suffered any injury. The next morning ... we buried our dead with heavy hearts.[29]

Finally, Captain Pouchot provided a rather garbled French version of this skirmish: "M. de Corbiere, a colonial captain [actually a lieutenant of French Marines] marched a detachment of 45 Indians, soldiers & Canadians in the direction of LoyalAnon. He encountered a forward party, which he estimated at 7 to 800 men & attacked it. It withdrew in disorder to the camp."[30]

Washington's account, although considerably more stirring than Forbes's rather stilted formal report to Abercromby, was written thirty years after the event, a period in which Washington had been extremely busy. Most likely, Forbes's account was the more accurate of the two, and is more realistic given our knowledge of Forbes's tactical acumen and skills. Attempting to surround a French force would have been an ambitious move, but is indicative of Forbes's determination to carry the fight to the enemy, and to inflict a stinging defeat upon them. Forbes might almost have welcomed the French raid, as it provided him with an fortuitous opportunity to inflict a substantial reverse upon his opponents, and launching a successful double enveloping attack would have provided Forbes an opportunity to gain just such a signal success.

Forbes's selection of the 1st and 2nd Virginia Regiments as the attacking forces is particularly intriguing. At first thought, it would be expected that Forbes would have placed greater confidence in the fighting abilities of his Highlanders, or Bouquet's Royal Americans. Surprisingly, he chose Washington's and Mercer's Virginians instead. Most likely, Forbes selected them based upon their years of service on the frontier, and upon Washington's and Mercer's considerable Indian fighting experience. In order to surround the French, Forbes needed leaders and soldiers well schooled in woods fighting, and he naturally turned to two young, energetic, ambitious officers who had been on nearly continuous military service on the frontier since 1754.

Unfortunately, Forbes was to be disappointed. The tactical and leadership skills of the

Virginia provincials were not well enough developed to execute such a difficult maneuver. As Captain Thomas Bulloch's account unabashedly states, Washington lost control of the situation, and his column collided with Mercer instead of the French and Indians. Although at least Mercer made contact with the French and held his own in the contest, capturing three prisoners in the process, the French were able to slip away, and the Virginian columns ended up engaging in each other in the dark. Some of the fighting with the French was still heavy, as Captain Shelby of the Maryland Battalion was reputed to have "killed with his own hand one of the leading chiefs of the enemy."[31]

What is interesting is that Washington's account is written to place himself and his 1st Virginia Regiment in a more favorable light. Whether or not he was attempting to avoid responsibility for a failed tactical command, or had forgotten the precise details in the thirty years since the incident, cannot be determined. Clearly Washington played a prominent and hazardous role in regaining control of the situation, but until the prisoners were brought in Forbes must have considered it to be yet another missed opportunity of the campaign. Certainly Forbes could not have been pleased with the performance of either Washington or his regiment.

Until, that is, sometime in the evening of November 12, when these three prisoners were hauled before Forbes in his small cabin just outside the east gate of Fort Ligonier. Forbes was a professional officer of long service, and a Scot on top of that, and it can be believed that he could well press an interrogation. He was fluent in French, as he and Bouquet regularly corresponded in that language. However, his use of French may not have proven necessary, as one of the prisoners carried an English name, Richard Johnson. Such a classic English name strongly suggests that he was a soldier who had deserted and joined the French. In so doing he had committed the capital offense of treason, for which the usual penalty was hanging. Scores of English deserters serving with the Jacobite Army at Culloden had been hanged for just such an offense, only twelve years previously. It can easily be believed that Johnson was forthcoming in his interview with Forbes, as the information that he had on Fort Duquesne would have been the only bargaining chip in his possession to save his life.

Thus, Forbes conducted an interrogation with a common prisoner that would determine the fate of the campaign. Following its conclusion, Forbes instructed that a complete written statement be made, which is provided in full. Rarely has such a succinct document had such a monumental impact upon an entire campaign:

> I, Richard Johnson, being made a prisoner near the English Camp at Loyalhanning upon the Request of Brigadier General Forbes, do confess the truth, relating to my self, and give the following just Intelligence of such Affairs of the French, and the present Condition of Fort DuQuesne according to the best of my Knowledge —
>
> It is now four Days past since I left The French Fort, and by Inquiry that I made while I was there of a Dutch Prisoner, He informed me that there were then about Two hundred French Troops in the Fort, Fourty of whom came in Consort with the Indians who appeared here Yesterday But to the best of my Judgement there did not appear to me, to be so many in the Fort as the Dutch Man reported —
>
> By making Inquiry also of the s^d [said] Dutch Man in regard to their Victualing, He gave me to know that they had not more than three Weeks provisions then in the Fort —
>
> And further signified, that if they had not a speedy Supply The Garrison threatened to divest the Fort —
>
> There was a report came to the Indians on the Road hither, that they would shortly have a fresh supply of Provisions at Fort DuQuesne That the English Fleet was defeated by the French and That the French Vessels had arrived safe at Canada with provisions, and that they expected Batteaus from thence loaded with Supplys of Provisions and Three hundred Men But my oppinion of this Report is that it was nothing but to encourage the Indians to be strong & vigilant. —

Forbes's cabin at Fort Ligonier, where the interview with Prisoner Johnson occurred. Reproduction, at Fort Ligonier Museum, Ligonier, Pennsylvania.

I also inquired of the afs^d [aforesaid] Dutchman in regards to their Ammunition He gave me to know that they had plenty and it appeared so to me for they staid [*sic*; I interpret this as meaning "staved"] their Caskes [i.e., powder casks or barrrels] and gave it to the Indians without measure —[32]

The French have lately erected a new Stockade Fort within ab^t [about] a hundred Yards from the old one, and to my Judgement, something larger, but of no considerable Strength as they have no great Guns mounted on it,

As to the Old Fort I cou'd have no Intelligence of what Number of Great guns it mounted, any other than by the French firing four different Guns as a Salutation to any approaching Friendly Indians— Standing by one of the Guns, I took up one of the Balls, I asked the Weight of and Was told it was of Six pound w^t [weight] I observed it was small w:^t, to which they replied it was large enough for the English —[33]

As to the Wall of the old Fort, it is built with a Foundation of Stone three feet high and the other part neatly done with large squared Loggs, I can't judge as to the Breadth of the Foundation [2 or 3 words totally blotted out and illegible] Top I think it about Six feet broad— There is a dry Ditch surrounds the Fort of Eight feet [one word blotted out and illegible — the last letter is clearly "d" and I surmise the word is "broad"] and about six deep, over which Ditch is a Draw Bridge [start of word blotted out and illegible — the last letters might be "ding" and I surmise the word is "leading"] to the Port of the Fort

[signed] Richard Johnson.[34]

For the first time, Forbes had real, definitive, timely human intelligence regarding Fort Duquesne. The information was but four days old, so it was current. Forbes now knew that only two hundred French regulars were at the fort, a comparatively small winter garrison. The French garrison was low on food, with only three weeks in stores, and was contemplating abandoning the fort. Clearly, this suggested that morale was poor at Fort Duquesne.

Additionally, the walls of the fort were only six feet thick, meaning that the 6-pounder cannon and 5½" howitzers with Forbes at the Loyalhanna Encampment could easily breach them.

In retrospect, this interview does not appear to have provided a substantial amount of military intelligence. But, in modern military language, it was "actionable intelligence," that is, it was military information that was timely, accurate, and credible enough that it could be acted upon. This human intelligence was precisely what Forbes had been attempting to gain the entire campaign: comprehensive information on the status and condition of both Fort Duquesne and its garrison. Forbes immediately reversed the decision of the council of war only the day before, and issued orders for a movement on Fort Duquesne the instant that he absorbed Johnson's testimony. The Orderly Book for November 13 instructed: "The line to hold themselves in readiness to March at an Hours warning and the Amunition to be Strictly reviewd and whatever deficiency there may be to be replac'd Immediately According to the Number before Orderd." Without hesitation, Forbes made his decision. He immediately organized his army to initiate the long-delayed third and final parallel against Fort Duquesne, with departure to begin early on the morning of November 15.[35]

• TEN •

"I will sleep in Fort Duquesne or in hell tonight"

The Final Movement on Fort Duquesne and the Occupation of the Forks of the Ohio

The last two weeks of November were the most hazardous of the entire campaign, as Forbes's army left Loyalhanna behind for its final movement upon Fort Duquesne. It was perilous in the extreme, for this movement forward was performed in the very face of the enemy, and every mile carried it closer to the bulwark of French strength, into terrain with which the French and Indian defenders were intimately familiar. It was during the final approach to the Forks of the Ohio three years previously that Braddock had met his demise. Enough officers and soldiers remained with Forbes who had been participants in that ill-fated campaign that Braddock's fate must have been regularly discussed, mournfully remembered, and greatly feared. Although correspondence from this final movement is regretably scarce, two Orderly Books, a scattering of letters, one short journal, and three tactical dispositions have survived which provide a comprehensive understanding of how Forbes executed this dangerous march.

Forbes's motley assemblage of Highlanders, British regulars, provincials, and Native Americans began their march forward on November 15. For this movement, Forbes formally divided his army into four detachments. Three of these detachments were organized as brigades and accompanied him on the movement forward. The fourth detachment remained within the fortifications at Loyalhanna to safeguard the supplies there, and provide Forbes a secure post to fall back upon should that prove either prudent, or necessary in the event of reverse.

The First Brigade, which moved with Forbes, was commanded by the inestimable Colonel Bouquet, and consisted of the three Pennsylvania Battalions and the Royal Americans. Bouquet's Brigade Major was Captain Joseph Shippen of the Pennsylvania Provincials, and Shippen maintained an Orderly Book from November 19 through December 3 that survives today.

The Second Brigade was commanded by Lt. Colonel Montgomery of the 77th Highlanders, and consisted of his own Highlanders and the 2nd Virginia Regiment. The brigade major was Lieutenant James Duff of the Highlanders. This Brigade directly accompanied Forbes, and as a result few written records survive from its officers and soldiers, presumably as most orders from Forbes must have been transmitted verbally.

Colonel Washington commanded the Third Brigade, the last component of Forbes's army destined for the Forks of the Ohio. This brigade consisted of his own 1st Virginia Provincials, along with two companies of artificers (under the command of Captains John Fields and John Posey), the North Carolina Battalion, the Lower Counties Battalion, and the "Royal" Maryland Battalion. The brigade major was Major Stewart of the Virginia provincials. Stewart maintained an Orderly Book throughout the entire advance, from 21 September to 24 November, which has also survived. The size of Washington's Brigade on November 20, which is the only brigade's strength that can be positively ascertained, was 929 officers and soldiers, broken up into 13 divisions composed of 39 platoons.[1]

Finally, what Forbes termed his "Reserve," but was more properly the Loyalhanna garrison, consisted of 200 Highlanders, 200 soldiers from the 2nd Virginia Regiment, and 200 of the Pennsylvania Provincials, the whole commanded by Colonel James Burd of Pennsylvania. This force remained within the Loyalhanna defenses to provide Forbes with a secure rear base, receive and process additional supplies from the east, forward necessary supplies and equipment to the advancing brigades, and receive and care for any wounded, sick or injured soldiers with Forbes's columns.

A light artillery train accompanied Montgomery's Highlanders with the 2nd Brigade.[2] The guns that Forbes took with him on this final advance were comparatively few, but Forbes must have felt that they were more than sufficient to handle Fort Duquesne, based upon the description that the prisoner Johnson had provided:

- twelve $4\frac{2}{5}$" (Coehorn) Mortars;
- four 6-pounder cannon; and
- two $5\frac{1}{2}$" (Royal) Howitzers.[3]

For the march, Montgomery, Bouquet and Washington were all appointed acting "brigadier generals." This was a brevet rank that carried a grandiose title but had no real meaning, except to ensure that they outranked any other officers within their respective brigades to avoid any difficulties of command that might conceivably arise. Forbes instructed, "The Commanding Officers of Corps to send to Captain Hays such a Number of Cartridges as will.... Compleat their Corps with 44 Rounds Per Man besides the 36 rounds which they carry." These additional rounds were packed carefully, clearly marked so that their correct battalions could be readily identified (a great concern given the variety of weapons with the various provincial commands), and loaded into ammunition wagons in such a manner that they would be readily accessible. A "basic load" of eighty rounds per man was an exceptionally large issue of ammunition, as Forbes anticipated that he would have to fight a general engagement before the French yielded Duquesne.[4]

Forbes was determined to move swiftly and relatively unencumbered. For that reason, "The Mens tents to be left pitched & a proportion of each Corps to guard them" were to be left at Loyalhanna Camp. Washington specifically issued Brigade Orders that "No Women are to March with Brigadier Washington's Division."[5] The only wagons that accompanied Forbes were those carrying ammunition and engineering tools.

Based upon a map located in Forbes's headquarters papers, Forbes initially planned a generally due west route, straight from the Loyalhanna Camp to Fort Duquesne. However, as his brigades marched forward, the terrain dictated a change in his course. Specifically, although there are no mountains to cross between Loyalhanna and the forks, there are numerous ridges and small tributaries of the three rivers. Accordingly, Forbes had to adopt a route that followed ridge tops as much as possible, to defer steep ascents and descents whenever possible, and to minimize stream crossings. Such defiles and crossings also presented the French with possible ambush points that Forbes would absolutely have wanted to avoid.

The result was that Forbes's route took a meandering path west from Loyalhanna. His only substantive impediment was Chestnut Ridge, the last of the real ridges of the Allegheny Mountains, and also the first obstacle that he would have to traverse after leaving the camp at Loyalhanna. Chestnut Ridge is about half the size of Laurel Ridge, which Forbes had been able to cross relatively easily. Once atop Chestnut Ridge the army stopped at the old "Grant's Paradise," a name which had apparently gone out of favor late in September. This road had been cut by Burd as early as September, and would have been well established by this time as the British had regularly sent detachments along it. The top of Chestnut Ridge is relatively wide, flat and dry and offered Forbes excellent marching. From here, the route followed the ridge tops and high ground as they took him, generally west, then northwest, then west, then northwest again, and finally due west along the Allegheny River.[6] The terrain here permitted good campsites, which were characteristically placed upon sloping ground to permit drainage when it rained; provided accessibility to a good water supply that could be readily protected; and had defensible ground surrounding the campsite. All these campsites were improved by the construction of simple fortifications established out of earth and logs. A headquarters memorandum provided Forbes's understanding of distances for his final route from his Papers:

From Loyalhanna camp to Chestnut Hill	7 Miles
From Chestnut Hill to the 4 Redoubts	9 Miles
From the Four Redoubts to Washington's Camp	11 Miles
From Washington's Camp to Bouquet's Camp	8 Miles
From Bouquet's Camp to Fort Duquesne	12 Miles
Total, Loyalhanna Camp to Fort Duquesne	47 Miles.[7]

These distances are actually quite accurate. Modern road mileage from Fort Ligonier Museum to Point State Park is fifty-one miles.

Forbes issued detailed instructions regarding the tactical dispositions that his army was to take. Three separate memorandums in Forbes's own hand, filed with his papers from 1758, survive. All three of these provide extremely detailed tactical formations and march instructions. The number of soldiers that they were written for indicates that they were prepared during the final march to Fort Duquesne. Taken together, these memorandums validate that Forbes had made great efforts to study warfare in the woods of North America, and had obviously been particular to inform himself regarding how Braddock and then Grant had been so badly mauled by the French and Indians. His dispositions are quite meticulous, as he certainly expected that he would have to engage the French and Indians on their ground and at the time of their own choosing, before he reached Fort Duquesne. One of these memorandums provides the order of march for the final advance on November 25. The other two appear to be more generic guidelines that the marching brigades were to follow, to prevent their being ambushed during their advance on Fort Duquesne, and to ensure that the brigades could rapidly defend themselves in case the French sallied forth against them. Both of these memorandums provide nearly "textbook" woods tactics, and predate the tactics employed by Henry Bouquet during his famous Bushy Run Campaign of 1763, and advance down the Ohio in 1764. The particular tactics that Bouquet subsequently employed to such advantage, and for which he receives deserved and great credit from numerous military historians and soldiers, were derived from these tactics that Forbes actually devised during the November approach march to Fort Duquesne. Forbes's first concern was with security of his column, based upon his hard-earned familiarity with the expertise of his opponents in the woods:

> As my chief dependence is upon the great number of small parties detachable to reconnoiter quite around us, & some of them always to be immediately upon the body of the enemy, for intelligence of their situation, and distance from us. I have made my disposition for forming the troops in front, taking it for granted that we shall always have timely information to have the army formed in order of battle & ready to receive them before they can attack us, as it is my opinion if the enemy are not discovered by any but the flanking parties ordered to cover the different columns of the main body of our army upon the order of march, that they will be in amongst our troops before they are formed, and immediately throw them into confusion, the fatal consequences of which I have severely experienced.

This last sentence, "the fatal consequences of which I have severely experienced," positively dates this memorandum after Grant's defeat of September 14. Forbes proceeded to order the tactical assignments of his army:

> The Highlanders & Royal Americans to be in the center of the first line, as their business will be to force the enemy by marching directly up to them. Their discipline being in the Regular manner, consequently more under their Officers command & their dependence probably not so great in aiming well & covering themselves with trees.
>   The most active & best woodsmen to be upon the flanks, who are to use their utmost indeavours to surround the enemy.
>   All small parties joining the main body are to fall in upon the right & left, indeavouring to get behind the enemy.
>   Upon the march, the advanced guard to follow the Light Horse as directed in my other plan, and as the leaves are now fallen from the trees, they will be able enough to keep at a proper distance for the columns of the Main Body to form.

That this memorandum was written "as the leaves are now fallen from the trees" certainly places it during the November advance, as leaves typically stay on the trees until late October in western Pennsylvania. Forbes thus broke his army down into small, maneuverable commands that were intended to avoid the panicked massing that in large part had resulted in Braddock's defeat three years earlier. Forbes also adapted the use of files, or soldiers marching in single ranks, to permit rapid movement through the heavily forested terrain west of Loyalhanna:

> The men in the different columns either in the first, or second line, the advanced or rear guards, are to keep as close up to each other as possible upon the march, by which means the line will be sooner formed.
>   An advanced guard form'd to the right & left from 12 columns marching two deep, 50 men in each, who are to take to trees.
>   The front line of the army form'd two deep from 10 columns four deep upon their march, each column having 176 men to be divided into 2 grand divisions, making 88 each & every grand division into two subdivisions, making 44 each, & every subdivision into 2 platoons making 22 each.
>   The second Line of the Army form'd to the right & left in a rank entire from 10 columns 2 deep upon their march. This line to be divided in the same manner as the first, every division containing just half the numbers.
>   The third Line of the army in 11 columns 32 in each, every column to march in an Indian File, a rank intire & are to form from the center to the right & left upon our extream flank of the Infantry in an Indian File, indeavouring to get round the enemy.
>   The Light Horse are to be upon their extream flanks & to gallop round the enemy, attacking them in the rear.
>   But provided that the General should choose to have this third line as a Corps de Reserve, to support the front of the main body. Take post upon strong grounds, as to cover the baggage & provisions in the rear, I would have them march two deep.

Forbes placed great emphasis on the use of flanking parties. In fact, his flank guards comprised nearly half the total strength of his army:

Flankers to the Main body in 8 Divisions, 40 men in each marching abreast, with their flank men next the main body of the Army. Marching upon the track, or path made by the extream divisions of the Advanced Guard. They are to form two deep upon the right & left of the front line, with their flanks from the main body advanced before the front line.

Reconnoitering Parties—120	
The Advanced Guard—600	
Flankers—320	
First Line—1,760	
Second Line—880	
Rear Guard—320	
Strength of the Army—4,000.	
880 men at four feet distance is 1,173 yards, 1 feet	
21 intervals of grand divisions at 6 yards each	126 yards
20 intervals of sub divisions at 4 yards each	80 yards
40 intervals of platoons at 2 yards each	80 yards
Entire of the Front besides flankers	1,459 yards, 1 feet
130 Light Horse & Guides 15 yards distance	1,950 yards.[8]

The Second Memorandum is relatively similar, but is every bit as instructive as the first.

- Small parties of Rangers, or woods men, disposed a considerable distance in the front, the flanks of some immediately upon the main body of the enemy & these parties are always to return upon the opposite wing to the one they marched from in order to cross the tracks of the enemy coming to reconnoiter our army. 148 men.
- 130 Light Horse Men & Guides, marching a breast at 15 yards distance from each other, extends 1,950 yards.
- Six columns of woods men 50 in each, marching two deep, who upon an alarm are to form to the right and left to take to trees, in order to cover the army in forming. These columns are to be furnished with small hatchets & bill hooks, to blaze the trees & open the thick brush, so as to make it passable, for the grand columns of the main body, who by following this course, will keep at a proper distance to form. 600 men.
- Six parties upon the flanks marching in an Indian file abreast, 50 men in each party with the flanks near the body of the army, upon the paths opened by the front columns that march upon the flanks of the light horse. 300 men.
- Four columns 50 men in each, marching in the paths of the columns of the main body in an Indian File, and forming a rear guard, in case they are attacked they are to take to the trees. 200 men, total 1,248.
- Sixteen columns, 172 men in each forming the main body of the army, marching four deep & in the paths opened by the advanced guard. They are to form to the right & the left, each column two deep, eight columns in the front line & eight in the rear, each column to be told off in two grand divisions, each grand division into two sub divisions & each sub division into two platoons, with considerable intervals between each divisions. Upon an attack all the parties either in the front, flank, rear or advanced, are to take post upon our flanks, & endeavour to surround the enemy, & to make it more expeditions, they are to form from the center to the right & left but those parties that make the advanced guard are not to quit their ground till the main body is formed.[9]

This tactical alignment makes extensive use of forces covering the front and flank of his advancing column, and the tactics are focused upon extending out upon the flanks if attacked to prevent the Indians from outflanking the main body. Indeed, these tactics are oriented upon outflanking the Indians by rapidly moving parties to either flank. Captain Pouchot, the experienced French commander, would note of Braddock's and Grant's advances against the Forks of the Ohio: "The English advanced only in the most fearful manner, and that when they were attacked, they could not estimate the numbers of their enemy because our men were always spread out and hidden behind trees. By contrast the English did not dare spread out in unknown territory & thus always remained in formation. As a result they were crushed by the fire of men who were excellent marksmen."[10] However, Forbes was well aware of this English tendency, and it is obvious that on his final march to Fort Duquesne he went to extraordinary lengths to ensure that this mistake was not repeated by his command.

His four brigades organized, ammunition and provisions issued, commanders appointed, and tactics established, Forbes's army was ready to advance. A significant advantage to facilitating Forbes's advance was that the full moon was November 14. Thus, Forbes advanced with good moonlight during the early stages of the advance, when additional light would be useful this late in the year for establishing camps and constructing roads, with the moon growing progressively darker as he approached Fort Duquesne. Forbes would not have wanted to reach Fort Duquesne under a full moon, since, if he needed to perform siege operations, he would want the cover of full darkness to conceal the construction of firing positions for his artillery and supporting trenches. The new moon was November 30, thus providing Forbes with desirable dark nights as he closed in on the French defenses.

Most likely to avoid choking the route with too many men and animals, and to avoid damaging the roads with excessive traffic, Forbes advanced his army by brigades, with staggered starting times and dates. Colonel Armstrong led the march with his Pennsylvanians, leaving Loyalhanna Camp at 8:00 A.M. on November 15. Washington's 3rd Brigade continued the advance at 4:00 P.M. the same day.[11] Washington had a relatively short journey for this day, as he only reached the top of Chestnut Ridge. Still, seven miles' march, considering that he left at 4:00 P.M. and only had one hour of full daylight remaining, is good time. Washington took advantage of the full moon to permit him to leave Loyalhanna Camp so late and still reach the top of Chestnut Ridge before he encamped.

Montgomery's battalion and Forbes remained at Loyalhanna on November 15. Forbes typically remained with the Highlanders for most of the campaign, and he accompanied Montgomery's 2nd Brigade during the advance. The Orderly Book for November 21 specified, "A Lieutenant of the Highland Battalion and 30 Men are to mount a Guard over General Forbes & the same Guard is to Continue upon that duty and not be relieved."[12] Considerable correspondence survives from the advance, primarily between Washington or Bouquet to Forbes, with none to Montgomery, suggesting that Forbes had no need to write Montgomery since he was with him and could presumably pass orders verbally.

On the first day, Armstrong advanced no less than sixteen miles to just beyond what would become known as the "Four Redoubts" camp. Here, he fortified an advanced post. The entrenchments that Armstrong constructed became almost immediately known as "the Four Redoubts." The Potts map depicts four fleches or redans (as they are alternately referred to), simple "V"-shaped entrenchments, constructed in a diamond pattern, with the salient points generally oriented north, east, south and southwest, or in the direction of anticipated attack. An English military engineer described the design and use of redans or fleches: "A work of two faces, usually raised in the field, to cover the quarter guards of a camp, or advanced posts, and often constructed before the glacis of a fortified place, when threatened with a siege, in order to keep the enemy as long at a distance as possible." Thus, Armstrong did not construct true redoubts, which as previously described must be closed fortifications. This engineer further specified that the size of a redan or fleche was determined based upon the terrain to be defended, the size of the defending force, and whether or not the defenders were equipped with artillery. The application of redans during Forbes's final advance is consistent with their intended use "to cover ... advanced posts."[13] And it should be stressed that Forbes ensured that his brigades entrenched every camp once they proceeded past Chestnut Ridge, so that his posts were always protected from attack.

The four fleches were oriented to provide flanking fires in all directions, across the points of the adjacent entrenchments. The size of the fleches cannot be determined, as their scale on his map is obviously exaggerated. Common practice, as for the redoubts previously described, was to adjust their size to the terrain. These redoubts were constructed on the top of a large flat-topped main hill that commanded the surrounding countryside.[14] These were earthen parapets, with fascines or cut log sides, and ditches in front. Since logs were readily available, they may have contained fraises or stockades. These four fleches would not have been large enough to permit an entire brigade to fight from behind them, but the open area within their center was scaled to provide protection for the baggage convoy of the artillery train, wagons, and animals (both draft and beeves). Forbes was pleased with this position, informing Colonel Burd at Loyalhanna, "This Camp ... [is] by nature extreamly strong, and fortifyed with four Redoubts...."[15]

The next morning, November 16, found Washington's two companies of artificers hard at work continuing the road to the west. On this day Washington still found the energy to recommend to Forbes, just one last time: "The keeping Fort DuQuesne ... in its present situation, will be attended with great advantages to the middle Colonies; and I do not know so effectual a way of doing it, as by the communication of Fort Cumberland and Genl Braddocks road."[16] Forbes tactfully ignored the recommendation, which was by this point about four months outdated. Washington constructed about six miles of good road from Chestnut Ridge to the west, following a route marked by the indomitable Captain Evan Shelby of the Maryland Battalion, who had been on a number of scouting parties to Fort Duquesne and was by now extremely familiar with the country between Loyalhanna and the forks. This road required considerable effort to construct. Washington would not reach Armstrong's "New Camp," which was also becoming known as the "Four Redoubts" camp, until "about 11 o'clock" on the evening of November 18. The full moon permitted Washington's men to work late into the night.

On November 16 Forbes issued instructions to Washington to quickly proceed past Armstrong: "[T]he General wishes that you could join him (in cutting the Road) to day, and march together or his Detachment before you as you may think best, and mark out an Incampment at about 20 or 22 miles from here.... You will then take the necessary Tools and march with a sufficient force to the heads of Turtle Creek where you will mark out and entrench your Camp — leaving to Col. Montgomery's Brigade the Road to cut to you."[17] Although these instructions are somewhat confusing, Forbes was in effect "leapfrogging" his brigades forward. That is, one brigade would move well forward and entrench a fortified camp to protect the army. Another brigade would construct the road actually behind the lead brigade, such that this lead brigade to their front could protect the work parties on the road. The third brigade would remain in the rear, so that the roads and encampments were not too crowded, but also performing an important logistical function in safeguarding and forwarding the ammunition and provisions. During the early stages of the advance, when Washington was cutting the road to Armstrong and his redoubts, Montgomery dispatched both axes and bullocks for beef forward to Washington's Brigade.[18]

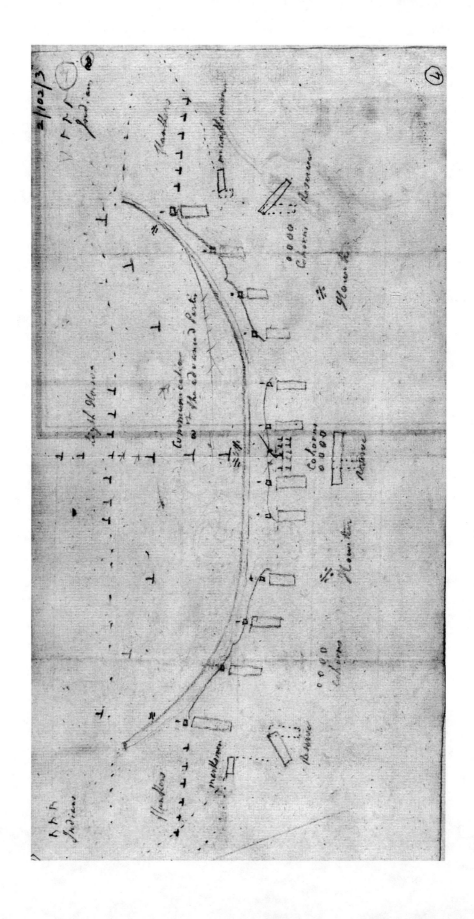

Although Forbes was vigorously pushing his army forward, his health remained precarious. Washington wrote him on November 17, "I was extremely sorry to hear of your Indisposition to-day."[19] Forbes noted that he had written his letter to Washington on November 20 "in my litter."[20] In addition to traveling the entire distance from Loyalhanna forward on his litter, he asked the brigades marching to the front to ensure that there was "a Chimney built for him in each of the extreme Camps."[21] Washington wrote from Armstrong's "Four Redoubts" camp on November 18, "Your chimney at this place is finished — I shall take care to put up one at the next Post." [22] Given Forbes's reduced physical condition, he was in a desperate plight for warmth every night to recoup his energy for the next day's trials.

Washington proceeded forward, leaving Armstrong's Camp at 3:00 A.M. on November 19 to march eleven miles to what would become known as "Washington's Camp" on Turtle Creek. On November 19, Montgomery and Forbes also left Loyalhanna Camp, reaching where Forbes noted "the Camp where they are building the redoubts" about 2:00 P.M. in the afternoon, suggesting that he might have actually left Loyalhanna on November 18.[23]

A portion of Bouquet's Brigade accompanied Washington forward, although Washington apparently laid out the encampment and this camp was named for him. Washington reached that camp on the evening of November 19, and began the construction of a single redan there the next day.[24] Also on November 20 the mundane logistical actions continued, without which Forbes's army could not advance, for the alarming fact was that Forbes was running out of whiskey. On this date Burd wrote Forbes that he had acted to alleviate this shortfall: "I have sent this afternoon 120 pack horses with flour & 12 pack horses with whiskey and 50 bullocks."[25]

In order to expedite his march, Forbes carried most of his supplies on pack horses during this final advance, and depended upon live cattle for his meat rations. Washington noted on November 17, "We have four Carriages with us that pass the Road we have made with great ease."[26] These "four carriages" were ammunition wagons transporting his brigade's spare musket cartridges. Bouquet's column required sixteen horses to draw the four six-pounder cannon accompanying him, along with fifteen wagons drawn by six horses each carrying coehorn mortars, ammunition, tools, rum, and forage for his brigade.[27] Forbes wrote Washington on November 20 regarding his logistical arrangements:

> I have sent forward 30 head of Cattle from the 90 that came from Loyal Hanning with the last Division [Montgomery's Highlanders] they have orders to make no stop until they reach you.... I have ordered 40 of the Waggon horses that arrived yesterday at Loyal Haning (Which are very fine) to be directly sent off with Eight loads of Flour in order to make the train quite easy and as there are a great number of Bats horses loaded with flour I should think the men ought to be putt again to their old Allowance, for otherwise our Cattle will not do and wee have flour enough.[28]

While Forbes's three brigades were hacking their way through the wilderness en route to Fort Duquesne, Burd's Brigade remained in the camp at Loyalhanna. This predominantly Pennsylvania Provincial brigade would never see Fort Duquesne or the Forks of the Ohio. They would never share in the glory of the final advance. But their role at Loyalhanna was critical, for they provided the logistical base upon which the entire British advance depended. One day's guard book survives from the entrenched camp, which could easily

Opposite: **Forbes's order of battle during final movement to Fort Duquesne (National Archives of Scotland, GD45/2/102).**

be referred to as "a day in the life of Loyalhanna." It comprehensively describes a typical day's events and activities as performed by Burd's Brigade, although it pre-dates the primary advance by about ten days.

A Report of the Guards at Lowall Hannon
Genl Forbes Commander in Chief of the Southern Forces
Nov. 6 1758
Parole Charles Town

Guards	Captains	Subalterns	Sergeants	Corporals	Drummers	Rank & File	Centries By Day	Centries By Night
Main Guard	1	1	2	2	1	48	10	10
Detacht from the main Guard	-	-	-	1	9			
Fort Guard	-	1	1	1	1	28	9	9
The West Guard	-	1	1	1	-	21	7	7
North West Guard	-	1	1	1	-	20	6	6
North Guard	-	1	1	1	-	20	6	6
East Guard	-	1	1	1	-	20	6	6
N. East Guard	-	1	1	1	1	20	6	6
Totall	1	7	8	9	3	186	50	50

Occurrances

John McDonold & John Kendall of the Virginians returned from Capt Woodows Detachment not being able to proceed 10 O'Clock A.M. Nov[r] 4th Major Jamison came in with a party of 150 men from the roads, 10 O'Clock A.M. 2 Sottling [Sutlers] waggons belonging to Mr. Smith came in to Camp at 11 O'Clock — Samuel Stellmaker & Guides came in with 2 waggons belonging to Col. Montgomeries & Byrd at 12 O'clock — Capt Sinclair of the Highlanders came with a Detachment of a 100 men from the Road at 2 P.M. — Mr. Bassett Ensign arrived at 2 P:M 1 Waggon belonging to Mr. Bassett came in at 3 O'Clock P.M. — Samson White of Col Byrdes Batt returned from Capt Woodsons Detachment being sick and not able to march. 3 Oclock P.M. 12 of the Volunteers belonging to Maryland left the camp having Discharges from Capt Shelby and 2 Waggonrs who had been Hunting Horses came in to camp at 4 P.M. 3 more of the Maryland Volunteers left the Camp having discharges from Capt. Shelby at 5 oClock P:M Charles Boyle of Capt. Thomson Light Horse came from RaysTown with letters to Sir John Sinclair at 8 Oclock A.M. Nov[r] the 5 1758 Mr. Sinclair Deputy Quartermaster Mr. Hoops & Mr. Clark Commissarys and Lt. Bryan with a party of 16 men came in with 97 pack Horses Loaded with flour & Oates at 12 O'clock

One of the Sentinels belonging to the N East Guard fired at two horses that passed by which he took for the enemy at 1 O'Clock this morning

Jn Dagworthy Lt. Col Maryland Forces.[29]

Thus passed a typical twenty-four hours within the environs of Forbes's principal advanced depot, including the maintenance of a relatively large guard detachment of two hundred soldiers manning fifty sentry posts, various wagons arriving and departing, soldiers detached from sundry commands coming and going, large trains of pack horses entering the stockades filled with supplies, letters being recieved and forwarded, and a nervous night sentry firing at shadows.

With Burd faithfully forwarding supplies and rendering assistance from the camp at Loyalhanna, Forbes could sustain his advance. The remainder of Bouquet's Brigade, commanded by Bouquet himself, moved up on November 20 to Washington's Camp. That day, Montgomery's Brigade remained at the Four Redoubts Camp, constructed the road from the Four Redoubts Camp forward to Washington, and improved the roads backwards (eastwards toward Loyalhanna). Additionally, on this date five scouting parties were dispatched towards Fort Duquesne, composed of one hundred men from the North Carolina and Maryland Battalions. Interestingly, they were directed to scout "at least twelve miles towards the

Fort" but only to send the middle party all the way to the fort. The other four parties were to guard its flanks and support it. This is a rather odd reconnaissance configuration. Presumably, the best scouts were in the center party, and Forbes wanted to protect it from being ambushed or attacked until it was close enough to be sent forward directly to Fort Duquesne. Even the most minor of Forbes's tactical dispositions were meticulously well planned, and carefully considered.

Shortly after arriving at the Four Redoubts Camp, Forbes learned that a Cherokee chief, the Little Carpenter, with a number of his warriors had left the camp and were heading home. Forbes wrote a furious letter to Colonel Burd, of which unfortunately only a portion survives today. Most likely, the ink literally scorched the parchment into ashes, as Forbes was absolutely incensed at such conduct this late in the campaign. The surviving letter fragment includes such passages as "astonished and amazed upon ... villanous desertion ... the methods he had used ... from our assistance at so critical a time." Forbes instructed Burd to strip the Little Carpenter and his warriors of all their weapons and ammunition, and a portion of their presents including horses that had been furnished them, although "their Blankets, shirts, silver truck, &c. are not of that consequence." Forbes suggested, although without much conviction, that Burd "try by gentle methods, before that rougher ones be made off."[30]

Even with the Little Carpenter's desertion, a number of Catawba Indians and Cherokees still accompanied the expedition, probably somewhere between thirty and eighty warriors.[31] These numbers were sufficient to provide Forbes with an effective scouting and screening force. Forbes noted on November 19 that three of the Indians had been sent towards Fort Duquesne on a scout. Forbes issued positive orders on November 20 to ensure that signals were well understood to avoid another "friendly fire" incident:

> The Troops are to be informed that any Partys of Indians whom they meet Carrying a red rag at the end of a Pole are to be received as friends and likewise any Single Indians wearing a blue and red badge ["about" or "above"] their heads as well as a Yellow one.[32]

With these scouting parties out, Forbes apparently felt confident enough to modify his approach tactics slightly. On November 21, Washington was ordered to begin cutting the road forward, while Bouquet's Brigade worked on constructing small defensive fleche at Washington's Camp, and also constructed the road forward from the camp. Washington performed this by moving his brigade forward about eight miles to what would become the next camp, and then dispatching work parties to his rear. The construction of a single fleche is rather odd, as it would have been considerably exposed to attack from the rear. Most likely, four such fleches were proposed here as at the "Four Redoubts Camp" but forward progress occurred so rapidly that the remaining entrenchments were never completed. Finally, Forbes and Montgomery's Brigade marched up to Washington's Camp, which was now becoming relatively crowded.

Forbes was generally displeased with the quality of the road construction, complaining to Bouquet on November 22, "I had no reason either to expect that that the road was better, or better open'd than what I had come, which was so monstrously and Carelessly done that I lost all manner of patience, and was oblidged to employ the artillery guard to make Bridges & Openings to let them pass."[33] To assist with the improvement and maintenance of the roads, Forbes on November 20 from the Four Redoubts Camp had written Colonel Burd at Loyalhanna to send forward "two hundred of your best men ... to take post at this Camp, in order to strengthen Convoys of Provisions &c. coming to the Army, and keep the Communication open."[34] It is interesting that Forbes was focused upon maintaining his combat power and thus had this rear detachment drawn from the Loyalhanna Camp and not his own force. Forbes must also have been confident that his advance would keep the French occupied, for otherwise two hundred men would be quite exposed after detachments for convoy and road duties had been made.

On November 22 the army continued its movement forward. The Orderly Books specified:

> The Army to march ToMorrow Morning in three Columns— The 1st [Bouquet's] & second [Montgomery's] Brigades to march at 7 o'Clock, the 1st Brigade to cover & to carry a small proportion of Axes & the 2d Brigade to open the Road. Mr. Gordon Engineer to attend the 1st Brigade, Mr. Basset to attend the 2nd. The 3rd Brigade [Washington's] to march at 8 o'Clock with the Train, when the Bullocks & heavy Baggage of the troops are to follow in the Rear under an Escort of one hundred Men.[35]

With this, Washington's Brigade now rotated to the rear, after having been predominantly in the van of Forbes's advance since the departure from Loyalhanna. Washington's soldiers were probably pleased with the respite, for they had been performing most of the hard labor of road construction to this date.

By nightfall of November 22, Bouquet had advanced eight miles to establish the next camp, which he entrenched with a single strong fleche oriented to the west in the direction of a presumed French advance. Forbes was close behind him, but because of problems with the condition of the road he stopped short of Bouquet's camp for the night. By early on the morning of November 23, Forbes had joined his entire army at what soon became known as "Bouquet's Camp." Forbes now changed his tactics of moving by brigade columns. Since he was only twelve miles from Fort Duquesne he wanted to amass his army, so that his combat power could be concentrated in case of contact. At this camp, Forbes was literally in the French backyard, and he accordingly issued strict orders to his soldiers:

> Any Soldier who fires his piece without his Officers orders Shall receive 200 Lashes upon the Spot without the Benefit of a Court Martial. ... the greatest Silence always to be observ'd in Camp at night and the Troops to be extreemly Alert upon their posts as we are now so near the Enemy we may expect frequent Alarms, in which Case the Troops are immediately to fall in upon their Incamping Ground, in the Greatest regularity and Silence and their [there] wait for orders & in Case the Alarm happens in the Night both the Divisions and Guards that Cover them are to retire 50 Yards behind the fires and there lay down in regular order on their Bellys— the Sentries are upon no Account to Quit their posts unless forced in by the Enemy.... The Troops to be under Arms at break of Day in the same disposition they Incampd & Continue ½ an Hour.[36]

Forbes further instructed that all men were to: "See that each Man clean his Pan & prime his gun a fresh out of their Horns & see that their Steels are in a proper condition to Strike fire." He issued provisions on this date, six days' worth of flour and four days' worth of meat, such that the army would not need further provisions until November 28. Forbes also had Indian scouting parties moving towards Fort Duquesne to provide him with information on the French, and his soldiers were again cautioned regarding their presence. Clearly, Forbes was preparing for the final movement on Fort Duquesne.

Forbes ensured that his loyal Indians established a protective screen around Bouquet's Camp, as well as using his own soldiers to ensure security for his encampment. He told Bouquet:

> I beg that the Indians be sent forward to morrow for Intelligence, with orders to lye out all next night and watch any force that the Enemy might either send to attack us or bring to their fort, and for the same purpose some of the very best of your Scouters ought to be sent out, with the like

orders.... I think some of the light horse might now be very usefully employed, particularly in gaining all the heights and reconnoitering the Grounds on the flanks.... I have sent the light horse to pass the night upon the tops of the Hills all around.

Forbes was determined to wrest dominance of the ground before Fort Duquesne from the French. During Braddock's advance over three years earlier the French had maintained such supremacy, and been able to surprise Braddock with their attack. Forbes told Washington, "I never doubted of the enemys scouting partys discovering us, but I think it highly necessary that wee discover them likewise, as also the sure knowledge, if ever they send out any force from their fort capable of attacking us."[37]

The French could not have been encouraged by what they saw. Instead of Braddock's ponderous column with poorly established scouting parties blundering naively through the woods, they found a relatively nimble army surrounded by a screen of Native American warriors, horsemen, and rifle-carrying frontiersmen. They must have watched Forbes advancing in loose columns that were capable of forming in short order and extending out to either flank in direct imitation of the Natives' favorite tactic, and been dismayed. The lack of baggage wagons must also have been ominous, as the French understood that Forbes could move as swiftly as they could. The French had achieved a great victory in September, but Forbes hadn't stopped. The French had launched a successful spoiling attack against the camp at Loyalhanna in October, and Forbes hadn't stopped. It must have been painfully obvious to them that this English general and his army had staying power, that they were perfectly well suited to the peculiar conditions of the wilderness, and that they meant business.

Forbes was taking no chances, and issued detailed instructions for the movement forward. Some of these instructions were issued in a shorter form in the Orderly Book for November 24:

When the Army marches it is to be in three Divisions, the 1st Brigade [Bouquet] on the Left, the 2d [Montgomery] in the Center & the 3d [Washington] upon the Right. — Each Brigade to march in 4 or more Columns according to the Nature of the ground, having 8 Light Horse belonging to each Brigade divided at the Head of their different columns besides 6 more upon each of the right & left Flanks of the 1st & 3d Brigades disposed as Flankers marching abreast. — The 4th part of each Brigade is to compose a Corps of Reserve to their respective Brigades & form a 2nd Line behind their Brigades & each to be under the Command of a Field Officer of their own Brigade. — In case the Enemy should appear, the Line of Battle to be formed in single Ranks, leaving the Distance of 150 Yards between the 1st & 2nd Lines, the right & left wings advancing more than the Center in order to surround the Enemy. — The Quarter Master General with a Detachment of 500 Men to march tomorrow at Day-Break in order to reconnoiter & open the Road[38];

A considerably more detailed tactical description is, however, located in Forbes's headquarters papers. Forbes most likely issued these more comprehensive instructions to his three brigadier generals. These orders are written for the three brigades to advance simultaneously. Since the brigades had moved out separately on every other day of the campaign to this point, and did not form a single army until this final day's march on the Forks, this order of march can only date to that planned for and executed on November 25:

Upon the firing of three Cannon, the troops are immediately to prepare for a March, by striking their tents, loading their Batt. Horses &c. and upon the Drums beating to Arms the Troops to assemble and march to their General Parade, the baggage on the rear of each Battalion, where the Commanding Officer of the Line will order them to march off in the following Manner, leaving one Officer and a proper command to take care of the things that may be left behind, which party will join when in readiness and follow the Line under the Command of the Senior Officer of the whole.

Forbes's orders of November 14 at Loyalhanna were that "the men's tents to be left in stores," and Bouquet would write on November 25, "We have neither Tents nor Baggage."[39] However, some limited number of tents were necessary to serve as hospitals for the sick and wounded; to protect stores and ammunition that would be damaged by exposure to the elements; to provide a covered location where provisions could be weighed and issued; and to serve as headquarters where maps and dispatches would have to be examined and letters written. Given Forbes's health problems, he positively required a marquee (a large officer's tent) brought along for his personal quarters, for his General Orders of November 26 would mention "at the General's Tent." Later General Orders also noted that a court-martial would be held at the "President's Tent," verifying that senior officers brought tents to be used as headquarters. These are the tents that Forbes is ordering to be struck.

Forbes's order continued:

1st The piquets of the whole under the Field Officer of the Day, as ane [an] advanced guard who will detach one officer and 25 men before him and likewise send out men at convenient distances upon his flanks to prevent skulking partys. Those flankers ought to be 10 or 15 paces from one another and about 20 or 25 paces upon each side of the main.

2d The Highland Battalion, beginning their March with the two center companies. Each Company in single files or 2 files as the road will allow and those followed by the other Companys upon the right & left so that when they come to halt and form, the two Center Companies keep the ground they are on, the other Companys forming upon their right & left, the whole two deep.

3rd. The first Virginia Battalion marching off by Companys from the right and forming upon the right of the Highlanders.

4th The 2d Virginia Battalion marching from the left and forming upon the left of the Highlanders.

5th The Detachments of the Pennsylvania Regiments, and in order to render the wings near equally strong to be divided upon the right and left of the Virginians, those going to the right marching from the right, and those to the left from the left.

6th The old Quarter Guards to form the rear Guard.

7th The Piquets to retreat to the flanks, and form facing outwards.

8th The Light Troops to send a detachment with one Officer and 25 men before the advance of the piquets, who is likewise to have a small advance and flankers, Alle [all] the rest are to take the right and left of the line as flankers, to the right and left of those of the infantry 30 or 40 yards posted at convenient distances, reconnoitering every where and guarding the heights and different passes until the line passes.

9th The Artillery to march as follows, Coehorns and 2 Six Pounders at the head of the Highlanders, Do at the Head of the Virginians upon our right and two 5 Inch [5½" or Royal] Howitzers on the head of the Virginians on the left.

10th The baggage to march in the rear, the Artillery & Waggons first and the rest in order as the line marches.

The greatest silence to be observed in marching & forming, the Officers to allow none to quit their ranks, and no firing on any pretence whatever.

This last paragraph is all but identical to the General Orders issued by Forbes for November 23: "The men are never to be allowed to carry their firelocks with the guard of the [illegible — probably "muskets" or "arms"] behind their shoulders, but are to carry them properly at all times, taking care in going."[40] In other words, Forbes wanted his soldiers to carry their arms ready for the immediate action that he anticipated at any moment.

The French were closely monitoring Forbes's advance. Pouchot reported, "M. de Corbiere encountered the enemy three leagues away from Fort du Quesne. He went back to warn M. de Lignery." The French commandant at Duquesne was French Marine Captain Francois-Marie Le Marchand de Lignery, whose actions upon Forbes's imminent arrival revealed a definite weakness of character and absence of resolution to resist. Pouchot continued:

...de Lignery who, finding himself short of both troops & supplies, immediately loaded onto his boats what remained of the munitions for the Illinois, together with the artillery, distributed the remaining trade goods to local Indians & himself withdrew with them to Sonnioto and the Riveire a la Roche [down the Ohio River for the French Illinois Colony]. M. de Corbiere, after burning Fort DuQuesne, took the land route to Fort Machault with a few Canadians & soldiers.[41]

The French governor of New France, de Vaudreuil, described Lignery's evacuation of Fort Duquesne in detail in a letter to Paris that he wrote early in 1759:

M. de Ligneris immediately assembled the officers of his garrison to deliberate on the measures he should take under the circumstances to which he was reduced. He had less than 300 men, a third of whom at the most were capable of taking the field. All these gentlemen [his officers] were of the opinion that they should prepare to evacuate the place. Accordingly, they began, from this day [November 19] to cut down the stakes around the new fort [the hornwork to the northeast of the main fort], in the part where there were no houses and where fire would not spread. M. de Ligneris saw that there was no longer any reason to flatter himself. He immediately ordered 8 days' provisions to be taken for the regulars and militia, who were intended to retreat with him to the Machault post. He had the cannon and munitions of war put in bateaux which he sent to the Illinois. When everyone had embarked, when the scouts had returned, and when all the bateaux had left, except one which he had kept, he had the fort set on fire. After this, he embarked to join his force of 192 men, who had orders to wait for him about a league above the fort. To blow up the fort, 50 or 60 barrels of spoiled powder were left in the powder magazine. As soon as M. de Ligneris heard the roar of this mine, he sent three men by land to see what damage it had done. They reported that the fort was entirely reduced to ashes and that the enemy would fall heir to nothing but the ironwork of the community buildings.[42]

As weak as he was, and even without the support of the Native warriors, de Lignery could have sortied aggressively from the fort, as he still had several hundred fighting men available to him. His available soldiers had demonstrated their superior woods fighting skills throughout the war and the campaign, and he could have hoped to have at least bloodied Forbes's advanced party. He could have remained in the fort and forced Forbes to initiate a formal siege. Had either of these tactics been utilized, and in fact both could have been employed sequentially, Lignery might easily have delayed Forbes one to two weeks. Given the onset of winter, which can arrive with full vengeance at any time in November in western Pennsylvania, even a single week's delay might have been sufficient to force Forbes to withdraw.

Instead, Lignery determined to destroy the fort, and flee with his garrison in two separate directions. Again, this decision by itself displayed an utter absence of resolution, as by fleeing both down the Ohio and up the Allegheny he automatically inserted the English between his two commands, ensuring that they could never again be joined. If Lignery planned to recapture the Forks of the Ohio in the spring, he needed to maintain his entire command as a cohesive force, with artillery and the necessary "munitions of war." Had he sent his artillery and ordnance supplies to Fort Machault, and split his command between Forts Niagara, Machault, Le Beouf and Presque Isle for the winter, he could have easily consolidated his command at Fort Machault early in the spring. Once reformed and reinforced from the other Ohio country garrisons, he could have expeditiously moved back down the Allegheny River to attack the British, gathering strengh as he moved south. If the winter was severe, provisions had run short, or sickness had broken out, the British garrison at the forks of the Ohio might well have been in difficult straits by the onset of spring. And the ice in the rivers would clear before the snow would melt in the high passes of the Allegheny Mountains.

Certainly the capture of Fort Frontenac had devastated French logistics from Fort de La

Presentation to the west. Supplies of all kinds, provisions and Indian trade goods in particular, were extremely limited. The other French posts on the Allegheny River route to Fort Duquesne were relatively small, although it must be acknowledged that Fort Niagara was a substantial post. Apparently Lignery did not feel that there were adequate supplies or winter quarters to dispatch his entire garrison to the north. Still, there were numerous French posts to the north, and the English threat was in that direction. Sending a portion of his command to the Illinois Territory permanently removed these soldiers and their arms from the theater of war, at a time when the French in Canada were desperately short of trained manpower and military stores. As discussed, Lignery's splitting his command into two wings practically meant that the Fort Duquesne garrison could never be reassembled. By dispersing his command among the many French forts to the north, it could have been relatively easily reformed in the spring, and even a small post should have been able to accommodate a slight increase in the size of its winter garrison. Lignery's decision, although driven by logistical considerations that he obviously considered paramount, was militarily unsound from both tactical (the ability to implement a spring offensive against the English at the forks of the Ohio) and strategic (the need for his men and munitions in New France) considerations.

Captain Lignery's tactics are inexplicable, and it is hard to arrive at any other determination except that the more resolute, determined commander achieved victory in the Ohio country in late November 1758. Lignery signaled this fact in dramatic fashion to Forbes by destroying Fort Duquesne on November 24, and fleeing ignominiously from the Forks of the Ohio in a manner that almost certainly guaranteed that he could never return.

On the evening of November 24, as the English army began to settle down for its last night's rest before it marched upon Fort Duquesne, his Indian scouts suddenly brought Forbes news that must have raced like fire through his Scottish blood. Bouquet related:

> The 23 we took post at 12 Miles from hence [Fort Duquesne] and halted the 24 for Intelligence. In the Evening our Indians reported that they had discovered a very thick smoak from the Fort [another transcription uses "Front"] extending in the bottom along the Ohio; a few hours after they sent word that the Enemies had abandoned their Fort after having burnt everything.[43]

Captain John Haslett, a Pennsylvanian Provincial Officer, wrote nearly an identical report:

> On the 24th, at night, we were informed by one of our Indian scouts, that he had discovered a cloud of smoke above the place, and soon after another came in with certain intelligence, that it was burnt and abandoned by the enemy.[44]

Some members of the column advised that a simple reconnaissance be sent in the direction of Duquesne. Forbes, who surmised precisely what that massive column of smoke meant, is said to have ordered the entire army to march at dawn with the invective, "I will sleep in Fort Duquesne or in hell tonight."[45] He also issued his usual meticulous orders: "The Light Horse are immediately to March & reconnoiter the French Fort if they find it abandoned they are to take possession of it. The Maryland Forces & Volunteers [presumably his scouts and Indians] are to March at the same time to support the Light Horse & the whole to March with Great precaution in Case of a Surprise."[46]

Sergeant Lindenmuth, with the 2nd Pennsylvania Provincials in Bouquet's Brigade, recalled the stirring events of that day from an infantryman in the ranks' perspective:

> Finally, it was eventually decided to march against the enemy with the entire army ... as the weather was very hard and cold, the march proceeded very poorly until finally on the [23rd] we arrived at Bouquet's encampment or Bouquet's Breastwork. On the morning of the [24th] in a deep snow orders were given for the entire army to march, but then a halt was called due to an

alarm because our leader or pilot had discovered a corps of Indians who however fled as quickly as they could. Immediately the cavalry with 50 men was sent off under Captain Hambrecht's [Captain John Hambright of the 2nd Pennsylvania Provincials, who commanded the Pennsylvania Light Horse] command. But before the infantry could set off, a shuddering was heard, that is to say like an earthquake. We then went in full march. In came the cavalry, however [they] rode forward very hard to about 8 miles this side of the fort, where they were met by a lad of 16 who had run off from them [the Indians], who said that they were occupied in burning everything, which put Captain Hambrecht into such a fervor that he immediately gave orders to set out and they rode with such speed that they still found 7 barrels of powder of which in one magazine one barrel was no further than one London inch from the fire, and also 8 barrels of pork which were saved. The pork was destroyed for fear it had been poisoned. And otherwise all the building were completely in flames. That evening in the night the infantry and cavalry arrived at 6 o'clock and took possession of the place in very hard weather and camped on the open field. The next day everything was inspected and the pickings were very poor. Everything was burned, and the cannons were all gone. We had the place in our possession but they left us nothing besides a destroyed site.[47]

At daybreak on November 25, Forbes's entire army marched forward. The route that he took for the final approach to Duquesne was relatively far to the north, with his right flank anchored on the Allegheny River.[48] Forbes probably selected this route so that at least one of his flanks could be protected against an enfilade attack, and to avoid ascending and then descending Grant's Hill. Quite possibly, he also wanted to avoid taking his men through the site of Grant's defeat, where the dead still lay rotting upon the ground. This would have been an extremely demoralizing sight, and it was certainly one that Forbes wanted to spare his army.

As the sun's rays began to turn scarlet and gold on the western horizon, Forbes's brigades finally reached the shattered, abandoned, still smoldering ruins of the fort. It had taken them eleven hours to march twelve miles while still finishing the road, which indicates that even though Forbes knew that the fort had been abandoned, he still maintained his careful tactical alignment, and marched ready for battle in the event of any French ambuscade. Forbes had run a cautious, carefully considered campaign from the very beginning, and he had no intentions of letting his guard down at the moment of triumph. Such a lack of caution at the very end of the campaign had, after all, cost Braddock his army, his life, and his reputation. But the French were well away, and Forbes had seen to it that the Indians had no interest in opposing his advance.

At some point late in the afternoon of November 25, Brigadier General John Forbes turned a bend or climbed a rise in the crude road hacked through the wilderness, and espied for the first time the deserted, charred remnants of an objective that he had spent eight months moving against, and for which he doubtless knew that he had sacrificed his own life. To a casual observer the blackened logs and ruined mounds of dirt and ditches that had less than twenty-four hours ago been among the most important fortifications in North America would have seemed unimpressive at best. John Ormsby of the Commissary Department would record, "The place had a most desolate appearance."[49] But it must have appeared to Forbes's eyes as the greatest sight that the world could ever, and would ever, offer him.

Bouquet reported that evening:

We marched this morning and found the Report true — they have blown up and destroyed all their Fortifications, Houses, Ovens and Magazines: all the Indian Goods burnt in their stores which seems to have been very considerable.

Captain Haslett, the Pennsylvania Provincial officer, wrote on November 26:

We arrived at 6 o'clock last night and found it in a great measure destroyed. There are two Forts, about 200 yards distant, the one built with immense labour, small, but a great deal of very strong works collected into very little room, and stands on the point of a very narrow neck of land at the confluence of the two great rivers. 'Tis square, and has two ravelins, gabions at each corner, &c. The other Fort stands on the bank of the Allegheny, in form of a parallelogram, but nothing so strong as the other; several of the outworks are lately begun and still unfinished. There are, I think, 30 stacks of chimneys standing, the houses all burnt down. They sprung 1 mine, which ruined one of their magazines. In the other we found 16 barrels of ammunition, a prodigious account of old carriage iron, barrels of guns, about a cartload of scalping knives, &c. They went off in such haste, that they could not make quite the havock of their works they intended.

Forbes issued General Orders from "Camp at Fort DuQuesne.... At 7 o'Clock P.M.:"

One Captain & 50 Men to mount Guard immediately in the Fort, they are to suffer no Body to come into the Fort or any Imbezzlement to be made of the things now in the Fort & to put out all the Fires, except the one for the Benefit of the Guards.[50]

It must have been with immense satisfaction that late that evening Forbes wrote his immediate military commanders, Generals Abercromby and Amherst, the various colonial governors, and William Pitt, the Royal Secretary of State:

I have the pleasure of acquainting you with Signal success of His Majesties Arms over all His Enemies on the Ohio, by having obliged them to burn, and abandon their Fort Duquesne, which they effectuated upon the 24th Instant; and of which I took possession with my light troops the same Evening, and with my little Army the next day —[51]

Having finally seized the Forks of the Ohio after such a long and arduous trial, John Forbes had absolutely no intention of relinquishing the post. Although his army was fearfully exposed to the elements at the site of Fort Duquesne, without tents or baggage, he still tarried long enough to begin the construction of the second British fort on the site of Fort Duquesne. This one would prove slightly more resilient than the small Virginian "Trent's Fort" that had existed on the Forks of the Ohio for only a few weeks in 1754.[52]

Not surprisingly, the first thing that Forbes did at the sight of Fort Duquesne was to give thanks for the victory that his "little Army" had achieved:

November 25th — All the Troops are to attend Divine Service tomorrow forenoon to return Thanks to Almighty God for the remarkable Superiority of His Majesty's Arms over his Enemies, in curbing their Power & Injustifiable Encroachments upon His Majesty's Rights of Dominion.—
November 26th — The Whole Line to attend Divine Services at one o'Clock at the General's Tent; the Rev Mr. Barclay [Beatty] to perform.[53]

On November 27 Forbes also ordered a traditional military salute, the "Fire of Joy" or ceremonial "running fire" to be fired by the army:

The Line to be under Arms tomorrow at 11 o'Clock to fire 3 Vollies on Account of our taking Fort DuQuesne. The Artillery to begin with firing 7 Guns & followed by the 1st Regt. on the Right, seconded by the Corps next to them, then by the 3rd Corps & so on regularly to the left of the Line.[54]

Necessary, and sorrowful, housekeeping was also in order. Knowing from previous scouting reports that Braddock's men remained unburied on the field of battle, Forbes dispatched a party on November 28:

Thirty Men from each of the 3 Brigades to parade Tomorrow Morning at 8 oClock with a proportion of Tools in order to march & bury the Bones upon the Field where General Braddock had his Engagement and any bones that they find upon the Road are likewise to be interred.[55]

A particularly poignant event occurred in conjunction with this event, as Major Halkett accompanied the party to Braddock's Field, where both his father and younger brother had been killed. With the assistance of a now friendly Indian who had been present at the engagement, obviously on the French side, Halkett was able to locate and identify the remains of both his father and brother, supposedly through a particular piece of dental work from his father's skull. Forbes, who had been a very close friend of Colonel Halkett, would have been deeply supportive of the major's mission, and he dispatched a bagpiper and drummer from Montgomery's Regiment to accompany the detachment. The legend is that Colonel and Lieutenant Halkett were given a traditional Scottish funeral on the field of battle, where they had fallen in defense of their King and Country.

The next day a similar party was ordered out to Grant's Hill, "A Detachment of an hundred men who have been in Major Grant's Affair to parade at 9 o'Clock Tomorrow Morning in the front of the 2nd Brigade, All the Officers, Serjts. Who were in that Affair to go to direct the party & to search for & bury the Dead."[56] The English were indignant at discovering that the French had never buried Grant's dead: "We have found numbers of dead bodies within a quarter mile of the Fort, unburied, so many monuments of French humanity."[57] Sadly enough, the frequently discussed and highly romantic story of the heads of Highlanders being found affixed to stakes outside of Fort Duquesne, with their kilts wrapped around them, forming an avenue into the entrance of the French fort has been well debunked.[58] Still, the sight of Grant's dead remaining above ground and scattered about so close to the French fort must have been distressing enough, and Forbes acted quickly to remove these scenes from his army's view.

With celebrations and burials underway or completed, Forbes turned his attention to more pressing matters. Specifically, he needed to prepare a post and garrison to maintain the British presence at the forks. He started this progress on November 28 by exploiting the remnants of Fort Duquesne:

> None of the Square Logs in or about the Camp are to be destroyed by the Soldiers. All the Working Tools are this afternoon to be sent to the Train & Mr. Ward will return the receipts. Twenty men Per Brigade to parade Tomorrow morning at 9 o'Clock in Order to sort the Iron Work in the Fort, And thirty men pr Brigade to parade at the same time in order to work for which they will be paid and to receive their Instructions from an Engineer. These Parties are to assemble in the front of the Royal Americans.[59]

Work having commenced, Forbes pitched upon a garrison, ordering on November 29:

> It is General Forbes's Orders that one Field Officer 2 Captains 6 Subs 8 Serjeants 2 Drums 200 Rank & File be left here to Garrison this Place & that half this Detachment be composed of the first Virginia Regiment & the other half of the two first Battalions of Pennsylvania.... The Garrison of this Place to be completed with good Arms & thirty six rounds of Ammunition each Man....The Troops who are to remain here are to be free of duty and to be employed in erecting their Barracks for which they will be paid.[60]

The commander of the fort was to become Colonel Hugh Mercer of the Pennsylvania Provincials. The fort itself was designed by Forbes's replacement chief engineer, Captain Harry Gordon. Forbes allocated funds in mid–December for Mercer's garrison, and the design and construction of the post.[61] As per the previous instructions, it is clear that substantial portions of Fort Duquesne were incorporated into its construction.

The fort was located approximately 1,000 feet upstream from the site of Fort Duquesne, which had been located nearly at the point where the rivers came together. It was located directly on the banks of the Monongahela River. Historical architect Charles Morse Stotz believed that already the English planned for a massive, permanent fortification at the forks, and that moving this fort so far upstream would remove it from the template of the future construction.[62] This may well be true, and certainly appears logical, but there is no evidence that any plans for the construction of the massive fortification that would later become known as Fort Pitt existed at this comparatively early date. Certainly Forbes had never been issued any instructions regarding the permanent possession of the site of Fort Duquesne. In fact, in the late fall Forbes had written numerous letters attempting to clarify the dispositions that he was to take at the forks in the event of his success. More likely, this position supported a rapid retreat should it become necessary. Being positioned to the southeast of the cleared Forks of the Ohio ensured that good observation could be maintained, so that any advancing French force could be easily spotted. Additionally, well-cleared fields of fire were available to facilitate the fort's being able to defend itself against an infantry attack or raid presumably coming down the Allegheny River. Mercer constructed a number of bateaux at the fort, and in the event of an overwhelming French advance he could use these boats to rapidly retreat up the Monongahela River and eventually back to Fort Cumberland, using waterways or the old Braddock Road as applicable.

The fort was a relatively small affair, originally planned for a garrison of only two hundred men. It was the traditional square, four-bastioned frontier fort, and was placed immediately on the bluff just above the banks of the Monongahela River. It was apparently not elevated to avoid the recurring freshets of the location; rather, the entire fort was constructed at ground level. Its four curtain walls were formed of barracks or storehouses, and its four bastions were a simple stockade. Officers' houses were placed in three of the bastions, and a magazine was placed in one of the southern bastions. It was a small post; the curtain walls were only seventy feet in length, and the officers' houses measured a mere ten by twenty feet. The total size of the fort was only 145 feet on a side.[63]

The storehouses were the most important component of this fort, for they contained the provisions, Indian trade goods, and ammunition that were integral to holding the position. On January 5 these storehouses contained 8,500 pounds of flour, 19,400 pounds of beef, 11,000 pounds of pork, and three bags of salt. Alarmingly, the storehouses were not initially equipped with that most important staple of Provincial frontier life, rum or whiskey. Mercer acted hastily to remedy this critical deficiency, and urgently requested "a Quantity of Rum from the Kings' Store."[64] How an error of this magnitude could possibly have been made after the experiences of a six months' campaign can only be attributed to the excitement of the final advance and occupation of Fort Duquesne, and the urgency of constructing the fortification.

A ditch was constructed around the exterior of the fort. Excavation of this ditch was quite difficult, as the frozen ground could not be penetrated with shovels or spades. Engineer Gordon recommended "with old Axes the Surface may be penetrated should the Frost be very strong, which I have practiced at Fort Edwards where the Frosts are much harder than in this Country."[65] Apparently these must have been very "old Axes" indeed, as using them for picks would immediately destroy whatever utility they might still possess as cutting instruments. Possibly facilitated by the sacrificial destruction of these tools, Mercer reported that the ditch "would be completed in two Days" on January 19.[66]

The fort was not heavily armed, and only six small 4⅖" (coehorn) mortars remained within its defenses. Mercer noted that he had two coehorn mortars mounted in each of the northern bastions, apparently in embrasures, "horizontally ... for firing grape shot," and the other two were placed within the fort to fire shells. In the event that the fort had to be abandoned, the British did not want to make a gift of any substantial artillery to the French.[67] By December 17 the fort was well underway, Mercer noted that "the works [were] carrying on with great expedition, the Barracks being raised & roofed & the Bastions almost inclosed. In a few days more the heaviest parts of our Work will be finished & two new battoes fitted up...."[68] On December 23 Mercer informed Bouquet:

The excessive cold weather is a great interruption to our Works & renders the Opening Ground for a Ditch impracticable. We are now employed in raising a Magazine in hanging the Gate and raising the Bankets [banquettes, or firing steps, in the bastions]. I expect in four Days to have the Place made capable of a tolerable Defence, and am fully determined to maintain the Post, or at least, make it as dear a Purchase to the Enemy as possible.[69]

Bouquet issued Mercer with very detailed instructions, to include extending a stockade from the fort down the banks to the Monongahela River "to prevent the Ennemies taking advantage of the high banks of the River to surprise you in the Night and it would be a good cover for your Battoes." He also advised that Mercer keep patrols out regularly, and advance sentries to the old Fort Duquesne site during the evenings, where they had good fields of observation up the Allegheny River. [70] Mercer stated on January 3 that he was adhering to these instructions.

The fort was expanded in January 1759 to accommodate a slightly larger command of 350 soldiers. This entailed constructing two additional barracks within the center of the fort, and "hutts ... raised in the front within the Intrenchment you have directed to be made."[71] Being located directly on the damp, wet banks of the Monongahela River, these small barracks could not have been particularly comfortable, and adding two more barracks within the fort must have crowded it considerably. Once these two barracks were finished the parade ground inside the fort was only thirty feet by fifty feet, so small that the entire garrison could not be assembled at any one time inside the fort. Given these extremely close quarters, when 150 hogs were sent forward from Loyalhanna in early January, the result could only have been utter chaos within Mercer's command, a scene which fortunately for modern sensibilities went unreported.[72]

Bouquet also directed Mercer in January to add a glacis and chevaux de frise.[73] A glacis was essentially a gently sloped, leveled, unobstructed grade that led from the edge of the ditch extending around the circumference of a fort to the limits of musketry range, thus providing the defenders with unobstructed vision and clear fields of fire in the event of an infantry attack. "Chevaux de frise" were wooden obstructions, with a central wooden post through which sharpened, perpendicular wooden stakes were placed. The pointed ends of the stakes were usually fitted with metal points, and the ends of the massive cross pieces were equipped with chains so that they could be locked to each other, or fastened securely to the ground. They provided portable protection against enemy infantry attack. These were relatively standard defensive measures that would increase the fort's strength against either a deliberate French attack or Indian raid. Exterior improvements to the fort included the construction of an Indian trading and council house outside of its walls, recognizing that allowing Indians access to the interior of the fort constituted a poor idea indeed.[74]

Certainly the fort was not capable of withstanding any sustained attack with artillery, but it could hold out against any Indian incursion or French infantry assault. The fort that was constructed was never formally named; correspondence from it is simply dated "Pittsburgh." Architect Charles Morse Stotz designated it "Fort Mercer" for its commanding officer, to distinguish it from the later Fort Pitt, but this nomenclature was never utilized during the fort's brief existence between 1758 and 1759.[75]

Forbes had first employed the traditional military stratagem of occupying the Forks of the Ohio with a garrison in a strong castle. To enhance his military preparations, and in keeping with Forbes's efforts throughout the campaign to establish a rapport with the Native Americans of the Ohio country, Forbes initiated diplomatic overtures with the Delawares, Shawnees, Mingoes and other Indian nations of the area. Immediately upon capturing Fort

Duquesne he sent out feelers to the various Indian communities and leaders, requesting that a council be held at the first opportunity at the point of the three rivers. Unfortunately, Forbes's health was so precarious, and the living conditions in the field so austere, that he could not remain until the Indians were able to reach him. Instead, he deputized Bouquet to remain in his stead to confer with the Indians upon their arrival.

On December 4, Bouquet met with various Delaware chiefs in the camp. The council followed the traditional mores of such events, with the presentation of presents, in this case gunpowder and lead, from Bouquet to the Indians to validate his earnestness. Once the presents were dispensed with, the conference continued with various greetings, lengthy oratory, and the exchange of strings or belts of wampum to serve as a record of the discussions. Bouquet told the Indians that the English had come merely to expel the French from the country, they would only maintain a small garrison to protect a trading post that they would erect at the point, and that they intended to immediately begin active trading with the Delawares. At this point the British government and army had made no firm decision to construct a massive fortification at the Forks of the Ohio, so possibly Bouquet even believed that he was telling the truth. The Delaware attested to their intent to abide by the provisions of the Treaty of Easton, and promised to assist the British garrison at the point, but stated that they could not guarantee their safety. The Delaware also promised to meet with other Indian nations regarding recent events in the Ohio country. Apparently Bouquet impressed the Indians, for one noted, "[W]e were taken to the commander's house; officers marched before us to keep back the crowd.... We found a fine man who, after the most agreeable of receptions, remained standing as he spoke to us. ... during the four days we were among them, we did not hear a single word which did not tend toward good." The council was never intended to do anything more than open a dialogue between the British and the Natives living west of the Alleghenies, and it succeeded admirably in this regard.[76]

The modern concept of civil-military affairs did not then exist, nor had the great Prussian General Von Clausewitz yet written, "War Does Not Consist of a Single Short Blow."[77] Yet, Forbes clearly comprehended that simply conquering Fort Duquesne would accomplish little, and that only the lodgement of a secure garrison at the site of the French fort would ensure possession of the Ohio country. And Forbes realized that for the English garrison to retain such possession, they would have to first establish and then maintain healthy relationships with the Native inhabitants who had until a short time previously been their armed and hostile opponents, and who greatly outnumbered them. Forbes and Bouquet fostered conditions such that the English could enjoy mutually beneficial and meaningful relationships with these Indians.

The English garrison provided warriors with employment throughout the winter by paying them liberally for fresh meat that they brought into the fort; helped the Natives' families survive the harsh northeastern winter by issuing the Indians with provisions; and earned their respect by requesting their aid and assistance in monitoring the French. As a result, a positive understanding was fostered between the inhabitants of the Ohio country and Mercer's garrison. Later, after the English had constructed a massive fortification at this site without the Natives' permission, and permitted a settlement to grow upon the slopes of the hill fertilized by Grant's dead, this relationship would again disintegrate into conflict. But that moment lay in the distant future, and for the time being Bouquet and Forbes had established a more constructive foundation for the shared occupation of the forks.[78]

Accordingly, another council was held between Lieutenant Colonel Mercer and nine chiefs of the Delawares, Shawnees, and Six Nations (Mingoes) early in January. Mercer reiterated Bouquet's pronouncements, and the Native chiefs responded in kind. Mercer completed his negotiations by providing a keg of rum for concluding festivities, which made the Natives "feel perfectly well again."[79] And proving once again, that absolutely nothing took place on the frontier that was not liberally lubricated with either rum or whiskey, or preferably both!

At this point in their discussions, the councils were being held at a comparatively lower level. The Indians were well aware that the politicians and not the soldiers held the real power. Neither party particularly expected anything monumental or even lasting to be decided upon. But it was of great significance simply that the various parties were now talking with each other. Opening such a dialogue had been a lengthy and complicated process, but it did much to retain English control of the Ohio country. This was a great contribution to peaceful relations; indeed, it was an accomplishment of the first magnitude, for which both Henry Bouquet and John Forbes deserve considerable commendation.

On December 1, Forbes issued those orders that remain today as his most enduring legacy in North America. Specifically, he named the posts upon which he had expended so much labor and effort:

> General Forbes has been pleased to name the different Posts as follows; & all Officers serving in this Army are desired to give them their several appelations either in Writing or otherwise;
>
> Late Fort DuQuesne = Pitsburgh [sic]
> Loyal Hannon   = Fort Ligonier
> Ray's Town   = Fort Bedford.[80]

Having successfully concluded the campaign, Forbes decided to finally relent to the wishes of the young Virginian colonel, and issued him orders to open the last few miles of the Braddock Road in General Orders for November 29:

> The Virginians to be served with ten Days Provisions & march for their own Frontier by General Braddock's Road, which they are to open from hence. A Proportion of Tools must therefore be delivered them bef[ore] they march.[81]

Washington responded to Bouquet on the same date:

> It has been represented to the General that it will be very inconvenient for the Virginia Troops to march along General Braddocks Road as their necessaries of every kind are at Loyal Hannon (Men as well as Officers) and that the advantages proposed in pursuing the old Road; viz. That of opening it, are very trivial; as this can always be done faster than a Body of Men can March (a little repair being wanted only) The general from these considerations seems now Inclined to Order us down by Loyal Hannon. I thought it expedient to inform you of this—[82]

It is surprising that after all the controversy and arguments regarding the opening of Braddock's Road from Virginia to the Forks of the Ohio, that Forbes finally gave Washington the chance to do just that in December 1758, and that Washington actually turned down the opportunity once it was proffered him! In all of his dealings with the business of the roads, Washington had proven that he was still a very young man, and a relatively inexperienced officer. Considerable maturing would be required before he could attain the greatness that he yearned for, and that in fact awaited him.

By early December the work of fortifying the site of Fort Duquesne was well under way, and the Indians had been placated for the time being. The Forks of the Ohio were firmly under English control. The weather was starting to turn solidly into winter, Bouquet on one day noting that the temperature was a frigid sixteen degrees Fahrenheit, and the soldiers were not adequately clothed or equipped for an extended winter stay in such an exposed location. Accordingly, on December 3 the return march began.[83] By this time Forbes was almost certainly terminally ill, and our friend Sergeant Lindenmuth recorded:

> As General Forbes was a sickly man, he did not stay long, but immediately gave orders to build barracks, most of the sick sent to Raystown, as most of the teamsters were going back there. December the [2nd] Captain Morgan received orders to take a command of 40 men and to march on the [3rd] one day ahead of the General to build him a schonsten [the precise meaning of this term is uncertain; presumably it meant a "lean-to" or section of a wall with chimney] to put up his tent against them because of the cold weather where it was necessary, under which command I was included.[84]

Sometime early in the morning of Monday, December 4, 1758, Brigadier General John Forbes departed his newly named Pittsburgh. He headed east into the rising sun whose glowing rays warmed his emaciated body, and offered him hope that he might yet survive to see the rugged green shores of his native land. Just to the east of the forks, as he ascended the first pinnacle that would soon swell and join with its brothers to become the endless ridges of the Allegheny Mountains, Forbes had his litter stopped and turned around. He gazed for the last time upon a crude encampment that was already being transformed into a substantial fortification. Forbes had just written Pitt of his earnest belief that "these dreary deserts will soon be the richest and most fertile of any possessed by the British in North America."[85] It was his reward, and Forbes's heart must have swelled. He now knew that he had conquered.

ELEVEN

"A willing sacrifice ... to King & Country"
Conclusions

The premier newspaper in the colony of Pennsylvania, the *Pennsylvania Gazette*, trumpeted Forbes's victory over Fort Duquesne:

> Blessed be God, the long look'd for Day is arrived, that has now fixed us on the Banks of the Ohio! With great Propriety called La Belle Riviere.... These Advantages have been procured for us by the Prudence and Abilities of General FORBES, without Stroke of Sword.... The Difficulties he had to struggle with were great. To maintain Armies in a Wilderness, Hundreds of Miles from the Settlements; to march them by untrodden Paths, over almost impassable Mountains, thro' thick Woods and dangerous Defiles, required both Foresight and Experience. ... consider [General Forbes's] long and dangerous Sickness, under which a Man of less Spirits must have sunk; and the advanced Season, which would have deterred a less determined Leader, and think that he has surmounted all these Difficulties, that he has conquered all this Country, has driven the French from the Ohio, and obliged them to blow up their Fort.... Thanks to Heaven, their [French] Reign on this Continent promises no long Duration![1]

With Colonel Mercer's force safely if not quite snugly ensconced in the newly christened Pittsburgh, Forbes and the army returned to more established winter quarters to the east. Garrisons were to be left along Forbes's new road, and arrangements were made for provisions to be convoyed to the Forks of the Ohio as the vagaries of weather permitted. Forbes and Bouquet settled in Philadelphia. Here, Forbes attempted to unravel the tangled accounts of his expedition, although his ravaged body limited his exertions. Major Halkett was dispatched across the Atlantic Ocean as Forbes's personal representative to Ligonier, William Pitt, and the Crown to document the victory. Those soldiers unfortunate enough to remain in the further western garrisons pulled up what was left of their collars and tugged their tattered sleeves down their wrists as they settled in for a long, cold winter in the crudely constructed stockades. Those lucky enough to return to the more settled townships of eastern Pennsylvania enjoyed considerably more comfortable barracks for the season. All of them knew that spring would bring another expedition into the wilderness. New France had been rocked back on its heels by the campaigns of 1758, and the new British commander, General Jeffery Amherst, would certainly strive for a knockout blow in 1759. More work awaited them.

Even with the campaign brought to a successful conclusion, St. Clair remained a thorn in Forbes's side. Almost immediately upon his return over the mountains, St. Clair rushed for British Army Headquarters in New York, to complain to Amherst of his treatment during the campaign. Wearily, Forbes wrote to his old comrade in arms, for Amherst and Forbes had served together on Lord Ligonier's staff for a number of years throughout the War of Austrian Succession in Flanders:

Sir John Sinclair being gone to York will attack you upon a subject upon which I must put you on your guard. He has taken it in his Noble mind, that as Quartermaster General he commands in the army wherever he comes, outposts, Detachments &c. are instantaneously to obey his sovereign will, and even Garrisons have been threatened with pains & penaltys for not attending him immediately on his arrival and receiving the parole & report of the State of their Garrison. This fancy tho never so absurd is not to be removed by me altho I told him that I had a longer experience than him in that office of Quartermaster General, and never lookt upon myself in the active military Capacity — but only as a person employed to take care of the Police of the Army. This has not hindered him from interfering with military command & putting several field officers in arrest for not complying with his immediate orders.... I beg if he talks to you, that you will set him right as to this affair.[2]

As regards Colonel Bouquet's impressions of St. Clair's accomplishments and performance throughout the campaign, he dispatched a long missive to Forbes on February 14, 1759, in which he at great length and in exhaustive detail scourged St. Clair's conduct:

Sir John's maneuvers do not surprise me. I have heard reports of so many deeds of this sort, and have seen so many myself, that there is nothing so low that I do not think him capable of.... General Amherst, not knowing him, may have let himself be imposed on by his audacity, but if he wants to cast his eye on the innumerable proofs which can be given of his incapacity and of his character, I do not think he would be much inclined to risk the success of an expedition with such a quartermaster general. He brought us within a hair's breadth of disaster by a total lack of forage, and he involved the government in very great expenses by the number of horses which perished and the wagons abandoned on this occasion. But on that important point he should be condemned ... with the whole army I can certify to the fact, which is that we had no other stores of forgage than those you yourself established in September, and that no one knows him ever to have taken any trouble or step about this. As to the roads, and the part he had in finding and opening them, I can furnish convincing proofs that this man's sole talent is to bring disorder and confusion wherever he is, and to delay and ruin the service as soon as he is given the slightest authority. At the time of his difference with Colonel Stephen, although I believed him in the wrong, I treated him with all possible consideration. ... he has not ceased to malign me secretly ever since, wherever he found people willing to listen to him. I abhor such infamous practices, and I spoke plainly enough to him at Ligonier to reduce to silence any man who had a trace of deceny and honesty left. He has spread his underhanded defamations too long. It is time to snatch away the mask and reveal the man as he is.[3]

No record is maintained of St. Clair's reception at Amherst's headquarters. Forbes and Amherst were friends of long standing, Forbes was known to be an extremely ill man who had just achieved a monumental victory for British arms, and Forbes and Amherst both enjoyed the patronage of Lord Ligonier, and through him William Pitt. John St. Clair was almost certainly disappointed in his intrigues. This can be inferred from the fact that although two years of major campaigning remained in North America, with subsequent expeditions by the same army in the West Indies, and further campaigns against the Indians participating in Pontiac's Rebellion, St. Clair was never again entrusted with a significant military or civil responsibility, or active command of soldiers.[4]

Colonel Henry Bouquet remained in western Pennsylvania. He would continue to play a leading role in subsequent campaigns, first to establish the large English fortification of Fort Pitt on the site of Fort Duquesne, and then to defend that fortification against an Indian uprising of staggering magnitude. His victory over the Indians at Bushy Run in early August 1763, and his ensuing 1764 campaign against the Indians of the Muskingham River Valley of Ohio, are canonized as textbook cases of successful wilderness operations. Nobody in the North American colonies was surprised. After all, Bouquet had studied under a master tutor. He would eventually be promoted to brigadier general in the British Army, and be appointed commander of the Southern District of North America. He died of yellow fever shortly after assuming this responsibility, at Pensacola, Florida, on September 2, 1765. It was a great loss to both England and America.

Surprisingly, upon his release from French captivity, Major James Grant would be chosen to lead another expedition against the Cherokee Indians in the Carolina back country. Grant would go on to an extremely distinguished career, to include serving as Royal Governor of East Florida, commanding an infantry brigade with Lord Howe in the War for American Independence, and holding an independent command of a British army in the West Indies. Grant eventually retired to his Scottish estate of Ballindalloch Castle as a well-respected and highly regarded major general. He died there in 1806. Why the British army ever again entrusted James Grant with an independent command after the disaster at Fort Duquesne must remain a mystery. He must have been one smooth talking, well-connected Scottish gentleman.[5]

Colonel Montgomery commanded his regiment the next year in the successful campaign that General Jeffery Amherst led against the French forts of Carillon at Ticonderoga, and St. Frederick at Crown Point. Montgomery led a punitive expedition against the Cherokee Indians in 1760, and then returned home to Scotland on account of poor health. He subsequently served as a minister of Parliament, and held numerous high-ranking civil and military appointments in England and Scotland. He became the Earl of Eglinton upon the death of his brother in 1776. He died a full general and colonel of the Royal Scots Grays on October 30, 1796, following a successful and highly distinguished career in the service of his country.[6]

Captain Francis Halkett carried news of Forbes's victory back to England, as the final bit of patronage that Forbes could provide to him. He was suitably rewarded, being given a permanent promotion to major in the 44th Foot. Unfortunately, he did not long enjoy his new rank, as he died in 1760. He was not married and had no children.[7]

In many ways, the Forbes campaign provided the training ground for the future Continental Army. It was a result that Forbes could never have foreseen, and would doubtless not have approved. But the military education that Forbes had provided so many provincial soldiers would have a momentous impact upon the ability of a new nation to conduct a successful contest of armed will within less than two decades.

The most prominent of these, of course, was young Colonel George Washington. Washington had done little to impress Forbes during this campaign; at one point Forbes told Bouquet, "His Behaviour about the roads, was no ways like a Soldier."[8] This was a crushing condemnation from a professional officer such as Forbes. Washington's performance on November 12, 1758, was likewise abysmal. Throughout the campaign, one gains the distinct impression that Forbes monitored Washington's performance very carefully, and pushed him quite hard. Washington had enjoyed a good relationship with Braddock, and had served Braddock as an aide de camp "in his own family." Washington had a drastically different relationship with Forbes, for he was a senior regimental commander under the command of a hard-driving and determined Scots officer. It is obvious that Washington never enjoyed the close and friendly personal relationship with Forbes that he had appreciated with Braddock. Still, Washington learned much from Forbes during the campaign. When Washington faced the challenge of forming his own national army from a disparate assemblage of state militias, one suspects that he gained from the example of John Forbes. As with Bouquet, Washington had studied under a master, and the lessons that he learned on this campaign would stand him in good stead as he moved to greatness commanding his own army less than two decades later.

Colonel John Armstrong continued to serve the British Army through the Seven Years' War and Pontiac's Rebellion. He subsequently became a surveyor, and was a prominent citizen of Carlisle and Cumberland County, Pennsylvania. He was an elder of the First Presbyterian Church in Carlisle. In March 1776 he was commissioned a brigadier general in the Continental Army. He played a prominent role in the defense of Charleston in 1776. He served throughout the 1776 and 1777 campaigns as a militia commander with Washington's Continental Army. Because of poor health, he then retired from active military service. He served as a member of Congress from Pennsylvania, both during the American Revolution, and from 1787 to 1788. For decades he was a leading and well respected citizen of Cumberland County, and state and national politicians and military and civil leaders regularly consulted with him. Armstrong was one of the founding fathers of Dickinson College in Carlisle, after the conclusion of the Revolution. He died in that city on March 9, 1795.[9]

Lieutenant Colonel Adam Stephen continued to serve throughout the Seven Years' War and Pontiac's Rebellion, and he also participated in pacification campaigns against the Southern Indians on several occasions. He ended his British military service as a Virginia regimental commander, and subsequently participated as a commanding officer in Dunmore's War. He ran for office in the Virginia House of Burgesses, and became a founding father of Frederick and Berkeley Counties, Virginia. He was an early and ardent patriot in Virginia, and fought in preliminary skirmishes to expel the British Royal Governor and his supporters. He became a brigadier general in the Continental Army, and as a brigade commander he served with considerable distinction at Trenton and Princeton. Promoted to major general, he served throughout the 1777 Philadelphia Campaign under George Washington, but was cashiered for misbehavior at the Battle of Germantown in October 1777. He returned to the county that he had formed, and died July 16, 1791, in Martinsburg, Virginia. His prominent stone home in Martinsburg (now in West Virginia) remains an important landmark in that community.[10]

Colonel Hugh Mercer served with great distinction and accomplishment as commander at Forbes's new post at Pittsburgh. He returned to his home of Fredericksburg, Virginia, following the cessation of the Seven Years' War and opened an apothecary shop that became prosperous. Mercer was one of the founding citizens of Fredericksburg and Caroline County, and was politically prominent. He was a founding member of the Fredericksburg Masonic Lodge, and served as master of that lodge for two years. An ardent American patriot, he joined the American Army quite early, raising the 3rd Virginia Regiment of the Continental Line in January 1776. He served with great distinction throughout the campaigns around New York and in New Jersey in 1776. Promoted to brigadier general, he commanded a brigade with considerable skill and courage at Trenton. Leading the American advance at Princeton, New Jersey, he was mortally wounded on January 3, 1777, and died there nine days later. He was considered to be the American hero of the battle, and his accomplishments remain commemorated by monuments at Princeton and Fredericksburg. His apothecary shop survives today in Fredericksburg, and is a popular tourist destination in that city's historic district.

Colonel James Burd served with the Pennsylvania Provincials and the British army until the conclusion of the Seven Years' War. He served the remainder of his life as a prominent judge and magistrate in Lancaster County, Pennsylvania. He played no role in the American Revolution. He was a leading member of his community and state. Colonel James Burd died at "Tinian," his farm near Highspire, Dauphin County, Pennsylvania, on October 5, 1793.[11]

A young doctor named John Morgan, only 23 years old, served as a first lieutenant in the Pennsylvania Provincials with Forbes. Although he was relatively undistinguished on the campaign, his military experience was to prove both formative and invaluable. Possibly after observing the problems of health and hygiene that plagued not only Forbes's army but indeed all 18th-century armies, he became one of the American colonies' foremost physicians. In 1765 he was a founder of the first colonial medical school, which eventually became the School of Medicine of the University of Pennsylvania. Also a prominent patriot, he served as director general and physician in chief of the Medical Department of the Continental Army during its formulative period from October 15, 1775, to January 9, 1777.[12] Although Morgan was a physician before the campaign, it is apparent that his experiences convinced him that the colonies required considerably better medical training and expertise, and he subsequently dedicated his life to that end.

And besides these prominent officers, many of the enlisted provincial soldiers and junior officers on the campaign later joined the Continental Army, either as officers or experienced NCOs. Sergeant Lindenmuth served as first a major and then a colonel with the Pennsylvania Militia, from 1775 through 1780. The accomplished Captain Bullett of Virginia fought as a lieutenant colonel in the Virginia Militia at the Battle of Great Bridge in Virginia in 1775, and served with the Continental Army as a field grade staff officer in 1776 and 1777.[13] Captain Evan Shelby of Maryland also had a particularly distinguished career. Shelby eventually moved to what was then southwestern Virginia, and became a founding father of the state of Tennessee. He served as one of the American leaders at the Battle of Kings Mountain in 1780 that decisively defeated a British army in South Carolina, and did much to win victory for the patriots in the south. Thomas Hutchins was a Lieutenant in the 3rd Battalion of the Pennsylvania Provincials during the Forbes Campaign. His contributions during the campaign itself were not particularly significant. His superlative performance as quartermaster for Mercer's Fort, throughout its short existence at the Forks of the Ohio, gained him considerable recognition. Hutchins would go on to participate in a number of military campaigns during the Seven Years' War with increasingly greater responsibility, became an ensign in the British Royal American Regiment (a substantial accomplishment for any American Colonial), provided excellent service to the Indian Department, and was recognized as an extremely accomplished and prominent surveyor in the early years of the United States.[14] Ensign William Crawford served with Washington's Virginia Regiment during this campaign. As with many officers and enlisted men, his service was apparently steady and reliable, but not significant enough to have garnered individual recognition. After the war Crawford settled along the Braddock Road, and along with Washington he was a strong advocate for Virginia's unsuccessful effort to expand into the area. He was a prominent early settler of the Ohio country. He served as justice and surveyor for the newly organized "Yohogania County" of Virginia. A colonel with the Continental Army, he was an accomplished regimental commander. In this capacity he served at Trenton and Princeton in 1776 and in the Philadelphia Campaign in 1777, and then on the western frontier. In 1782 he led an unsuccesful expedition west into the Ohio terrority in the course of which he was captured by hostile Indians, brutally tortured and eventually killed. The number of junior officers and enlisted men who served under Forbes and Bouquet, and went on to careers both distinguished and important, is remarkable.

However, some other officers were not so fortunate. Lieutenant Colonel George Mercer of Virginia was elected to the Virginia House of Burgesses following the end of the Seven Years' War. He accepted what promised to be a financially and politically lucrative position as the official representative of the Ohio Company to England in 1763. Unfortunately, he remained isolated in England with these duties while patriotic fervor began to grow in the colonies. He accepted the position of stamp collector for the colonies of Virginia and Maryland in 1765, and became the subject of much discord and garnered considerable ill feelings from his fellow colonists as a result of his perceived support of the wildly unpopular Stamp Act. He had fallen into deep debt on behalf of the Ohio Company in England, eventually became bankrupt, and was now universally disliked in his home colony. He remained in England, desperately attempting to reverse his financial decline, and slowly and inexorably slid into insanity. He died alone and forgotten in London in April 1784.[15]

As regards the querulous Quartermaster John St. Clair, he remained in America for nearly another decade, only briefly returning once to his native Scotland. His remaining years of military service and civilian life in North America were entirely undistinguished in every possible way. Presumably, he spent the time bungling whatever assignments were entrusted to him, browbeating his subordinates, arguing with his peers, and complaining to and conspiring against his superiors. He died at Belville, Union County, New Jersey, on November 26, 1767.[16]

The saga of Colonel William Byrd III of Virginia is perhaps the saddest of all. A superlative regimental commander who had served Forbes well, he continued to command with skill and aplomb throughout the Seven Years' War. He enjoyed a reputation as a congenial gentleman, and was quite well regarded in Virginia. Yet Byrd enjoyed a dissolute lifestyle, and amassed gambling debts of staggering magnitude. Although he was the senior member of one of the most prominent and prosperous families in the North American colonies, he squandered the family fortune, and was bankrupt by 1769. Most of his life was spent struggling with his massive debts. He remained loyal to King George III, fled to England at the onset of the Revolutionary War, and committed suicide in London on January 1, 1777.[17] It was a depressing end for a gallant officer and distinguished gentleman.

Forbes and Bouquet ran nearly a perfect campaign; only one single error of any magnitude was made, and that by Colonel Bouquet. This single greatest mistake was the authorization by Bouquet for Major James Grant to proceed with his September attack upon Fort Duquesne. Still, Bouquet ameliorated his risky decision by issuing Major Grant with prohibitive and peremptory orders for the conduct of his independent expedition. Grant himself must bear the overwhelming majority of the blame for this debacle, for he blatantly and gratuitously violated Bouquet's instructions, and displayed stunningly flawed tactics and incredibly poor decision-making once he arrived before the French fort. Although this would eventually comprise an operational victory for the campaign, it was a crushing tactical defeat of the same magnitude of Braddock's defeat three years earlier, and could easily have resulted in the failure of the entire effort. Bouquet's justifications to Forbes appear weak and unconvincing, and clearly Forbes would never have approved of Grant's expedition. Although Bouquet is traditionally considered by historians to have been one of the most effective frontier commanders of the British Army, and his 1763 and 1764 campaigns against the Indians are particularly well regarded, this was a fearfully poor decision, and he deserved considerably stronger censure than Forbes actually issued.

This is the only substantial error that these two leaders made throughout the campaign. It should be noted that a pair of modern historians have challenged Forbes's and Bouquet's resorting to impressment to obtain wagons and horses to support the campaign.[18] These historians go so far as to suggest that this impressment directly contributed to revolutionary fervor in Pennsylvania some ten and fifteen years later. However, without wagons and horses the campaign would have failed, and it is difficult to understand what other alternatives were available to Forbes and Bouquet. The British Army of 1758 was not organized, funded, equipped, or even permitted to purchase, operate or maintain their own transportation wagons, teamsters and horses. The only authorized carriages were the ammunition wagons, powder carts and traveling forges in the artillery train that actually belonged to the Board of Ordnance; but even these were not permitted horses or teamsters, which had to be locally procured. Before Forbes could purchase his own wagons or horses, or have wagons manufactured for him and shipped from England, he would have had to receive authorization from his immediate superior, British commander in chief General James Abercromby. Abercromby was a long-serving British army officer not exactly renowned for his innovative or creative approach to problem solving, as his actions before Fort Ticonderoga in July 1758 well demonstrate. Even if Abercromby authorized the direct purchase of wagons and horses, in itself extremely unlikely, such a diametric shift in British military policy and expenditures would have had to have receive final approval from England, meaning that a year's delay would certainly ensue. And Forbes and Bouquet would still have been without horses, for transportation of large numbers of animals across the Atlantic Ocean remained a difficult and frequently unsuccessful operation.

The price paid for the wagons, fifteen shillings a day, certainly appeared to be a more than adequate compensation. At one time, Forbes even permitted the Pennsylvanians to set their own price, "leaving the price to be paid them by us, to themselves, only begging that there might be no time lost in the execution."[19] Forbes would write to Governor Denny, "I know ... that several Waggoners has been abused by Officers. No Driver ever made his Complaint but the Person who abused him was punished." Forbes and Bouquet exhaustively corresponded with the various county officials in their attempts to obtain sufficient wagons, from the absolute commencement of the campaign, and more than adequate notice was provided to the farmers. The campaign's successful conclusion was absolutely integral to the safety and security of the colony, and Pennsylvania would be certain to reap immediate and dramatic commercial and economic benefits from the campaign's success. Fair wages were offered, along with liberal contractual terms. The wagons were routinely placed under the supervision of local wagonmasters rather than British officers, and every effort was made to ensure that the teamsters were not abused. Still, the wagons and teams were not forthcoming.

The record of the Pennsylvanians is not exactly pristine in their relationship with the army. Forbes was quite frustrated, at one point complaining to Bouquet, "I believe neither you nor I.... Interest ourselves either with Virginia or Pennsylvania, which last I hope will be damn'd for their treatment of us with the Waggons, and every other thing where they could profit by us from their impositions, altho at the risk of our perdition."[20] Certainly it appears that Forbes and Bouquet made every effort to obtain wagons through contract, before they finally resorted to draconian measures. After reading about the perfidy of the Pennsylvanians, one is led to believe that they almost deserved it. And the coupling by these two modern historians of Revolutionary ardor in Pennsylvania to the impressment of wagons for this campaign is not only tenuous, but imaginary, for no primary source documentation has been located that validates such claims.

Forbes's victory was attributable to a number of reasons, both external and internal to the campaign. The single greatest external factor that was outside of Forbes's influence was Bradstreet's capture of Fort Frontenac. The ensuing destruction of French supplies and transportation assets on Lake Ontario had an immediate, direct, and significant effect upon the French ability to logistically maintain and thus defend Fort Duquesne. In particular, the massive loss of provisions and Indian trade goods was devastating. French Commander Pouchot would go so far as to state, "The loss of Fort Frontenac ... caused the loss of Fort duQuesne."[21] Perhaps this was an exaggeration, but Bradstreet certainly did much to assist Forbes with his successful expedition to the Catarqui River.

With this exception, the success of the campaign was entirely due to factors that Forbes and Bouquet directly influenced. The first of these was of course the smooth working relationship between these two senior officers. Although Forbes and Bouquet had only met for the first time at Philadelphia in early May at the very commencement of the campaign, they instantaneously formed a bond. Their voluminous correspondence documents a relaxed, comfortable relationship with Forbes clearly in command, but confident enough to delegate all necessary responsibility and authority to Bouquet to guide the advanced components of the army. Forbes in turn assumed the considerably more onerous and less glorious position of staying in the rear of the army to push the cornucopia of soldiers, provisions, ammunition, arms, wagons, horses, whiskey, rum and military equipment forward to Bouquet, who would then apply them to advancing towards Fort Duquesne.

To many military amateurs, logistics receives little attention and generates even less interest. Academic historians find the clash of armies guided by charismatic leaders and besotten villains replete with aggressive tactical evolutions, glorious deeds, dashing charges and spectacular failures to be considerably more fascinating, while many military buffs tend to wallow in the microanalysis of uniform and weapon details. Analyzing identical barrels of salt pork ensconced in a ramshackle wilderness storehouse so freshly constructed that it still oozes pine tar does not readily lend itself to the formulation of particularly interesting history. But without those monotonous rows and stacks of slowly moldering barrels of salt pork, the soldiers would never make it to the battlefield. A squeaking, badly worn Pennsylvania farm wagon creeping across a muddy valley carrying a load of these same barrels, one wagon in several score of a convoy, is similarly boring and repetitous. But until something moves, no military campaign happens. Forbes well understood that purchasing, moving, inventorying and distributing the contents of those barrels of salt pork was infinitely more important to his campaign than delving into the facing colors of the Pennsylvania Provincials' coats, or correcting the particular weaving of the regimental lace of Montgomery's Highlanders. Succinctly, regimental buttons cannot be eaten. Salt pork can. And Forbes was well aware of this. Without his exhaustive attention to the logistics portion of the campaign, it would never have succeeded.

The colony of Pennsylvania had never before supported a military campaign. There were no established military contractors, vendors or suppliers in Philadelphia. The tradesmen, factories and manufacturers in the province were not familiar with British army pricing, contractual and payment procedures. Not one soldier was stationed in Philadelphia on April Fools' Day, 1758. When Forbes arrived in Philadelphia in April, only a single preparation had been made for the campaign. And that single preparation, the recruitment of Southern Indians for the campaign, was absolutely untimely, as no arrangements had been made in turn for their reception.

Forbes had to personally ensure that every single item required by his army, from the simplest linchpin for an ammunition wagon, to more familiar military items such as muskets, cannon balls, and uniforms, was available.[22] The tabular list of ordnance equipment alone provided in Appendix B documents the complexity and magnitude of this effort.

Competent, trustworthy suppliers had to be located; negotiations for terms and prices performed; legally binding contracts issued; prototypes received and inspected; final productions delivered and approved; the items packaged and transported to the appropriate military organization, and finally properly issued so that accountability could be maintained. An entire army had to be recruited, assembled, properly mustered, uniformed, armed and equipped, receive at least some rudimentary discipline and training, and then be dispatched to Bouquet.

And even with that monumental task accomplished, if Forbes departed Philadelphia before all necessary logistical and transportation arrangements had been completed, then the campaign would grind to a rapid cessation. Additionally, by spending a considerable amount of time in Philadelphia, Forbes was able to formulate a smooth working relationship with key individuals such as the many contractors and businessmen, the proprietary governor of Pennsylvania, representatives of the Colonial Assembly, and even Quaker merchants such as Pemberton. Forbes's decision to remain in the rear throughout the formulative stages of the campaign, where little commendation but much tedium and aggravation would be found, was the second internal reason for the success of the campaign.

Third, Forbes commanded what in modern military terms would be referred to as a "joint task force," or perhaps more properly a "multinational coalition." His army contained provincials from five separate colonies, English recruits led by predominantly German officers, British artillerymen, Highlanders, and Native Americans of at least three different nations. None of these men had ever served together before. In such a fractious force, discord could easily erupt, and literally tear the entire army apart. The potential for such disharmony clearly existed, as the example of the controversy of whether a new road would be constructed from Pennsylvania, or the Braddock Road would be used from Virginia, well demonstrated. Surviving records from the earlier Braddock campaign convey that Braddock's army never became an integrated whole; rather, it functioned as a discordant assemblage of provincials, regular independent companies, and the British regulars that Braddock brought with him from Ireland. Forbes expended considerable efforts to prevent his army from degenerating into such a segmented collection of disparate armed entities, striving instead to construct a homogenous force. When Quartermaster St. Clair almost single-handedly dismembered Forbes's carefully constructed coalition, Bouquet rebuked him in unmistakable terms by reminding him that Forbes considered the maintenance of harmony between the regulars and provincials to be a central tenet of his army. With these exceptions, the extensive correspondence between the provincial officers and regular officers that survive in various papers suggests that Forbes succeeded admirably in forming a truly unified army.

Fourth, Forbes's decision to proceed due west from Ray's Town, across Allegheny Mountain and the Laurel Ridge, was the single most important decision that he made during the entire campaign. Forbes's selection, already exhaustively analyzed in this treatise, was perhaps most significant for the deception effect that it had upon the French at Fort Duquesne. Their attention was totally focused upon the old Braddock Road, and Forbes was fully established at Loyalhanna before Grant's debacle revealed his avenue of advance to the French. The route that Forbes finally selected was clearly a shorter distance from the Philadelphia logistical base that he had established. Given the length of time that it took Forbes to finally reach Fort Duquesne by this more direct route, a decision to utilize the longer Braddock Road would probably have doomed the campaign, at least for the year.

This choice was Forbes's and Forbes's alone, one that was made while he was dreadfully ill. And it was clearly the right decision.

Next, Forbes's campaign plan was well considered, and executed as planned. His policy of developing two primary advanced depots at "about forty mile" distances at Ray's Town and Loyalhanna permitted Forbes to stockpile supplies as far forward as possible to support the next movement, without being so advanced that these stockpiles could not be organized given the limits of transportation and challenges of terrain. Forbes's establishment of small intermediate posts such as Fort Duart and Stony Creek Crossing improved the security of his line of communications by stationing parties at key points, facilitated the repair and maintenance of the road once constructed, provided overnight protection to convoys and work parties, and secured rest and maintenance stops to these convoys. Construction of these relatively small posts did not require much time or effort, and locally available materials such as timber, earth, sod and fascines were used. The relatively small garrisons did not absorb much of Forbes's overall strength, and the advantage gained for the security of the road was worth the expenditure. Because of this firmly established logistical chain from Carlisle west, the French were never able to mount an effective raid upon the road. In fact, not one instance of Forbes's supply route's being interdicted by the French for even a moment was recorded. Forbes's campaign approach ensured that even a local tactical reverse would not defer his advance.

Perhaps the most significant aspect of Forbes's campaign plan was his intent to approach in late fall after the leaves had left the trees, and at a time when the Native Americans were departing upon their important winter hunt. From the beginning of the campaign, Forbes had planned to attack at this time. On September 2, when writing to Bouquet regarding the timing of his advance, he stated, "I think it would be Imprudent yet for some time. Because from what I can learn that the strength of the Indians at Fort Duquesne are from the Detroit and Westward of the Lakes, they are now weary and must return by the latter end of September for taking care of their Hunting and for fear of the Frosts." He similarly corresponded with William Pitt late in October:

> I was assured by every one, and made believe that the Months of October and November were the two best Months in the year for an Expedition, because of the trees losing their leaves, by which one can see a litle thro' the woods, and prevent the Enemy's surprizes, which is their only strength, and likewise, that in those two Months the Indians leave the French as it is their chief hunting Season, in which they provide for their familys during the winter. This last was of great consequence to me, as the Enemy's Numbers had all along been represented to me, not only equall, but even to exceed what I could carry against them....[23]

Additionally, Grant's repulse from the hill above the forks, although it had clearly constituted a significant check to Forbes's advance and was a stinging tactical defeat, turned out to be a strategic victory. Grant had brought 37 officers and 805 men to Fort Duquesne on September 13. Nearly three years before, Braddock had brought not that many more forward, possibly about 1,300 men, although because of his crushing defeat, his exact numbers at the Battle of Monongahela are unknown.[24] To the Indians, the defeats of Braddock and Grant must have appeared similar in scope and scale. For a Native warrior, a successful summer at war entailed taking scalps, capturing prisoners, and gaining plunder and loot. Grant's defeat had certainly provided the Native American warriors with an abundance of all of those things. Pennsylvanian James Smith had been taken captive by Delaware Indians in 1755, and carried by them past Fort Duquesne and into the Ohio Valley for adoption. Smith lived a number of years with his family of Delawares, and he reported of the timing of warriors from his village in 1756:

Towards the last of this time, which was in June 1756, they were all engaged in preparing to go to war against the frontiers of Virginia; when they were equipped, they went through their ceremonies, sung their war songs &c. They all marched off.... The warriors had come in, and brought with them on horse-back, a quantity of meat. These warriors had divided into different parties, and all struck at different places in August county. They brought in with them a considerable number of scalps, prisoners, horses, and other plunder.... About the time that these warriors came in, the green corn was beginning to be of use [August].

Smith then suggests that the warriors "became lazy" and enjoyed the fall harvest after their return.[25] Smith documented nearly an identical pattern the next year: "About the middle of June [1757] the Indians were almost all gone to war, from sixteen to sixty.... Some time in August the warriors returned, and brought in with them a great many scalps, prisoners, horses and plunder."[26] With Grant's defeat, the Native warriors had fulfilled all of their expectations of a season on the warpath.

Finally, Smith specifically reported the aftermath of Grant's defeat:

After this defeat the Indians held a council, but were divided in their opinions. Some said that General Forbes would now turn back, and go home the way that he came, as Dunbar had done when General Braddock was defeated: others supposed he would come on. The French urged the Indians to stay and see the event: but it was hard for the Indians to be absent from their squaws and children, at this season of the year, a great many of them returned home to their hunting. After this, the remainder of the Indians, some French regulars, and a number of Canadians, marched off in quest of General Forbes. They met his army near Fort Ligonier, and attacked them, but were frustrated in their design. When they returned from the battle to Fort DuQuesne, the Indians concluded that they would go to their hunting."[27]

Taken in this context, Anderson's recounting of the Delaware refusal to accept a French war belt on November 20 indicates not so much admission of a peace with the English, or lack of support for the French, as the simple indication that it was in fact well past time to depart on the winter hunt. The Delawares told the French officers to "let him go with his young men; he boasted much of their fighting; now let us see his fighting. We have often ventured our lives for him...." If the French officers wished to fight in winter, the Delaware welcomed them to do so, and in fact invited them to do so, but the French would have to do it on their own. The Delaware had more important things to do, such as hunting for their very survival.[28]

Forbes also went to great efforts to train his army to operate in the wilderness conditions that it would encounter during its advance on Fort Duquesne. Marksmanship training with live ball was stressed, and regularly conducted by the Pennsylvania Provincials at Fort Augusta and the entire army at Ray's Town. Bouquet performed extensive drills and exercises at Carlisle and Ray's Town, and he incorporated movements specifically adapted to woods fighting into this training. The improvement in the ability of Forbes's army to traverse the wilderness was validated when Grant's large expedition was able to reach the very ditch of Fort Duquesne without being detected by the French. Forbes established carefully considered orders of march and formations for the final movement upon the French fort. Such tactical alignments resulted in a flexible column that could easily respond to a French attack, which accordingly never came. These tactical configurations that Forbes established became the basis of the tactics that Bouquet would employ so successfully in subsequent campaigns. During his advance Forbes also surrounded his army with small parties of Native American warriors and provincial frontier scouts used to operating in difficult terrain, again ensuring that his army would not be surprised by the French as Braddock's army had been. Finally, the extensive usage of pack horses on the final march to the

Forks of the Ohio provided Forbes with a relatively light, mobile column that was not encumbered by numerous heavy wagons. The end result was not only a well-trained army by European standards, but a smoothly functioning entity that was well suited to operating in the peculiar western Pennsylvania and North American conditions. Forbes's army was clearly never an equal in woods fighting abilities to the French and their Native allies; this had been proven at Grant's defeat, and at Loyalhanna on two separate occasions. Still, the army that Forbes compiled was considerably better than Braddock's army; and it was strong, flexible, alert and capable enough that the French never seriously considered attacking it during the final movement on Duquesne.

The success of Forbes, Bouquet, and Bosomworth in maintaining good relationships with the Cherokees and Catawbas was instrumental to the success of the campaign. This was not achieved without exhaustive efforts, and the prodigal expenditure of Indian trade goods in the form of presents. Forbes and Bouquet were at times quite frustrated in their dealings with the Natives, and felt that the Indians were capricious allies at best. Yet the simple fact that Forbes's army had maintained any Native warriors at all, kept them throughout the entire campaign, and was able to regularly utilize them in raiding and scouting parties, was a major accomplishment for any British army in North America. The presence of these warriors with Forbes facilitated the dispatching of the regular scouting parties that Forbes utilized, and clearly enhanced the security of his command. Certainly Forbes was considerably disappointed in the numbers of Indians that accompanied him on the final movement to Fort Duquesne. But their worth was proved when they carried back the first word to Forbes that the French had abandoned and destroyed their fort.

Forbes's insistence that Pennsylvania initiate negotitiations with the Delawares and other western Indians, finally achieving fruition in the Treaty of Easton, also contributed to his victory. Numerous historians have suggested that the various Indian negotiations culminating in the Treaty of Easton directly resulted in the seizure of Fort Duquesne by Forbes and his army. Dr. Fred Anderson titled the chapter on the Forbes Campaign in his study of the Seven Years' War, "Indian Diplomacy and the Fall of Fort Duquesne."[29] Forbes's advance upon the Forks of the Ohio occupies a mere two pages in Anderson's study, while he devotes nearly twenty pages to Indian diplomacy. He concludes, "The French emissary ... sent word back warning Lignery not to expect help from his [Delaware] allies. When the unwelcome news arrived at the Forks, the commandant took the only option left to him and ordered the fort evacuated and destroyed."[30] Forbes's presence with his army a mere ten miles from the fort had no effect upon Lignery's decision, according to Anderson. Francis Jennings similarly stated: "The remainder of [Lignery's] Indians abandoned him to attend the great peace council at Kuskuski, where a French captain labored in vain to disrupt the proceedings. On the twenty-fourth of November, Lignery burned and blew up the fort...."[31] Jennings devotes an entire chapter, nearly forty pages, to Indian diplomacy, and a mere four pages to the remainder of Forbes's campaign. Commandant Lignery did have choices available to him, as previously discussed, and his failure to mount an effective defense must be attributed more to lack of resolution than the Indians' desertion. However, when combined with the wide range of other decision factors that Forbes had formulated, the Treaty of Easton and all of its implications deeply shook French confidence and supremacy at a critical moment, and that in and of itself contributed to British victory in the Ohio country.

The Prussian Von Clausewitz properly noted that "effects in war seldom result from a single cause; there are usually several concurrent causes. It is therefore not enough to trace, however honestly and objectively, a sequence of events back to their origin; each identifiable cause still has to be correctly assessed."[32] This was certainly true of Forbes's campaign across the western wilds of the colony of Pennsylvania in 1758, for the success of British arms resulted from not a single factor, but rather a compilation of successful tactics and strategies. The fall of Fort Frontenac at a providential time rendered great assistance to Forbes's

Forbes's grave inside Christ Church, Philadelphia.

advance. Forbes's relationship with Bouquet and the provincial officers, the relatively well-organized and -trained army that Forbes established within only a couple of months, Forbes's meticulous attention to logistical matters, his efforts to retain Native American allies, Forbes's timing of the expedition, his carefully established tactics that rendered his army impervious to surprise or ambush, a well-chosen route with a well-considered campaign plan, coupled with Grant's defeat, and a failure of French leadership, all combined to result in the French abandonment of Fort Duquesne. Indian diplomacy culminating at the Treaty at Easton certainly smoothed Forbes's path, but it was not the ultimate decision factor. That

Monument to the Forbes Campaign, located at the site of General Forbes's victory, Fort Pitt Museum, Point Park, Pittsburgh. A bridge over the Monongahela River is to the rear.

had been predominantly due to Forbes's own leadership and decision-making, along with the strategic good fortune and timing of Fort Frontenac's fall and Grant's defeat.

The successful campaign was due, finally, to the leadership team of Forbes and Bouquet working together, one pulling from the front, one pushing from the rear. Bouquet was effusive in his praise of Forbes, as he wrote to two intimate friends following the capture of Fort Duquesne:

Interpretive signage in honor of Brigadier General John Forbes, located at the site of his greatest victory, Fort Pitt Museum, Point Park, Pittsburgh. A bridge over the Monongahela River is to the rear.

The Glory of our success must after God be allowed to our General, who from the beginning took those wise measures which deprived the French of their chief strength, and by the treaty of Easton kept such a number of Indians idle during the whole campaign, and procured a peace with those inveterate enemies, more necessary and beneficial to the safety and welfare of the Provinces than the driving the French from the Ohio. His prudence in all measures, in the numberless difficulties he had to surmount, deserves the highest praises.

After God the success of this Expedition is entirely due to the General, who by bringing about the Treaty of Easton, has struck the blow which has knocked the French in the head, in temporizing wisely to expect the Effects of that Treaty, in securing all his posts, and giving nothing to chance; and not yielding to the urging instances for taking Braddock's Road, which would have been our destruction; In all these measures I say that he has shown the greatest prudence, firmness and ability; Nobody is better informed of the Numberless difficulties he had to surmount than I am, who had an opportunity to see every step that was taken from the beginning and every obstruction that was thrown in his way. I wish the Nation may be as sensible of his service as he really deserves and give him the only reward that can flatter him; The pleasure of seeing them pleased and satisfied.[33]

On Sunday, March 11, 1759, Colonel Bouquet wrote in a sorrowful letter to General Jeffery Amherst:

It is with the utmost grief I am to inform your Excellency that Brigadier General Forbes died this morning. Tho' in the cruel situation he was reduced, his death only could put an End to his miseries. The Shock is not less sensible to me. He had honoured me with his Confidence as my General, and with a tender affection as a friend. I hope your Excellency will forgive these free Expressions of my sensibility to the loss of a man to whom I was so sincerely devoted, and for whose memory I Shall always entertain the highest respect.

Amherst responded sadly two days later: "This moment I receive your Letter ... with the account of the death of poor Forbes, whose loss I feel and condole with you, as I had the pleasure of being intimately acquainted with him, and I lament his death from my heart."[34]

Forbes's conduct had earned him the respect and admiration of the entire Philadelphia community, which was deeply shocked and saddened at his passing. The colony of Pennsylvania arranged for Forbes to be buried underneath the chancel of the most prominent church in the city, Christ Church, following a spectacular and somber ceremony. Joseph Shippen wrote to his father on March 14, "General Forbes is to be interred this afternoon, with great pomp."[35] His funeral reflected the esteem with which he was held, and symbolized the epochs of his life as expressed in the funerary traditions of the times:

The form and order of march at his funeral was as follows.
I. The Pioneers.
II. The Seventeenth Regiment, and two companies of Colonel Montgomery's Regiment, the colours with [black] crapes; the drums covered with black; and the officers with crapes on their arms.
III. Two pieces of cannon, with Commanding Officers of artillery.
IV. The Engineers.
V. The Staff.
VI. The Servants, in mourning, uncovered, two and two.
VII. A led horse, covered with black, conducted by a groom.
VIII. The Surgeons.
IX. The Physicians.
X. The Clergy and Chaplains of the army.
XI. The Corpse and the pall held by six field officers.
XII. The mourners.
XIII. The Governor, the Council, the Speaker, and members of the Assembly, the Judges, the magistrates, and gentlemen of the Province and city, two by two.
XIV. The Officers from the different garrisons, two and two.

The minute guns were fired from the time the corpse was brought out until the interment was over; and the whole ended by a triple discharge of the small arms.[36]

Among the field officers who served as pallbearers were Colonels Bouquet and Montgomery, who had served Forbes so nobly on his penultimate journey across the Allegheny Mountain, and now carried him on his final journey.

The base of an impressive marble sepulcher at Christ Church in Philadelphia bears the following inscription, which was Forbes's epitaph in this world:

By a steady pursuit of well conducted measures in defiance of disease and numberless obstructions, he brought to a happy issue a most extraordinary campaign, resulting in the evacuation of Fort Duquesne, and made a willing sacrifice of his own life to what he loved more, the interest of his King & Country.

Per Tot Discrimina, Ohio Britannica Consilio Manuque.

Appendix A

A Compilation of Indian Trade Goods Presented to the Cherokee and Catawba Warriors During the Forbes Campaign, 1758

Forbes and Bouquet went to great lengths to attract Cherokee and Catawba warriors to their army. Their papers are replete with Indian councils, meetings with Indian chiefs, and gifts bestowed upon Native warriors. Presents were an essential commodity to facilitate the employment and maintain the support of Native American fighters. Upon their arrival at the English camp, the Natives would have been given some small presents in recognition of the length of their journey that they had made to join the British army, and to thank them for their presence. When Native leaders and British officers met to discuss a potential raid or patrol, presents would have been first provided to validate the sincerity, honesty and good intentions of the English officers. Before any Indian scouting parties departed, they would have been equipped with necessaries to sustain them, including food, ammunition, clothing, and similar gear such as blankets and powder horns. Upon their return, these parties would also have expected gifts as a token of recognition of the hardships that they had overcome, and in appreciation of their accomplishments. Significant feats of arms such as taking a prisoner or a scalp would have been important enough to garner supplemental and particularly valuable gifts. Any equipment that had been lost, worn out or broken upon their mission would have been replaced or repaired. Finally, when the Natives departed for home they would have expected substantial generosity from the British, essentially as payment for their services. By going to war for the summer, the Native men had not been able to provide for their families by hunting or fishing. The presents compensated them for this sacrifice, and also served as a means to validate their courage and bravery to their families and communities upon their return home.

The type and quantity of Indian presents made during this campaign may be the most complete of any 18th-century North American military campaign in which Southern Indian nations participated. These lists, compiled at Forbes's express orders to validate expenditures of his impromptu Indian department, provide an excellent and relatively scarce record of what Cherokee and Catawba warriors in 1758 desired, and expected to receive, for their military contributions. Accordingly, this appendix will detail the gifts that the Southern warriors received as payment for their services. This record also documents the colonial tradesmen and vendors who created and supplied many of these goods, predominantly from the Philadelphia mercantile area. Thus, these lists also serve to record the ability of Pennsylvania to support the Indian trade, and provide a glimpse into that colony's economic and manufacturing community.

Even before the campaign began, when William Byrd III was recruiting these Indians in the Natives' towns in the Carolinas, he would report, "I fitted out the warriors I turn'd back, according to my agreement, with a match coat, boots, paint, a knife apiece & a few trifles for the seven women."[1] Early in the spring, provincial officers were already working with Natives to scout the French at Fort Duquesne. Lieutenant Colonel Byrd wrote Governor Denny of Pennsylvania from Fort August on April 26, 1758: "...three of our Indian Warriors vizt: Hambus, Thekeachemus and Sisockappee, arrived here from Fort DuQuesne the 21st last. Our Warriors brought me a French scalp that they took just by the New Fort. They intended to have brought the person prisoner, but the Enemy rushed out so quick upon them they could not effect it. I rewarded the Indians in part by giving each of them a new Blanket and Shirt...."

The first formal record of presents formally issued to the Cherokees and Catawbas on this campaign appears in the *Papers of Henry Bouquet*, for gifts distributed by Captain Edward Ward, Second Battalion (Armstrong's) of the Pennsylvania Regiment, at Fort Littleton to Cherokees on May 10 and 28, 1758:

4 Shirts
12 yards of Red Ribbon
31 Shirts "Delivered to Two Parties of Cherokees Per My Order"
21 Pair of Shoes
21 Pair of Buckals [buckles]
"To Cherokees Chiefs Son" [possibly referring to Okuola or Ucahala, son of the Cherokee Chief
    Old Hop, who was serving as a Scout to Forbes at this time]
    1 Red Coat
    1 Hat
    1 Pair of Stockings
    1 Pair of Shoes
    1 Shirt
    1 Pair of Buckles
    1 Pair of Breeches
1 Pair of Buckles to Another Cherokee
"Liquor at sundery times" [8 pounds' sterling worth of liquor, a large amount]
1 Rifle Gun
1 Broad Cloth Stroud
2 Ruffled Shirts
24 Pounds of Sugar
10 Gallons of Rum.[2]

Forbes penned to Quartermaster John St. Clair on May 23, 1758, from Philadelphia:

I believe I wrote you that I had bought a pretty large quantity of Indian Goods here, which I sent up the Country ten days ago, with Captain Bosomworth, who I desired should proceed from Carlisle to Winchester and let you know what he had done, and in every place to make out a list of the Indian goods that has been provided and by whom, the distribution that has been made, and what remains, by which one may judge what is further necessary to be provided — I am sorry to find that they are so bent upon returning home, but still hope by a prudent management they may be kept.

Accompanying this letter were two lists of these Indian Goods.[3]

A List of Goods Sent by William West to Captain Bosomworth by Order of His Excellency General Forbes

38 pieces of Strouds
43½ pieces of half thicks
13 Single Matchcoats

527 plain shirts
21 fine ruffled shirts
3 pieces fine Holland with Cambrick & thread to make 22 ruffled shirts
500 pounds FF gunpowder
500 pounds Powder from the General's Magazine
25 weight Bar Lead
5 weight Swan Shot
5500 best French Common Gun Flints
121 Guns
32 pair Pistolls
96 Dozen Clasp Knives
4 Gross Brass Jews Harps
4½ Gross Morris Bells
3 Gross Indian Awl Blades
16 Gross Tobacco Pipes
72 pieces Ribbon
42 gross garters
2 gross fine broad garters
20 gross bed lace
20 dozen scissors
12 dozen razors
29 pounds brass wire
7 dozen small looking glasses
25 pounds red lead [used by the Indians to create red paint]
1 piece red bunting
1 piece blue bunting
46 thousand 7 hundred black wampum
6 thousand 6 hundred white wampum
1000 light tomhawks [*sic*]
17 tin kettles sent by Mr. Andrew Elliot

A List of Goods Bought by Captain Bosomworth & William West not yet sent off but will be ready on Thursday next May 23rd 1758

14 pieces blue strouds
2 pieces strip'd [striped] flannel
2 pieces half thicks
3 single match coats
426 plain shirts
39 ruffled shirts
2 dozen gun locks
12 dozen large French Cutto Knives
6 pounds brass wire
24 fine laced hats
3 thousand 3 hundred black wampum
3 thousand 4 hundred white wampum
30 Gorgets, 5 breastplates, 5 half moons—are bespoke of several silver smiths to be made as soon as possible—Captain Bosomworth has wrote to me from Lancaster to send for 10 thousand white wampum more which I have done—and Captain Bosomworth has bought in Lancaster 28 thousand black wampum

Indian presents continued to flow as a result of Forbes's instructions to make every attempt to placate the Indians and maintain them with his army. Forbes, as per his previous instructions to Captain Bosomworth, instructed that meticulous records be maintained of what Indian presents were purchased and disbributed.

Invoice of Sundry Goods sent to Captain Bosomworth per order of General Forbes per Robert Keech's Waggon, May 25th 1758

[First mark—a "W" with "4" at top and "XX" below]—A Case containing 4 pieces strouds
2 pieces strip'd flannels

2 pieces half thicks
3 single match coats
6½ pounds brass wire
2 dozen gunlocks & pins
12 dozen large french cuttoe knives
150 check shirts

[Second mark — a double "WW" with "4" at top and "XX" below] — No. 6 — A Case
151 plain shirts white
31 fine ruffled shirts white
100 check shirts

[Third mark — a "W" with "4" at top and "XX" below] — A Trunk (containing) No. 3 on the bottom
24 Fine (silver laced) hats
27 Check Shirts
10 Shirts unmade, with thread to make them

N.B. In the List of Goods sent to Captain Bosomworth with the 17th May I mention'd 21 Ruffled Shirts, which shoud have been 29: having in a hurry put up 8 ruffled shirts & call'd them plain — I was oblig'd to send up nine shirts unmade, with the thread, & as I have in my former Account charg'd for making these nine shirts: I have put up linen for another shirt, to make up for the charge of making the nine. The above list goods with those formerly sent, makes up the full compliment of goods that I have charged to the General except a few thousands of wampum which I expect daily from New York

Wm. West.

St. Clair reported to George Washington from York, Pennsylvania, on May 7 regarding Indian goods intended for the Virginia colony, "I have got 360 Match Coats & a Dozn more light Guns with some Vermillion [paint], I shall send them off to morrow for Winchester."[4] A more expansive list was provided early in May, of goods for the same purpose:

A List of Goods Bought by Capt Bosomworth and William West for the Cherokee Indians by Order of General Forbes:
52 pieces of Stroud, about 11 strouds in a piece
55½ pieces half thick
2 pieces striped flannel
16 single match coats
953 plain shirts
60 fine ruffled shirts
3 pieces fine holland [linen] sent unmade with cambrick it will make 22 ruffled shirts
500 FF Gunpowder
25 cwt small bar lead
56 wt swan shot
5500 gun flints
121 guns
32 pair pistols
2 dozen gun locks
105 dozen clasp knives
4 gross brass Jews harps
18½ gross Morris bells
3 gross Indian Awl Blades
16 Gross Tobacco Pipes
72 Pieces Ribbons
42 Gross Garters
2 Gross fine broad garters
28 gross bed lace
28 dozen Scissors
12 dozen razors
35 lbs. brass wire

7 dozen Indian looking glasses
25 lbs. Red Lead
24 fine laced hats
1 piece red bunting
1 piece blue bunting
50 m black wampum
10 m white wampum
1000 light Indian tomahawks
170 Tin Kettles
Tin Measures bought by Mr. Elliot and by him sent up
28 m [common 18th-century abbreviation for thousand] black wampum bought by Captain
    Bosomworth in Lancaster
10 m more white wampum which he directed me to write for

May 1758, Wm West

A List of Goods Bought by Sir John St. Clair Taken From a List Delivered to me by Capt. Bosomworth

312 fuzees
28 pieces match coats, 20 in a piece
703 dressed deer skins for moccasins
140 kettles
500 powder horns
8 pieces strouds
12 pieces half thicks
94 pounds vermillion
10 red lead
50 m black wampum
10 m white wampum
150 dozen silver broaches
100 arm bands
100 bracelets
200 shirts
3 gross red lace
1½ gross garters

The Amount of the two foregoing lists

60 pieces stroud
57½ pairs half thicks
2 pieces strip'd flannel
28 pieces match coat, 20 in a piece
16 singles match coats
1235 shirts
500 pounds FF powder
500 pounds ditto from the magazine
25 Ct Wt small bar lead
56 swan shot
5500 gun flints
433 guns
32 pair pistols
2 dozen gun locks
108 dozen clasp knives
4 gross brass Jew harps
4½ gross Morris bells
3 gross Indian Awl Blades
16 gross Tobacco Pipes
72 Pieces Ribbons
45½ Gross Garters
23 Gross Bed Lace
28 dozen scissors

12 dozen razors
35 pounds brass wire
7 dozen Indian looking glasses
94 pounds vermillion
35 red lead to mix with it
24 fine laced hats
274 kettles
500 powder horns
Tin measures
128 m black wampum
30 m white wampum
150 dozen silver broaches
100 arm bands
100 bracelets
903 dressed deerskins
1000 light Indian Tomahawks
1 Piece Red narrow bunting
1 Piece Blue narrow bunting
40 gorgets[,] half moons &c. ordered by the General[5]

Numerous purchases were made from merchants in Philadelphia to obtain these Indian goods, as carefully delineated in Forbes's headquarters papers. This list is particularly valuable, as it provides the names of Philadelphia merchants, and the types of goods that they could provide in the spring of 1758.

Philadelphia, May 8, 1758
Mr. William West
By the Order of General Forbes, bought off Oswell Eve
16 pair pistols

Philadelphia 5 May 1758
William West for Account: General Forbes
Bought Jeremiah Warder
5 lb. Brass ware
25 Hundred Bar Lead
6 Dozen Black Spring Knives
9 Dozen Cuttoe Spring Knives
23 Dozen Cuttoe Larger Spring Knives
2 Dozen Very Large Spring Knives
2 Gross Very Broad Star Gartering [gartering with a woven star pattern]
1 piece Stroud
13 Black Striped Match Coats, Little Damaged
20 gross Bed Lace
26 Gross Star Gartering
7 gross Scarlet Gartering
¾ Gross Broader Scarlet Gartering
40 Pieces Stroud
8 dozen Scizzors No. 32
6 dozen Scizzors No. 33
12 doz. Red Scale Razors
6 dozen Small Scizzors
12 dozen combs
12 dozen combs, no. 2
31 pieces Ribands [ribbons]
N.B. All the small goods are in a case marked—[mark]
N: 1
Lead in 5 Casks Marked IW.

Philadelphia May 9th 1758

Mr. William West

By Order of the General

Bought of Samuel Neaves

6 Dozen Cuttoe Knives
4 Dozen Large Cuttoe Knives
2 Gross Brass Jews Harps
[illegible] Gross Indian Awl Blades
Box Pipes MN No. 20

Philadelphia 9th May 1758

Captain Bosomworth

Bought of William West for the Cherokee Indians

8 pieces Fine Tanden Linen — The above pieces is deliver'd out to be made into 60 Ruffled Shirts
  for the Indian Chiefs

14 yards low priced cambrick to ruffle the shirts
4 yards finer cambrick to ruffle the shirts
½ pound fine thread to make the shirts
31 pieces white ⅞ linen 836 yards deliver'd out to be made into 257 shirts
10 pieces ⅞ linen checked 431 yards
42 pieces strong cotton 1,833 yards
Total 2,264 yards
Deliver'd the above check linen out to be made into shirts at 3¼ yards to a shirt will be 696 shirts

6 pounds white thread for the plain white & check shirts
2 pounds finer white thread for the plain white & check shirts
½ pound finer white thread for the plain white & check shirts

To the making of the shirts which I have agreed for as follows:
696 checked shirts
257 plain white shirts
Total 953 Shirts
30 fine ruffled shirts
30 finer ruffled shirts
Total 1,013 ruffled and plain shirts in all

To 3 pieces superfine Tanden Holland, 25 yard each, packed up unmade
2 patches cambrick to ruffle them
3 ounces fine white thread
4½ gross Morris Bells
2 Gross Brass Jews Harps
4 Pieces Blue Stroud Cloth, 96 yards
4 thousand common gun flints
15 hundred best French flints
1 dozen small looking glasses

Philadelphia 10th May 1758

His Excellency General Forbes

To William West For Sundry Goods Bought by his Order for the Cherokee Indians, as per the several bills of parcels herewith deliver'd

Of Whom Bought
Andrew Elliott	4½ pieces half thick
Francis Harris & Co.	6 pieces half thick
Daniel Curry	2 pieces half thick
Philip Benezet	3 pieces half thick
York & Potts	8 pieces half thick & 2 pieces strip'd linsey
John Head	3 pieces half thick

Daniel Rundle	11 pieces half thick
W.B. White	16 pairs pistols & 2 guns
McJannett & Co.	31 fuzees
Oswald Eve	16 pairs pistols
William Henry	7 guns
Hughes & Jones	16 dozen clasp knives
Samuel Neave	10 dozen clasp knives, 2 gross Jews Harps, 3 gross Indian Awl blades, & 1 box pipes
John Carson	41 pieces Ribbon & 16 pounds brass wire
Abraham Mitchell	4 pieces blue strouds
Robrt & Ames Strettell	3 Match Coats
Jeremiah Warder	Strouds, Lead, Etc.
William West	Sundry Linens, Etc.
Charles Cox	2 pieces half thick
James & Drinker	6 dozen looking glasses

N.B. By Direction of Captain Bosomworth I have wrote to a Gentleman in N. York for sixty thousand wampum — we have also order'd 170 tin kettles &c. to be made here — neither of these articles are in the above Account — Wm. West.[6]

Bosomworth also bought still more goods from West in Philadelphia, in mid–May:

50 m black wampum
10 m white wampum
25 red lead at 6d per pound & bag 4d
12 shillings, 10 pence
[thus this means 25 pounds of red lead]
6 pieces best (Indian) half thick [wool]
24 English Castor Hats, lined with silk
2 pounds Scotch thread, deliver'd to make up the Shirts since the former bill was deliver'd
12 doz Large French Cuttoe Knives
2 Dozen Gunlocks & Pins
4 Pieces Blue Stroud Cloth quantity 100 yards (will make 50 strouds).[7]

In addition to these acquisitions, Quartermaster John St. Clair also made his own direct purchases of Indian goods:

May 10	72¾ yds Yellow Stuff
May 15	108 Plain Shirts
	21 Dozen Silver Brooches
	Carriage for two bundles from Philadelphia to Lancaster
May 16	Cash paid the Gun Smith for Mending & Cleaning 38 Guns
	15 Silver Arm Bands Broad
	36 Baubles
May 24	24 Pair Silver Ear Bobbs
	17 Plain Bobb
	3 Dozen Silver Rings
	25 Dozen Broaches
	7 Large Hair Plates
	5 Large Arm Bands
	[two illegible entries]
	35,500 Black and White Wampum
May 29	9 Silver Half Moons
May 30	45 Dozen Silver Broaches
	12 Arm Bands.[8]

Bouquet would specifically write to Forbes from Carlisle on June 3 for a large number of stores for the army, including "30 Silver Arm Plates & 50 Bracelets for Presents to the Indian Chiefs."[9] Governor James Glen of South Carolina, Forbes's cousin who accompanied the army, would write of some of these Native allies on July 26, 1758:

As for Indian Affairs I saw that those with Byrd were extremely spoil'd and ruined, and therefore I avoided intermeddling with them from the beginning. Mr. Campbell came hither with 8 or 10 of them three or four days ago there pretext of coming was to get some necessaries altho they needed none having already received blankets, shirts, leggings, some silver, gorgets, armplates, paint, guns, powder, bullets they behaved with the greatest insolence insisting to have over and above the 40 weight of leather for staying with us the Campaign, 56 silver gorgets as many silver breastplates as many wristbands, 56,000 wampum near 300 matchcoats &c. &c[10]

Governor William Denny of Pennsylvania would write Forbes on July 28: "The Union Flaggs, and a parcel of yellow shalloon fillets, are made up, and Mr. Peters will forward them from Bethlehem, for which place he sets out immediately in order to procure one or more Indians to be sent for Intelligence to the Friendly Tribes on the Ohio."[11] Major George Armstrong with the Pennsylvania Provincials wrote to Bouquet on July 29: "[O]ur Indians eats the Divel and all of our provisions and talks of going back if the following necessary's are not sent to them Viz: 4 Shirts 4 pr. Legins and Paint and Mockasons."[12] Bouquet would note on August 11, "Captain Bullen with 31 Catawbas and 27 Tascaroroas are expected at Cumberland. Some blankets are needed to outfit them, and especially some vermilion."[13]

Another list of goods was compiled on July 24, for "the use of the Cherokee Indians with Colonel Byrd at Fort Cumberland and Sent by Orders of Colonel Bouquet:"

57 Knives
30 Arm Bands
20 Wrist Bands
60 Brooches
5 Pieces of Ribbon
22,500 Black Wampum
5 Pieces of Half Thick [wool]
2 Ruffled shirts
55 plain White shirts
57 Check shirts
4 [pounds] Vermillion
12 Stroud Mantles
8 Gorgets
2 Breast Plates
2 Shells [not otherwise identified, presumably some type of silver ornament]
4,000 Black Wampum
1,800 White Wampum.[14]

The value of these goods was also calculated on July 23 in a document titled "Proportion of Presents agreed to be given to each Indian for his Service during the Campaign." This list was prepared to ascertain the expenses of outfitting each Indian warrior:

5 Stroud Mantles	20 shillings apiece	5 pounds
1 Pair Stockings	3 shillings, 9 pence	
2 Knives	2 shillings	
1 Shirt	7 shillings, 6 pence	
1 Breech Clout and Cap	5 shillings, 9 pence	
Silver Truck, Wampum, Gartering, Vermillion, &c.	3 pounds	
Sub-total	8 pounds, 17 shillings	
Necessary to equip them for Service	1 pound, 10 shillings	
Total	10 pounds, 7 shillings.[15]	

Bosomworth reported the following Indian trade goods in stores at Raystown on July 12:

90 Cutlasses
14 dozen & 10 Scalping Knives
86 Dozen & 8 Clasp Knives
3500 Flints

10 Gross & 5 pieces of Gartering
8 dozen horn combs
¾ gross morris bells
26 pieces of ribbon
8½ dozen scissors
3 pipe hatchetts
1 dozen & five razors
1 dozen & 10 screw boxes
3 gross awl blades
11 pounds brass wire
1 piece red bunting
1 piece blue bunting
1 spear
34 yards stroud in remnants
2 gross & 4½ dozen Jew Harps
30 pieces 22 Yards half thick
25 pounds red lead
497 check shirts
149 white plain shirts
56 white ruffled shirts
2 dozen gunlocks
2 pieces strip'd flannel
27 matchcoats
212 drest [dressed] dear [deer] skins
1 box & 23 pounds swan shot
2 boxes lead
2 casks lead & an half cask about 250 pounds lead
72 guns
19 pistols
2 tin pints [measures or cups]
5 tin kettles
25 powder horns
1 hogshead & ⅓ of a hogshead of tobacco
1 bag & 1 small cask of tobacco
120 Tin Quart Potts
24 fine silver laced hats
500 tomahawks
22 blankets
60 pieces and half pieces of yellow quality binding
6 half pieces of ribbon
94 arm bands
63 wrist bands
24 dozen & 4 brooches
6 gorgets or half moons
7 pounds vermillion
1600 white wampum
36,400 black wampum
5 half barrels powder
some silver lace

This is an Exact Return as examined by Captain A. Bosomworth.

Bosomworth also provided "A List of Goods wanting to equip three hundred more Indians expected to join for the Service of the Expedition:"

60 pieces of Stroud mostly blue and black, but few red amongst them
30 pieces of Dusseld's or striped matchcoats, 20 [maybe 10, blotted] matchcoats in a piece, take care they don't send us blankets instead of matchcoats
150 pounds vermillion, necessary to be sent immediately as there is no fitting Warriors out without it

50 pieces single [?] ribbon, red, blue, green, yellow of each an equal quantity
75 gross bedlace, one half yellow, ¼ red, ¼ green
Guns, N.B. the guns remaining in store are fit for soldiers but too heavy for Indians & therefore light guns will be wanted
5 barrels double FF powder
12 dozen low priced small tooth combs
24 dozen looking glasses at about 18/per dozen
about 100 pounds worth low priced callico, 18 yards in a piece of the gayest colours
200 plain white shirts
50 m [50,000] beads, one half small white, the other half small of different colours
100,000 black wampum.[16]

As the campaign continued, similar goods were regularly purchased and distributed. Forbes wrote to Philadelphia in late August, "Let Mr. West purchase 50 lb. Weight of Vermillion, and sent it off, with the first waggons that come from Mr. Howell, with proper directions."[17] At the conclusion of the campaign, the following Indian goods remained in the King's Storehouse at Fort Bedford. These stores were specifically identified for issue to the Ohio country Indians in the winter and spring of 1759, as the majority of these goods were ordered to Pittsburgh on January 1, 1759:

20 Guns with Locks
5 Guns without Locks
99 dozen and 8 Clasp Knives
21 dozen and 8 Scalping Knives
23 Gun Locks
15 Pounds of Thread
13 Pieces of Gartering, 60 Yards
19 Pieces of Yellow Binding
2½ pounds of Wire
300 Flints
2 Gross of Awl Blades
12 Dozen & 9 Jews Harps
1 Remnant of a Piece of White Linen about 3 Shirts
26 Check Shirts
22 Silver Laced Hats
16 Tin Quarts [probably drinking cups, possibly measures]
45 Tin Pints [probably drinking cups, possibly measures]
14 Yards of Flannel, Striped
110 Cutlasses
2 Pistols
15 Pieces of Half Thick [Wool]
7 Yards of Half Thick [Wool]
11 Breech Clouts
9 Strouds
3 Pair of Half Thick [Wool] Stockings
8 Pounds of Vermillon
200 Pounds Tobacco
500 Hatchets
1 Box of Bullets, 60 Pounds
1 Box of Bullets, 40 Pounds
1 Box of Bullets, 30 Pounds
2 Casks of Lead, 500 Pounds Each
4 Boxes of Bar Lead
1 Box of Swan Shot and 6 Bags
10 Yards of Calico
4½ Pounds of Black and White Beads
30 Dozen of [Silver Brooch] Rings
3 Dozen of Shoulder Buttons

46 Pipe Tomahawks
518 Blankets
60 English Match Coats
80 White French Match Coats, Very Coarse
120 Brown French Match Coats, Very Coarse
19 Silver Hair Bobs
26 Silver Gorgets
4 Wrist Bands
6,000 White Wampum.[18]

While Lieutenant Colonel Hugh Mercer commanded the post at Pittsburgh following the fall of Fort Duquesne, he specifically noted: "Some Canoes may be purchased of the Indians—for this purpose as well as gaining Intelligence, black Wampum is the readiest traffick, will come cheaper to us than Goods.... And is more agreeable to the Indians."[19]

These records reveal some interesting facets of British-Indian relations. First, social and leadership distinctions within the Native ranks were acknowledged by the British, and recognized Native leaders were presented with distinctive items such as fine ruffled shirts of higher quality cloth, silver laced hats lined with silk, gorgets (a traditional badge of officer's rank, usually made of silver), silver lace for decoration, silver arm plates and bracelets, pistols, shoes with buckles, and in at least one case a red coat. The distribution of fine white ruffled shirts in particular seemed to be limited to higher-ranking Indian leaders.

The common Native warriors were issued a catalogue of items. Rations and liquor were routinely dispersed to the Natives, along with tobacco and pipes. Given the vagaries of time and location during the campaign, sites where the presents were being distributed, and nature of the present gifting, the specific items issued at any one time varied widely. However, typical trade goods included:

- Un-ruffled or plain white or checked linen shirts (most common) or calico shirts (less common), or white or checked cotton shirts (less common);
- "Half thick" wool for leggings;
- Deer skins for moccasins (which they presumably made themselves);
- Stroud wool for matchcoats, or already manufactured matchcoats;
- White or black wampum [colored wampum is only mentioned once];
- Gunpowder, bullets, lead shot;
- Lead for casting their own musket balls;
- Light muskets or rifles, in some cases just gun locks (presumably most likely to break, and most difficult for a Native to repair or replace);
- Hatchets or tomahawks, in some cases swords or cutlasses;
- Knives;
- Other military equipment such as powder horns, tin or brass mess kettles;
- Blankets;
- Decorations such as red paint, ribbons, garters, buttons, brass wire, bells, lace, mirrors, horn combs;
- Fancier decorations, typically of silver, including gorgets, ear bobs, arm bands, and bracelets;
- Tools such as razors, awls, scissors, pins;
- Entertainment items such as bells and jew's harps; and
- Various types of British flags and colored bunting for signaling to the English soldiers as discussed in the narrative.

Other interesting facts are that the shirts were sewn using 3¼ yards of linen per shirt, and were exclusively made with white thread regardless of whether the shirts were checked, white or calico.

Colors and more specific details are only rarely recorded. However, the following hues were identified:

- Scarlet gartering;
- Red ribbon;

- Red, blue, green and yellow ribbon;
- Blue stroud (most commonly mentioned);
- Black or red stroud (considerably less commonly mentioned);
- Red lace;
- Calico "of the gayest colours;"
- Striped match coats (quite common);
- White French match coats; and
- Brown French match coats.

It is interesting to note that only black and white wampum was issued, and only red paint. No other colors of these two items were distributed.

Managing and dispersing this diverse quantity of material to such difficult customers must have been a tough and time-consuming job. But watching a war party of Natives pass by in all their regalia must well have made all the effort and trouble seem worthwhile. These warriors must truly have been a magnificent sight. And of greatest significance to the success of this British Army on this campaign, it was one that the English, Scottish and provincial soldiers saw from the very initiation of the campaign all the way to the Forks of the Ohio.

Appendix B
List of Ordnance Supplies on the Forbes Campaign[1]

The following is as accurate a list as can be compiled of Ordnance Stores that Forbes's army carried across the wilderness road during the campaign.

Light Brass Ordnance Mounted on Traveling Carriages Compleat with Limbers Ammunition Boxes & Elevating Screws	12 Pounders	4
	6 Pounders	6
Brass Mortars Mounted on their Beds compleat with Lashing Ropes		
	4⅖ Inches	12
[Note: these are Coehorn mortars]		
Spare Hind Wheels	12 Pounders	1
Spare Hind Wheels	6 Pounders	1
Spare Hind Axletrees	12 Pounders	1
Spare Hind Axletrees	6 Pounders	1
Ladles with Staves	12 Pounders	4
Ladles with Staves	6 Pounders	6
Sponges with Rammers & Staves	12 Pounders	4
Sponges with Rammers & Staves	6 Pounders	6
Sponges for Mortars	4⅖ Inches	12
Sponge Bags, Painted		22
Wadhooks with Rammers	12 Pounders	4
Wadhooks with Rammers	6 Pounders	6
Spare Sponges & Rammerheads	12 Pounders	2 each
Spare Sponges & Rammerheads	6 Pounders	3 each
Tarpaulins	12 Pounders	4
Tarpaulins	6 Pounders	6
Field Tampeons with Collars	12 Pounders	4
Field Tampeons with Collars	6 Pounders	6
Copper Powder Measures from 3 Pound to ¼ Ounce, sets		2
Corn Powder for flannel cartridges for 12 & 6 Pounders	185 barrels	
Corn Powder for copper hooped whole barrels for filling & throwing shells		75
Empty Shells for Mortars, Corked	4⅖ Inch	8,387
Match, cwt [hundredweight]		3
Aprons of Lead for Guns		10
Aprons of Lead for Mortars		12
Funnels of Plate		2
Muzzel Caps for Mortars		12

Hand Grenades Fixed		1,000
Powder Horns		22
Priming Irons		66
Linstocks Without Cocks		22
Budge Barrels Copper Hooped		3
Handspikes		24
Grease, Firkins		2
Crows of Iron		2
[Crowbars, as previously introduced in narrative]		
Hand Screws, Small		2
Hair Cloths		6
Wadmill Tilts		6
[Wadmill Tubs: these were used to manufacture wadding for the cannon shells]		
Tanned Hides		12
Sheep Skins, Dozens		2
Steel Spikes for Nailing Guns		25
Nails, 40d		500
Nails, 30d		500
Nails, 20d		1000
Nails, 10d		1000
Nails, 6d		1000
Nails, 4d		1000
Nails, Clout		500
Nails, Dog		200
Nails, Copper		100
Ammunition Wagons		2
Forge Carts, Compleat		1
Barr Iron of Sorts, cwt [hundredweights]		2
Steel, cwt		½
Twine, cwt		6
Packthread, cwt		6
Coals for Smiths, Chaldron		½
Horse Harness, Shill		13
Horse Harness, Trace		20
Horse Harness, Bitt Halters		33
Horse Harness, Wanty's		13
Drag Ropes with Pins	12-pounder pairs	4
Drag Ropes with Pins	6-pounder pairs	6
Men's Harness 12 to a set		20 sets
Tryangle Gyn, Compleat		1
Iron Gyn Blocks with Brass Sheaves	Double	1
Iron Gyn Blocks with Brass Sheaves	Trible	1
White Rope	5-Inch	1 coil
White Rope	3½ Inch	1 coil
White Rope	2 Inch	1 coil
Tarr'd Rope	2½ Inch	1 coil
Tarr'd Marline [skeins]		10 skains
Hambro'd line [skeins]		10 skains

[This presumably means hawser-laid rope, also referred as common-laid rope. This would have been a general use rope.][2]

Lanthorn [lantern]	Muscovy	2
Lanthorn	Tin	4
Lanthorn	Dark	4
Earth Rammers		4
Large Wood Mauls		4
Intrenching Tools	Pickaxes helved	125

Intrenching Tools	Spades	200
Intrenching Tools	Shovels	50
Intrenching Tools	Hand Hatchets	50
Intrenching Tools	Hand Bills	50
Intrenching Tools	Felling Axes	50
Intrenching Tools	Spare Helves Pickaxes	25
Intrenching Tools	Wheelbarrows	75
Intrenching Tools	handbarrows	12
Ballast Baskets		30
Grind Stone with Trough		1
Leather Buckets		12
Cross Cut Saws		2
Pails		6
Whole Deals [narrow wooden boards],	12 Feet	25
Whole Deals	10 Feet	25
Slit Deals	12 Feet	20
Slit Deals	10 Feet	20
Sand Baggs	Bushel	2000
Sand Baggs	½ Bushel	5000
Tallow	Cwt.	½
Punches for the Vents of Guns	12 Pounders	8
Punches for the Vents of Guns	6 Pounders	12
Hammers for the Vents of Guns		10
Perpendiculars of the New Pattern		2

[Note: these are gunners' quadrants for aiming, the "new pattern" suggests they might be spirit levels]

Spare Forelock Keys		100
Spare Forelock Rings		50
Spare Clouts of Sorts		104
Couples for Chain Traces		100
Spring Keys, Pairs		8
Spare Linchpins		20
Spare Washers		20
Spare Tug Pins		8
Musquets with Bayonets & tann'd leather slings		2000
Cartrouch Boxes 18 holes		2000
Halberts		60
Drums		40
Musquet Shot	12 tons, 6 cwt [hundredweight]	
Corn Powder in Copper Hoop'd, whole barrels		125
Fine Paper	Reams, Qrs	17, 8
Musquet Flints		40,000
Spare Ash Ramrods		1,000
Foot Tents Compleat with Poles Pines & Mallets		1,000
Laboratory Stores		

Tin Cases Filled With Iron Shot Fixed with Wood Bottoms, & Flannel Cartridges Filled with Powder & Parchments Caps & Covers [canister or case shot]

12 Pounders		400
6 Pounders		600

Round Shot Fixed with Wood Bottoms & Flannel Cartridges Filled with Powder & Parchments Caps & Covers

12 Pounders		1600
6 Pounders		2400
Tin Tubes, Fixed	12-Pounders	2200
Tin Tubes, Fixed	6-Pounders	3300
Spare Flannel Cartridges, Empty	12-Pounders	200
Spare Flannel Cartridges, Empty	6-Pounders	300

Fixed Fuzes Including Spare	4⅖ Inch	10,560
Spare Fixed Fuzes for Hand Grenadoes		100
Portfires, Small Long	Dozens	20
Portfire Sticks		20
Green Soap	Pounds	25
Cutting Knives		6
Scizors [Scissors]	Pairs	6
Mealed Powder	Pounds	100
Barrels for Mealed Powder, Copper Hooped	1 Whole	
Barrels for Mealed Powder, Copper Hooped	1 Half	
Spirits of Wine	Quarts	4
White Wine Vinegar	Quarts	4
Quick Match, Cotton For Fuzes	Pounds	20
Quick Match, Worsted for Tubes	Pounds	6
Boxes for Quick Match		2
Paper, Cartridges	Quires	10
Paper, Brown	Reams	2
Paper, Blue	Quires	10
Barras [I don't know what this is]	Yards	6
Thin Canvas for Capping Fuzes	Yards	20
Brass Quadrants		2
Kit [I don't know what this means]	Pounds	50
Kit Kettle with Iron Trevet	Each	1
Kit Brushes		6
Flax	Pounds	10
Rasps	½ Round	12
Pincers for Drawing Fuzes	Pairs	2
Brass Weights	3 Pound Pile	1
Copper Salting Boxes		4
Copper Funnels for Filling Shells	4⅖ Inch	6
Three Square Files [triangular files]		12
Mallets of Wood for Setting Fuzes	4⅖ Inch	12
Setters of Wood for Setting Fuzes	4⅖ Inch	24
Twine	Pounds	8
Cartrouches of Leather	12-Pounders	4
Cartrouches of Leather	6-Pounders	6
Tin Boxes with Straps for Tubes	12-Pounders	8
Tin Boxes with Straps for Tubes	6-Pounders	12
Tenant Saws for Cutting Fuzes		2
Brass Portfire Mold		1
For the Portfire Mold	Iron Former	1
For the Portfire Mold	Iron Drifts, Brass Tipped	4
For the Portfire Mold	Setters of Brass	1
For the Portfire Mold	Ladle	1
Portfire Composition	Pounds	50
Cartridge Paper for Portfires	Quires	10
Scraper for Shells	4⅖ Inch	4
Seive of Hair with Top & Bottom		1
Lead Plummets		3
Laboratory Chests with Padlocks & Keys		1

For Artificers

Sets of Tools for Carpenters	2
Sets of Tools for Wheelers	2
Sets of Tools for Smiths	2
Set of Tools for Cooper	1
Sets of Tools for Collarmaker	1

For Artillery, Engineer, Civil Officers & Artificers

Tents, Compleat with Poles, Pins and Mallets
— Officers   5
— Horsemens   10
— Foot   6
— Bell   1
Camp Kettles with Frying Pan Covers   10
Tin Canteens   48
Double Hammocks   34
Double Hammocks Bedding   34

Chapter Notes

Chapter 1

1. For two succinct discussions of the effects and successes of these French raids, refer to Matthew C. Ward, "The European Method of Warring Is Not Practiced Here: The Failure of British Military Policy in the Ohio Valley, 1755–1759," *War in History* 4, no. 3 (1997): 247–251; and Matthew C. Ward, "Fighting the Old Women: Indian Strategy on the Virginia and Pennsylvania Border, 1754–1758," *Virginia Magazine of History and Biography* 103, no. 3 (1995): 297–320.

2. Brigadier General John Forbes, *Writings of General John Forbes, Relating to His Service in North America*, ed. Alfred Procter James (Menasha, Wisconsin: The Collegiate Press, 1938; reprint edition, Arno Press, 1971), 54.

3. Rex Whitworth, *Field Marshal Lord Ligonier: A Story of the British Army, 1702–1770* (Oxford: University Press, 1958), 152, 154.

4. Ibid., 241, 393.

5. Brigadier General John Forbes, *Letters of General John Forbes Relating to the Expedition Against Fort Duquesne in 1758*, ed. Irene Stewart (Pittsburgh: Colonial Dames of America, 1927; reprint edition, Pennsylvania State University Press, 2006), 13.

6. Nearly all of Forbes's biographical information is derived from three sources: his will dated February 13, 1759; an obituary published in the *Pennsylvania Gazette* of March 15, 1759; and a biographical sketch prepared by Dr. Alfred Proctor James. All three of these sources are located at *The Writings of General John Forbes*, ix–xii, 299–300, 301–302.

7. "Sheriff, Court of Fife Deeds, 1715–1809," Accessed online at http://www.fifefhs.org/Records/Court/fife.htm on September 23, 2006.

8. Burd S. Patterson, *The Head of Iron: A Romance of Colonial Pennsylvania* (Pittsburgh: T.M. Walker, 1908), 294–295.

9. The author thanks Ms. Linda Gibson, Curator of the Pittencrieff House, Fife, Scotland, for this interpretation.

10. Forbes's commissions are located in his Headquarters Papers at the University of Virginia, Charlottesville, Virginia. Janet Linde and William H. Runge, eds., *A Calendar of The Headquarters Papers of Brigadier-General John Forbes Relating to the Expedition against Fort Duquesne in 1758, in the Tracy W. McGregor Library, The Keepsake of an Exhibition 6 November–15 January* (Charlottesville: Department of Special Collections, University of Virginia Library, 1988), 1–3.

11. Forbes Headquarters Papers, "Undated, untitled manuscript, regarding Forbes's financial matters [note: In Forbes's own hand, appears to be a rough draft]."

12. There is a frequently recounted story that Forbes fought the Jacobite rebels under the Duke of Cumberland at Culloden in April 1746. However, by that time Forbes was Ligonier's deputy quartermaster general. Forbes's regiment, the Royal Scots Grays, never left Flanders and were not engaged in operations in Scotland against the Jacobite Rebellion. Although General Ligonier was present for early operations in Scotland and England, he was not present at Culloden, being in London at that time. The author has been unable to locate any confirmation that Forbes was present at Culloden, and as neither his regiment nor his senior officer were present there, it is also unlikely that Forbes would have been on that field of battle. Whitworth, *Lord Ligonier*, 114–115.

13. John Forbes, "Letters," in Papers of Lord Charles Hays. National Library of Scotland, Edinburgh, Scotland.

14. *The Writings of General John Forbes*, 1.

15. Ibid., 65.

16. Ibid., 5, 21, 27, 37.

17. Forbes Papers, Dalhousie Muniments, File #69 — Miscellaneous Financial Records. Forbes bought numerous camp equipages, and a cask of port wine, at the same time.

18. Dr. Edward Shippen, *Memoir of Henry Bouquet 1719–1765: Brigadier General in America and Colonel of the Royal American Regiment in the French and Indian War* (Philadelphia: G.H. Buchanan and Company, 1900), 7.

19. Henry Bouquet, *The Papers of Colonel Henry Bouquet*, ed. Sylvester E. Stevens, *et al.*, 19 vols. (Harrisburg: Pennsylvania Historical Commission and Works Progress Administration, 1940–1944), 2: 608.

20. Shippen, *Memoir of Henry Bouquet 1719–1765*, 7. Whitehead was the second Episcopal Bishop of Pittsburgh, serving in that post between 1882 and 1922.

Chapter 2

1. *The Papers of Henry Bouquet*, 1: 246–247.

2. Nearly all biographical information on Bouquet's early life is provided by C.G.F. Dumas, "Sketch of the Life of Henry Bouquet," and Paul-Emile Schazmann, "Henry Bouquet in Switzerland," in *The Papers of Henry Bouquet*, 1: xvi–xxvii. Some limited additional information is provided by Louis M. Waddell, "The American Career of Henry Bouquet," *The Swiss-American Historical Society Newsletter* 17 (1981): 13–15. Earlier sources, which relied heavily on Dumas and provide little new scholarship on Bouquet's early life, are George Harrison Fisher, "Brigadier General Henry Bouquet," *The Penn-*

sylvania Magazine of History and Biography 3, no. 2 (1879): 121–123; Shippen, *Memoir of Henry Bouquet 1719–1765,* and E. Douglas Branch, "Henry Bouquet: Professional Soldier," *The Pennsylvania Magazine of History and Biography* 62, no. 1 (January 1938): 41–42.

3. Major Patrick H. Hannum, *Henry Bouquet: A Study of Three Military Campaigns in North America, 1758–1764* (Fort Leavenworth, Kansas: U.S. Army Command and General Staff College, 1991), 2–3.

4. The only history of the War of the Austrian Succession in the Italian Piedmont is Spenser Wilkinson, *The Defence of Piedmont, 1742–1748: A Prelude to the Study of Napoleon* (Oxford: Clarendon Press, 1927). This book supports the widely held premise that Bouquet gained considerable experience in mountain warfare, road building, and fighting with and against irregular forces during the war.

5. *The Papers of Henry Bouquet,* 1: 333.

6. *The Writings of General John Forbes,* 141.

7. *The Writings of General John Forbes,* 1, 14–15, 21, 24, 25, 40.

8. Forbes Headquarters Papers, "Memorandum of Brigade Major Halkett [undated]."

9. Martin West, transcriber., *George Washington Remembers: Reflections on the French and Indian War* (Lanham, Boulder, New York, Toronto and Oxford: Rowman & Littlefield Publishers, 2004), 41.

10. The only biographical sketch of St. Clair is Charles R. Hildeburn, "Sir John St. Clair, Baronet, Quarter Master General in America, 1755 to 1767," *The Pennsylvania Magazine of History and Biography* 9, no. 1 (1885). Unfortunately this brief biography is both quite limited and badly outdated.

11. Forbes Headquarters Papers, "Instructions for the Quarter Master General in the Southern Provinces, 1758 [undated]."

12. *The Writings of General Forbes,* 1.

13. Ibid., 114.

14. Ibid., 128, 139.

15. Alfred Proctor James and Charles Morse Stotz, *Drums in the Forest, Decision at the Forks, Defense in the Wilderness* (Pittsburgh: Historical Society of Western Pennsylvania, 1958; revised edition, Pittsburgh: Western Pennsylvania Historical Society, 2005), 90.

16. *The Writings of General John Forbes,* 199.

17. Ibid., 70–71.

18. Donald Cornu, "Captain Lewis Ourry, Royal American Regiment of Foot," *Pennsylvania History* 19 (July 1932): 252–259.

19. *The Papers of Henry Bouquet,* 1: 171.

20. Stewart, Editor, *Letters of General John Forbes,* 17.

21. *The Papers of Henry Bouquet,* 1: 333; and 2: 308–310.

22. Forbes Headquarters Papers, "A Sketch of the Number of Troops Under General Forbes Encamped Carlisle 17th July 1758."

23. E.M. Lloyd, "The Raising of the Highland Regiments in 1757," *English Historical Review* 17, no. 67 (July 1902): 466–469.

24. *The Papers of Henry Bouquet,* 2: 120–122.

25. Information on the officers of the 77th Foot is provided by Ian Macpherson McCulloch, *Sons of the Mountains: The Highland Regiments in the French and Indian War, 1756–1767* (Fleischmanns, New York: Purple Mountain Press, 2006), 2: 51–66. For Grant, see Paul David Nelson, *General James Grant: Scottish Soldier and Royal Governor of East Florida* (Gainesville: University Press of Florida, 1993), 1–16.

26. Reel 30, James Grant of Ballidalloch Papers, Library of Congress, Washington, D.C.

27. *The Papers of Henry Bouquet,* 1: 177, 184–185.

28. Ibid., 1: 197.

29. Forbes Headquarters Papers, "Letter, William Byrd III to Forbes, Charlestown, South Carolina, March 21, 1758."

30. *Writings of General Forbes,* 77.

31. Forbes Papers, Dalhousie Muniments, Scottish Record Office, Edinburgh, United Kingdom. File #51—Letters of Allen McLean, 77th Highlanders.

32. Forbes Headquarters Papers, "Letter, Forbes to Bouquet, dated Philadelphia June 8th, 1758" and Stewart, *Letters of General John Forbes,* 21.

33. Forbes Headquarters Papers, "Field Return of the 1st Highlander Battalion Commanded by the Honourable Colonel Archibald Montgomery, Camp near Philadelphia, June 13th 1758."

34. For discussions of the challenges faced by the Colony of Pennsylvania in raising a military defense, refer to Francis Jennings, "The Seven Years' War in Pennsylvania" in William G. Shade, ed., *Revisioning the British Empire in the Eighteenth Century: Essays from Twenty-Five Years of the Lawrence Henry Gibson Institute for Eighteenth-Century Studies* (Bethlehem, Pennsylvania: Lehigh University Press, 1998), 55–75; Charles M. Stotz, *Outposts of the War for Empire* (1985; revised edition, Pittsburgh, Pennsylvania: Western Pennsylvania Historical Society, 2005), 37–38; and Matthew C. Ward, "An Army of Servants," *Pennsylvania Magazine of History and Biography* 119 (1995): 76–79.

35. Ward, "An Army of Servants," 79–86, 89–93.

36. "Journal of Colonel James Burd, February 16–March 10, 1758." Colonel James Burd Papers, Western Pennsylvania Historical Society, Pittsburgh, Pennsylvania.

37. *Writings of General John Forbes,* 205.

38. Forbes Headquarters Papers, "Total of the Pennsylvania Regiment [less] Detachments for the Frontier Camps."

39. Forbes Headquarters Papers, "Letter, James Glen to Forbes, dated Raystown, July 26, 1758."

40. W.W. Abbot, ed., *The Papers of George Washington, Colonial Series* (Charlottesville: University Press of Virginia, 1988), 5: 134, 144–146.

41. Mary Vernon Mish, "General Adam Stephen, Founder, Martinsburg, West Virginia," *West Virginia History* 22, no. 2 (January 1961): 63–65; and Harry M. Ward, *Major General Adam Stephen and the Cause of American Liberty* (Charlottesville: University Press of Virginia, 1989).

42. *The Papers of George Washington,* 5: 135.

43. Wilbur R. Jacobs, ed., *The Appalachian Indian Frontier: The Edmond Atkin Report and Plan of 1755* (University of South Carolina Press: 1954; revised edition, University of Nebraska Press: 1967), xxvi.

44. Alfred P. James, "George Mercer of the Ohio Company, A Study in Frustration," *The Western Pennsylvania Historical Magazine* 46, no. 1 (January 1963): 2, 11–19.

45. John Ferling, "Soldiers for Virginia: Who Served in the French and Indian War?" *The Virginia Magazine of History and Biography* 94, no. 3 (July 1986): 308–309, 317; and Matthew C. Ward, *Breaking the Backcountry: The Seven Years War in Virginia and Pennsylvania, 1754–1765* (Pittsburgh: University of Pittsburgh Press, 2003), 97–99, 108–110.

46. Forbes Headquarters Papers, "Letter, St. Clair to Forbes, dated Winchester May 19, 1758."

47. Forbes Headquarters Papers, "Letter, St. Clair to Forbes, dated Winchester, May 21, 1758."

48. Forbes Headquarters Papers, "Letter from Colonel Byrd to Forbes, dated Winchester, May 29, 1758."

49. Forbes Headquarters Papers, "Letter from Colonel Byrd to Forbes, dated Winchester, June 3, 1758."

50. Forbes Headquarters Papers, "Letter from Colonel Byrd to Forbes, dated Fort Cumberland, August 3, 1758."

51. *The Papers of Henry Bouquet*, 2: 336, 339, 673–675.

52. *The Papers of George Washington*, 5: 198–199.

53. Forbes Headquarters Papers, "A Sketch of the number of Troops under General Forbes Encamped Carlisle 17th July 1758."

54. William Hand Browne, ed., *Archives of Maryland, Correspondence of Governor Horatio Sharpe* (Baltimore: Maryland Historical Society, 1890), 2: 182–184.

55. The Maryland Assembly failed to pass a single act in the spring session of 1758. An extremely lengthy and detailed discourse regarding the machinations of the Maryland Assembly, as viewed from Sharpe's perspective to Forbes, can be found ibid., 198–203.

56. *Writings of General John Forbes*, 103–104.

57. *Correspondence of Governor Sharpe*, 205.

58. *Writings of General John Forbes*, 117, 190.

59. Forbes Headquarters Papers, "A Sketch of the Number of Troops Under General Forbes Encamped Carlisle 17th July 1758."

60. Forbes Headquarters Papers, "Letter, Forbes to St. Clair, dated Philadelphia June 16, 1758."

61. Forbes Headquarters Papers, "Letter, St. Clair to Forbes, dated Carlisle June 23, 1758."

62. Donald Eugene Becker, *North Carolina, 1754–1763: An Economic, Political, and Military History of North Carolina During the Great War for the Empire* (Ph.D. dissertation, University of North Carolina at Chapel Hill, 1971), 277.

63. Forbes Headquarters Papers, "A Sketch of the Number of Troops Under General Forbes Encamped Carlisle 17th July 1758."

64. *Writings of General John Forbes*, 139.

65. John R. Maass, "'All This Poor Province Could Do': North Carolina and the Seven Years' War, 1757–1762," *The North Carolina Historical Review* 89, no. 1 (January 2002): 53.

66. *Writings of General John Forbes*, 147, 201, 205.

67. John C. Van Horne and George Reese, eds., *The Letter Book of James Abercromby, Colonial Agent 1751–1773* (Richmond: Virginia State Archives and Library, 1991), 297, 345. Abercromby was colonial agent for North Carolina throughout the timeframe of the Forbes Campaign.

68. *The Papers of Henry Bouquet*, 2: 256.

69. Forbes Headquarters Papers, "A Return of Part of the North Carolina Troops."

70. Maass, "All This Poor Province Could Do," 60.

71. *The Papers of Henry Bouquet*, 2: 210.

72. Ibid., 1: 380, 382.

73. Samuel Hazard, ed., *Pennsylvania Archives* (Philadelphia: Joseph Severns & Company, 1853), 3: 397–398, 401.

74. Forbes Headquarters Papers, "Return of the Officers and Men Military and Civil of the Detachment of the Royal Regiment of Artillery Commanded by Captain Lieutenant George Anderson, June 13, 1758."

75. *Writings of General John Forbes*, 169; and *The Papers of Henry Bouquet* 2: 322.

76. *The Papers of Henry Bouquet*, 2: 17.

77. Forbes Headquarters Papers, "[List of] Artillery [not dated]."

78. Forbes, Dalhousie Muniments, "File #37 — Miscellaneous Returns of Stores, Ordnance, and Barracks Room Furniture, 1757–1759." For artillery being left behind, refer to *Pennsylvania Archives*, 3: 492.

79. *Writings of General John Forbes*, 217; *The Papers of Henry Bouquet*, 2: 439.

80. *The Papers of Henry Bouquet*, 2: 423–434.

81. Ibid., 2: 386.

82. *Writings of General John Forbes*, 110, 225; and *The Papers of Henry Bouquet*, 2: 530.

83. *Writings of General John Forbes*, 220, 225

84. Ibid., 225.

85. *The Papers of Henry Bouquet*, 2: 103.

86. Marion Tinling, ed., *The Correspondence of The Three William Byrds of Westover, Virginia, 1684–1776* (Charlottesville: Virginia Historical Society, 1977), 2: 638–645.

87. *Writings of General John Forbes*, 68.

88. *The Papers of George Washington*, 5: 138.

89. *Writings of General John Forbes*, 239.

90. *The Papers of Henry Bouquet*, 1: 339.

91. The premier authority on rifles in the early British army is DeWitt Bailey, *British Military Flintlock Rifles, 1740–1840* (Lincoln, Rhode Island: Andrew Mowbray Publishers, 2002). For rifles in the Forbes campaign, refer to 11–16.

92. Forbes Headquarters Papers, "[List of] Artillery [not dated]."

93. *The Papers of Henry Bouquet*, 2: 17.

94. For a detailed description and high-quality photographs of this rifle, refer to DeWitt Bailey, *British Military Flintlock Rifles*, 17, 198.

95. *The Papers of Henry Bouquet*, 2: 28.

96. Ibid., 2: 368–369.

97. Ibid., 2: 50.

98. Ibid., 2: 564.

99. *The Papers of George Washington*, 6:157.

Chapter 3

1. *Writings of General John Forbes*, 239–240.

2. Michel Brisebois, "Books from General Wolfe's Library at the National Library of Canada." *National Library News* 28, no. 2 (February 1996), accessed online at: http://www.collectionscanada.ca/bulletin/015017-9602-15-e.html; and William Coolidge Lane, *A Catalogue of the Washington Collection in the Boston Athenaeum* (Boston: The Boston Athenaeum, 1897),541.

3. Captain Joseph Otway, *An Essay on the Art of War, Translated from the French of Count Turpin, in Two Volumes* (London: A. Hamilton, 1761).

4. Otway, *An Essay on the Art of War*, 2: 99–101.

5. St. Clair's Letterbook remained in Forbes's Headquarters Papers. Linde and Runge, eds., *A Calendar of the Headquarters Papers of Brigadier-General John Forbes*, 2–3.

6. G.D. Scull, ed., *Collections of the New York Historical Society for the Year 1881: The Montrose Journals* (New York: New York Historical Society, 1882), 62.

7. John Muller, *The Attac and Defence of Fortified Places* (1757; revised edition, Arlington, Virginia: The Invisible College Press, 2004), ix–x.

8. Otway, *An Essay on the Art of War*, 2: 102–107.

9. Ross D. Netherton, "The Carlyle House Conference: An Episode in the Politics of Colonial Union." In James Allen Braden, ed., *Proceedings of Northern Virginia Studies Conference, 1983, Alexandria: Empire to*

Commonwealth (Alexandria: Northern Virginia Community College, 1984), 57, 66.

10. *The Papers of Henry Bouquet*, 1: 372–373.

11. Forbes Headquarters Papers, "Letter of Governor Glen, Camp at Reas Town, Aug' 8th 1758."

12. *The Papers of Henry Bouquet*, 2: 74.

13. Headquarters Papers of Forbes, Letterbook of Sir John St. Clair, "p. 155 [St. Clair to Colonel Napier, Fort Cumberland, August 15, 1755]."

14. John Flexer Walzer, "Transportation in the Philadelphia Trading Area, 1740–1775" (Madison: University of Wisconsin M.A. thesis, 1968), 7.

15. T.H. Breen, *The Marketplace of Revolution: How Consumer Politics Shaped American Independence* (Oxford University Press, 2004), 111.

16. Ray's Town, now modern Bedford, was named for the Indian trader John Ray. Participants in the campaign most commonly referred to it as "Raes Town." The proper "Ray's Town" will be used throughout this study. Williams, *Bouquet's March to the Ohio*, 83.

17. *Writings of General John Forbes*, 117–118.

18. Forbes Headquarters Papers, "Troops Destined for the Ohio, Fort DuQuesne or Other Operations to the Southward" [not dated, c. 1757].

19. Archer Butler Hulbert, *Historic Highways of America*, Volume 5: *The Old Glade (Forbes) Road* (Cleveland, Ohio: The Arthur H. Clark Company, 1903), 15–33.

20. Forbes Headquarters Papers, "Letter, Forbes to St. Clair, dated Philadelphia, May 30, 1758."

21. *Writings of General John Forbes*, 239.

22. Frank G. Speck, *Midwinter Rites of the Cayuga Long House* (Philadelphia: University of Pennsylvania Press, 1949; revised edition, Lincoln: University of Nebraska Press, 1995), 36.

23. Lewis Henry Morgan, *The League of the Iroquois* (1851; revised edition, North Dighton, Massachusetts: JG Press, 1995), 197–199, 336–338.

24. Johann Georg Kohl, *Kitchi-Gami: Life Among the Lake Superior Ojibway* (1860; revised edition Minnesota Historical Society Press, 1985), 342.

25. Jacobs, ed., *The Appalachian Indian Frontier*, 82–83.

26. Steven F. Johnson, *Ninnouck (The People): The Algonkian People of New England* (Marlborough, Massachusetts: Bliss Publishing Company, 1995), 21–22.

27. *Scoouwa: James Smith's Indian Captivity Narrative*, 66, 96.

28. Forbes Headquarters Papers, "[Undated, untitled manuscript]."

29. Forbes Papers, Dalhousie Muniments, File #74 — Unsigned, Undated Memorandum on Conduct of Campaign.

30. *The Papers of Henry Bouquet*, 2: 74.

31. *Writings of General John Forbes*, 171.

32. Hulbert, *The Old Glade Road*, 131.

Chapter 4

1. *The Papers of Henry Bouquet*, 1: 301–302, 322–323, 333.

2. Ibid., 1: 342, 345.

3. Ibid., 1: 347–349. Forbes regularly used "ane" instead of "an," indicating that he both spoke and wrote with a strong Scottish brogue.

4. Derived from Forbes, Dalhousie Muniments, File #72 —1758 — Notes of Stages and Distances on the road from Pittsburgh to New York. I have utilized Forbes's perceived distances throughout this manuscript, rather than topographically precise modern mileages that were of course never available to Forbes, his subordinate officers, or his engineers.

5. *Writings of General John Forbes*, 94–95.

6. Forbes, Dalhousie Muniments. File #51— Letters of Allen McLean, 77th Highlanders.

7. *The Papers of Henry Bouquet*, 1: 362.

8. *Writings of General John Forbes*, 100–101.

9. *The Papers of Henry Bouquet*, 1: 387, 402.

10. Captain Thomas Simes, *A Military Course for the Government and Conduct of a Battalion* (London: 1778), 203.

11. *The Papers of Henry Bouquet*, 2: 660.

12. Ibid., 2: 149.

13. Ibid., 2: 165.

14. Niles Anderson, "The General Chooses a Road: The Forbes Campaign of 1758 to Capture Fort Duquesne." *Western Pennsylvania Historical Magazine*, 42 (June, September, December 1959): 132.

15. *The Papers of Henry Bouquet*, 2: 82.

16. Captain Evan Shelby Papers, The Shelby Family Collection, Archives of Appalachia, East Tennessee State University, Johnson City, Tennessee.

17. *Correspondence of Governor Sharpe*, 206, 211–215, 221–223.

18. *Writings of General John Forbes*, 145.

19. Ibid., 110.

20. Quoted in McCulloch, *Sons of the Mountains*, 1: 116.

21. Stewart, ed., *Letters of General John Forbes*, 21; *Writings of General John Forbes*, 113; Forbes Headquarters Papers, "Letter, Forbes to St. Clair, dated Philadelphia June 16th 1758."

22. *The Papers of Henry Bouquet*, 1: 399.

23. Ibid., 1: 361.

24. *Pennsylvania Archives*, 3: 402–403.

25. *The Papers of Henry Bouquet*, 1: 389–390.

26. *Writings of General John Forbes*, 106.

27. This is the author's assumption. No records are known to be available documenting the shoe production capacity of Philadelphia in 1758. For background information on this topic, refer to David L. Salay, "Marching to War: The Production of Leather and Shoes in Revolutionary Pennsylvania," *Pennsylvania History* 60, no. 1 (January 1993): 72. Supporting this assumption is that archaeological investigations at Fort Ligonier between 1960 and 1965 recovered 155 pairs of shoes. These shoes displayed 22 different styles of quarter straps and 25 different styles of vamp tongues. Clearly, large numbers of manufacturers were engaged in producing shoes for Forbes's army. Jacob L. Grimm, *Archaeological Investigation of Fort Ligonier, 1960–1965* (Pittsburgh, Pennsylvania: Annals of Carnegie Museum, 1970), 107.

28. *Writings of General John Forbes*, 108.

29. *The Papers of Henry Bouquet*, 2: 662.

30. *Writings of General John Forbes*, 115.

31. *The Papers of Henry Bouquet*, 2: 64.

32. Forbes Headquarters Papers, "Letter, Forbes to St. Clair," dated Philadelphia June 16th 1758.

33. *The Papers of Henry Bouquet*, 2: 135.

34. *Colonial Records of Pennsylvania* (Philadelphia: J. Severn, 1852), 8: 79–80, 83–84.

35. Marion Tinling, ed., "Some Unpublished Correspondence of William Byrd III," *The Virginia Magazine of History and Biography* 88 (July 1980): 286.

36. "Journal of Joseph Shippen, 1758," Shippen Family Papers, Historical Society of Pennsylvania, Philadelphia, Pennsylvania.

37. *The Papers of Henry Bouquet*, 2: 22.

38. *Writings of General John Forbes*, 100.

39. *The Papers of Henry Bouquet*, 2: 28–29.

40. *The Papers of Henry Bouquet*, 2: 107; and *Correspondence of Governor Sharpe*, 197, 238.

41. "Military Letters of Captain Joseph Shippen," 457.

42. *Pennsylvania Archives*, 3: 483.

43. Reverend Thomas Barton, *Journal of an Expedition to the Ohio, Commanded by His Excellency Brigadier General Forbes, in the Year of our Lord 1758* (Philadelphia, Pennsylvania: Historical Society of Pennsylvania), August 19, 1758.

44. *The Papers of Henry Bouquet*, 1: 347; *Writings of General John Forbes*, 106, 107, 115.

45. *Writings of General John Forbes*, 192–193.

46. *The Papers of Henry Bouquet*, 2: 16.

47. *The Papers of Henry Bouquet*, 2: 112; and *Pennsylvania Archives*, 3: 410.

48. *Writings of General John Forbes*, 133.

49. Lieutenant Colonel Thomas G. Tousey, *Military History of Carlisle and Carlisle Barracks* (Richmond, Virginia: The Dietz Press, 1939), 27.

50. *The Papers of Henry Bouquet*, 2: 7.

51. *The Papers of George Washington*, 5: 257.

52. Ibid., 5: 152–153. "Half Thick" is a type of coarse wool, commonly used for leggings.

53. Garland R. Quarles, *George Washington and Winchester, Virginia, 1748–1758* (Winchester, Virginia: Winchester-Frederick County Historical Society, 1974), 38.

54. *The Papers of Henry Bouquet*, 2: 174, 183.

55. *The Papers of George Washington*, 5: 290–291.

56. Ibid., 5: 257; and *The Papers of Henry Bouquet*, 2: 158.

57. *The Papers of Henry Bouquet*, 2: 89.

58. Forbes Headquarters Papers, "Letter from Colonel Byrd to Forbes, dated Winchester, May 29, 1758."

59. Forbes Headquarters Papers, "Letter, Colonel Byrd to Forbes, dated Winchester, June 3, 1758."

60. *The Papers of Henry Bouquet*, 2: 136.

61. Tinling, ed., *Correspondence of Three William Byrds*, 2: 660–661.

62. For the role of chaplains and religion in the British Army of the Seven Years' War, refer to Paul E. Kopperman, "Religion & Religious Policy in the British Army, c. 1700–1776," *The Journal of Religious History* 15 (1987): 390–405.

63. *The Papers of Henry Bouquet*, 2: 145–146.

64. Robert G. Crist, *John Armstrong: Proprietors Man* (Ph.D. thesis, Pennsylvania State University, 1981), 108.

65. *Writings of General John Forbes*, 132.

66. Interpretation of the Reverend Barton's intent was generously provided by my brother, the Rev. Robert Kaylor, an elder in the United Methodist Church, while studying in the 18th-century chapel of the Rev. John Wesley in London, England, during the summer of 2006.

67. David W. Rial, *The Old Forbes Road* (Pittsburgh: Western Pennsylvania Historical Society, 1995), 62–63.

68. *The Papers of Henry Bouquet*, 2: 544.

69. Ibid., 2: 661, 669.

70. For women with the army, refer to Paul E. Kopperman, "The British High Command and Soldiers' Wives in America, 1755–1783," *Journal of the Society for Army Historical Research* 60 (1982): 14–34; and Holly A. Mayer, "From Forts to Families: Following the Army into Western Pennsylvania, 1758–1766," *Pennsylvania Magazine of History and Biography* 130, no. 1 (January 2006).

71. *The Papers of Henry Bouquet*, 2: 680, 684.

72. The best source on training of the British Army during this timeframe is J. Houlding, *Fit for Service: The Training of the British Army, 1715–1795* (Oxford: Clarendon Press, 1981).

73. *The Papers of Henry Bouquet*, 2: 35.

74. Brigitte Burkett, transcriber and translator, *The Journal of Johann Michael Lindenmuth, 1737–1812* (Rockport, Maine: Picton Press, 2000), 29.

75. Stotz, *Outposts of the War for Empire*, 116.

76. *The Papers of Henry Bouquet*, 2: 337.

77. Charles E. Brodine, Jr., "Henry Bouquet and British Infantry Tactics on the Ohio Frontier, 1758–1764," in David C. Skaggs and Larry L. Nelson, eds., *The Sixty Year's War for the Great Lakes, 1754–1814* (East Lansing: Michigan State University Press, 2001), 61.

78. *The Papers of Henry Bouquet*, 2: 1.

79. Forbes, Dalhousie Muniments, File #51, "Letter of Allen McLean, 77th Highlanders, dated Lancaster, May 10, 1758." For additional discussions, refer to Brodine, "Henry Bouquet and British Infantry Tactics on the Ohio Frontier," 49–50, 59. Brodine correctly discusses the initial shortages of lead balls, but fails to record that the arrival of the store ship alleviated this concern.

80. *The Papers of Henry Bouquet*, 2: 136.

81. Ibid., 2: 658.

82. Quoted in Joseph R. Rilling, *The Art and Science of War in America: A Bibliography of American Military Imprints, 1690–1800* (Alexandria Bay, New York: Museum Restoration Service, 1990), 4.

83. *The Papers of Henry Bouquet*, 2: 670, 672, 675–677; Barton, *Journal*, August 8–13, 1758.

84. For a detailed discussion of these tactics, refer to Brodine, "Henry Bouquet and British Infantry Tactics on the Ohio Frontier," 43–61.

85. *The Papers of Henry Bouquet*, 2: 397.

86. Forbes Headquarters Papers, "A Calculation of Provisions for Six Thousand Men for Three Months or 84 Days Philadelphia May 1st 1758."

87. *The Papers of Henry Bouquet*, 2: 96, 683.

88. Ibid., 2: 208.

89. Forbes Headquarters Papers, "A Calculation of Provisions for Six Thousand Men for Three Months or 84 Days, Philadelphia May 1st 1758."

90. Forbes Headquarters Papers, "Survey on Provisions at Carlisle June 6th 1758."

91. Forbes Headquarters Papers, "Letter, Commissary Draper S. Woods to Forbes, dated Carlisle, June 9th 1758."

92. *The Papers of Henry Bouquet*, 2: 361.

93. Forbes Headquarters Papers, "A Calculation of Provisions Now in Stores & Time it will serve six thousand Men, dated Carlisle, Pennsylvania, August 4, 1758."

94. *The Papers of Henry Bouquet*, 2: 355.

95. Ibid., 3: 24–25.

96. Ibid., 2: 21.

97. John E. Guilday, "Animal Remains from Archaeological Excavations at Fort Ligonier," *Annals of the Carnegie Museum* 42 (1970), 177–186.

98. *The Papers of Henry Bouquet*, 2: 335.

99. Forbes Headquarters Papers, "A Return of Provisions in Store at the Camp and Fort near Raystown August the 1st 1758"; "A Calculation of Provisions Now in Store at Sundry Places, and the Time it will serve six thousand men"; "A Return of Provisions in Store at the Fort Near Ray's Town August the 8th 1758."

100. Forbes Headquarters Papers, "Letter, Draper S. Wood to St. Clair, dated Alexandria May 15, 1758."

101. Forbes Headquarters Papers, "Letter from Forbes to Mr. Joshua Howell, dated Shippensburg, 15th August 1758."

102. Dora Mae Clark, "The British Treasury and the Administration of Military Affairs in America, 1754–1774," *Pennsylvania History* 2, no. 4 (October 1935): 201.

103. *The Papers of Henry Bouquet*, 1: 352, 364. A hogshead contained 63 gallons, according to A Society of Gentlemen in Scotland, *Encyclopedia Britannica, or a Dictionary of Arts and Sciences* (Edinburgh: A. Bell and C. Macfarquhar, 1768–1771) 2: 788.

104. *The Papers of Henry Bouquet*, 2: 158.

105. Ibid., 2: 75, 102.

106. Ibid., 2: 102.

107. Forbes Headquarters Papers, "Letter, St. Clair to Forbes, dated Carlisle June 17th 1758."

108. For a well-researched and analytical discussion of wagons on the Braddock Campaign, refer to Whitfield J. Bell Jr. and Leonard W. Labaree, "Franklin and the 'Wagon Affair,' 1755," *Proceedings of the American Philosophical Society* (December 19, 1957): 551–558.

109. *Writings of General John Forbes*, 63.

110. Ibid., 88–89.

111. Ibid., 111.

112. *The Papers of Henry Bouquet*, 1: 371.

113. *Writings of General John Forbes*, 107, 115.

114. Ibid., 116.

115. *The Papers of Henry Bouquet*, 2: 106.

116. Ibid., 2: 230.

117. Ibid., 2: 33.

118. Ibid., 2: 122.

119. Ibid., 2: 180.

120. Ibid., 2: 163–164. Managing of wagons and other transportation of the army was a critical role of the quartermaster.

121. For a simplistic and not particularly insightful view of the challenges faced by Forbes and Bouquet in the acquisition of transportation, and their eventually having to resort to impressment, refer to J. Alan Rogers, "Impressment in Western Pennsylvania, 1755–1759," *The Western Pennsylvania Historical Magazine* 52 (July 1969): 259–260, 262. For another modern treatment, similarly flawed, see Charles Brodine, "Civil-Military Relations in Pennsylvania, 1758–1760: An Examination of John Shy's Thesis," *Pennsylvania History* 62 (April 1995): 219–222, 226–227.

122. *The Papers of Henry Bouquet*, 1: 405.

123. Ibid., 1: 378–379.

124. Ibid., 1: 386–387.

125. Ibid., 2: 26–28; and *Pennsylvania Archives*, 3: 409.

126. Painting by Thomas Gainsborough, *Open Landscape in Suffolk with a Wagon on a Track*, in Linda Doeser, *The Life and Works of Gainsborough* (New York: Shooting Star Press, 1995), 28–29. The most comprehensive source on these wagons is Don H. Berkehile, "Conestoga Wagons in Braddock's Campaign, 1755," in *Bulletin 218: Contributions from the Museum of History and Technology* (Washington, D.C.: Smithsonian Institution, 1959), 144–146, 150.

127. *Writings of General John Forbes*, 88–89.

128. *The Papers of Henry Bouquet*, 2: 5, 50.

129. Forbes Papers, Dalhousie Muniments, File #37 — Miscellaneous Returns of Stores, Ordnance, and Barracks Room Furniture, 1757–1759.

130. John Muller, *A Treatise of Artillery, 1780* (1757; 1780 edition reprinted by Alexandria Bay, New York: Museum Restoration Service, 1977), 125–143.

131. *Writings of General John Forbes*, 204, 207, 216.

132. *The Papers of Henry Bouquet*, 2: 121, 124.

133. Ibid., 2: 135.

134. Forbes Headquarters Papers, "Letter from St. Clair to Forbes, dated Lancaster May 10, 1758."

135. *Writings of General John Forbes*, 168–169.

136. Ibid., 174.

137. *The Papers of Henry Bouquet*, 2: 221, 224.

138. Ibid., 2: 180.

139. Ibid., 2: 5.

140. Ibid., 1: 362.

141. Tousey, *Military History of Carlisle and Carlisle Barracks*, 17.

142. Ibid., 24.

143. Stotz, *Outposts of the War for Empire*, 108–109.

144. Tousey, *Military History of Carlisle and Carlisle Barracks*, 25.

145. Forbes Headquarters Papers, "Report of the State of Carlisle Fort."

146. Hayes R. Eschenmann, *Forbes Expedition, Carlisle to Cowan's Gap* (privately printed, 1999), 18, 23.

147. Tousey, *Military History of Carlisle and Carlisle Barracks*, 32.

148. Barton, *Journal*, July 20, 1758.

149. Hulbert, *The Old Glade Road*, 56.

150. F.R. Reece, ed., "Colonel Eyre's Journal of His Trip from New York to Pittsburgh, 1762," *Western Pennsylvania Historical Magazine* 27 (1944): 41.

151. Forbes Headquarters Papers, "Memorandum of the Fort at Shippensburg Aug 13th 1758."

152. *The Papers of Henry Bouquet*, 2: 47.

153. A slender history of Fort Loudon, well intentioned but not particularly useful, is Gary T. Hawbaker, *Fort Loudon on the Frontier* (Hershey, Pennsylvania: privately printed, 1976).

154. Barton *Journal*, July 21, 1758.

155. *The Papers of Henry Bouquet*, 2: 73.

156. Ibid., 2: 88, 121.

157. Three local history works, of marginal interest and dubious accuracy, have attempted to address this portion of the Forbes Road. Eschenmann, *Forbes Expedition, Carlisle to Cowan's Gap*; Eschenmann, *Forbes Expedition, Cowan's Gap to Juniata Crossing* (Privately printed, 2003): and Harry E. Foreman, *Forbes Road, Parnell's Knob to Burnt Cabins* (Chambersburg, Pennsylvania: privately printed, 1954). The single most valuable description of the Forbes Road route, exhaustively researched and based upon numerous historic maps of the road, is Edward G. Williams, ed., *Bouquet's March to the Ohio: The Forbes Road (From the Original Manuscripts in the William L. Clements Library)* (Pittsburgh: Historical Society of Western Pennsylvania, 1975). Williams's exemplary work is the basis for discussions of the Forbes campaign route in this study.

158. Reginald P. Briggs, "Conquest of the Allegheny Mountains in Pennsylvania: The Engineering Geology of Forbes Road: 1758–1764." *Environmental & Engineering Geoscience* 4, no. 3 (Fall 1998): 403.

159. Stotz, *Outposts of the War for Empire*, 110.

160. Barton, *Journal*, July 22, 1758.

161. Ibid., July 23, 1758.

162. *The Papers of Henry Bouquet*, 2: 73, 121.

163. Barton, *Journal*, July 23, 1758.

164. *The Papers of Henry Bouquet*, 2: 122, 126.

165. Stotz, *Outposts of the War for Empire*, 110–112.

166. This discussion of redoubts is adapted from Douglas R. Cubbison, *Historic Structures Report: The Redoubts of West Point* (West Point, New York: United States Military Academy, Directorate of Public Works, 2004).

167. Lewis Lochee, *Elements of Field Fortification* (London: T. Cadell and T. Egerton, 1783); Jean Louis La Cointe, *The Science of Military Posts; For the use of Regimental Officers, Who Frequently Command Detached*

Parties, in Which Is Shown the Manner of Attacking and Defending Posts, with Cuts, Explaining the Construction of Field-Forts and Intrenchments (London: Printed for T. Payne, at the Mews Gate, 1761); Lieutenant J.C. Pleydell, *An Essay on Field Fortification: Intended Principally for the Use of Officers of Infantry, showing how to trace out on the ground and construct in the easiest manner, all sorts of Redoubts and other field works, translated from the original manuscript of an officer of experience in the Prussian Service* (London: Printed for J. Nourse, Bookseller to His Majesty; 1768; New Edition, London: Printed for F. Wingrave, 1790); and Sir James Young, *An Essay on the Command of Small Detachments* (London, 1766).

168. For examples of this refer to Guillaume Le-Blond, *The Elements of Fortification, Translated from the French* (Philadelphia: Printed for the War Office by C.P. Wayne, 1801), 27, 29–30, 32, 42; and Sebastien LePrestre de Vauban, translated by George A. Rothrock, *A Manual of Siegecraft and Fortification* (1740; reprint edition, Ann Arbor: University of Michigan Press, 1968), 155.

169. Marchel Sebastien LePrestre de Vauban. *The New Method of Fortification, published in English by Abel Swall, London, 1691* (Ann Arbor, Michigan: University Microfilms, Inc, 1963), 18.

170. *The Papers of Henry Bouquet*, 2: 122–123.

171. The most comprehensive study of 18th-century roads is provided by Philip Lord Jr., *War Over Walloomscoick: Land Use and Settlement Pattern on the Bennington Battlefield, 1777* (Albany, New York: New York State Museum, 1989), 20–31. Another valuable archaeological study of an 18th-century road is Ronald F. Kingsley and James Rowe Jr., "In Search of the Eighteenth Century Rowley Road, Shoreham Township, Addison County, Vermont," *Journal of Vermont Archaeology* 3 (2000): 61–68.

172. Walzer, "Transportation in the Philadelphia Trading Area," 150, 152; and Lord, *War Over Walloomscoick*, 25. For contemporary length of a rod refer to Society of Gentlemen in Scotland, *Encyclopedia Britannica*, 3: 553.

173. Charles Fisher and Lois M. Feister, *Archaeology of the Colonial Road at the John Ellison House, Knox's Headquarters State Historic Site, Vail's Gate, New York* (Albany, New York: Bureau of Historic Sites, 2000), 13.

174. Lord, *War Over Walloomscoick*, 32–34.

175. *Correspondence of Governor Sharpe*, 211.

176. Grimm, *Archaeological Investigation of Fort Ligonier, 1960–1965*, 21.

177. Cornu, "Captain Lewis Ourry," 257.

178. Williams, *Bouquet's March to the Ohio*, 40.

179. For this, refer to Fisher, *Archaeology of the Colonial Road at the John Ellison House*, 6–7, 10–11, 23.

180. Forbes, Dalhousie Muniments, "File #37 — Miscellaneous Returns of Stores, Ordnance, and Barracks Room Furniture, 1757–1759."

181. An interesting journal documenting early commercial use of the Forbes Road is John W. Jordan, ed., "James Kenny's Journal to the Westward, 1758–1759," *Pennsylvania Magazine of History and Biography* 37 (1913): 395–449.

182. Williams, *Bouquet's March*, 42.

183. *The Papers of Henry Bouquet*, 2: 142.

184. Barton, *Journal*, July 24, 1758.

185. *The Papers of Henry Bouquet*, 2: 126, 142.

186. Ibid., 1: 366–368.

187. Barton, *Journal*, August 22, 1758.

188. "Military Letterbooks of Joseph Shippen, 1756–1758," Shippen Family Papers, Historical Society of Pennsylvania, Philadelphia, Pennsylvania.

189. *The Papers of Henry Bouquet*, 2: 217.

190. Ibid., 2: 356, 675.

191. Barton, *Journal*, August 13, 1758.

192. *The Papers of Henry Bouquet*, 2: 187, 221.

193. John Muller, *A Treatise Containing the Elementary Part of Fortification* (London: J. Nourse, 1746; reprint edition, Ottawa, Ontario, Canada: Museum Restoration Service, 1968), 217.

194. *The Papers of Henry Bouquet*, 2: 672.

195. Ibid., 2: 219.

196. Forbes Headquarters Papers, "Letter, Governor James Glen to Forbes, dated Raystown, July 22nd 1758."

197. The most descriptive source on Fort Bedford, which was not given this name until after the campaign had ended, is Stotz, *Outposts of the War for Empire*, 113–117.

198. Captain Joseph Shippen, "Military Letters of Captain Joseph Shippen on the Provincial Service, 1756–1758," *Pennsylvania Magazine of History and Biography* 36 (1912): 462.

199. *The Papers of Henry Bouquet*, 2: 659–660, 662, 664, 667, 672.

200. Ibid., 2: 106.

201. Forbes Headquarters Papers, "Letter from Forbes to Joshua Howell, dated Shippensburgh, 26th August 1758."

202. *The Papers of Henry Bouquet*, 2: 4–5, 18, 24.

203. Ibid., 2: 313.

204. Ibid., 2: 227–228.

205. Forbes Headquarters Papers, "Letter from St. Clair to Forbes, dated Winchester, May 21, 1758."

206. Forbes Headquarters Papers, "Letter, Forbes to St. Clair, dated Philadelphia, May 25, 1758."

207. *Pennsylvania Archives*, 3: 446–447.

208. *Writings of General John Forbes*, 146.

209. Ibid., 157–158. In 18th-century verbiage, to speak "roundly" meant that Forbes was speaking "plain, free, without delicacy or reserve, almost rough." E.L. McAdam Jr. and George Milne, eds., *Johnson's Dictionary: A Modern Selection* (New York: Pantheon Books, 1963), 351.

210. Becker, *North Carolina*, 221, 239.

211. *Writings of General John Forbes*, 103, 92.

212. Forbes Headquarters Papers, "Letter from Abraham Bosomworth to Forbes, Dated May 2, 1758 from Philadelphia."

213. Forbes Headquarters Papers, "Instructions, Forbes to Bosomworth, dated Philadelphia, May 12, 1758."

214. Forbes Headquarters Papers, "Proclamation at Virginia by Sir John St. Clair, dated Winchester, May 16, 1758."

215. *The Papers of Henry Bouquet*, 2: 36–38.

216. Forbes Headquarters Papers, "Letter, Forbes to St. Clair, dated Philadelphia, May 30, 1758."

217. Forbes Headquarters Papers, "Letter, Adam Hoops to Forbes, dated Lancaster, May 29th 1758."

218. *The Papers of Henry Bouquet*, 2: 136.

219. Ibid., 2: 209.

220. Ibid., 2: 74, 95, 97, 102.

221. Ibid., 2: 37, 49, 75, 144, 173.

222. Ibid., 2: 227.

223. Ibid., 2: 96, 181.

224. *Writings of General John Forbes*, 115.

225. Forbes Headquarters Papers, "Letter, Forbes to St. Clair, dated Philadelphia June 16th 1758."

226. The most comprehensive and meticulously researched analysis of these negotiations is Francis Jennings, *Empire of Fortune: Crown, Colonies & Tribes in the*

Seven Years' War in America (New York: W.W. Norton & Company, 1988), 374–384. Additional information is provided by Walter T. Champion Jr., "Christian Frederick Post and the Winning of the West," *Pennsylvania Magazine of History and Biography* 104 (1980): 315.

227. *Writings of General John Forbes*, 115.
228. *The Papers of Henry Bouquet*, 2: 209.

Chapter 5

1. This decision has been well analyzed by Anderson, "The General Chooses a Road," 109–138, 241–258, 383–401.
2. Hulbert, *The Old Glade Road*, 95.
3. *The Papers of Henry Bouquet*, 2: 112.
4. *Writings of General John Forbes*, 143.
5. *The Papers of Henry Bouquet*, 2: 123.
6. *Writings of General John Forbes*, 141.
7. *The Papers of Henry Bouquet*, 2: 180, 290–291.
8. Forbes Headquarters Papers, "Rohr Report on Road, July 31, 1758."
9. Forbes Headquarters Papers, "Instructions for Scouting Parties, July 7, 1758."
10. Forbes Headquarters Papers, "A Report of Captain Ward sent to Reconnoiter the Road to the Westward [undated]."
11. Hulbert, *The Old Glade Road*, 141.
12. *The Papers of Henry Bouquet*, 2: 328, 337.
13. Anderson, "The General Chooses a Road," 130–131.
14. Forbes Headquarters Papers, Sir John St. Clair Letterbook, "p. 155 [St. Clair to Colonel Napier, Fort Cumberland, August 15, 1755]."
15. James P. Myers, "General Forbes's Road to War," *Westmoreland History* 7, no. 2 (September 2002): 45.
16. *The Papers of Henry Bouquet*, 2: 328.
17. Ibid., 2: 349.
18. *Writings of General John Forbes*, 173.
19. Ibid., 203.
20. Captain Pierre Pouchot, *Memoirs on the Late War in North America Between France and England*, translated by Michael Cary, edited and annotated by Brian Leigh Dunnigan (1781; revised edition, Youngstown, New York: Old Fort Niagara Association, 1994), 424.
21. *The Papers of George Washington*, 5: 318, 320–322, 324–326, 353–361.
22. *The Papers of Henry Bouquet*, 2: 291.
23. *The Papers of George Washington*, 5: 360–361.
24. Ibid., 5: 370.
25. *Writings of General John Forbes*, 171, 199.
26. Hulbert, *The Old Glade Road*, 124–141.
27. *Writings of General John Forbes*, 171.
28. *The Papers of Henry Bouquet*, 2: 345.
29. *Writings of General John Forbes*, 173.
30. *Pennsylvania Archives*, 3: 552.
31. *The Papers of Henry Bouquet*, 2: 264–266. Throughout this study the author has used Forbes's own distances, rather than absolutely accurate modern geographical mileage, as Forbes was basing his decision upon the mileage as he understood it.
32. Ibid., 2: 277.
33. *Writings of General John Forbes*, 156–157. This paragraph was contained in a letter written by Byrd to Bouquet on July 9: "I have some reason to think the whole Party [of Indians at Fort Cumberland] may be kept to be of Service to the General on the Expedition, provided he goes by the old Road, otherwise I am afraid they will return; for they tell me they will not go by Ray's Town." *The Papers of Henry Bouquet*, 2: 173.

34. *Writings of General John Forbes*, 173.
35. Forbes Headquarters Papers, "Letter, James Glen to Forbes, dated Raystown, July 26, 1758."
36. *The Papers of Henry Bouquet*, 2; 294–295.

Chapter 6

1. For a contemporary opinion of how gravely ill Forbes was in early September, see letter from Captain James Young to Bouquet on September 10, 1758, in *The Papers of Henry Bouquet*, 2: 489.
2. *Writings of General John Forbes*, 154.
3. Ibid., 161. Presumably, the "physick" was some sort of laxative that, given the quality of medical care available at the time, probably did little to assist the general and may well have done much to harm him.
4. Ibid., 163.
5. William M. McBride, "'Normal' Medical Science and British Treatment of the Sea Scurvy, 1753–75," *Journal of the History of Medicine and Allied Sciences* 46, no. 2 (1991): 158–177.
6. Forbes papers, Dalhousie Muniments, Scottish Record Office, Edinburgh, File #77, "Directions for General Forbes" [not signed or dated].
7. *Writings of General John Forbes*, 166, 169.
8. Ibid., 170.
9. Ibid., 172.
10. Ibid., 177.
11. Ibid., 193.
12. Ibid., 197.
13. *The Papers of Henry Bouquet*, 2: 202.
14. Ibid., 2: 225.
15. Barton, *Journal*, September 15, 1758.
16. Williams, *Bouquet's March to the Ohio*, 85.
17. Ibid., 86.
18. Briggs, "Conquest of the Allegheny Mountains," 407.
19. *The Papers of Henry Bouquet*, 2: 341.
20. Stotz, *Outposts of the War of Empire*, 113.
21. Williams, *Bouquet's March to the Ohio*, 93.
22. Ibid.
23. *The Papers of Henry Bouquet*, 2: 283, 285.
24. Ibid., 2: 290–291.
25. Forbes Headquarters Papers, "Letter, Captain George Armstrong, Pennsylvania Provincials to Colonel Bouquet, Edmonds Swamp, 25th July 1758."
26. *The Papers of Henry Bouquet*, 2: 323.
27. Ibid., 2: 341.
28. Ibid., 2: 349.
29. Ibid., 2: 360. *Encyclopaedia Britannica*, 2: 293.
30. *The Papers of Henry Bouquet*, 2: 361.
31. Ibid., 2: 475.
32. Ibid., 2: 373.
33. Ibid., 2: 373.
34. Ibid., 2: 430–431.
35. Ibid., 2: 336.
36. Ibid., 2: 320.
37. Ibid., 2: 492.
38. Ibid., 2: 282.
39. *Writings of General John Forbes*, 168.
40. Ibid., 198.
41. *The Papers of Henry Bouquet*, 2: 433, 464.
42. Forbes Headquarters Papers, "Letter from Governor Glen to Forbes, Ray's Town, August 8, 1758."
43. Barton, *Journal*, September 4, 1758.
44. *The Papers of Henry Bouquet*, 2: 434.
45. Ibid., 2: 436.
46. The whole sordid affair is well documented ibid., 2: 430–436.

47. Ibid., 2: 496.
48. Thomas Simes, *The Military Guide for Young Officers, Containing a System for the Art of War, Parade, Camp, Field Duty, Manoeuvres, Standing and General Orders, Warrants, Regulations, Returns, Tables, Forms, Extracts from Military Acts, Battles, Sieges, Forts, Posts, Military Dictionary* (1776; reprint edition, Uckfield, East Sussex, United Kingdom: The Naval & Military Press in association with the Royal Armouries, 2006), 7–8.
49. *The Papers of Henry Bouquet*, 2: 418.
50. Ibid., 2: 582.
51. Letterbook of Colonel Burd, 9 September 1758.
52. *Writings of General John Forbes*, 206–207.
53. *Colonial Records of Pennsylvania*, 8: 167–169
54. Barton, *Journal*, September 5, 1758.
55. *The Correspondence of Governor Sharpe*, 271–275.
56. Barton, *Journal*, September 22, 1758.
57. *The Papers of Henry Bouquet*, 2: 677–678.
58. Barton, *Journal*, September 24–26, 1758.
59. Ibid., September 25, 1758.
60. Ibid., August 24, 1758.
61. *The Papers of Henry Bouquet*, 2: 397.
62. Ibid., 2: 678–679.
63. Ibid., 2: 674.
64. Ibid., 2: 673.
65. Ibid., 2: 336.
66. Ibid., 2: 397.
67. Ibid., 2: 406–408. Burd certainly complied with Bouquet's instructions to maintain a journal, and a fragment of this document survives in the Shippen Family Papers, Historical Society of Pennsylvania, Philadelphia, Pennsylvania.
68. Burd, "Letterbook of Colonel James Burd."
69. Ibid.
70. Stotz, *Outposts of the War for Empire*, 148.
71. *The Papers of Henry Bouquet*, 2: 396.
72. The two principal sources on the design and construction of Fort Ligonier are Stotz, *Outposts of the War of Empire*, 118–120, 146–189; and Grimm, *Archaeological Investigation of Fort Ligonier*, 7–46.
73. *The Papers of Henry Bouquet*, 2: 492.
74. *Writings of General John Forbes*, 228.
75. Stotz, *Outposts of the War of Empire*, 176.
76. *The Papers of Henry Bouquet*, 2: 551.
77. Ibid., 2: 543–544.
78. Ibid., 2: 408–409.
79. Ibid., 2: 418–419.
80. Forbes Headquarters Papers, "Letter from Draper Wood to Forbes, Dated Philadelphia May 6th, 1758."
81. Ibid., "Letter, Forbes to St. Clair, dated Philadelphia 23 May 1758."
82. Ibid., "Letter, Forbes to St. Clair, dated Philadelphia June 16th 1758."
83. *The Papers of Henry Bouquet*, 2: 313.
84. Ibid., 2: 315.
85. Forbes Headquarters Papers, "Letter from Governor Glen to Forbes, Ray's Town, August 8, 1758."
86. Forbes, Dalhousie Muniments, File #60, "Two reports of Scouts to Fort Duquesne." A similar, but not identical, transcription of Allen's scout is located in *Papers of Henry Bouquet*, 2: 324–326, and Chew's scout is located ibid., 400–404. A copy of map of Fort Duquesne, most likely that prepared by Chew, is located with the Forbes Papers, Dalhousie Muniments and is provided at the rear of this chapter.
87. Forbes Papers, Dalhousie Muniments, File #62, "Letter of Colonel Wm Byrd of Virginia, August 24, 1758."
88. *The Papers of Henry Bouquet*, 2: 329.
89. Ibid., 2: 337.
90. Ibid., 2: 374–375.
91. Ibid., 2: 450–451.
92. Ibid., 2: 459–460.
93. Ibid., 2: 546.
94. "Letterbook of Colonel James Burd, 1756–1758," Shippen Family Papers, Historical Society of Pennsylvania, Philadelphia, Pennsylvania.
95. *Writings of General John Forbes*, 198.
96. Anderson devotes an entire chapter to Bradstreet's raid upon Fort Frontenac. Fred Anderson, *Crucible of War: The Seven Years' War and the Fate of Empire in British North America, 1754–1766* (New York: Alfred A. Knopf, 2000), 259–266. For additional information, refer to Pouchot, *Memoirs on the Late War in North America*, 153–154,161–162.
97. Pouchot, *Memoirs on the Late War in North America Between France and England*, 161–162.

Chapter 7

1. *The Papers of Henry Bouquet*, 2: 222.
2. *Writings of General John Forbes*, 220.
3. Forbes Dalhousie Muniments, File #78 — Letters of Colonel John Armstrong, Pennsylvania Provincials.
4. *The Papers of Henry Bouquet*, 2: 518; and *The Partisan or, The Art of Making War in Detachment with Plans proper to facilitate the understanding of the several Dispositions and Movements necessary to Light Troops, in order to accomplish their Marches, Ambuscades, Attacks and Retreats with Success. Translated from the French of Mr. de Jeney By an Officer in the Army* (London, 1760). Jeney was first published in French in 1749.
5. *Writings of General John Forbes*, 177–178.
6. Ibid., 164.
7. *The Papers of Henry Bouquet*, 2: 493, 517.
8. *The Journal of Johann Michael Lindenmuth*, 31–33.
9. The *Papers of Henry Bouquet*, 2: 479, 482, 493, 517.
10. Ibid., 2: 493, 517.
11. Ibid., 2: 493, 518.
12. Forbes Headquarters Papers, "Indian Intelligence Camp at Ray's Town 20th July 1758." 13. *The Papers of Henry Bouquet*, 2: 518.
14. Colonel James Burd, "Letterbook of Colonel James Burd, 1756–1758," Shippen Family Papers, Historical Society of Pennsylvania, Philadelphia, Pennsylvania.
15. *The Papers of Henry Bouquet*, 2: 493.
16. La Cointe, *The Science of Military Posts*, 219–221.
17. Ibid., 154–158.
18. *The Papers of Henry Bouquet*, 2: 508–509.
19. La Cointe, *The Science of Military Posts*, 158.
20. "Barton, Journal," September 11, 1758.
21. *The Papers of Henry Bouquet*, 2: 493.
22. Howard H. Peckham, ed., "Thomas Gist's Indian Captivity, 1758–1759," *The Pennsylvania Magazine of History and Biography* (July 1956): 290.
23. *The Papers of Henry Bouquet*, 2: 519.
24. Reel 30, James Grant of Ballidalloch Papers, Library of Congress, Washington, D.C.
25. Peckham, ed., "Thomas Gist's Indian Captivity," 290.
26. Ibid.
27. *The Papers of Henry Bouquet*, 2: 499–500.
28. Peckham, Editor, "Thomas Gist's Indian Captivity," 290.
29. The three primary sources for Grant's defeat are the account of Ensign Gist, Peckham, ed., "Thomas

Gist's Indian Captivity," 291–294; a letter from Grant to Forbes; and Bouquet's report to Forbes. The last two in *The Papers of Henry Bouquet*, 2: 500–504, and 517–520.

30. McCulloch, *Sons of the Mountains*, 1: 123.

31. *The Papers of Henry Bouquet*, 2: 328.

32. Ibid., 2: 328.

33. Neville B. Craig, *The History of Pittsburgh* (Pittsburgh: J.R. Weldin Company, 1917), 61.

34. Stotz, *Outposts of the War of Empire*, 83, 85, 87.

35. Captain Alexander McDonald, 77th Foot, "Letterbook of Captain Alexander McDonald, of the Royal Highland Emigrants, 1775–1779," in *Collections of the New York Historical Society for the Year 1882* (New York: New York Historical Society, 1883), 442.

36. *The Papers of George Washington*, 6: 38, 44.

37. Craig, *History of Pittsburgh*, 60.

38. *The Papers of George Washington*, 6: 38–39, 44.

39. McCulloch, *Sons of the Mountains*, 1: 125.

40. Ian McCulloch and Timothy Todish, eds., *Through So Many Dangers: The Memoirs and Adventures of Robert Kirk[wood], Late of the Royal Highland Regiment* (Fleischmanns, New York: Purple Mountain Press, 2004), 40–41. Kirkwood claimed that the Indians used canoes to outflank the Highlanders, based upon seeing Indians emerge from the banks of the Monongahela River. This is somewhat fanciful, as the Indians were more than adept at flanking maneuvers, and Captive Smith's account clarifies that the Indians used the steep banks of the rivers for both cover and concealment.

41. Houlding, *Fit for Service*, 318–321.

42. Craig, *History of Pittsburgh*, 61.

43. John J. Barsotti, ed., *Scoouwa: James Smith's Indian Captivity Narrative* (1780; reprint edition, Ohio Historical Society, 1996), 117.

44. *Scoouwa: James Smith's Indian Captivity Narrative*, 161. Note that this account of Smith's explains Kirkwood's belief, as also told to Sergeant Lindenmuth by the Pennsylvania survivors, that the Indians had used canoes to outflank the Highlanders, as Kirkwood apparently saw the Indians emerging from the banks of the Monongahela River to engage McKenzie's company.

45. Colonel James Burd Papers, "Letter of Captain Daniel Clark, Ray's Town, September 21, 1758."

46. *The Papers of George Washington*, 6: 39.

47. Alastair Macpherson Grant, *General James Grant of Ballindalloch, 1720–1806* (London: A.M. Grant, 1930), 57.

48. These tactics are well documented in Leroy V. Eid, "'A Kind of Running Fight:' Indian Battlefield Tactics in the Late Eighteenth Century," *The Western Pennsylvania Historical Magazine* 71, no. 2 (April 1988): 147–171.

49. McCulloch and Todish, *Through So Many Dangers*, 40–41.

50. Captain Alexander McDonald, 77th Foot, "Letterbook of Captain Alexander McDonald, of the Royal Highland Emigrants, 1775–1779," in *Collections of the New York Historical Society for the Year 1882* (New York: New York Historical Society, 1883), 442.

51. Craig, *History of Pittsburgh*, 61.

52. *The Papers of George Washington*, 6: 39, 44.

53. McCulloch, *Sons of the Mountains*, 2: 70.

54. *The Papers of Henry Bouquet*, 2: 499.

55. *The Journal of Johann Michael Lindenmuth*, 33–35.

56. Pouchot, *Memoirs on the Late War in North America Between France and England*, 157–158.

57. *The Journal of Johann Michael Lindenmuth*, 33.

58. *The Papers of Henry Bouquet*, 2: 511–512.

59. The five unwounded officers who were prisoners of the French were exchanged in 1759. Pouchot, *Memoirs on the Late War in North America Between France and England*, 158.

60. *The Papers of Henry Bouquet*, 2: 508–509; *The Papers of George Washington*, 6: 39; and McCulloch, *Sons of the Mountains*, 2: 51–80.

61. *The Papers of Henry Bouquet*, 2: 521.

62. "Military Letterbooks of Joseph Shippen, 1756–1758."

63. *Writings of General John Forbes*, 220. "Tra Mon tane" can be translated as "Over the Mountains" or "Beyond the Mountains." Although his meaning cannot positively be determined, Forbes is apparently telling Bouquet that Grant must have gone "out of his head" or "over the mountains." In other words, Forbes believed that Grant must have lost his senses on the battlefield.

64. *Pennsylvania Archives*, 3: 551.

65. *The Papers of Henry Bouquet*, 2: 520.

66. McCulloch and Todish, *Through So Many Dangers*, 41–44.

Chapter 8

1. *The Papers of Henry Bouquet*, 2: 555–556.

2. James, *Decision at the Forks*, 51.

3. Journal of Joseph Shippen, 1758, Shippen Family Papers, Historical Society of Pennsylvania, Philadelphia, Pennsylvania.

4. *The Papers of Henry Bouquet*, 2: 552.

5. Ibid., 2: 567.

6. Colonel James Burd, "Fragments of Journal Kept at Loyal Hannon," Shippen Family Papers, Historical Society of Pennsylvania, Philadelphia, Pennsylvania.

7. *The Correspondence of Governor Sharpe*, 305.

8. Burd, "Fragments of Journal Kept at Loyal Hannon."

9. McCulloch, *Sons of the Mountains*, 1: 131.

10. *The Papers of Henry Bouquet*, 2: 558.

11. Ibid., 2: 556.

12. Pouchot, *Memoirs on the Late War in North America Between France and England*, 158–160.

13. *The Papers of Henry Bouquet*, 2: 555.

14. *Writings of General John Forbes*, 232, 236.

15. Pouchot, *Memoirs on the Late War in North America Between France and England*, 159–160. The English reported 36 of their men killed or missing (and presumed dead). This suggests that the crafty Native American warriors were able to separate each scalp into three scalps, for morale and reward purposes.

16. Thomas Balch, *Letters and Papers Relating Chiefly to the Provincial History of Pennsylvania* (Philadelphia: Crissy & Markley, 1855), 142. A similar list is provided *The Papers of Henry Bouquet*, 2: 567.

17. *The Papers of Henry Bouquet*, 2: 560.

18. Sylvanus Urban, ed., *The Gentleman's Magazine* 28 (December 1758): 611.

19. *The Papers of Henry Bouquet*, 2: 592.

Chapter 9

1. "Military Letterbooks of Joseph Shippen, 1756–1758."

2. *Writings of General John Forbes*, 174–175.

3. Forbes Headquarters Papers, "Letter from Major James Grant to Forbes, Fort Loudon August 16th 1758."

4. Cadwallader Colden, *Letters and Papers of Cadwallader Colden in Collections of the New York Historical*

Society for the Year 1922 (New York: New York Historical Society, 1923, 5: 257–258.

  5. *Writings of General John Forbes*, 176.
  6. *The Papers of Henry Bouquet*, 2: 356.
  7. These negotiations are exhaustively covered in
Anderson, *Crucible of War*, 267–285; Jennings, *Empire
of Fortune*, 374–407; Michael McConnell, *A Country
Between: The Upper Ohio Valley and Its Peoples, 1724–
1774* (Lincoln: University of Nebraska Press, 1992),
128–141; and Champion, "Post and the Winning of the
West." The narrative in this volume is intended only to
be an overview of these treaty negotiations, and the cited
sources should be perused for more comprehensive information.
  8. *Writings of General John Forbes*, 180–181.
  9. Ibid., 233.
  10. Burd, "Letterbook of Colonel James Burd."
  11. *The Papers of Henry Bouquet*, 2: 573.
  12. Forbes, Dalhousie Muniments, "File #69 — Miscellaneous Financial Records."
  13. *The Papers of Henry Bouquet*, 2: 557.
  14. Ibid., 2: 568.
  15. *Pennsylvania Archives*, 3: 552.
  16. *Writings of General John Forbes*, 233, 244, 249,
250.
  17. *Pennsylvania Archives*, 3: 552.
  18. *Writings of General John Forbes*, 175.
  19. *The Papers of George Washington*, 6: 27–30.
  20. *Writings of General John Forbes*, 235.
  21. Ibid., 242.
  22. Ibid., 246–247.
  23. Balch, *Pennsylvania Letters*, 147.
  24. Simes, *The Military Guide for Young Officers*, Military Dictionary.
  25. *The Papers of Henry Bouquet*, 2: 600–601.
  26. *Writings of General John Forbes*, 255–256.
  27. *George Washington Remembers*, 23. Washington
allegedly provided a nearly identical version of the tale
to a resident of Ligonier, Pennsylvania. *The Papers of
George Washington*, 6: 120–121.
  28. Thomas W. Bullitt, *My Life at Oxmoor: Life on a
Farm in Kentucky Before the War* (1911; reprint edition:
privately printed 1995), 120.
  29. *The Journal of Johann Michael Lindenmuth*, 35.
  30. Pouchot, *Memoirs on the Late War in North America Between France and England*, 160.
  31. Shelby Family Papers.
  32. In other words, when the French were outfitting
the raiding party, they opened up the powder casks to
the Indians, and let them take as much gunpowder as
they desired.
  33. Note that a 6-pounder cannon is not a standard
French artillery size, but it is a standard English cannon
size. The statement "it was large enough for the English"
could have been bluster on the part of the French soldiers, or it could have meant literally that this size of gun
was large enough for the English to carry to Fort
Duquesne. Thus, this might well have been one of the
6-pounders captured at Braddock's defeat.
  34. Forbes Papers, Dalhousie Muniments, Folder #63.
  35. *The Papers of George Washington*, 6: 123–126.

Chapter 10

  1. *The Papers of George Washington*, 6: 149–150.
  2. Ibid., 6: 126.
  3. Forbes, Dalhousie Muniments, File #37 — Miscellaneous Returns of Stores, Ordnance, and Barracks
Room Furniture, 1757–1759; and Forbes Headquarters
Papers, "Order of March, [Tactical Instructions in
Forbes Own Hand, Not Dated]."
  4. *The Papers of George Washington*, 6: 126.
  5. Ibid., 6: 127–128.
  6. Briggs, "Engineering Geology of Forbes Road,"
409–412; Williams, *Bouquet's March to the Ohio*, 95–
100, 140–147; and George B. Ravis, "Youngstown [Penn-
sylvania] and the Forbes Road," *Westmoreland History* 2,
no. 1 (Spring 1996): 15–22.
  7. Forbes Papers, Dalhousie Muniments, File #72 —
1758 — Notes of Stages and Distances on the road from
Pittsburgh to New York.
  8. Forbes Headquarters Papers, "Explanation to the
Plan of the Line of Battle [undated]."
  9. Forbes Headquarters Papers, "Explanation of an
Order of March for Four Thousand Infantry, one hundred & thirty Light Men and Guides [undated]."
  10. Pouchot, *Memoirs on the Late War in North America Between France and England*, 160.
  11. *The Papers of George Washington*, 6: 126–127, 129.
  12. Ibid., 6: 151; Shippen Orderly Book, November 21,
1758.
  13. Pleydell, *An Essay on Field Fortifications*, 7–9.
  14. Harold A. Thomas, "Site of Forbes's Last Three
Breastworks," *Western Pennsylvania Historical Magazine*
47 (1964): 60.
  15. *Writings of General John Forbes*, 258.
  16. *The Papers of George Washington*, 6: 131.
  17. *Writings of General John Forbes*, 254.
  18. *The Papers of George Washington*, 6: 132–133, 136–
138.
  19. Ibid., 6: 139.
  20. *The Papers of Henry Bouquet*, 2: 604.
  21. *Writings of General John Forbes*, 254.
  22. *The Papers of George Washington*, 6: 142.
  23. Ibid., 6: 144.
  24. Thomas, "The Sites of Forbes's Last Three Breastworks," 62–64.
  25. Burd, "Letterbook of Colonel James Burd."
  26. *The Papers of George Washington*, 6: 135–136.
  27. Anderson, "New Light on the 1758 Campaign,"
96.
  28. *Writings of General John Forbes*, 259–260.
  29. Forbes Papers Dalhousie Muniments, File #35.
  30. *Writings of General John Forbes*, 256–257.
  31. Ibid., 259; and *The Papers of George Washington*,
6: 145–146.
  32. *The Papers of George Washington*, 6: 148; and
Shippen Orderly Book, November 20, 1758. One word
is different in the two Orderly Books, as noted, although
the meaning of the Indians' markings is not altered.
  33. *Writings of General John Forbes*, 261.
  34. Ibid., 258.
  35. *The Papers of George Washington*, 6: 151; and Shippen Orderly Book, November 21, 1758.
  36. *The Papers of George Washington*, 6: 155–156; and
Shippen Orderly Book, November 23, 1758.
  37. *Writings of General John Forbes*, 259, 261–262.
  38. *The Papers of George Washington*, 6: 156–157; and
Shippen Orderly Book, November 24, 1758.
  39. *The Papers of George Washington*, 6: 126; and *The
Papers of Henry Bouquet*, 2: 609.
  40. Forbes Headquarters Papers, "Order of March
[Tactical Instructions in Forbes Own Hand, Not Dated]."
  41. Pouchot, *Memoirs on the Late War in North America Between France and England*, 107, 160–161.
  42. As quoted in Stotz, *Outposts of the War of Empire*,
45.
  43. *The Papers of Henry Bouquet*, 2: 610.

44. Samuel Hazard, ed., *The Register of Pennsylvania* (Philadelphia: William F. Geddes, 1830), 6: 226–227.

45. As related in Hulbert, *The Old Glade Road*, 158.

46. *The Papers of George Washington*, 6: 157; and Shippen Orderly Book, November 24, 1758.

47. *The Journal of Johann Michael Lindenmuth*, 35–39.

48. Rial, "The Old Forbes Road," 61, 63; and Thomas, "The Last Two Campsites of Forbes's Army," 46–47. Forbes's route essentially followed the modern Penn Avenue in Pittsburgh.

49. Craig, *The History of Pittsburgh*, 64.

50. Shippen Orderly Book, November 25, 1758.

51. *Writings of General John Forbes*, 262–269.

52. Stotz, *Outposts of the War of Empire*, 91.

53. Shippen Orderly Book, November 25, 1758.

54. Shippen Orderly Book, November 26, 1758.

55. Ibid. This party was originally to parade on November 27th, but was delayed a day, apparently to permit the soldiers to participate in the celebratory fire.

56. Shippen Orderly Book, November 28, 1758.

57. Hazard, *The Register of Pennsylvania*, 227.

58. Kenneth A. White, "The Phantom Atrocity." *Western Pennsylvania Historical Magazine* 66 (1983): 382–388; and McCulloch, *Sons of the Mountains*, 1: 137.

59. Shippen Orderly Book, November 27, 1758.

60. Shippen Orderly Book, November 29, 1758.

61. *Writings of General John Forbes*, 299.

62. Stotz, *Outposts of the War for Empire*, 121.

63. This fort is well characterized by Stotz, *Outposts of the War for Empire*, 121–125.

64. *The Papers of Henry Bouquet*, 3: 19, 78.

65. Ibid., 3: 11.

66. Ibid., 3: 59.

67. Forbes, Dalhousie Muniments, "File #37 — Miscellaneous Returns of Stores, Ordnance, and Barracks Room Furniture, 1757–1759"; and *The Papers of Henry Bouquet*, 3: 9, 11.

68. *The Papers of Henry Bouquet*, 2: 635.

69. Ibid., 2: 640.

70. Ibid., 2: 643.

71. Ibid., 3: 10.

72. Ibid., 3: 39.

73. Ibid., 3: 44.

74. Ibid., 2: 55–56.

75. Stotz, *Outposts of the War for Empire*, 121.

76. *The Papers of Henry Bouquet*, 2: 621–626.

77. General Carl Von Clausewitz, *On War*, Michael Howard and Peter Paret, ed. and trans. (New York: Alfred P. Knopf, Everyman's Library Edition, 1973), 87.

78. The author feels obliged to insert an editorial comment that current affairs in another distant land, conquered by a "single short blow" and inhabited by large numbers of recently hostile citizens, suggest that modern military and political commanders at the highest echelons could learn much from this sick and emaciated but still brilliant man who lived 250 years ago, and possessed considerable wisdom in the strategies of both warfare and peace. Similar wisdom sadly appears to be lacking in many of today's military and political leaders.

79. *The Papers of Henry Bouquet*, 3: 26–32.

80. Shippen Orderly Book, December 1, 1758.

81. Shippen Orderly Book, November 29, 1758.

82. *The Papers of George Washington*, 6: 160–161.

83. *The Papers of Henry Bouquet*, 2: 620; and Shippen Orderly Book, December 2 and 3, 1758.

84. *The Journal of Johann Michael Lindenmuth*, 39.

85. *Writings of General John Forbes*, 269–270.

Chapter 11

1. As quoted in James P. Myers Jr., "Notes and Documents, The New Way to the Forks of the Ohio: Reflections on John Pott's Map of 1758," *Pennsylvania Magazine of History and Biography* 122, no. 4 (October 1998): 409.

2. *Writings of General John Forbes*, 287–288.

3. *The Papers of Henry Bouquet*, 3: 122–124.

4. Hildeburn, "Sir John St. Clair."

5. For the further adventures of James Grant, the author recommends the fine biography by Nelson, *General James Grant: Scottish Soldier and Royal Governor of East Florida.*

6. Refer to sketch of Montgomery in McCulloch, *Sons of the Mountains*, 2: 51–52.

7. Thomas Carter, *Historical Record of the Forty-Fourth: Or the East Essex Regiment* (Chatham, England: Gale & Polden, Brompton Works, 1887), 12; and Charles H. Maclean and George Robinson, *Cases Decided by the House of Lords on Appeals and Writs of Error* (London: Saunders and Benning, Law Booksellers, 1840), 58–59.

8. *Writings of General John Forbes*, 199.

9. Colonel Armstrong's business papers are located at the Archives and Special Collections, Dickinson Library, Carlisle; and his surveying papers are located at the Cumberland County Historical Society, Carlisle. Unfortunately, Armstrong's papers were destroyed in a 1768 fire, and none of his known papers address the Forbes campaign timeframe. No book-length biography has been prepared for Armstrong. The only scholarly study is Crist, *John Armstrong: Proprietors Man*, which unfortunately only addressed Armstrong's life to 1774.

10. For more information on Adam Stephen, refer to the excellent biography by Harry M. Ward, *Major General Adam Stephen and the Cause of American Liberty* (Charlottesville: University Press of Virginia, 1989).

11. For a complete narrative of Burd's life, see Lily Lee Nixon, *James Burd: Frontier Defender, 1726–1793* (Philadelphia: University of Pennsylvania Press, 1941).

12. Stanhope B. Jones, *The Evolution of Preventive Medicine in the United States Army, 1607–1939* (Washington, D.C.: Office of the Surgeon General of the Department of the Army, 1968), 23–25.

13. *The Journal of John Michael Lindenmuth*, 6–8; and Bullitt, *My Life at Oxmoor*, 121.

14. Anna M. Quattrocchi, "Thomas Hutchins in Western Pennsylvania," *Pennsylvania History* 16 (January 1949): 31–38.

15. The best biography of George Mercer is Alfred P. James, "George Mercer of the Ohio Company, a Study in Frustration," *The Western Pennsylvania Historical Magazine* 46, no. 1 (January 1963): 1–43; and 46, no. 2 (April 1963): 141–183.

16. Hildeburn, "Sir John St. Clair, Baronet."

17. A fine sketch of Byrd is provided by Tinling, *The Correspondence of The Three William Byrds*, 2: 603–614.

18. Rogers, "Impressment in Western Pennsylvania;" and Brodine, "Civil-Military Relations in Pennsylvania," 213–233.

19. *Writings of General John Forbes*, 213.

20. Ibid., 213.

21. Pouchot, *Memoirs on the Late War in North America*, 161–162.

22. The linchpin was used to secure the wheel of the carriage onto the axle.

23. *Writings of General John Forbes*, 194, 237–238.

24. Paul E. Kopperman, *Braddock at the Monongahela* (University of Pittsburgh Press, 1977), 31.

25. *Scoouwa: James Smith's Indian Captivity Narrative*, 61–65.

26. Ibid., 94–97.

27. Ibid., 117–118.

28. Anderson, *Crucible of War*, 282–283.

29. Ibid., 267.

30. Ibid., 282–283.

31. Jennings, *Empire of Fortune*, 409.

32. Clausewitz, *On War*, 182.

33. *The Papers of Henry Bouquet*, 2: 608, 611.

34. Ibid., 3: 186, 196.

35. Balch, *Pennsylvania Letters*, 152.

36. *Writings of General John Forbes*, 301–302.

Appendix A

1. Tinling, ed., *Correspondence of Three William Byrds*, 2: 647.

2. *The Papers of Henry Bouquet*, 1: 341–342.

3. Forbes Headquarters Papers, "Letter, Forbes to St. Clair, dated Philadelphia 23 May 1758."

4. *The Papers of George Washington*, 5: 168–169.

5. Forbes Headquarters Papers, "A List of Goods Bought by Capt Bosomworth and William West for the Cherokee Indians by Order of General Forbes [not dated, early May 1758]."

6. Forbes Headquarters Papers, "Numerous Invoices, May 1758."

7. Forbes Headquarters Papers, "Account, Captain Bosomworth, Bought of William West, Philadelphia, May 18th 1758."

8. Forbes Headquarters Papers, "St. Clair Accounts with Joseph Simons, May 10–30, 1758."

9. *The Papers of Henry Bouquet*, 2: 21.

10. Forbes Headquarters Papers, "Letter, James Glen to Forbes, dated Raystown, July 26, 1758."

11. Forbes Headquarters Papers, "Letter from Governor William Denny of Pennsylvania to Forbes, dated Philadelphia 28 July 1758."

12. *The Papers of Henry Bouquet*, 2: 286.

13. Ibid., 2: 356.

14. Colden, *Letters and Papers of Cadwallader Colden*, 5: 249.

15. *Letters and Papers of Cadwallader Colden*, 5: 248.

16. Forbes Headquarters Papers, "A Return of the Indian Stores at the Camp at Ray's Town July the 12th 1758."

17. *Writings of General John Forbes*, 193.

18. *The Papers of Henry Bouquet*, 3: 4–5.

19. Ibid., 3: 9–10.

Appendix B

1. Forbes Headquarters Papers, "A Proportion of Ordnance and Stores for Pensilvania."

2. Samuel Eliot Morison, *The Ropemakers of Plymouth: A History of the Plymouth Cordage Company, 1824–1949* (Boston: Houghton Mifflin Company, 1950), 12.

Bibliography

Primary Sources

Abbott, W.W., ed. *The Papers of George Washington, Colonial Series.* 5 (October 1757–September 1758) and 6 (October 1758–December 1758). Charlottesville: University Press of Virginia, 1988.

Armstrong, Colonel John. Business Papers. Archives and Special Collections, Dickinson College, Carlisle, Pennsylvania.

_____. Surveying Papers. Cumberland County Historical Society, Carlisle, Pennsylvania.

Balch, Thomas. *Letters and Papers Relating Chiefly to the Provincial History of Pennsylvania.* Philadelphia: Crissy & Markley, 1855. (Primarily extracts from Shippen Papers in Pennsylvania Archives.)

Barsotti, John J., ed. *Scoouwa: James Smith's Indian Captivity Narrative.* 1780. Reprint, Ohio Historical Society, 1996.

Barton, Reverend Thomas. *Journal of an Expedition to the Ohio, Commanded by His Excellency Brigadier General Forbes, in the Year of our Lord 1758.* Philadelphia: Historical Society of Pennsylvania.

Bouquet, Henry. Henry Bouquet Papers, Letter dated April 29, 1765. U.S. Army Military History Institute, Carlisle Barracks, Pennsylvania.

_____. *The Papers of Colonel Henry Bouquet.* Edited by Sylvester E. Stevens, *et al.* 19 vols. Harrisburg: Pennsylvania Historical Commission and Works Progress Administration, 1940–1944.

_____. *The Papers of Henry Bouquet.* Vol. 1. Edited by Sylvester E. Stevens, *et al.* Harrisburg: Pennsylvania Historical and Museum Commission, 1972.

_____. *The Papers of Henry Bouquet.* Vol. 2, *The Forbes Expedition.* Edited by Sylvester E. Stevens, *et al.* Harrisburg: Pennsylvania Historical and Museum Commission, 1951.

_____. *The Papers of Henry Bouquet.* Vol. 3. Edited by Sylvester E. Stevens, *et al.* Harrisburg: Pennsylvania Historical and Museum Commission, 1976.

Browne, William H., ed. *Archives of Maryland, Correspondence of Governor Horatio Sharpe.* Vol. 2, 1757–1761. Baltimore: Maryland Historical Society, 1890.

Bullitt, Thomas W. *My Life at Oxmoor: Life on a Farm in Kentucky Before the War.* 1911. Reprint edition: privately printed, 1995.

Burd, Colonel James. Colonel James Burd Papers. Western Pennsylvania Historical Society, Pittsburgh, Pennsylvania.

_____. "Fragment of Journal Kept at Loyal Hannon." Shippen Family Papers, Historical Society of Pennsylvania, Philadelphia, Pennsylvania.

_____. "Journal of Colonel James Burd, February 16–March 10, 1758." Colonel James Burd Papers, Western Pennsylvania Historical Society, Pittsburgh, Pennsylvania.

_____. "Letterbook of Colonel James Burd, 1756–1758." Shippen Family Papers, Historical Society of Pennsylvania, Philadelphia, Pennsylvania.

Burkett, Brigitte, trans. *The Journal of Johann Michael Lindenmuth, 1737–1812.* Rockport, ME: Picton Press, 2000.

Colden, Cadwallader. *Letters and Papers of Cadwallader Colden in Collections of the New York Historical Society for the Year 1922.* New York: New York Historical Society, 1923.

Colonial Records of Pennsylvania. Vol. 8. Philadelphia: J. Severn, 1852.

Doeser, Linda. *The Life and Works of Gainsborough.* New York: Shooting Star Press, 1995.

Forbes, Brigadier General John. Forbes Headquarters Papers, University of Virginia Library, Charlottesville, Virginia. Microfilm Copy at David Library of the American Revolution, Washington Crossing, Pennsylvania.

_____. Forbes Papers. Dalhousie Muniments, Scottish Record Office, Edinburgh. Microfilm Copy at David Library of the American Revolution, Washington Crossing, Pennsylvania.

_____. Letters. Papers of Lord Charles Hay. National Library of Scotland, Edinburgh, Scotland.

_____. *Letters of General John Forbes Relating to the Expedition Against Fort Duquesne in 1758.* Edited by Irene Stewart. Pittsburgh: Colonial Dames of America, 1927.

_____. *Writings of General John Forbes Relating to His Service in North America.* Edited by Alfred Proctor James. Menasha, WI: The Collegiate Press, 1938.

Grimm, Jacob L. *Archaeological Investigation of Fort Ligonier, 1960–1965.* Pittsburgh, PA: Annals of Carnegie Museum, 1970.

Haslet, Captain John. "Letter from Fort DuQuesne,

November 26, 1758." In Samuel Hazard, ed., *The Register of Pennsylvania.* Vol. 6. Philadelphia: William F. Geddes, 1830.

Hazard, Samuel, ed. *Pennsylvania Archives.* 1st Series, Vol. 3. Philadelphia: Joseph Severns, 1853.

_____. *The Register of Pennsylvania.* Philadelphia: William F. Geddes, 1830.

Hunter, William A., ed. "Thomas Barton and the Forbes Expedition." *The Pennsylvania Magazine of History and Biography* 95 (1971): 431–483.

Jordan, John W., ed. "James Kenny's Journal to the Westward, 1758–1759." *Pennsylvania Magazine of History and Biography* 37 (1913): 395–449.

La Cointe, Jean Louis. *The Science of Military Posts; For the Use of Regimental Officers, Who Frequently Command Detached Parties, in Which Is Shown the Manner of Attacking and Defending Posts, with Cuts, Explaining the Construction of Field-Forts and Intrenchments.* London: Printed for T. Payne, at the Mews Gate, 1761. Reprint edition: East Sussex, England: Naval & Military Press, 2006.

LeBlond, Guillaume. *The Elements of Fortification, Translated from the French.* Philadelphia: Printed for the War Office by C.P. Wayne, 1801.

Linde, Janet, and William H. Runge, eds. *A Calendar of the Headquarters Papers of Brigadier-General John Forbes Relating to the Expedition Against Fort Duquesne in 1758, in the Tracy W. McGregor Library, The Keepsake of an Exhibition 6 November–15 January.* Charlottesville: Department of Special Collections, University of Virginia Library, 1988.

Lochee, Lewis. *Elements of Field Fortification.* London: T. Cadell and T. Egerton, 1783.

McAdam, E.L., Jr., and George Milne, eds. *Johnson's Dictionary: A Modern Selection.* New York: Pantheon Books, 1963.

McCulloch, Ian, and Timothy Todish, eds. *Through So Many Dangers: The Memoirs and Adventures of Robert Kirk, Late of the Royal Highland Regiment.* Fleischmanns, NY: Purple Mountain Press, 2004.

McDonald, Captain Alexander, 77th Foot. "Letterbook of Captain Alexander McDonald, of the Royal Highland Emigrants, 1775–1779." In *Collections of the New York Historical Society for the Year 1882.* New York: New York Historical Society, 1883.

Muller, John. *The Attac and Defence of Fortified Places.* 1757. Reprint, Arlington, VA: The Invisible College Press, 2004.

_____. *A Treatise Containing the Elementary Part of Fortification.* London: J. Nourse, 1746. Reprint edition, Ottawa, Ontario, Canada: Museum Restoration Service, 1968.

_____. *A Treatise of Artillery, 1780.* 1757. 1780 edition reprinted by Alexandria Bay, New York, and Bloomfield, Ontario, Canada: Museum Restoration Service, 1977.

Myers, James P., Jr. "Notes and Documents, The New Way to the Forks of the Ohio: Reflections on John Pott's Map of 1758." *Pennsylvania Magazine of History and Biography* 122, no. 4 (October 1998): 385–410.

Otway, Captain Joseph. *An Essay on the Art of War, Translated from the French of Count Turpin, in Two Volumes.* London: A. Hamilton for W. Johnston, 1761.

The Partisan: or, The Art of Making War in Detachment with Plans Proper to Facilitate the Understanding of the Several Dispositions and Movements Necessary to Light Troops, in Order to Accomplish Their Marches, Ambuscades, Attacks and Retreats with Success. Translated from the French of Mr. de Jeney by an Officer in the Army. London, 1760.

Peckham, Howard H., ed. "Thomas Gist's Indian Captivity, 1758–1759." *The Pennsylvania Magazine of History and Biography* (July 1956): 285–311.

Pleydell, Lieutenant J.C. *An Essay on Field Fortification: Intended Principally for the Use of Officers of Infantry, Showing How to Trace Out on the Ground and Construct in the Easiest Manner, All Sorts of Redoubts and Other Field Works, Translated from the Original Manuscript of an Officer of Experience in the Prussian Service.* London: Printed for J. Nourse, Bookseller to His Majesty; 1768; New Edition, London: Printed for F. Wingrave, 1790.

Pouchot, Captain Pierre. *Memoirs on the Late War in North America Between France and England.* 1781. Translated by Michael Cary, edited and annotated by Brian Leigh Dunnigan. Youngstown, NY: Old Fort Niagara Association, 1994.

Reece, F.R., ed. "Colonel Eyre's Journal of His Trip from New York to Pittsburgh, 1762." *Western Pennsylvania Historical Magazine* 27 (1944): 37–50.

Scull, G.D., ed. *Collections of the New York Historical Society for the Year 1881: The Montrose Journals.* New York: New York Historical Society, 1882.

Shelby, Captain Evan. *Papers.* The Shelby Family Collection, Archives of Appalachia, East Tennessee State University, Johnson City, Tennessee.

"Sheriff, Court of Fife Deeds, 1715–1809." Accessed online at *http://www.fifefhs.org/Records/Court/fife.htm* on September 23, 2006.

Shippen, Captain Joseph. *Letters, 1758.* Shippen Family Papers, Historical Society of Pennsylvania, Philadelphia, Pennsylvania.

_____. "Military Letterbook of Joseph Shippen, 1756–1758." Shippen Family Papers, Historical Society of Pennsylvania, Philadelphia, Pennsylvania.

_____. "Military Letters of Captain Joseph Shippen on the Provincial Service, 1756–1758." *Pennsylvania Magazine of History and Biography* 36 (1912): 367–378, 385–463.

_____. "Orderly Book, 1758." Shippen Papers, American Philosophical Society, Philadelphia, Pennsylvania.

Simes, Captain Thomas. *A Military Course for the Government and Conduct of a Battalion.* London: 1778.

_____. *The Military Guide for Young Officers, Containing a System for the Art of War, Parade, Camp, Field Duty, Manoeuvres, Standing and General*

Orders, Warrants, Regulations, Returns, Tables, Forms, Extracts from Military Acts, Battles, Sieges, Forts, Posts, Military Dictionary. 1776. Reprint edition, Uckfield, East Sussex, United Kingdom: The Naval & Military Press in association with the Royal Armouries, 2006.

Society of Gentlemen in Scotland, A. *Encyclopedia Britannica, or a Dictionary of Arts and Sciences.* 3 vols. Edinburgh: A. Bell and C. Macfarquhar, 1768–1771.

Tinling, Marion, ed. *The Correspondence of the Three William Byrds of Westover, Virginia, 1684–1776.* 2 vols. Charlottesville: Virginia Historical Society, 1977.

_____. "Some Unpublished Correspondence of William Byrd III." *The Virginia Magazine of History and Biography* 88 (July 1980): 277–300.

Urban, Sylvanus, ed. *The Gentleman's Magazine* 28 (1758).

Van Horne, John C., and George Reese, eds. *The Letter Book of James Abercromby, Colonial Agent, 1751–1773.* Richmond: Virginia State Library and Archives, 1991.

Vauban, Marchel Sebastien LePrestre de. *A Manual of Siegecraft and Fortification.* Translated by George A. Rothrock. 1740. Reprint edition, Ann Arbor: University of Michigan Press, 1968.

_____. *The New Method of Fortification, Published in English by Abel Swall, London, 1691.* Ann Arbor, MI: University Microfilms, 1963.

West, Martin, transcriber. *George Washington Remembers: Reflections on the French and Indian War.* Lanham, Boulder, New York, Toronto and Oxford: Rowman & Littlefield, 2004.

Williams, Edward G. "A Survey of Bouquet's Road, 1764: Samuel Finley's Field Notes." *Western Pennsylvania Historical Magazine* 66 (April, July, October 1983): 129–168, 237–269, 347–367; 67 (January, April 1984): 33–63, 133–152.

_____, ed. *Bouquet's March to the Ohio: The Forbes Road (From the Original Manuscripts in the William L. Clements Library).* Pittsburgh: Historical Society of Western Pennsylvania, 1975.

Williams, Samuel C., ed. *Lieutenant Henry Timberlake's Memoirs, 1757–1765.* Johnson City, TN: The Watauga Press, 1927.

Young, Sir James. *An Essay on the Command of Small Detachments.* London, 1766.

Secondary Sources

Anderson, Fred. *Crucible of War: The Seven Years' War and the Fate of Empire in British North America, 1754–1766.* New York: Alfred A. Knopf, 2000.

Bailey, DeWitt. *British Military Flintlock Rifles, 1740–1840.* Lincoln, RI: Andrew Mowbray, 2002.

Becker, Donald Eugene. *North Carolina, 1754–1763: An Economic, Political, and Military History of North Carolina During the Great War for the Empire.* Ph.D. dissertation, University of North Carolina at Chapel Hill, 1971.

Bell, Raymond M. *The Brothers and Sisters of Colonel John Armstrong, 1717–1795 and of His Wife Rebecca, 1717–1797 of Carlisle, Pennsylvania.* Washington, PA: R.M. Bell, 1990.

Breen, T.H. *The Marketplace of Revolution: How Consumer Politics Shaped American Independence.* Oxford University Press, 2004.

Brodine, Charles E., Jr. "Henry Bouquet and British Infantry Tactics on the Ohio Frontier, 1758–1764." In David C. Skaggs and Larry L. Nelson, eds., *The Sixty Years' War for the Great Lakes, 1754–1814.* East Lansing: Michigan State University Press, 2001.

Carter, Thomas. *Historical Record of the Forty-Fourth: Or the East Essex Regiment.* Chatham, England: Gale & Polden, Brompton Works, 1887.

Clausewitz, General Carl von. *On War.* Edited and translated by Michael Howard and Peter Paret. New York: Alfred P. Knopf, 1973. Everyman's Library Edition.

Cleland, Hugh. *George Washington in the Ohio Valley.* Pittsburgh: University of Pittsburgh Press, 1955.

Cort, Cyrus. *Colonel Henry Bouquet and His Campaigns of 1763 and 1764.* Lancaster, PA: Steinman & Hensel, Printers, 1883.

Craig, Neville B. *The History of Pittsburgh.* Pittsburgh: J.R. Weldin Company, 1917.

Crist, Robert G. *John Armstrong: Proprietors Man.* Ph.D. thesis, Pennsylvania State University, 1981.

Cubbison, Douglas R. *Historic Structures Report: The Redoubts of West Point.* West Point, NY: United States Military Academy, Directorate of Public Works, 2004.

Doerflinger, Thomas M. "Farmers and Dry Goods in the Philadelphia Market Area, 1750–1800." In Ronald Hoffman, *et al.,* eds. *The Economy of Early America: The Revolutionary Period, 1763–1790.* Charlottesville: University Press of Virginia, 1988.

Eschenmann, Hayes R. *Forbes Expedition, Carlisle to Cowan's Gap.* Privately printed, 1999.

_____. *Forbes Expedition, Cowan's Gap to Juniata Crossing.* Privately printed, 2003.

Foreman, Harry E. *Forbes Road, Parnell's Knob to Burnt Cabins.* Chambersburg, PA: privately printed, 1954.

Grant, Alastair Macpherson. *General James Grant of Ballindalloch, 1720–1806.* London: A.M. Grant, 1930.

Hannum, Major Patrick H. *Henry Bouquet: A Study of Three Military Campaigns in North America, 1758–1764.* Fort Leavenworth, KS: U.S. Army Command and General Staff College, 1991.

Hawbaker, Gary T. *Fort Loudon on the Frontier.* Hershey, Pennsylvania: privately printed, 1976.

Houlding, J. *Fit for Service: The Training of the British Army, 1715–1795.* Oxford: Clarendon Press, 1981.

Huidekoper, Frederic Louis. "The Struggle Between the French and English for the Valley of the Ohio, 1749–1758, Address delivered before The Society of Colonial Wars in the District of Columbia on Thursday, March 5, 1914." In *Some Important Colonial Military Operations.* Washington, D.C.:

Society of Colonial Wars in the District of Columbia, Press of Gibson Brothers, 1914.

Hulbert, Archer Butler. *Historic Highways of America*. Vol. 5: *The Old Glade (Forbes) Road*. Cleveland, OH: Arthur H. Clark, 1903.

Hunter, William A. "Armstrong's Victory at Kittanning." Harrisburg: Pennsylvania Historical and Museum Commission, Historic Pennsylvania Leaflet No. 17, 1956.

Hutton, Sir Edward. *Colonel Henry Bouquet, 60th Royal Americans, 1756–1765.* Winchester, England: Warren, 1911.

James, Alfred Proctor, and Charles Morse Stotz. *Drums in the Forest, Decision at the Forks, Defense in the Wilderness*. Pittsburgh: Historical Society of Western Pennsylvania, 1958. Revised edition, Pittsburgh: Western Pennsylvania Historical Society, 2005.

Jennings, Francis. *Empire of Fortune: Crown, Colonies & Tribes in the Seven Years' War in America*. New York: W.W. Norton, 1988.

_____. "The Seven Years' War in Pennsylvania." In William G. Shade, ed., *Revisioning the British Empire in the Eighteenth Century: Essays from Twenty-Five Years of The Lawrence Henry Gibson Institute for Eighteenth-Century Studies*. Bethlehem, PA: Lehigh University Press, 1998.

Jones, Stanhope B. *The Evolution of Preventive Medicine in the United States Army, 1607–1939*. Washington, D.C.: Office of the Surgeon General of the Department of the Army, 1968.

Klein, Randolph Shipley. *Portrait of an Early American Family: The Shippens of Pennsylvania Across Five Generations*. Philadelphia: University of Pennsylvania Press, 1975.

Kopperman, Paul E. *Braddock at the Monongahela*. Pittsburgh: University of Pittsburgh Press, 1977.

Lane, William Coolidge. *A Catalogue of the Washington Collection in the Boston Athenaeum*. Boston: The Boston Athenaeum, 1897.

Maclean, Charles H., and George Robinson. *Cases Decided by the House of Lords on Appeals and Writs of Error*. London: Saunders and Benning, Law Booksellers, 1840.

McConnell, Michael. *Army & Empire: British Soldiers on the American Frontier, 1758–1775*. Lincoln and London: University of Nebraska Press, 2004.

_____. *A Country Between: The Upper Ohio Valley and Its Peoples, 1724–1774*. Lincoln: University of Nebraska Press, 1992.

McCulloch, Ian Macpherson. *Sons of the Mountains: The Highland Regiments in the French and Indian War, 1756–1767*. 2 vols. Fleischmanns, NY: Purple Mountain Press, 2006.

Morison, Samuel Eliot. *The Ropemakers of Plymouth: A History of the Plymouth Cordage Company, 1824–1949*. Boston: Houghton Mifflin, 1950.

Nelson, Paul David. *General James Grant: Scottish Solider and Royal Governor of East Florida*. Gainesville: University Press of Florida, 1993.

Netherton, Ross D. "The Carlyle House Conference: An Episode in the Politics of Colonial Union." In

James Allen Braden, ed., *Proceedings of Northern Virginia Studies Conference, 1983, Alexandria: Empire to Commonwealth*. Alexandria: Northern Virginia Community College, 1984.

Nixon, Lily L. *James Burd: Frontier Defender*. Philadelphia: University of Pennsylvania Press, 1941.

Odintz, Mark F. *The British Officer Corps, 1754–1783*. Ph.D. dissertation, University of Michigan, 1988.

Patterson, Burd S. *The Head of Iron: A Romance of Colonial Pennsylvania*. Pittsburgh: T.M. Walker, 1908.

Quarles, Garland R. *George Washington and Winchester, Virginia, 1748–1758*. Winchester, VA: Winchester-Frederick County Historical Society, 1974.

Rankin, George H. "George H. Rankin Collection, 1913–1957." Western Pennsylvania Historical Society, Pittsburgh.

Rial, David W. *The Old Forbes Road*. Pittsburgh: Western Pennsylvania Historical Society, 1995.

Rilling, Joseph R. *The Art and Science of War in America: A Bibliography of American Military Imprints, 1690–1800*. Alexandria Bay, NY: Museum Restoration Service, 1990.

Robinson, W. Stitt. *James Glen: From Scottish Provost to Royal Governor of South Carolina*. Westport, CT: Greenwood Press, 1996.

Shippen, Edward. *Memoir of Henry Bouquet, 1719–1765: Brigadier General in America and Colonel of the Royal American Regiment in the French and Indian War*. Philadelphia: G.H. Buchanan, 1900.

Shultz, Dr. James H. *General John Forbes and the Forbes Road in Fulton County, Pennsylvania*. McConnellsburg, PA: Fulton County Historical Society, 1999.

Stephenson, Robert S. *"An Extreme Bad Collection": Signs of Professionalism in the Pennsylvania Regiment, 1757–1759*. Master's thesis, University of Virginia, 1990. Transcript at the David Library of the American Revolution, Washington's Crossing, Pennsylvania.

Stotz, Charles M. *Outposts of the War for Empire*. 1985. Revised edition, Pittsburgh: Western Pennsylvania Historical Society, 2005.

Titus, James R.W. *The Old Dominion at War: Society, Politics, and Warfare in Late Colonial Virginia*. Columbia: University of South Carolina Press, 1991. (Book is based upon Ph.D. thesis.)

_____. "Soldiers When They Choose to Be So: Virginians at War, 1754–1763." Ph.D. dissertation, Rutgers University, 1983.

Tousey, Lieutenant Colonel Thomas G. *Military History of Carlisle and Carlisle Barracks*. Richmond, VA: The Dietz Press, 1939.

Walzer, John Flexer. "Transportation in the Philadelphia Trading Area, 1740–1775." Madison: University of Wisconsin master's thesis, 1968.

Ward, Harry M. *Major General Adam Stephen and the Cause of American Liberty*. Charlottesville: University Press of Virginia, 1989.

Ward, Matthew C. *Breaking the Backcountry: The Seven Years War in Virginia and Pennsylvania,*

1754–1765. Pittsburgh: University of Pittsburgh Press, 2003.

Western Pennsylvania Historical Survey. *Guidebook to Historic Places in Western Pennsylvania*. Pittsburgh: University of Pittsburgh Press, 1938.

Whitworth, Rex. *Field Marshal Lord Ligonier: A Story of the British Army, 1702–1770*. Oxford: Oxford University Press, 1958.

Wilkinson, Spenser. *The Defence of Piedmont, 1742–1748: A Prelude to the Study of Napoleon*. Oxford: Clarendon Press, 1927.

Periodical Articles

Anderson, Niles. "The General Chooses a Road: The Forbes Campaign of 1758 to Capture Fort Duquesne." *Western Pennsylvania Historical Magazine* 42 (June, September, December 1959): 109–138, 241–258, 383–401.

_____. "New Light on the 1758 Forbes Campaign." *Western Pennsylvania Historical Magazine* 50 (1967): 89–103.

Bell, Whitfield J., Jr., and Leonard W. Labaree. "Franklin and the 'Wagon Affair,' 1755." *Proceedings of the American Philosophical Society* (December 19, 1957): 551–558.

Berger, J. Alfred, Catherine A. Hawks, and Jacob L. Grimm. "The Metallurgical Study of Fort Ligonier Bayonet Sections, Hand Forged Spikes, and Copper Powder Keg Hoop Sections." *Northeast Historical Archaeology* 5 (Spring 1976): 34–39.

Branch, E. Douglas. "Henry Bouquet: Professional Soldier." *Pennsylvania Magazine of History and Biography* 62 (January 1938): 41–51.

Briggs, Reginald P. "Conquest of the Allegheny Mountains in Pennsylvania: The Engineering Geology of Forbes Road: 1758–1764." *Environmental & Engineering Geoscience* 4, no. 3 (Fall 1998): 397–414.

Brisebois, Michel. "Books from General Wolfe's Library at the National Library of Congress." *National Library News* 28, no. 2 (February 1996). Accessed online at: *http://www.collectionscanada.ca/bulletin/015017–9602–15-e.html*.

Brodine, Charles. "Civil-Military Relations in Pennsylvania, 1758–1760: An Examination of John Shy's Thesis." *Pennsylvania History* 62 (April 1995): 213–233.

Bruce, B.B. "Colonel Thomas Lloyd: Commandant of Fort Ligonier." *Westmoreland History* 8, no. 3 (December 2003): 20–25.

Champion, Walter T., Jr. "Christian Frederick Post and the Winning of the West." *Pennsylvania Magazine of History and Biography* 104 (1980): 308–325.

Clark, Dora Mae. "The British Treasury and the Administration of Military Affairs in America, 1754–1774." *Pennsylvania History* 2, no. 4 (October 1935): 197–204.

Cornu, Donald. "Captain Lewis Ourry, Royal American Regiment of Foot." *Pennsylvania History* 19 (July 1932): 249–261.

_____. "The Historical Authenticity of Dr. Johnson's 'Speaking Cat.'" *Review of English Studies* New Series 2, no. 8 (October 1951): 358–370.

Donehoo, George P. "Christian Frederick Post's Part in the Capture of Fort Duquesne and in the Conquest of the Ohio." *The Penn Germania* 2, no. 1 (January 1913): 1–6.

Eid, Leroy V. "'A Kind of Running Fight': Indian Battlefield Tactics in the Late Eighteenth Century." *The Western Pennsylvania Historical Magazine* 71, no. 2 (April 1988): 147–171.

Ferling, John. "Soldiers for Virginia: Who Served in the French and Indian War?" *Virginia Magazine of History and Biography* 94 (July 1986): 307–328.

Fisher, George Harrison. "Brigadier-General Henry Bouquet." *The Pennsylvania Magazine of History and Biography* 3, no. 2 (1879): 121–143.

Giblin, John F. "The Other Forbes Road." *Westmoreland History* 1, no. 1 (Spring 1995): 33–34.

Giddens, Paul H. "The Cooperation of the Southern Colonies in the Forbes Expedition Against Fort DuQuesne." *Virginia Magazine of History and Biography* 36 (1928): 1–16, 145–160.

Guilday, John E. "Animal Remains from Archaeological Excavations at Fort Ligonier." *Annals of the Carnegie Museum* 42 (1970): 177–186.

Hildeburn, Charles R. "Sir John St. Clair, Baronet, Quarter-Master General in America, 1755 to 1767." *The Pennsylvania Magazine of History and Biography* 9, no. 1 (1885).

Huidekoper, Frederic Louis. "Provincial Negotiations with the Western Indians, 1754–1758." *Pennsylvania History* 18, no. 3 (July 1951): 2–8.

James, Alfred P. "Decision at the Forks." *The Western Pennsylvania Historical Magazine* 41 (1958): 1–56.

_____. "Fort Ligonier, Additional Light from Unpublished Documents." *The Western Pennsylvania Historical Magazine* 17 (December 1934): 259–285.

_____. "George Mercer of the Ohio Company, A Study in Frustration." *The Western Pennsylvania Historical Magazine* 46, no. 1 (January 1963): 1–43; and 46, no. 2 (April 1963): 141–183.

Kiefer, Anna. "The Logistics of Supply and the Forbes Campaign of 1758." Accessed online at *http://web.hardynet.com/~gruber/supplies_forbes_road.html* on October 10, 2005.

Kopperman, Paul E. "The British High Command and Soldiers' Wives in America, 1755–1783." *Journal of the Society for Army Historical Research* 60 (1982): 14–34.

_____. "Religion & Religious Policy in the British Army, c. 1700–1776." *The Journal of Religious History* 15 (1987): 390–405.

Lloyd, E.M. "The Raising of the Highland Regiments in 1757." *English Historical Review* 17 (July 1902): 466–469.

Maass, John R. "'All This Poor Province Could Do:' North Carolina and the Seven Years' War, 1757–1762." *The North Carolina Historical Review* 79, no. 1 (January 2002): 50–89.

Mayer, Holly A. "From Forts to Families: Following

the Army into Western Pennsylvania, 1758–1766." *Pennsylvania Magazine of History and Biography* 130, no. 1 (January 2006).

McBride, William M. "'Normal' Medical Science and British Treatment of the Sea Scurvy, 1753–75." *Journal of the History of Medicine and Allied Sciences* 46, no. 2 (1991): 158–177.

McConnell, Michael. "New Tales from the Wild East: Fort Ligonier in Perspective." Accessed on the Internet at http://www.fortligonier.org/raising.htm on November 18, 2003.

Mish, Mary Vernon. "General Adam Stephen, Founder, Martinsburg, West Virginia." *West Virginia History* 22, no. 2 (January 1961): 63–75.

Morton, Richard L. "Benjamin Franklin and the Parliamentary Grant for 1758." *The William and Mary Quarterly*, 3rd Series, 23 (1966): 575–595.

Myers, James P. "General Forbes' Road to War." *Westmoreland History* 7, no. 2 (September 2002): 43–51.

_____. "Research Notes: Bewitched by Maps: A Caveat." *Pennsylvania History* 65 (Spring 1998): 203–213.

_____. "The Reverend Thomas Barton's Conflict with Colonel John Armstrong, c. 1758." *Cumberland County History* 10, no. 1 (Summer 1983): 3–14.

Nixon, Lily Lee. "Colonel James Burd in the Forbes Campaign." *Pennsylvania Magazine of History and Biography* 59 (April 1935): 106–133.

Norkus, Nellie. "Virginia's Role in the Capture of Fort Duquesne, 1758." *Western Pennsylvania Historical Magazine* 45 (December 1962): 291–308.

Quattrocchi, Anna M. "Thomas Hutchins in Western Pennsylvania." *Pennsylvania History* 16 (January 1949): 31–38.

Ravis, George B. "Youngstown [Pennsylvania] and the Forbes Road." *Westmoreland History* 2, no. 1 (Spring 1996): 15–22.

Rogers, J. Alan. "Impressment in Western Pennsylvania, 1755–1759." *Western Pennsylvania Historical Magazine* 52 (July 1969): 255–262.

Russell, Marvin F. "Thomas Barton and Pennsylvania's Colonial Frontier." *Pennsylvania History* 46, no. 4 (October 1979): 313–334.

Salay, David L. "Marching to War: The Production of Leather and Shoes in Revolutionary Pennsylvania." *Pennsylvania History* 60, no. 1 (January 1993): 51–72.

Stephenson, Robert S. "Pennsylvania Provincials in the Seven Years' War." *Pennsylvania History* 62 (1995): 196–212.

Stokesbury, James L. "John Forbes and His Wilderness Road." *American History Illustrated* 9 (1974), 28–40.

Stotz, Charles Morse. "Forbes Conquers the Wilderness: A Modern Odyssey." *Western Pennsylvania Historical Magazine* 67 (October 1984): 309–322.

_____. "The Reconstruction of Fort Ligonier: The Anatomy of a Frontier Fort." *Bulletin of the Association of Preservation Technology* 4 (1974): 2–103.

Thomas, Harold A. "The Last Two Campsites of Forbes's Army." *Western Pennsylvania Historical Magazine* 46 (1963): 45–56.

_____. "Site of Forbes's Last Three Breastworks." *Western Pennsylvania Historical Magazine* 47 (1964): 55–66.

Waddell, Louis M. "The American Career of Henry Bouquet, 1755–1765." *The Swiss-American Historical Society Newsletter* 17 (1981): 13–38.

Walkinshaw, Lewis C. "As Forbes Trailed Through." *Western Pennsylvania Historical Magazine* 19 (1936): 135–142, 221–228.

Ward, Matthew C. "An Army of Servants." *Pennsylvania Magazine of History and Biography* 119 (1995): 75–93.

_____. "'The European Method of Warring Is Not Practiced Here': The Failure of British Military Policy in the Ohio Valley, 1755–1759." *War in History* 4, no. 3 (1997): 247–263.

_____. "Fighting the Old Women: Indian Strategy on the Virginia and Pennsylvania Border, 1754–1758." *Virginia Magazine of History and Biography* 103, no. 3 (1995): 297–320.

White, Kenneth A. "The Phantom Atrocity." *Western Pennsylvania Historical Magazine* 66 (1983): 382–388.

Background Research Sources

Native Americans

Jacobs, Wilbur R., ed. *The Appalachian Indian Frontier: The Edmond Atkin Report and Plan of 1755.* University of South Carolina Press, 1954. Revised edition, University of Nebraska Press, 1967.

Johnson, Steven F. *Ninnuock (The People): The Algonkian People of New England.* Marlborough, MA: Bliss, 1995.

Kohl, Johann Georg. *Kitchi-Gami: Life Among the Lake Superior Ojibway.* 1860. Reprint edition, Minnesota Historical Society Press, 1985.

Morgan, Lewis Henry. *The League of the Iroquois.* 1851. Reprint edition North Dighton, Massachusetts: JG Press, 1995.

Speck, Frank G. *Midwinter Rites of the Cayuga Long House.* Philadelphia: University of Pennsylvania Press, 1949. Reprint edition, Lincoln: University of Nebraska Press, 1995.

Roads and Wagons

Berkebile, Don H. "Conestoga Wagons in Braddock's Campaign, 1755." In *Bulletin 218: Contributions from the Museum of History and Technology.* Fisher, Charles, and Lois M. Feister. *Archaeology of the Colonial Road at the John Ellison House, Knox's Headquarters State Historic Site, Vail's Gate, New York.* Albany, NY: Bureau of Historic Sites, 2000.

Kingsley, Ronald F., and James Rowe Jr. "In Search of the Eighteenth Century Rowley Road, Shoreham Township, Addison County, Vermont." *Journal of Vermont Archaeology* 3 (2000): 61–68.

Kirkorian, Cecilia S., and Joseph D. Zeranski. "Investigations of a Colonial New England Roadway." *Northeast Historical Archaeology* 10 (1981): 1–10.

Kral, Cynthia, and John Boback. *Report on the Location and Status of the Extant Segments of the Braddock Road, Fayette County, Pennsylvania.* Privately printed, 2003.

Lord, Philip, Jr. *War Over Walloomscoick: Land Use and Settlement Pattern on the Bennington Battlefield, 1777.* Albany, NY: New York State Museum, 1989.

Shumway, George, and Howard C. Frey, *Conestoga Wagon 1750–1850: Freight Carrier for 100 Years of America's Westward Expansion.* 3rd ed. Privately published, 1968.

Index